Li...ger Memorial Library

THE APOSTOLIC FATHERS

II

LCL 25

THE APOSTOLIC FATHERS

VOLUME II

THE SHEPHERD OF HERMAS
THE MARTYRDOM OF POLYCARP
THE EPISTLE TO DIOGNETUS

WITH AN ENGLISH TRANSLATION BY

KIRSOPP LAKE

HARVARD UNIVERSITY PRESS
CAMBRIDGE, MASSACHUSETTS
LONDON, ENGLAND

First published 1913
Reprinted 1917, 1924, 1930, 1946, 1948, 1950, 1959, 1965, 1970,
1976, 1992

ISBN 0-674-99028-5

Printed in Great Britain by St Edmundsbury Press Ltd,
Bury St Edmunds, Suffolk, on acid-free paper.
Bound by Hunter & Foulis Ltd, Edinburgh, Scotland.

CONTENTS

THE APOSTOLIC FATHERS

THE SHEPHERD OF HERMAS

THE APOSTOLIC FATHERS

THE SHEPHERD OF HERMAS

THE Shepherd of Hermas is in form an apocalypse.
It consists of a series of revelations made to Hermas
by the Church, who appears in the form of a woman,
first old, and afterwards younger; by the shepherd,
or angel of repentance; and by the great angel, who
is in charge of Christians. Each revelation is accom-
panied by an explanation, and from these it can be
seen that though the form of the book is apocalyptic
and visionary, its object is practical and ethical. The
main problem, which constantly recurs, is that of sin
after baptism. In the circle to which Hermas belonged
the belief obtained that Christians after baptism were
capable of leading sinless lives, and that if they fell
they could not again obtain forgiveness. Experience,
however, had shown that in this case few indeed
would be saved, and the message of Hermas was
that for sin after baptism there was still the possi-
bility of forgiveness for those who repented, though
this repentance would not avail more than once.
A great part of the book is taken up in developing
the details of this doctrine of repentance, which is
entrusted to an angel called the Shepherd, who
gives his name to the book, and it is obvious that

2

we have here the beginning of the Catholic doctrine of penance.

The Shepherd is divided into Visions (in the last of which the Shepherd appears), Commandments or Mandates, as they are more usually called, and Parables or Similitudes. It may roughly be said that in the Visions the necessity for repentance is enforced, in the Mandates the life required from the penitent is explained, and in the Similitudes the working and theological doctrine of repentance is developed.

The date and provenance of the Shepherd is fixed by the list of canonical books in the Muratorian canon, which rejects the Shepherd of Hermas, though some accepted it as a canonical apocalypse, on the ground that it was written "quite recently, in our own time in the city of Rome, by Hermas, while his brother Pius was sitting on the throne of the church of the city of Rome." Pius was Pope about 148 A.D., so that the Shepherd must have been written in Rome at about that time. Many critics, however, think that it may have been written at intervals during the twenty or thirty years preceding this date, and that traces can be seen of varying dates in the three divisions of the book. This question, which can probably never be decided satisfactorily, and in any case depends on the consideration of a mass of details which cannot be discussed shortly, may best be studied in Harnack's *Chronologie* and in Zahn's *Der Hirt des Hermas*.

The authorities for the text of the Shepherd are as follows :—

ℵ, Codex Sinaiticus, containing Vis. I. i. 1. to Mandate IV. iii. 6. written in the fourth century, probably in Alexandria or the neighbourhood.

3

A, Codex Athous, a MS of the fifteenth century, originally containing ten leaves, of which six are still in the convent of S. Gregory on Mt. Athos, three are at Leipsic, and one, the last, has been lost.

The text of this MS was copied on Mt. Athos by the celebrated forger Simonides, who brought back with him the three leaves now at Leipsic, and later on was collated rather hastily by Georgandas, but it is very difficult to read, and both the copy of Simonides and the collation of Georgandas are very inaccurate. A photographic reproduction and transcript of the Athos fragment have recently been published at the Clarendon Press.

H, a small fragment of vellum MS, containing Sim. IV. 6–7 and V. 1–5, now in Hamburg, published in the *Sitzungsberichten d. Berliner Akademie*, 1909, pp. 1077 ff.

Fragments of the text have also been found in the following papyri quoted as P^{am}, P^{ox}, etc. :—

> Amherst papyri, CXC. containing Vis. I. 1, 2–3, 1 ; III. 12, 3 and 13, 3–4. Mand. XII. 1, 1 and 1, 3. Sim. IX. 2, 1–2 and 4–5. IX. 12, 2–3 and 5 ; IX. 17, 1 and 3 ; IX. 30, 1–2 and 3–4. Published by Grenfell and Hunt in *Amherst Papyri*, ii.
>
> Oxyrh. No. 404, containing Sim. X. 3, 2–5. Published by Grenfell and Hunt in *Oxyrynchus Papyri*, iii.
>
> Oxyrh. Pap. 1172, containing Sim. II. 4–10. Published by Hunt in *Oxyrynchus Papyri*, ix.
>
> Berlin Pap. 5513, containing Sim. II. 7–10 and Sim. IV. 2–5. Published in *Berliner Klassiker Texte*, vi.

THE SHEPHERD OF HERMAS

Berlin Pap. 6789, containing Sim. VIII. 1, 1–12. Published in *Berliner Klassiker Texte*, vi.

Besides these Greek MSS and fragments, there are three extant versions.

L_1, the Vulgate version found in many MSS., published in the Editio Princeps of Faber, Paris, 1513.

L_2, the Palatine version found in Cod. Vat. Palatin. 150, and published in the *Patrum Apostolicorum Opera* of von Gebhardt, Harnack and Zahn.

L, without qualification, is used for the consensus of L_1 and L_2.

E, an Ethiopic translation found by d'Abbadie and published in the *Abhandl. d. deutschen morgenland. Gesellsch.* Bd. II. Nr. 1.

C, a few fragments of a Sahidic Coptic version have also been found in Papyri now in the Bib. Nat. at Paris and in the library of the Louvre, and have been published in the *Sitzungsberichten d. Berlin Akad.*, 1903, pp. 261 ff., in the *Revue de l'Orient Chrétien*, 1905, pp. 424 ff., and in the *Z. f. Aeg. Spr. und Altertumskunde* 1910, pp. 137 ff. Some evidence is also given by the numerous citations in Clement of Alexandria, pseudo-Athanasius, and Antiochus of Palestine, quoted as Clem., Athan., and Ant.

The text of Hermas is probably far from good : the evidence of the papyri shows that neither א nor A is completely trustworthy, and it is unfortunate that for so large a part of the book A is the only continuous Greek text. The evidence of LE and the Patristic quotations, though often valuable, is too free to be used with confidence.

ΠΟΙΜΗΝ

I

1. Ὁ θρέψας με πέπρακέν με Ῥόδῃ τινὶ [1] εἰς Ῥώμην. μετὰ πολλὰ ἔτη ταύτην ἀνεγνωρισάμην καὶ ἠρξάμην αὐτὴν ἀγαπᾶν ὡς ἀδελφήν. 2. μετὰ χρόνον τινὰ λουομένην εἰς τὸν ποταμὸν τὸν Τίβεριν εἶδον καὶ ἐπέδωκα αὐτῇ τὴν χεῖρα καὶ ἐξήγαγον αὐτὴν ἐκ τοῦ ποταμοῦ. ταύτης οὖν ἰδὼν τὸ κάλλος διελογιζόμην ἐν τῇ καρδίᾳ μου λέγων· Μακάριος ἤμην, εἰ τοιαύτην γυναῖκα εἶχον καὶ τῷ κάλλει καὶ τῷ τρόπῳ. μόνον τοῦτο ἐβουλευσάμην, ἕτερον δὲ οὐδὲ ἕν. 3. μετὰ χρόνον τινὰ πορευομένου μου εἰς Κώμας [2] καὶ δοξάζοντος τὰς κτίσεις τοῦ θεοῦ, ὡς μεγάλαι καὶ ἐκπρεπεῖς καὶ δυναταί εἰσιν, περιπατῶν ἀφύπνωσα. καὶ πνεῦμά με ἔλαβεν καὶ ἀπήνεγκέ με δι᾽ ἀνοδίας τινός, δι᾽ ἧς ἄνθρωπος οὐκ ἐδύνατο ὁδεῦσαι· ἦν δὲ ὁ τόπος κρημνώδης καὶ ἀπερρηγὼς ἀπὸ τῶν

---

[1] πρὸς γυναῖκά τινα AL₁, omitting the mention of her name
[2] κώμας ℵ AE, civitatem Ostiorum L, the editors emend to Κούμας (Cumae). It is probable that Cumae is the meaning of the text, but it is not impossible the spelling κώμας is original. The alternative is that πορευομένου εἰς κώμας means the same as the modern Italian "Villeggiatura" (summer holiday in the country).

6

THE SHEPHERD

Vision 1

I

1. He who brought me up sold me to a certain Rhoda at Rome. After many years I made her acquaintance again, and began to love her as a sister.[1] 2. After some time I saw her bathing in the river Tiber, and gave her my hand and helped her out of the river. When I saw her beauty I reflected in my heart and said: " I should be happy if I had a wife of such beauty and character." This was my only thought, and no other, no, not one. 3. After some time, while I was going to Cumae, and glorifying the creation of God, for its greatness and splendour and might, as I walked along I became sleepy. And a spirit seized me and took me away through a certain pathless district, through which a man could not walk, but the ground was precipitous and broken up by the

---

[1] As it stands this is hardly intelligible : presumably the meaning is that Hermas was born a slave, and that his owner sold him to Rhoda. It is implied that he then passed out of her possession, and later on made her acquaintance again. The alternative is that ἀνεγνωρισάμην merely means "came to know her properly."

ὑδάτων. διαβὰς οὖν τὸν ποταμὸν ἐκεῖνον ἦλθον εἰς τὰ ὁμαλὰ καὶ τιθῶ τὰ γόνατα καὶ ἠρξάμην προσεύχεσθαι τῷ κυρίῳ καὶ ἐξομολογεῖσθαί μου τὰς ἁμαρτίας. 4. προσευχομένου δέ μου ἠνοίγη ὁ οὐρανός, καὶ βλέπω τὴν γυναῖκα ἐκείνην, ἣν ἐπεθύμησα, ἀσπαζομένην με ἐκ τοῦ οὐρανοῦ, λέγουσαν· Ἑρμᾶ χαῖρε. 5. βλέψας δὲ εἰς αὐτὴν λέγω αὐτῇ· Κυρία, τί σὺ ὧδε ποιεῖς; ἡ δὲ ἀπεκρίθη μοι· Ἀνελήμφθην, ἵνα σοῦ τὰς ἁμαρτίας ἐλέγξω πρὸς τὸν κύριον. 6. λέγω αὐτῇ· Νῦν σύ μου ἔλεγχος εἶ; Οὔ, φησίν, ἀλλὰ ἄκουσον τὰ ῥήματα, ἅ σοι μέλλω λέγειν. ὁ θεὸς ὁ ἐν τοῖς οὐρανοῖς κατοικῶν καὶ κτίσας ἐκ τοῦ μὴ ὄντος τὰ ὄντα καὶ πληθύνας καὶ αὐξήσας ἕνεκεν τῆς ἁγίας ἐκκλησίας αὐτοῦ ὀργίζεταί σοι, ὅτι ἥμαρτες εἰς ἐμέ. 7. ἀποκριθεὶς αὐτῇ λέγω· Εἰς σὲ ἥμαρτον; ποίῳ τόπῳ[1] ἢ πότε σοι αἰσχρὸν ῥῆμα ἐλάλησα; οὐ πάντοτέ σε ὡς θεὰν[2] ἡγησάμην; οὐ πάντοτέ σε ἐνετράπην ὡς ἀδελφήν; τί μου καταψεύδῃ, ὦ γύναι, τὰ πονηρὰ ταῦτα καὶ ἀκάθαρτα; 8. γελάσασά μοι λέγει· Ἐπὶ τὴν καρδίαν σου ἀνέβη ἡ ἐπιθυμία τῆς πονηρίας. ἢ οὐ δοκεῖ σοι ἀνδρὶ δικαίῳ πονηρὸν πρᾶγμα εἶναι, ἐὰν ἀναβῇ αὐτοῦ ἐπὶ τὴν καρδίαν ἡ πονηρὰ ἐπιθυμία; ἁμαρτία γέ ἐστιν, καὶ μεγάλη, φησίν. ὁ γὰρ δίκαιος ἀνὴρ δίκαια βουλεύεται. ἐν τῷ οὖν δίκαια βουλεύεσθαι αὐτὸν κατορθοῦται ἡ δόξα αὐτοῦ ἐν τοῖς οὐρανοῖς καὶ εὐκατάλλακτον ἔχει τὸν κύριον ἐν παντὶ πράγματι αὐτοῦ· οἱ δὲ πονηρὰ βουλευόμενοι ἐν ταῖς καρδίαις αὐτῶν θάνατον καὶ αἰχμαλωτισμὸν ἑαυτοῖς ἐπισπῶνται, μάλιστα οἱ τὸν αἰῶνα τοῦτον

Ps. 2, 4; 123, 1;

Gen. 1, 28; 8, 17; 9, 1; 28, 3 etc.

---

[1] τόπῳ ℵ* L₁, τρόπῳ ℵ^cAL₂(E). [2] θυγατέρα A, dominam E.

streams of water. So I crossed that river, and came
to the level ground and knelt down and began to
pray to the Lord and to confess my sins. 4. Now
while I was praying the Heaven was opened, and I
saw that woman whom I had desired greeting me
out of the Heaven and saying: "Hail, Hermas."
5. And I looked at her, and said to her: "Lady,
what are you doing here?" and she answered me:
"I was taken up to accuse you of your sins before
the Lord." 6. I said to her: "Are you now accusing
me?" "No," she said, "but listen to the words
which I am going to say to you. 'God who dwells
in Heaven' and created that which is out of that
which is not, and 'increased and multiplied it' for
the sake of his Holy Church, is angry with you
because you sinned against me." 7. I answered and
said to her: "Did I sin against you? In what place,
or when did I speak an evil word to you? Did I
not always look on you as a goddess? Did I not
always respect you as a sister? Why do you charge
me falsely, Lady, with these wicked and impure
things?" 8. She laughed and said to me: "The
desire of wickedness came up in your heart. Or do
you not think that it is an evil deed for a righteous
man if an evil desire come up in his heart? Yes,
it is a sin," said she, "and a great one. For the
righteous man has righteous designs. So long then
as his designs are righteous his repute stands fast in
Heaven, and he finds the Lord ready to assist him
in all his doings. But they who have evil designs in
their hearts bring upon themselves death and cap-
tivity, especially those who obtain this world for

The Vision
of Rhoda
speaking
from
Heaven

περιποιούμενοι καὶ γαυριῶντες ἐν τῷ πλούτῳ
αὐτῶν καὶ μὴ ἀντεχόμενοι τῶν ἀγαθῶν τῶν
μελλόντων. 9. μετανοήσουσιν αἱ ψυχαὶ αὐτῶν,
οἵτινες οὐκ ἔχουσιν ἐλπίδα, ἀλλὰ ἑαυτοὺς ἀπεγνώ-
κασιν καὶ τὴν ζωὴν αὐτῶν. ἀλλὰ σὺ προσεύχου
πρὸς τὸν θεόν, καὶ ἰάσεται τὰ ἁμαρτήματά σου
καὶ ὅλου τοῦ οἴκου σου καὶ πάντων τῶν ἁγίων.

Deut. 30 ,3
cf. Jer. 3, 22

II

1. Μετὰ τὸ λαλῆσαι αὐτὴν τὰ ῥήματα ταῦτα
ἐκλείσθησαν οἱ οὐρανοί· κἀγὼ ὅλος ἤμην πεφρικὼς
καὶ λυπούμενος. ἔλεγον δὲ ἐν ἐμαυτῷ· Εἰ αὕτη
μοι ἡ ἁμαρτία ἀναγράφεται, πῶς δυνήσομαι
σωθῆναι; ἢ πῶς ἐξιλάσομαι τὸν θεὸν περὶ τῶν
ἁμαρτιῶν μου τῶν τελείων; ἢ ποίοις ῥήμασιν
ἐρωτήσω τὸν κύριον, ἵνα ἱλατεύσηταί μοι;
2. ταῦτά μου συμβουλευομένου καὶ διακρίνοντος
ἐν τῇ καρδίᾳ μου, βλέπω κατέναντί μου καθέδραν
λευκὴν ἐξ ἐρίων χιονίνων γεγονυῖαν μεγάλην·
καὶ ἦλθεν γυνὴ πρεσβῦτις ἐν ἱματισμῷ λαμπρο-
τάτῳ, ἔχουσα βιβλίον εἰς τὰς χεῖρας, καὶ ἐκάθισεν
μόνη καὶ ἀσπάζεταί με· Ἑρμᾶ, χαῖρε. κἀγὼ
λυπούμενος καὶ κλαίων εἶπον· Κυρία, χαῖρε.
3. καὶ εἶπέν μοι· Τί στυγνός, Ἑρμᾶ; ὁ μακρόθυμος καὶ ἀστομάχητος, ὁ πάντοτε γελῶν, τί
οὕτω κατηφὴς τῇ ἰδέᾳ καὶ οὐχ ἱλαρός; κἀγὼ
εἶπον αὐτῇ· Ὑπὸ γυναικὸς ἀγαθωτάτης λεγούσης,
ὅτι ἥμαρτον εἰς αὐτήν. 4. ἡ δὲ ἔφη· Μηδαμῶς
ἐπὶ τὸν δοῦλον τοῦ θεοῦ τὸ πρᾶγμα τοῦτο. ἀλλὰ
πάντως ἐπὶ τὴν καρδίαν σου ἀνέβη περὶ αὐτῆς.

themselves, and glory in their wealth, and do not lay hold of the good things which are to come. 9. Their hearts will repent; yet have they no hope, but they have abandoned themselves and their life. But do you pray to God, and 'He shall heal the sins of yourself' and of all your house and of all the saints."

II

1. AFTER she had spoken these words the Heavens were shut, and I was all shuddering and in grief. And I began to say in myself: "If this sin is recorded against me, how shall I be saved? Or how shall I propitiate God for my completed sins? Or with what words shall I beseech the Lord to be forgiving unto me?" 2. While I was considering and doubting these things in my heart I saw before me a white chair of great size made of snow-white wool; and there came a woman, old and clothed in shining garments with a book in her hand, and she sat down alone and greeted me: "Hail, Hermas!" And I, in my grief and weeping, said: "Hail, Lady!" 3. And she said to me: "Why are you gloomy, Hermas? You who are patient and good-tempered, who are always laughing, why are you so downcast in appearance and not merry?" And I said to her: "Because of a most excellent lady, who says that I sinned against her." 4. And she said: "By no means let this thing happen to the servant of God; but for all that the thought did enter your

The vision of the ancient lady

11

THE APOSTOLIC FATHERS

ἔστιν μὲν τοῖς δούλοις τοῦ θεοῦ ἡ τοιαύτη βουλὴ
ἁμαρτίαν ἐπιφέρουσα· πονηρὰ γὰρ βουλὴ καὶ
ἔκπληκτος εἰς πάνσεμνον πνεῦμα καὶ ἤδη δεδο-
κιμασμένον, ἐὰν ἐπιθυμήσῃ πονηρὸν ἔργον, καὶ
μάλιστα Ἑρμᾶς ὁ ἐγκρατής, ὁ ἀπεχόμενος πάσης
ἐπιθυμίας πονηρᾶς καὶ πλήρης πάσης ἁπλότητος
καὶ ἀκακίας μεγάλης.

III

1. Ἀλλ' οὐχ ἕνεκα τούτου ὀργίζεταί σοι ὁ θεός,
ἀλλ' ἵνα τὸν οἶκόν σου τὸν ἀνομήσαντα εἰς τὸν
κύριον καὶ εἰς ὑμᾶς τοὺς γονεῖς αὐτῶν ἐπιστρέψῃς.
ἀλλὰ φιλότεκνος ὢν οὐκ ἐνουθέτεις σου τὸν οἶκον,
ἀλλὰ ἀφῆκες αὐτὸν καταφθαρῆναι,¹ διὰ τοῦτό
σοι ὀργίζεται ὁ κύριος· ἀλλὰ ἰάσεταί σου
πάντα τὰ προγεγονότα πονηρὰ ἐν τῷ οἴκῳ σου·
διὰ γὰρ τὰς ἐκείνων ἁμαρτίας καὶ ἀνομήματα σὺ
κατεφθάρης ἀπὸ τῶν βιωτικῶν πράξεων. 2. ἀλλ'
ἡ πολυσπλαγχνία τοῦ κυρίου ἠλέησέν σε καὶ τὸν
οἶκόν σου καὶ ἰσχυροποιήσει σε καὶ θεμελιώσει
σε ἐν τῇ δόξῃ αὐτοῦ. σὺ μόνον μὴ ῥαθυμήσῃς,
ἀλλὰ εὐψύχει καὶ ἰσχυροποίει σου τὸν οἶκον. ὡς
γὰρ ὁ χαλκεὺς σφυροκοπῶν τὸ ἔργον αὐτοῦ περιγίνεται τοῦ πράγματος οὗ θέλει, οὕτω καὶ ὁ λόγος
ὁ καθημερινὸς ὁ δίκαιος περιγίνεται πάσης πονηρίας. μὴ διαλίπῃς οὖν νουθετῶν σου τὰ τέκνα.
οἶδα γάρ, ὅτι, ἐὰν μετανοήσουσιν² ἐξ ὅλης καρδίας
αὐτῶν, ἐνγραφήσονται εἰς τὰς βίβλους τῆς ζωῆς

¹ καταφθαρῆναι ℵ* Pᵃᵐ, καταφθαρῆναι δεινῶς ALE.
² μετανοήσουσιν ℵ, μετανοήσωσιν A.

12

heart concerning her. It is such a design as this which brings sin on the servants of God. For it is an evil and mad purpose against a revered spirit and one already approved, if a man desire an evil deed, and especially if it be Hermas the temperate, who abstains from every evil desire and is full of all simplicity and great innocence.

III

1. "But it is not for this that God is angry with you, but in order that you should convert your family, which has sinned against the Lord, and against you, their parents. But you are indulgent, and do not correct your family, but have allowed them to become corrupt. For this reason the Lord is angry with you, but he will heal all the past evils in your family, for because of their sins and wickednesses have you been corrupted by the things of daily life. 2. But the great mercy of the Lord has had pity on you and on your family, and will make you strong and will establish you in his glory; only do not be slothful, but have courage and strengthen your family. For as the smith, by hammering his work, overcomes the task which he desires, so also the daily righteous word overcomes all wickedness. Do not cease, then, correcting your children, for I know that if they repent with all their heart, they will be inscribed in the books of

Why God is angry

μετὰ τῶν ἁγίων. 3. μετὰ τὸ παῆναι αὐτῆς τὰ
ῥήματα ταῦτα λέγει μοι· Θέλεις ἀκοῦσαί μου
ἀναγινωσκούσης; λέγω κἀγώ· Θέλω, κυρία. λέγει
μοι· Γενοῦ ἀκροατὴς καὶ ἄκουε τὰς δόξας τοῦ
θεοῦ. ἤκουσα μεγάλως καὶ θαυμαστῶς, ὃ οὐκ
ἴσχυσα μνημονεῦσαι· πάντα γὰρ τὰ ῥήματα
ἔκφρικτα, ἃ οὐ δύναται ἄνθρωπος βαστάσαι.
τὰ οὖν ἔσχατα ῥήματα ἐμνημόνευσα· ἦν γὰρ

Ps. 58, 6;
etc.

ἡμῖν σύμφορα καὶ ἥμερα· 4. Ἰδού, ὁ θεὸς τῶν
δυνάμεων, ὃν ἀγαπῶ,[1] δυνάμει κραταιᾷ καὶ τῇ
μεγάλῃ συνέσει αὐτοῦ κτίσας τὸν κόσμον καὶ τῇ
ἐνδόξῳ βουλῇ περιθεὶς τὴν εὐπρέπειαν τῇ κτίσει
αὐτοῦ καὶ τῷ ἰσχυρῷ ῥήματι πήξας τὸν οὐρανὸν

Ps. 135, 6

καὶ θεμελιώσας τὴν γῆν ἐπὶ ὑδάτων καὶ τῇ ἰδίᾳ
σοφίᾳ καὶ προνοίᾳ κτίσας τὴν ἁγίαν ἐκκλησίαν
αὐτοῦ, ἣν καὶ ηὐλόγησεν, ἰδού, μεθιστάνει τοὺς
οὐρανούς, καὶ τὰ ὄρη καὶ τοὺς βουνοὺς καὶ τὰς
θαλάσσας, καὶ πάντα ὁμαλὰ γίνεται τοῖς ἐκλεκτοῖς
αὐτοῦ, ἵνα ἀποδῷ αὐτοῖς τὴν ἐπαγγελίαν, ἣν
ἐπηγγείλατο μετὰ πολλῆς δόξης καὶ χαρᾶς, ἐὰν
τηρήσωσιν τὰ νόμιμα τοῦ θεοῦ, ἃ παρέλαβον ἐν
μεγάλῃ πίστει.

IV

1. Ὅτε οὖν ἐτέλεσεν ἀναγινώσκουσα καὶ ἠγέρθη
ἀπὸ τῆς καθέδρας, ἦλθαν τέσσαρες νεανίαι καὶ
ἦραν τὴν καθέδραν καὶ ἀπῆλθον πρὸς τὴν
ἀνατολήν. 2. προσκαλεῖταί δέ με καὶ ἥψατο τοῦ

---

[1] ὃν ἀγαπῶ ℵ, qui invisibili (= ἀοράτῳ) L₁, qui omnia
virtute sustentabili L₂, "in his pity and in his love" E.
The text is clearly corrupt, and cannot be restored with
certainty.

life with the saints." 3. After she had ceased these
words she said to me : " Would you like to hear me The lady
reads to
read aloud ? " and I said : " I should like it, Lady." Hermas
She said to me : " Listen then, and hear the glory
of God." I heard great and wonderful things which
I cannot remember ; for all the words were frightful,
such as a man cannot bear. So I remembered the
last words, for they were profitable for us and gentle :
4. " Lo, 'the God of the powers,' whom I love, by
his mighty power, and by his great wisdom ' created
the world,' and by his glorious counsel surrounded
his creation with beauty, and by his mighty word
' fixed the Heaven and founded the earth upon the
waters,' and by his own wisdom and forethought
created his holy Church, which he also blessed—
Lo, he changes the heavens, and the mountains and
the hills and the seas, and all things are becoming
smooth for his chosen ones, to give them the promise
which he made with great glory and joy, if they
keep the ordinances of God, which they received
with great faith."

IV

1. So, when she had finished reading, and rose The close
of the
from the chair, there came four young men, and vision
took up the chair and went away towards the East.
2. And she called me and touched my breast and said

στήθους μου καὶ λέγει μοι· Ἤρεσέν σοι ἡ
ἀνάγνωσίς μου; καὶ λέγω αὐτῇ· Κυρία, ταῦτά
μοι τὰ ἔσχατα ἀρέσκει, τὰ δὲ πρῶτα[1] χαλεπὰ καὶ
σκληρά. ἡ δὲ ἔφη μοι λέγουσα· Ταῦτα τὰ ἔσχατα
τοῖς δικαίοις, τὰ δὲ πρῶτα τοῖς ἔθνεσιν καὶ
τοῖς ἀποστάταις. 3. λαλούσης αὐτῆς μετ᾽ ἐμοῦ δύο
τινὲς ἄνδρες ἐφάνησαν καὶ ἦραν αὐτὴν τῶν ἀγκώ-
νων καὶ ἀπῆλθαν, ὅπου ἡ καθέδρα, πρὸς τὴν
ἀνατολήν. ἱλαρὰ δὲ ἀπῆλθεν καὶ ὑπάγουσα λέγει
μοι· Ἀνδρίζου, Ἑρμᾶ.

Ὅρασις β´.

I

1. Πορευομένου μου εἰς Κώμας[2] κατὰ τὸν
καιρόν, ὃν καὶ πέρυσι, περιπατῶν ἀνεμνήσθην τῆς
περυσινῆς ὁράσεως, καὶ πάλιν με αἴρει πνεῦμα
καὶ ἀποφέρει εἰς τὸν αὐτὸν τόπον, ὅπου καὶ πέρυσι. 2. ἐλθὼν οὖν εἰς τὸν τόπον τιθῶ τὰ γόνατα
καὶ ἠρξάμην προσεύχεσθαι τῷ κυρίῳ καὶ δοξάζειν
αὐτοῦ τὸ ὄνομα, ὅτι με ἄξιον ἡγήσατο καὶ
ἐγνώρισέν μοι τὰς ἁμαρτίας μου τὰς πρότερον.
3. μετὰ δὲ τὸ ἐγερθῆναί με ἀπὸ τῆς προσευχῆς
βλέπω ἀπέναντί μου τὴν πρεσβυτέραν, ἣν καὶ
πέρυσιν[3] ἑωράκειν, περιπατοῦσαν καὶ ἀναγινώ-
σκουσαν βιβλαρίδιον, καὶ λέγει μοι· Δύνῃ ταῦτα

Ps. 85, 9, 12;
Is. 24, 15;
66, 5;

---

[1] πρότερα ℵᵃ A (L priora). ℵ* omits, but the next line
(where A also reads πρότερα) suggests that its archetype read
πρῶτα.
[2] κώμας ℵAE, regionem Cumanorum L, but see the note on
Vis. I, 1. 3.   [3] πέρυσιν ALₗ, πρότερον ℵ, om. ELₗ.

to me ; "Did my reading please you?" and I said to her : "Lady, this last part pleases me, but the first part was hard and difficult." And she said to me : "This last part is for the righteous, but the first part was for the heathen and the apostates." 3. While she was speaking with me two men appeared, and took her by the arm and they went away towards the East, whither the chair had gone. But she went away cheerfully, and as she went said to me, "Play the man, Hermas."

Vision 2

I

1. While I was going to Cumae, at about the same time as the year before, as I walked along I remembered the vision of the previous year, and the spirit again seized me and took me away to the same place, where I had been the previous year. 2. So when I came to the place, I knelt down and began to pray to the Lord and 'to glorify his name,' because he had thought me worthy, and had made known to me my former sins. 3. But after I rose from prayer I saw before me the ancient lady, whom I had seen the year before, walking and reading out from a little book. And she said to

The second vision at Cumae

The ancient lady returns

τοῖς ἐκλεκτοῖς τοῦ θεοῦ ἀναγγεῖλαι; λέγω αὐτῇ·
Κυρία, τοσαῦτα μνημονεῦσαι οὐ δύναμαι· δὸς δέ
μοι τὸ βιβλίδιον, ἵνα μεταγράψωμαι αὐτό. Λάβε,
φησίν, καὶ ἀποδώσεις μοι. 4. ἔλαβον ἐγώ, καὶ
εἴς τινα τόπον τοῦ ἀγροῦ ἀναχωρήσας μετεγρα-
ψά-
μην πάντα πρὸς γράμμα· οὐχ ηὕρισκον γὰρ τὰς
συλλαβάς. τελέσαντος οὖν[1] τὰ γράμματα τοῦ
βιβλιδίου ἐξαίφνης ἡρπάγη μου ἐκ τῆς χειρὸς
τὸ βιβλίδιον· ὑπὸ τίνος δὲ οὐκ εἶδον.

II

1. Μετὰ δὲ δέκα καὶ πέντε ἡμέρας νηστεύσαν-
τός μου καὶ πολλὰ ἐρωτήσαντος τὸν κύριον
ἀπεκαλύφθη μοι ἡ γνῶσις τῆς γραφῆς. ἦν δὲ
γεγραμμένα ταῦτα· 2. Τὸ σπέρμα σου, Ἑρμᾶ,
ἠθέτησαν εἰς τὸν θεὸν καὶ ἐβλασφήμησαν εἰς τὸν
κύριον καὶ προέδωκαν τοὺς γονεῖς αὐτῶν ἐν
πονηρίᾳ μεγάλῃ καὶ ἤκουσαν προδόται γονέων καὶ
προδόντες οὐκ ὠφελήθησαν, ἀλλὰ ἔτι προσέθηκαν ταῖς ἁμαρτίαις αὐτῶν τὰς ἀσελγείας καὶ
συμφυρμοὺς πονηρίας, καὶ οὕτως ἐπλήσθησαν αἱ
ἀνομίαι αὐτῶν. 3. ἀλλὰ γνώρισον ταῦτα τὰ
ῥήματα τοῖς τέκνοις σου πᾶσιν καὶ τῇ συμβίῳ
σου τῇ μελλούσῃ[2] ἀδελφῇ· καὶ γὰρ αὕτη οὐκ
ἀπέχεται τῆς γλώσσης, ἐν ᾗ πονηρεύεται· ἀλλὰ
ἀκούσασα τὰ ῥήματα ταῦτα ἀφέξεται καὶ ἕξει[3]
ἔλεος. 4. μετὰ τὸ γνωρίσαι σε ταῦτα τὰ ῥήματα
αὐτοῖς, ἃ ἐνετείλατό μοι ὁ δεσπότης ἵνα σοι

----

[1] οὖν א, οὖν μου A.
[2] μελλούσῃ א, μελλούσῃ σου A(L).   [3] ἕξεις א.

18

me: "Can you take this message to God's elect ones?" I said to her: "Lady, I cannot remember so much; but give me the little book to copy." "Take it," she said, "and give it me back." 4. I took it and went away to a certain place in the country, and copied it all, letter by letter, for I could not distinguish the syllables.[1] So when I had finished the letters of the little book it was suddenly taken out of my hand; but I did not see by whom.

The little book

II

1. BUT after fifteen days, when I had fasted and prayed greatly to the Lord, the knowledge of the writing was revealed to me. And these things were written: 2. Your seed, Hermas, have set God at naught, and have blasphemed the Lord, and have betrayed their parents in great wickedness, and they are called the betrayers of parents, and their betrayal has not profited them, but they have added to their sins wanton deeds and piled up wickedness, and so their crimes have been made complete. 3. But make these words known to all your children and to your wife, who shall in future be to you as a sister. For she also does not refrain her tongue, with which she sins; but when she has heard these words she will refrain it, and will obtain mercy. 4. After you have made known these words to them, which the

The contents of the little book

---

[1] Hermas no doubt means that it was written, like most early MSS., in a continuous script with no divisions between the words.

ἀποκαλυφθῇ, τότε[1] ἀφίενται αὐτοῖς αἱ ἁμαρτίαι
πᾶσαι, ἃς πρότερον ἥμαρτον, καὶ πᾶσιν τοῖς
ἁγίοις τοῖς ἁμαρτήσασιν μέχρι ταύτης τῆς ἡμέρας,
ἐὰν ἐξ ὅλης τῆς καρδίας μετανοήσωσιν καὶ ἄρωσιν
ἀπὸ τῆς καρδίας[2] αὐτῶν τὰς διψυχίας. 5. ὤμοσεν
γὰρ ὁ δεσπότης κατὰ τῆς δόξης αὐτοῦ ἐπὶ τοὺς
ἐκλεκτοὺς αὐτοῦ· ἐὰν ὡρισμένης τῆς ἡμέρας
ταύτης ἔτι ἁμάρτησις γένηται, μὴ ἔχειν αὐτοὺς
σωτηρίαν· ἡ γὰρ μετάνοια τοῖς δικαίοις ἔχει
τέλος· πεπλήρωνται αἱ ἡμέραι μενανοίας πᾶσιν
τοῖς ἁγίοις· καὶ τοῖς δὲ ἔθνεσιν μετάνοιά ἐστιν
ἕως ἐσχάτης ἡμέρας. 6. ἐρεῖς οὖν τοῖς προηγουμένοις τῆς ἐκκλησίας, ἵνα κατορθώσωνται
τὰς ὁδοὺς αὐτῶν ἐν δικαιοσύνῃ, ἵνα ἀπολάβωσιν
ἐκ πλήρους τὰς ἐπαγγελίας μετὰ πολλῆς δόξης.
7. ἐμμείνατε οὖν οἱ ἐργαζόμενοι τὴν δικαιοσύνην
καὶ μὴ διψυχήσητε, ἵνα γένηται ὑμῶν ἡ πάροδος
μετὰ τῶν ἀγγέλων τῶν ἁγίων. μακάριοι ὑμεῖς,
ὅσοι ὑπομένετε τὴν θλῖψιν τὴν ἐρχομένην τὴν
μεγάλην καὶ ὅσοι οὐκ ἀρνήσονται τὴν ζωὴν αὐτῶν.
8. ὤμοσεν γὰρ κύριος κατὰ τοῦ υἱοῦ αὐτοῦ, τοὺς
ἀρνησαμένους τὸν Χριστὸν[3] αὐτῶν ἀπεγνωρίσθαι
ἀπὸ τῆς ζωῆς αὐτῶν, τοὺς νῦν μέλλοντας ἀρνεῖσθαι ταῖς ἐρχομέναις ἡμέραις· τοῖς δὲ πρότερον

Ps. 15, 2; Acts 10, 35; Heb. 11, 33

---

[1] τότε AL₁E, πότε ℵ L₂.
[2] τῆς καρδίας ℵ, τῶν καρδιῶν A(L).
[3] Χριστόν ℵ*, κύριον ℵᶜ AL₂, filium L₁.

Master commanded me to reveal to you, all the sins which they have formerly committed shall be forgiven them, and they shall be forgiven to all the saints who have sinned up to this day,[1] if they repent with their whole heart, and put aside double-mindedness from their heart. 5. For the Master has sworn to his elect by his glory that if there be still sin after this day has been fixed, they shall find no salvation; for repentance for the just has an end; the days of repentance have been fulfilled for all the saints, but for the heathen repentance is open until the last day. 6. You shall say, then, to the leaders of the Church, that they reform their ways in righteousness, to receive in full the promises with great glory. 7. You, therefore, 'who work righteousness,' must remain steadfast and be not double-minded, that your passing may be with the holy angels.[2] Blessed are you, as many as endure the great persecution which is coming, and as many as shall not deny their life. 8. For the Lord has sworn by his Son that those who have denied their Christ have been rejected from their life, that is, those who shall now deny him in the days to come.

[1] This is the main point of the "Shepherd." The primitive teaching was that for sin after baptism no repentance is possible (cf. Heb. vi.). Hermas now states that it has been revealed to him that "up to this day," i.e. the time of his revelation, sin will be forgiven to the repentant. But this offer of forgiveness will not be made a second time.

[2] Cf. Herm. Sim. ix, 25. and Martyr. Polycarp. ii 3 with the note on the latter passage as to the doctrine of a transformation of the just into angels after their death.

ἀρνησαμένοις, διὰ τὴν πολυσπλαγχνίαν ἵλεως
ἐγένετο αὐτοῖς.

III

1. Σὺ δέ, Ἑρμᾶ, μηκέτι μνησικακήσῃς τοῖς
τέκνοις σου μηδὲ τὴν ἀδελφήν σου ἐάσῃς, ἵνα
καθαρισθῶσιν ἀπὸ τῶν προτέρων ἁμαρτιῶν
αὐτῶν. παιδευθήσονται γὰρ παιδείᾳ δικαίᾳ, ἐὰν
σὺ μὴ μνησικακήσῃς αὐτοῖς. μνησικακία θάνατον
κατεργάζεται. σὺ δέ, Ἑρμᾶ, μεγάλας θλίψεις
ἔσχες ἰδιωτικὰς διὰ τὰς παραβάσεις τοῦ οἴκου
σου, ὅτι οὐκ ἐμέλησέν σοι περὶ αὐτῶν· ἀλλὰ
παρενεθυμήθης καὶ ταῖς πραγματείαις σου συν-
ανεφύρης ταῖς πονηραῖς· 2. ἀλλὰ σώζει σε τὸ
Heb. 3, 11 μὴ ἀποστῆναί σε ἀπὸ θεοῦ ζῶντος καὶ ἡ ἁπλότης
σου καὶ ἡ πολλὴ ἐγκράτεια· ταῦτα σέσωκέν σε,
ἐὰν ἐμμείνῃς, καὶ πάντας σώζει τοὺς τὰ τοιαῦτα
ἐργαζομένους καὶ πορευομένους ἐν ἀκακίᾳ καὶ
ἁπλότητι. οὗτοι κατισχύσουσιν[1] πάσης πονηρίας
Ps. 106, 3; 15, 2 καὶ παραμενοῦσιν εἰς ζωὴν αἰώνιον. 3. μακάριοι
πάντες οἱ ἐργαζόμενοι τὴν δικαιοσύνην. οὐ δια-
φθαρήσονται ἕως αἰῶνος. 4. ἐρεῖς δὲ Μαξίμῳ·
Ἰδού, θλῖψις ἔρχεται· ἐάν σοι φανῇ, πάλιν
ἄρνησαι. Ἐγγὺς κύριος τοῖς ἐπιστρεφομένοις, ὡς
Eldad and Modat γέγραπται ἐν τῷ Ἐλδὰδ καὶ Μωδάτ,[2] τοῖς προ-
φητεύσασιν ἐν τῇ ἐρήμῳ τῷ λαῷ.

---

[1] κατισχύουσιν ℵ.
[2] Ἐλδὰδ καὶ Μωδάτ ℵ, Ἐλὰδ καὶ Μωδάδ A, Heldam et
Modal L₁, Heldat et Modat L₂, Eldad et Mudath A.

But those who denied him formerly have obtained forgiveness through his great mercy.

III

1. "But, Hermas, no longer bear a grudge against your children, nor neglect your sister, that they may be cleansed from their former sins. For they will be corrected with righteous correction, if you bear no grudge against them. The bearing of grudges works death. But you, Hermas, had great troubles of your own because of the transgressions of your family, because you did not pay attention to them. But you neglected them and became entangled in their evil deeds. 2. But you are saved by not 'having broken away from the living God,' and by your simplicity and great temperance. These things have saved you, if you remain in them, and they save all whose deeds are such, and who walk in innocence and simplicity. These shall overcome all wickedness and remain steadfast to eternal life. 3. 'Blessed' are all they 'who do righteousness'; they shall not perish for ever. 4. But you shall say to Maximus: 'Behold, persecution is coming, if it seems good to you deny the faith again.' 'The Lord is near those that turn to him,' as it is written in the Book of Eldad and Modat,[1] who prophesied to the people in the wilderness."

[1] This book is mentioned among the Apocrypha of the N.T. in the Athanasian Synopsis and in the Stichometry of Nicephorus, but is not extant. It is thought to be quoted in II Clem. xi. 2. Eldad and Modat are mentioned in Numbers xi. 26.

IV

1. Ἀπεκαλύφθη δέ μοι, ἀδελφοί, κοιμωμένῳ ὑπὸ νεανίσκου εὐειδεστάτου λέγοντός μοι· Τὴν πρεσβυτέραν, παρ' ἧς ἔλαβες τὸ βιβλίδιον, τίνα δοκεῖς εἶναι; ἐγώ φημι· Τὴν Σίβυλλαν. Πλανᾶσαι, φησίν, οὐκ ἔστιν. Τίς οὖν ἐστιν; φημί. Ἡ Ἐκκλησία, φησίν. εἶπον αὐτῷ· Διατί οὖν πρεσβυτέρα; Ὅτι, φησίν, πάντων πρώτη ἐκτίσθη· διὰ τοῦτο πρεσβυτέρα· καὶ διὰ ταύτην ὁ κόσμος κατηρτίσθη. 2. μετέπειτα δὲ ὅρασιν εἶδον ἐν τῷ οἴκῳ μου. ἦλθεν ἡ πρεσβυτέρα καὶ ἠρώτησέν με, εἰ ἤδη τὸ βιβλίον δέδωκα τοῖς πρεσβυτέροις. ἠρνησάμην δεδωκέναι. Καλῶς, φησίν, πεποίηκας· ἔχω γὰρ ῥήματα προσθεῖναι. ὅταν οὖν ἀποτελέσω τὰ ῥήματα πάντα, διὰ σοῦ γνωρισθήσεται τοῖς ἐκλεκτοῖς πᾶσιν. 3. γράψεις οὖν[1] δύο βιβλαρίδια καὶ πέμψεις ἓν Κλήμεντι καὶ ἓν Γραπτῇ. πέμψει οὖν Κλήμης εἰς τὰς ἔξω πόλεις, ἐκείνῳ γὰρ ἐπιτέτραπται· Γραπτὴ δὲ νουθετήσει τὰς χήρας καὶ τοὺς ὀρφανούς. σὺ δὲ ἀναγνώσῃ εἰς ταύτην τὴν πόλιν μετὰ τῶν πρεσβυτέρων τῶν προϊσταμένων τῆς ἐκκλησίας.

Ὅρασις γ΄.

I

1. Ἣν εἶδον, ἀδελφοί, τοιαύτη. 2. νηστεύσας πολλάκις καὶ δεηθεὶς τοῦ κυρίου, ἵνα μοι φανε-

---

[1] γράψεις οὖν ℵᶜ AL₁, γράψεις ℵ*, καὶ γράψεις L₂F.

IV

1. AND a revelation was made to me, brethren, while I slept, by a very beautiful young man who said to me, " Who do you think that the ancient lady was from whom you received the little book?" I said, "The Sibyl." "You are wrong," he said, "she is not." "Who is she, then?" I said. "The Church," he said. I said to him, "Why then is she old?" "Because," he said, "she was created the first of all things. For this reason is she old; and for her sake was the world established." 2. And afterwards I saw a vision in my house. The ancient lady came and asked me if I had already given the book to the elders. I said that I had not given it. "You have done well," she said, "for I have words to add. When, therefore, I have finished all the words they shall be made known by you to all the elect. 3. You shall therefore write two little books and send one to Clement and one to Grapte. Clement then shall send it to the cities abroad, for that is his duty; and Grapte shall exhort the widows and orphans; but in this city you shall read it yourself with the elders who are in charge of the church."

The revelation as to the ancient lady

The ancient lady returns

Vision 3.

I

1. THE third vision which I saw, brethren, was as follows: 2. I had fasted for a long time, and prayed

The ancient lady comes again

ρώσῃ τὴν ἀποκάλυψιν, ἥν μοι ἐπηγγείλατο
δεῖξαι διὰ τῆς πρεσβυτέρας ἐκείνης,[1] αὐτῇ τῇ
νυκτί μοι ὦπται ἡ πρεσβυτέρα καὶ εἶπέν μοι·
Ἐπεὶ οὕτως ἐνδεὴς εἶ καὶ σπουδαῖος εἰς τὸ γνῶναι
πάντα, ἐλθὲ εἰς τὸν ἀγρόν, ὅπου χονδρίζεις, καὶ
περὶ ὥραν πέμπτην ἐμφανισθήσομαί σοι καὶ
δείξω σοι, ἃ δεῖ σε ἰδεῖν. 3. ἠρώτησα αὐτὴν
λέγων· Κυρία, εἰς ποῖον τόπον τοῦ ἀγροῦ; Ὅπου,
φησίν, θέλεις. ἐξελεξάμην τόπον καλὸν ἀνα-
κεχωρηκότα. πρὶν δὲ λαλῆσαι αὐτῇ καὶ εἰπεῖν
τὸν τόπον, λέγει μοι· Ἥξω[2] ἐκεῖ, ὅπου θέλεις.
4. ἐγενόμην οὖν, ἀδελφοί, εἰς τὸν ἀγρὸν καὶ
συνεψήφισα τὰς ὥρας καὶ ἦλθον εἰς τὸν τόπον,
ὅπου διεταξάμην αὐτῇ ἐλθεῖν, καὶ βλέπω συμψέλιον κείμενον ἐλεφάντινον, καὶ ἐπὶ τοῦ συμψελίου ἔκειτο κερβικάριον λινοῦν καὶ ἐπάνω
λέντιον ἐξηπλωμένον λινοῦν καρπάσιον. 5. ἰδὼν
ταῦτα κείμενα καὶ μηδένα ὄντα ἐν τῷ τόπῳ
ἔκθαμβος ἐγενόμην, καὶ ὡσεὶ τρόμος με ἔλαβεν
καὶ αἱ τρίχες μου ὀρθαί· καὶ ὡσεὶ φρίκη μοι
προσῆλθεν μόνου μου ὄντος. ἐν ἐμαυτῷ οὖν
γενόμενος καὶ μνησθεὶς τῆς δόξης τοῦ θεοῦ καὶ
λαβὼν θάρσος, θεὶς τὰ γόνατα ἐξωμολογούμην τῷ
κυρίῳ πάλιν τὰς ἁμαρτίας μου[3] ὡς καὶ πρότερον.
6. ἡ δὲ ἦλθεν μετὰ νεανίσκων ἕξ, οὓς καὶ πρότερον ἑωράκειν, καὶ ἐστάθη[4] μοι καὶ κατηκροᾶτο
προσευχομένου καὶ ἐξομολογουμένου τῷ κυρίῳ
τὰς ἁμαρτίας μου. καὶ ἁψαμένη μου λέγει·

---

[1] ἐκεινης om. א.   [2] Om. א*.
[3] ἁμαρτίας μου—ἁμαρτίας μου om. per homoiot. אL₂.
[4] ἐστάθη A, stetit post me L₁E, ἐπεστάθη is accepted by
most editors as an emendation.

the Lord to explain to me the revelation which he had promised to show me through that ancient lady ; and in the same night the ancient lady appeared to me and said to me : " Since you are so importunate and zealous to know everything, come into the country, where you are farming, and at the fifth hour I will appear to you, and show you what you must see." 3. I asked her, saying, " Lady, to what part of the field ? " " Where you like," she said. I chose a beautiful secluded spot ; but before I spoke to her and mentioned the place she said to me, " I will be there, where you wish." 4. I went, therefore, brethren, to the country, and I counted the hours, and I came to the spot where I had arranged for her to come, and I saw a couch of ivory The couch placed there, and on the couch there lay a linen of ivory pillow, and over it a covering of fine linen was spread out. 5. When I saw these things lying there, and no one in the place I was greatly amazed, and, as it were, trembling seized me and my hair stood on end. And, as it were, panic came to me because I was alone. When therefore I came to myself, and remembered the glory of God and took courage, I knelt down and confessed my sins again to the Lord, as I had also done before. 6. And she came with The six six young men, whom I had also seen on the former young men occasion, and stood by me, and listened to me praying and confessing my sins to the Lord. And

Ἑρμᾶ, παῦσαι περὶ τῶν ἁμαρτιῶν σου πάντα
ἐρωτῶν· ἐρώτα καὶ περὶ δικαιοσύνης, ἵνα
λάβῃς μέρος τι ἐξ αὐτῆς εἰς τὸν οἶκόν σου.
7. καὶ ἐξεγείρει με τῆς χειρὸς καὶ ἄγει με πρὸς
τὸ συμψέλιον καὶ λέγει τοῖς νεανίσκοις· Ὑπάγετε
καὶ οἰκοδομεῖτε. 8. καὶ μετὰ τὸ ἀναχωρῆσαι
τοὺς νεανίσκους καὶ μόνων ἡμῶν γεγονότων λέγει
μοι· Κάθισον ὧδε. λέγω αὐτῇ· Κυρία, ἄφες τοὺς
πρεσβυτέρους πρῶτον καθίσαι. Ὅ σοι λέγω,
φησίν, κάθισον. 9. θέλοντος οὖν μου καθίσαι εἰς
τὰ δεξιὰ μέρη οὐκ εἴασέ με, ἀλλ᾽ ἐννεύει μοι τῇ
χειρί, ἵνα εἰς τὰ ἀριστερὰ μέρη καθίσω. διαλογι-
ζομένου[1] μου οὖν καὶ λυπουμένου, ὅτι οὐκ εἴασέ
με εἰς τὰ δεξιὰ μέρη καθίσαι, λέγει μοι· Λυπῇ,
Ἑρμᾶ; ὁ εἰς τὰ δεξιὰ μέρη τόπος ἄλλων ἐστίν,
τῶν ἤδη εὐαρεστηκότων τῷ θεῷ καὶ παθόντων
εἵνεκα τοῦ ὀνόματος·[2] σοὶ δὲ πολλὰ λείπει ἵνα
μετ᾽ αὐτῶν καθίσῃς· ἀλλὰ ὡς μένεις[3] τῇ
ἁπλότητί σου, μεῖνον, καὶ καθιῇ μετ᾽ αὐτῶν καὶ
ὅσοι ἐὰν ἐργάσωνται τὰ ἐκείνων ἔργα καὶ
ὑπενέγκωσιν, ἃ καὶ ἐκεῖνοι ὑπήνεγκαν.

II

1. Τί, φημί, ὑπήνεγκαν; Ἄκουε, φησίν· μάστιγας, φυλακάς, θλίψεις μεγάλας, σταυρούς, θηρία
εἵνεκεν τοῦ ὀνόματος· διὰ τοῦτο ἐκείνων ἐστὶν τὰ

[1] διαλογιζ. א*, λογιζομ. A (א* om. per homoiot. ἀλλ᾽ ἐννεύει—εἴασέ με).
[2] μου τοῦ ὀνόματος א*, τοῦ ὀνόματός μου א^c, τοῦ ὀνόματος αὐτοῦ AL₂E, τοῦ ὀνόματος L₁. [3] μένεις א*, ἐμμένεις א^cA.

28

she touched me and said : " Hermas ! stop asking
all these questions about your sins, ask also
concerning righteousness, that you may take presently
some part of it to your family." 7. And she raised
me up by the hand and took me to the couch and said
to the young men : " Go and build." 8. And after
the young men had gone away and we were alone,
she said to me : " Sit here." I said to her : " Lady,
let the elders sit first.[1] " She said : " Do what I tell
you, and sit down." 9. Yet when I wished to sit Hermas
on the right hand she would not let me, but signed couch
to me with her hand to sit on the left. When therefore I thought about this, and was grieved because
she did not let me sit on the right hand, she said to
me : " Are you sorry, Hermas ? The seat on the The place
right is for others, who have already been found martyrs
well-pleasing to God and have suffered for the Name.
But you fall far short of sitting with them. But
remain in your simplicity as you are doing, and you
shall sit with them, and so shall all who do their
deeds and bear what they also bore."

II

1. " What," I said, " did they bear ? " " Listen,"
she said : " Stripes, imprisonments, great afflictions,
crucifixions, wild beasts, for the sake of the Name.

[1] The meaning is obscure : ' the elders ' is often explained
as ' the Elders of the Church,' but it is more probably a
mere formula of politeness ' seniores priores.'

δεξιὰ μέρη τοῦ ἁγιάσματος καὶ ὃς ἐὰν πάθη διὰ
τὸ ὄνομα· τῶν δὲ λοιπῶν τὰ ἀριστερὰ μέρη ἐστίν.
ἀλλὰ ἀμφοτέρων, καὶ τῶν ἐκ δεξιῶν καὶ τῶν
ἀριστερῶν καθημένων, τὰ αὐτὰ δῶρα καὶ αἱ αὐταὶ
ἐπαγγελίαι· μόνον ἐκεῖνοι ἐκ δεξιῶν κάθηνται καὶ
ἔχουσιν δόξαν τινά. 2. σὺ δὲ κατεπιθυμεῖς καθίσαι ἐκ δεξιῶν μετ' αὐτῶν, ἀλλὰ τὰ ὑστερήματά
σου πολλά. καθαρισθήσῃ δὲ ἀπὸ τῶν ὑστερημά-
των σου· καὶ πάντες[1] οἱ μὴ διψυχοῦντες καθαρ-
ισθήσονται ἀπὸ πάντων τῶν ἁμαρτημάτων εἰς
ταύτην τὴν ἡμέραν. 3. ταῦτα εἴπασα ἤθελεν
ἀπελθεῖν· πεσὼν δὲ αὐτῆς πρὸς τοὺς πόδας
ἠρώτησα αὐτὴν κατὰ τοῦ κυρίου, ἵνα μοι ἐπιδείξῃ
ὃ ἐπηγγείλατο ὅραμα. 4. ἡ δὲ πάλιν ἐπελάβετό
μου τῆς χειρὸς καὶ ἐγείρει με καὶ καθίζει ἐπὶ τὸ
συμψέλιον ἐξ εὐωνύμων· ἐκαθέζετο δὲ καὶ αὐτὴ
ἐκ δεξιῶν. καὶ ἐπάρασα ῥάβδον τινὰ λαμπρὰν
λέγει μοι· Βλέπεις μέγα πρᾶγμα; λέγω αὐτῇ·
Κυρία, οὐδὲν βλέπω. λέγει μοι· Σύ, ἰδού, οὐχ
ὁρᾷς κατέναντί σου πύργον μέγαν οἰκοδομούμενον
ἐπὶ ὑδάτων λίθοις τετραγώνοις λαμπροῖς; 5. ἐν
τετραγώνῳ δὲ ᾠκοδομεῖτο ὁ πύργος ὑπὸ τῶν ἐξ[2]
νεανίσκων τῶν ἐληλυθότων μετ' αὐτῆς· ἄλλαι δὲ
μυριάδες ἀνδρῶν παρέφερον λίθους, οἱ μὲν ἐκ τοῦ
βυθοῦ, οἱ δὲ ἐκ τῆς γῆς, καὶ ἐπεδίδουν τοῖς ἐξ[2]
νεανίσκοις· ἐκεῖνοι δὲ ἐλάμβανον καὶ ᾠκοδόμουν.
6. τοὺς μὲν ἐκ τοῦ βυθοῦ λίθους ἑλκομένους
πάντας οὕτως ἐτίθεσαν εἰς τὴν οἰκοδομήν· ἡρμοσμένοι γὰρ ἦσαν καὶ συνεφώνουν τῇ ἁρμογῇ μετὰ
τῶν ἑτέρων· καὶ οὕτως ἐκολλῶντο ἀλλήλοις,
ὥστε τὴν ἁρμογὴν αὐτῶν μὴ φαίνεσθαι. ἐφαίνετο

---

[1] πάντες א*, πάντες δὲ א°A.   [2] ἓξ א° ALE, ἑξήκοντα א*.

Therefore is it given to them to be on the right
hand of the Holiness, and to everyone who shall
suffer for the Name; but for the rest there is the left
side. But both, whether they sit on the right
or the left, have the same gifts, and the same
promises, only the former sit on the right and have
somewhat of glory. 2. And you are desirous of
sitting on the right hand with them, but your
failings are many. But you shall be cleansed from
your failings, and all who are not double-minded
shall be cleansed from all sins, up to this day."
3. When she had said this she wished to go away,
but I fell at her feet and besought her by the Lord,
to show me the vision which she had promised.
4. And she again took me by the hand and lifted The vision
me up, and made me sit on the couch on the left of the town
and she herself sat on the right. And she lifted up
a certain glittering rod, and she said to me: " Do
you see a great thing?" I said to her: " Lady, I
see nothing." She said to me: " Behold, do you
not see before you a great tower being built on the
water with shining square stones?" 5. Now the
tower was being built four-square by the six young
men who had come with her; but tens of thousands
of other men were bringing stones, some from the
deep sea, and some from the land, and were giving
them to the six young men, and these kept taking
them and building. 6. The stones which had been The stones
dragged from the deep sea, they placed without
exception as they were into the building, for they
had all been shaped and fitted into the joins with
the other stones. And they so fastened one to the
other that their joins could not be seen. But the

31

δὲ ἡ οἰκοδομὴ τοῦ πύργου ὡς ἐξ ἑνὸς λίθου
ᾠκοδομημένη. 7. τοὺς δὲ ἑτέρους λίθους τοὺς
φερομένους ἀπὸ τῆς ξηρᾶς τοὺς μὲν ἀπέβαλλον,
τοὺς δὲ ἐτίθουν εἰς τὴν οἰκοδομήν· ἄλλους δὲ
κατέκοπτον καὶ ἔρριπτον[1] μακρὰν ἀπὸ τοῦ πύργου.
8. ἄλλοι δὲ λίθοι πολλοὶ κύκλῳ τοῦ πύργου[2]
ἔκειντο, καὶ οὐκ ἐχρῶντο αὐτοῖς ἐπὶ[3] τὴν οἰκοδομήν·
ἦσαν γάρ τινες ἐξ αὐτῶν ἐψωριακότες, ἕτεροι δὲ
σχισμὰς ἔχοντες, ἄλλοι δὲ κεκολοβωμένοι, ἄλλοι
δὲ λευκοὶ καὶ στρογγύλοι, μὴ ἁρμόζοντες εἰς τὴν
οἰκοδομήν. 9. ἔβλεπον δὲ ἑτέρους λίθους ῥιπτομένους μακρὰν ἀπὸ τοῦ πύργου καὶ ἐρχομένους εἰς
τὴν ὁδὸν καὶ μὴ μένοντας ἐν τῇ ὁδῷ, ἀλλὰ κυλιομένους ἐκ τῆς ὁδοῦ εἰς τὴν ἀνοδίαν· ἑτέρους δὲ
ἐπὶ πῦρ ἐμπίπτοντας καὶ καιομένους· ἑτέρους δὲ
πίπτοντας ἐγγὺς ὑδάτων καὶ μὴ δυναμένους
κυλισθῆναι εἰς τὸ ὕδωρ, καίπερ θελόντων κυλισθῆναι καὶ ἐλθεῖν εἰς τὸ ὕδωρ.

III

1. Δείξασά μοι ταῦτα ἤθελεν ἀποτρέχειν.
λέγω αὐτῇ· Κυρία, τί μοι ὄφελος ταῦτα ἑωρακότι
καὶ μὴ γινώσκοντι, τί ἐστιν τὰ πράγματα;
ἀποκριθεῖσά μοι λέγει· Πανοῦργος εἶ ἄνθρωπος,
θέλων γινώσκειν τὰ περὶ τὸν πύργον. Ναί, φημί,
κυρία, ἵνα τοῖς ἀδελφοῖς ἀναγγείλω καὶ ἱλαρώτεροι
γένωνται καὶ ταῦτα[4] ἀκούσαντες γινώσκωσιν τὸν

---

[1] ἔρριπτον ALE, ἐτίθουν ℵ.
[2] τοῦ πύργου—τοῦ πύργου om. per homoiot. ℵ.
[3] ἐπὶ ℵ*, εἰς ℵcA.
[4] ἱλαρώτεροι γένωνται, καὶ ταῦτα AL, om. ℵE which also alter
the next sentence to ἐν πολλῇ δόξῃ, ἔφη, ἀκούσονται κ.τ.λ.

building of the tower appeared as if it had been built of a single stone. 7. Of the other stones, which were being brought from the dry ground, they cast some away, and some they put into the building and others they broke up and cast far from the tower. 8. And many other stones were lying round the tower, and they did not use them for the building, for some of them were rotten, and others had cracks, and others were too short, and others were white and round and did not fit into the building. 9. And I saw other stones being cast far from the tower, and coming on to the road, and not staying on the road, but rolling from the road into the rough ground. And others were falling into the fire, and were being burnt, and others were falling near the water, and could not be rolled into the water, although men wished them to be rolled on and to come into the water.

III

1. When she had showed me these things she wished to hasten away. I said to her : " Lady, what does it benefit me to have seen these things, if I do not know what they mean ? " She answered me and said : " You are a persistent man, wanting to know about the tower." " Yes," I said, " Lady, in order that I may report to my brethren, and that they may be made more joyful, and when they hear these

The explanation of the vision

κύριον ἐν πολλῇ δόξῃ. 2. ἡ δὲ ἔφη· Ἀκούσονται
μὲν πολλοί· ἀκούσαντες δέ τινες ἐξ αὐτῶν
χαρήσονται, τινὲς δὲ κλαύσονται· ἀλλὰ καὶ οὗτοι,
ἐὰν ἀκούσωσιν καὶ μετανοήσωσιν, καὶ αὐτοὶ
χαρήσονται. ἄκουε οὖν τὰς παραβολὰς τοῦ πύρ-
γου· ἀποκαλύψω γάρ σοι πάντα. καὶ μηκέτι μοι
κόπους πάρεχε περὶ ἀποκαλύψεως· αἱ γὰρ ἀποκαλύψεις αὗται τέλος ἔχουσιν· πεπληρωμέναι γάρ
εἰσιν. ἀλλ' οὐ παύσῃ αἰτούμενος ἀποκαλύψεις·
ἀναιδὴς γὰρ εἶ. 3. ὁ μὲν πύργος, ὃν βλέπεις
οἰκοδομούμενον, ἐγώ εἰμι ἡ Ἐκκλησία, ἡ ὀφθεῖσά
σοι καὶ νῦν καὶ τὸ πρότερον· ὃ ἂν οὖν θελήσῃς,
ἐπερώτα περὶ τοῦ πύργου, καὶ ἀποκαλύψω σοι,
ἵνα χαρῇς μετὰ τῶν ἁγίων. 4. λέγω αὐτῇ· Κυρία,
ἐπεὶ ἅπαξ ἄξιόν με ἡγήσω τοῦ πάντα μοι ἀπο-
καλύψαι, ἀποκάλυψον. ἡ δὲ λέγει μοι· Ὃ ἐὰν
ἐνδέχηταί σοι ἀποκαλυφθῆναι, ἀποκαλυφθήσεται.
μόνον ἡ καρδία σου πρὸς τὸν θεὸν ἤτω καὶ μὴ
διψυχήσεις, ὃ ἂν ἴδῃς. 5. ἐπηρώτησα αὐτήν· Διατί
ὁ πύργος ἐπὶ ὑδάτων ᾠκοδόμηται, κυρία; Εἶπά
σοι, φησίν, καὶ τὸ πρότερον, καὶ ἐκζητεῖς ἐπι-
μελῶς· ἐκζητῶν οὖν εὑρίσκεις τὴν ἀλήθειαν. διατί
οὖν ἐπὶ ὑδάτων ᾠκοδόμηται ὁ πύργος, ἄκουε· ὅτι
ἡ ζωὴ ὑμῶν διὰ ὕδατος ἐσώθη καὶ σωθήσεται.
τεθεμελίωται δὲ ὁ πύργος τῷ ῥήματι τοῦ παντο-
κράτορος καὶ ἐνδόξου ὀνόματος, κρατεῖται δὲ ὑπὸ
τῆς ἀοράτου δυνάμεως τοῦ δεσπότου.

IV

1. Ἀποκριθεὶς λέγω αὐτῇ· Κυρία, μεγάλως
καὶ θαυμαστῶς ἔχει τὸ πρᾶγμα τοῦτο· οἱ δὲ

34

things may know the Lord in great glory."
2. And she said : "Many indeed shall hear, but
some of them shall rejoice when they hear, and
some shall mourn. But these also, if they hear and
repent, even they shall rejoice. Hear then, the
parables of the tower, for I will reveal everything to
you. And no longer trouble me about revelation,
for these revelations are finished, for they have been
fulfilled. Yet you will not cease asking for
revelations, for you are shameless. 3. The tower
which you see being built is myself, the Church,
who have appeared to you both now and formerly.
Ask, therefore, what you will about the tower, and I The tower
will reveal it to you, that you may rejoice with the
saints." 4. I said to her : "Lady, since you have
once thought me worthy to reveal everything to me,
proceed with the revelation." And she said to me :
"What is permitted to be revealed to you shall be
revealed ; only let your heart be turned towards God
and do not be double-minded as to what you see."
5. I asked her : "Why has the tower been built on
the water, Lady ? " "As I told you before, you are
seeking diligently," said she, "and so by seeking you
are finding out the truth. Hear, then, why the tower
has been built upon the water : because your life was
saved and shall be saved through water, and the tower
has been founded by the utterance of the almighty
and glorious Name, and is maintained by the unseen
power of the Master."

IV

1. I answered and said to her : "Lady, great and The six
wonderful is this thing. But, Lady, who are the six young men

35

νεανίσκοι οἱ ἐξ[1] οἱ οἰκοδομοῦντες, τίνες εἰσίν,
κυρία; Οὗτοί εἰσιν οἱ ἅγιοι ἄγγελοι τοῦ θεοῦ οἱ
πρῶτοι κτισθέντες, οἷς παρέδωκεν ὁ κύριος πᾶσαν
τὴν κτίσιν αὐτοῦ αὔξειν καὶ οἰκοδομεῖν καὶ
δεσπόζειν τῆς κτίσεως πάσης· διὰ τούτων οὖν
τελεσθήσεται ἡ οἰκοδομὴ τοῦ πύργου. 2. Οἱ δὲ
ἕτεροι οἱ παραφέροντες τοὺς λίθους, τίνες εἰσίν;
Καὶ αὐτοὶ ἅγιοι ἄγγελοι τοῦ θεοῦ· οὗτοι δὲ οἱ ἐξ
ὑπερέχοντες αὐτούς εἰσιν· συντελεσθήσεται οὖν
ἡ οἰκοδομὴ τοῦ πύργου, καὶ πάντες ὁμοῦ εὐφρανθή-
σονται κύκλῳ τοῦ πύργου καὶ δοξάσουσιν τὸν
θεόν, ὅτι ἐτελέσθη ἡ οἰκοδομὴ τοῦ πύργου. 3.
ἐπηρώτησα αὐτὴν λέγων· Κυρία, ἤθελον γνῶναι
τῶν λίθων τὴν ἔξοδον καὶ τὴν δύναμιν αὐτῶν,
ποταπή ἐστιν. ἀποκριθεῖσά μοι λέγει· Οὐχ ὅτι
σὺ ἐκ πάντων ἀξιώτερος εἶ, ἵνα σοι ἀποκαλυφθῇ.
ἄλλοι γάρ σου πρότεροί εἰσιν καὶ βελτίονές σου,
οἷς ἔδει ἀποκαλυφθῆναι τὰ ὁράματα ταῦτα· ἀλλ'
Ps. 86, 9. 12 ἵνα δοξασθῇ τὸ ὄνομα τοῦ θεοῦ, σοὶ ἀπεκαλύφθη
καὶ ἀποκαλυφθήσεται διὰ τοὺς διψύχους, τοὺς δια-
λογιζομένους ἐν ταῖς καρδίαις αὐτῶν, εἰ ἄρα ἔστιν
ταῦτα ἢ οὐκ ἔστιν.[2] λέγε αὐτοῖς, ὅτι ταῦτα πάντα
ἐστὶν ἀληθῆ καὶ οὐδὲν ἔξωθέν ἐστιν τῆς ἀληθείας,
ἀλλὰ πάντα ἰσχυρὰ καὶ βέβαια καὶ τεθεμελιωμένα
ἐστίν.

V

1. Ἄκουε νῦν περὶ τῶν λίθων τῶν ὑπαγόντων
εἰς τὴν οἰκοδομήν. οἱ μὲν οὖν λίθοι οἱ τετράγωνοι

---

[1] ἐξ ℵᶜ AL, ἑξήκοντα ℵ*, om. E. (but in the next verse ℵ
also reads ἐξ).   [2] εἰ ἄρα . . . οὐκ ἔστιν om. ℵ*.

36

young men who are building?" "These are the
holy angels of God, who were first created, to whom
the Lord delivered all his creation to make it increase,
and to build it up, and to rule the whole creation.
Through them, therefore, the building of the tower
shall be completed." 2. "But who are the others, who
are bringing the stones?" "They also are holy angels
of God, but these six are greater than they. Therefore the building of the tower shall be completed,
and all shall rejoice together around the tower, and
shall glorify God because the building of the tower
has been completed." 3. I asked her saying:
"Lady, I would like to know the end of the stones,
and what kind of force [1] they have." She answered
me and said: "It is not because you are more worthy
than all others that a revelation should be made to
you, for there were others before you and better
than you, to whom these visions ought to have been
revealed. But in order that 'the name of God might
be glorified' they have been, and shall be, revealed
to you because of the double-minded who dispute in
their heart whether these things are so or not. Tell
them, that all these things are true, and that there
is nothing beyond the truth, but that all things are
strong and certain and well-founded.

V

1. "Listen then concerning the stones which go The stones
into the building. The stones which are square and

---

[1] Here almost the equivalent of 'meaning.'—'What is
their meaning in the vision?'

καὶ λευκοὶ καὶ συμφωνοῦντες ταῖς ἁρμογαῖς
αὐτῶν, οὗτοί εἰσιν οἱ ἀπόστολοι καὶ ἐπίσκοποι
καὶ διδάσκαλοι καὶ διάκονοι οἱ πορευθέντες κατὰ
τὴν σεμνότητα τοῦ θεοῦ καὶ ἐπισκοπήσαντες καὶ
διδάξαντες καὶ διακονήσαντες ἁγνῶς καὶ σεμνῶς
τοῖς ἐκλεκτοῖς τοῦ θεοῦ, οἱ μὲν κεκοιμημένοι, οἱ δὲ
ἔτι ὄντες· καὶ πάντοτε ἑαυτοῖς συνεφώνησαν καὶ
ἐν ἑαυτοῖς εἰρήνην ἔσχον καὶ ἀλλήλων ἤκουον· διὰ
τοῦτο ἐν τῇ οἰκοδομῇ τοῦ πύργου συμφωνοῦσιν αἱ
ἁρμογαὶ αὐτῶν. 2. Οἱ δὲ ἐκ τοῦ βυθοῦ ἑλκόμενοι
καὶ ἐπιτιθέμενοι εἰς τὴν οἰκοδομὴν καὶ συμφωνοῦντες ταῖς ἁρμογαῖς αὐτῶν μετὰ τῶν ἑτέρων
λίθων τῶν ἤδη ᾠκοδομημένων, τίνες εἰσίν; Οὗτοί
εἰσιν οἱ παθόντες ἕνεκεν τοῦ ὀνόματος τοῦ κυρίου.[1]
3. Τοὺς δὲ ἑτέρους λίθους τοὺς φερομένους ἀπὸ τῆς
ξηρᾶς θέλω γνῶναι, τίνες εἰσίν, κυρία. ἔφη·
Τοὺς μὲν εἰς τὴν οἰκοδομὴν ὑπάγοντας καὶ
μὴ λατομουμένους, τούτους ὁ κύριος ἐδοκίμασεν,
ὅτι ἐπορεύθησαν ἐν τῇ εὐθύτητι τοῦ κυρίου καὶ
κατωρθώσαντο τὰς ἐντολὰς αὐτοῦ. 4. Οἱ δὲ
ἀγόμενοι καὶ τιθέμενοι εἰς τὴν οἰκοδομήν, τίνες
εἰσίν; Νέοι εἰσὶν ἐν τῇ πίστει καὶ πιστοί. νουθε-
τοῦνται δὲ ὑπὸ τῶν ἀγγέλων εἰς τὸ ἀγαθοποιεῖν,
διότι εὑρέθη[2] ἐν αὐτοῖς πονηρία. 5. Οὓς δὲ
ἀπέβαλλον καὶ ἐρίπτουν, τίνες εἰσίν; Οὗτοί εἰσιν
ἡμαρτηκότες καὶ θέλοντες μετανοῆσαι· διὰ τοῦτο
μακρὰν οὐκ ἀπερίφησαν ἔξω τοῦ πύργου, ὅτι
εὔχρηστοι ἔσονται εἰς τὴν οἰκοδομήν, ἐὰν μετανοήσωσιν. οἱ οὖν μέλλοντες μετανοεῖν, ἐὰν μετανοήσωσιν, ἰσχυροὶ ἔσονται ἐν τῇ πίστει, ἐὰν νῦν
μετανοήσωσιν, ἐν ᾧ οἰκοδομεῖται ὁ πύργος. ἐὰν

---

[1] κυρίου AL, θεοῦ ℵ.   [2] εὑρέθη ℵ₂, οὐχ εὑρέθη AL₁E.

38

white and which fit into their joins are the Apostles and bishops and teachers and deacons who walked according to the majesty of God, and served the elect of God in holiness and reverence as bishops and teachers and deacons ; some of them are fallen asleep and some are still alive. And they always agreed among themselves, and had peace among themselves, and listened to one another ; for which cause their joins fit in the building of the tower."
2. " But who are they who have been brought out of the deep sea, and added on to the building, and agree in their joins with the other stones which have already been built ? " " These are they who have suffered for the name of the Lord." 3. " But I should like to know, Lady, who are the other stones which are being brought from the dry land ? " She said : " Those which go into the building without being hewed are they whom the Lord approved because they walked in the uprightness of the Lord and preserved his commandments." 4. " But who are they who are being brought and placed in the building ? " " They are young in the faith and faithful ; but they are being exhorted by the angels to good deeds, because wickedness has been found in them." 5. " But who are they whom they The rejected were rejecting and throwing away ? " " These are stones they who have sinned and wish to repent ; for this reason they have not been cast far away from the tower, because they will be valuable for the building if they repent. Those, then, who are going to repent, if they do so, will be strong in the faith if they repent now, while the tower is being built ;

δὲ τελεσθῇ ἡ οἰκοδομή, οὐκέτι ἔχουσιν τόπον, ἀλλ'
ἔσονται ἔκβολοι· μόνον δὲ τοῦτο ἔχουσιν, παρὰ
τῷ πύργῳ κεῖσθαι.

VI

1. Τοὺς δὲ κατακοπτομένους καὶ μακρὰν ῥιπτομένους[1] ἀπὸ τοῦ πύργου θέλεις γνῶναι; οὗτοί εἰσιν
οἱ υἱοὶ τῆς ἀνομίας· ἐπίστευσαν δὲ ἐν ὑποκρίσει, καὶ πᾶσα πονηρία οὐκ ἀπέστη ἀπ' αὐτῶν·
διὰ τοῦτο οὐκ ἔχουσιν σωτηρίαν, ὅτι οὐκ εἰσὶν
εὔχρηστοι εἰς οἰκοδομὴν διὰ τὰς πονηρίας αὐτῶν.
διὰ τοῦτο συνεκόπησαν καὶ πόρρω ἀπερίφησαν
διὰ τὴν ὀργὴν τοῦ κυρίου, ὅτι παρώργισαν αὐτόν.
2. τοὺς δὲ ἑτέρους, οὓς ἑώρακας πολλοὺς κειμένους, μὴ ὑπάγοντας εἰς τὴν οἰκοδομήν, οὗτοι οἱ
μὲν ἐψωριακότες εἰσίν, οἱ ἐγνωκότες τὴν ἀλήθειαν,
μὴ ἐπιμένοντας[2] δὲ ἐν αὐτῇ.[3] 3. Οἱ δὲ τὰς
σχισμὰς ἔχοντες, τίνες εἰσίν; Οὗτοί εἰσιν οἱ
I Thess. 5,
18, cf. Mk. 9,
50
κατ' ἀλλήλων ἐν ταῖς καρδίαις ἔχοντες καὶ μὴ
εἰρηνεύοντες ἐν ἑαυτοῖς, ἀλλὰ πρόσωπον εἰρήνης
ἔχοντες, ὅταν δὲ ἀπ' ἀλλήλων ἀποχωρήσωσιν,
αἱ πονηρίαι αὐτῶν ἐν ταῖς καρδίαις ἐμμένουσιν·
αὗται οὖν αἱ σχισμαί εἰσιν, ἃς ἔχουσιν οἱ λίθοι.
4. οἱ δὲ κεκολοβωμένοι, οὗτοί εἰσιν πεπιστευκότες μὲν καὶ τὸ πλεῖον μέρος ἔχουσιν[4] ἐν τῇ
δικαιοσύνῃ, τινὰ δὲ μέρη ἔχουσιν τῆς ἀνομίας·
διὰ τοῦτο κολοβοὶ καὶ οὐχ ὁλοτελεῖς εἰσιν. 5.

---

[1] καὶ μακρὰν ῥιπτομένους om. ℵ.
[2] ἐπιμένοντας ℵ, ἐπιμείναντας Α.
[3] αὐτῇ ℵL₂E, αὐτῆ, μηδὲ κολλώμενοι τοῖς ἀγίοις. διὰ τοῦτο
ἄχρηστοί εἰσιν ΑL₁.   [4] ἔχουσιν ℵ, ἔχοντες Α.

but if the building be finished, they no longer have a place, but will be cast away. But they have only this,—that they lie beside the tower."

VI

1. "Do you wish to know who are those which are being broken up and cast far from the tower? These are the sons of wickedness; and their faith was hypocrisy, and no wickedness departed from them. For this cause they had no salvation, for because of their wickedness they are not useful for the building. Therefore they were broken up and cast far away, because of the anger of the Lord, for they had provoked his anger. 2. But the others of whom you saw many left lying and not going into the building, of these those which are rotten are they who have known the truth, but are not remaining in it." 3. "And who are they which have the cracks?" "These are they who bear malice in their hearts against one another, and are not 'at peace among themselves,' but maintain the appearance of peace, yet when they depart from one another their wickednesses remain in their hearts. These are the cracks which the stones have. 4. And those which are too short are they which have believed, and they live for the greater part in righteousness, but have some measure of wickedness. Therefore they are short and not perfect." 5. "But who, Lady, are the white

The stones which were broken up

The stones put on one side

THE APOSTOLIC FATHERS

Οἱ δὲ λευκοὶ καὶ στρογγύλοι καὶ μὴ ἁρμόζοντες εἰς τὴν οἰκοδομήν, τίνες εἰσιν, κυρία; ἀποκριθεῖσά μοι λέγει· Ἕως πότε μωρὸς εἶ καὶ ἀσύνετος, καὶ πάντα ἐπερωτᾷς καὶ οὐδὲν νοεῖς; οὗτοί εἰσιν ἔχοντες μὲν πίστιν, ἔχοντες δὲ καὶ πλοῦτον τοῦ αἰῶνος τούτου· ὅταν γένηται θλῖψις, διὰ τὸν πλοῦτον[1] αὐτῶν καὶ διὰ τὰς πραγματείας ἀπαρνοῦνται τὸν κύριον αὐτῶν. 6. καὶ ἀποκριθεὶς αὐτῇ λέγω· Κυρία, πότε οὖν εὔχρηστοι ἔσονται εἰς τὴν οἰκοδομήν; Ὅταν, φησίν, περικοπῇ αὐτῶν ὁ πλοῦτος ὁ ψυχαγωγῶν αὐτούς, τότε εὔχρηστοι ἔσονται τῷ θεῷ. ὥσπερ γὰρ ὁ λίθος ὁ στρογγύλος, ἐὰν μὴ περικοπῇ καὶ ἀποβάλῃ ἐξ αὐτοῦ τι, οὐ δύναται τετράγωνος γενέσθαι, οὕτω καὶ οἱ πλουτοῦντες ἐν τούτῳ τῷ αἰῶνι, ἐὰν μὴ περικοπῇ αὐτῶν ὁ πλοῦτος, οὐ δύνανται τῷ κυρίῳ εὔχρηστοι γενέσθαι. 7. ἀπὸ σεαυτοῦ πρῶτον γνῶθι· ὅτε ἐπλούτεις, ἄχρηστος ἦς, νῦν δὲ εὔχρηστος εἶ καὶ ὠφέλιμος τῇ ζωῇ. εὔχρηστοι γίνεσθε τῷ θεῷ· καὶ γὰρ σὺ αὐτὸς χρᾶσαι ἐκ τῶν αὐτῶν λίθων.[2]

VII

1. Τοὺς δὲ ἑτέρους λίθους, οὓς εἶδες μακρὰν ἀπὸ τοῦ πύργου ῥιπτομένους καὶ πίπτοντας εἰς τὴν ὁδὸν καὶ κυλιομένους ἐκ τῆς ὁδοῦ εἰς τὰς ἀνοδίας· οὗτοί εἰσιν οἱ πεπιστευκότες μέν, ἀπὸ δὲ τῆς διψυχίας αὐτῶν ἀφίουσιν τὴν ὁδὸν αὐτῶν τὴν ἀληθινήν· δοκοῦντες οὖν βελτίονα ὁδὸν δύ-

[1] τοῦ αἰῶνος . . . πλοῦτον om. ℵ.
[2] καὶ γὰρ . . . λίθων om. ℵ.

and round ones which do not fit into the building?" The round She answered and said to me, "How long will stones you be stupid and foolish, and ask everything and understand nothing? These are they which have faith, but have also the riches of this world. When persecution comes, because of their wealth and because of business they deny their Lord." 6. And I answered and said to her, "Lady, but then when will they be useful for the building?" "When," she said, "their wealth, which leads their souls astray, shall be cut off from them, then they will be useful to God. For just as the round stone cannot become square, unless something be cut off and taken away from it, so too they who have riches in this world cannot be useful to the Lord unless their wealth be cut away from them. 7. Understand it first from your own case; when you were rich, you were useless, but now you are useful and helpful for the Life. Be useful to God, for you yourself are taken from the same stones.[1]

VII

1. "But as for the other stones which you saw The stones being cast far from the tower, and falling on to the thrown away from road, and rolling from the road on to the rough the tower ground; these are they who have believed, but because of their double-mindedness leave their true road. They think that it is possible to find a better

---

[1] This appears to be the meaning; but the Greek is obscure and the early translations all paraphrase it so freely that they cannot be used to suggest any emendation.

THE APOSTOLIC FATHERS

περιπατοῦντες ἐν ταῖς ἀνοδίαις. 2. οἱ δὲ πίπτ-
οντες εἰς τὸ πῦρ καὶ καιόμενοι, οὗτοί εἰσιν οἱ
εἰς τέλος ἀποστάντες τοῦ θεοῦ τοῦ ζῶντος, καὶ
οὐκέτι αὐτοῖς ἀνέβη ἐπὶ τὴν καρδίαν τοῦ μετανοῆσαι διὰ τὰς ἐπιθυμίας τῆς ἀσελγείας αὐτῶν
καὶ τῶν πονηριῶν ὧν εἰργάσαντο. 3. τοὺς δὲ
ἑτέρους τοὺς πίπτοντας ἐγγὺς τῶν ὑδάτων καὶ
μὴ δυναμένους κυλισθῆναι εἰς τὸ ὕδωρ θέλεις
γνῶναι, τίνες εἰσίν; οὗτοί εἰσιν οἱ τὸν λόγον
ἀκούσαντες καὶ θέλοντες βαπτισθῆναι εἰς τὸ
ὄνομα τοῦ κυρίου· εἶτα ὅταν αὐτοῖς ἔλθῃ εἰς
μνείαν ἡ ἁγνότης τῆς ἀληθείας, μετανοοῦσιν καὶ
πορεύονται πάλιν ὀπίσω τῶν ἐπιθυμιῶν αὐτῶν
τῶν πονηρῶν. 4. ἐτέλεσεν οὖν τὴν ἐξήγησιν τοῦ
πύργου. 5. ἀναιδευσάμενος ἔτι αὐτὴν ἐπηρώτησα, εἰ ἄρα πάντες οἱ λίθοι οὗτοι οἱ ἀποβεβλημένοι καὶ μὴ ἁρμόζοντες εἰς τὴν οἰκοδομὴν τοῦ
πύργου, εἰ ἔστιν αὐτοῖς μετάνοια καὶ ἔχουσιν
τόπον εἰς τὸν πύργον τοῦτον. Ἔχουσιν, φησίν,
μετάνοιαν, ἀλλὰ εἰς τοῦτον τὸν πύργον οὐ δύνανται ἁρμόσαι· 6. ἑτέρῳ δὲ τόπῳ ἁρμόσουσιν
πολὺ ἐλάττονι, καὶ τοῦτο ὅταν βασανισθωσιν καὶ
ἐκπληρώσωσιν τὰς ἡμέρας τῶν ἁμαρτιῶν αὐτῶν.
καὶ διὰ τοῦτο μετατεθήσονται, ὅτι μετέλαβον τοῦ
ῥήματος τοῦ δικαίου. καὶ τότε αὐτοῖς συμβήσεται
μετατεθῆναι ἐκ τῶν βασάνων αὐτῶν, διὰ[1] τὰ
ἔργα ἃ εἰργάσαντο πονηρά. ἐὰν δὲ μὴ ἀναβῇ ἐπὶ
τὴν καρδίαν αὐτῶν, οὐ σώζονται διὰ τὴν σκληρο-
καρδίαν αὐτῶν.

Heb. 3, 12

Mk. 4, 18; Mt. 13, 20. 22

Acts 19, 5 (10, 48; 2, 38)

Ecclus. 18, 30

[1] διά אL₂, ἐὰν ἀναβῇ ἐπὶ τὴν καρδίαν αὐτῶν AL₁E. The text of אL₂ can scarcely be quite correct, but the other is clearly an emendation.

44

road, and err and wander miserably in the rough ground. 2. And they who are falling into the fire and are being burnt, these are they who finally 'apostatise from the living God' and it no longer enters into their hearts to repent because of their licentious lusts, and the crimes which they have committed. 3. But do you wish to know who are the others which are falling near the water and cannot be rolled into the water? 'These are they who have heard the Word' and wish to be baptised 'in the name of the Lord.' Then, when the purity of the Truth comes into their recollection they repent and go again 'after their evil lusts.'" 4. So she ended the explanation of the tower. 5. I was still unabashed and asked her whether really all these stones which have been cast away, and do not fit into the building of the tower,—whether repentance is open to them, and they have a place in this tower. "Repentance," she said, "they have, but they cannot fit into this tower. 6. But they will fit into another place much less honourable, and even this only after they have been tormented and fulfilled the days of their sins, and for this reason they will be removed,[1] because they shared in the righteous Word. And then [2] it shall befall them to be removed from their torments, because of the wickedness of the deeds which they committed. But if it come not into their hearts they have no salvation, because of the hardness of their hearts."

The end of the rejected stones

[1] *I.e.* from their punishment.
[2] Apparently the meaning is 'Then, *i.e.* if they repent,' but the text is obscure, and probably some words have been lost.

VIII

1. Ὅτε οὖν ἐπαυσάμην ἐρωτῶν αὐτὴν περὶ πάντων τούτων, λέγει μοι· Θέλεις ἄλλο ἰδεῖν; κατεπίθυμος ὢν τοῦ θεάσασθαι περιχαρὴς ἐγενόμην τοῦ ἰδεῖν. 2. ἐμβλέψασά μοι ὑπεμειδίασεν καὶ λέγει μοι· Βλέπεις ἑπτὰ γυναῖκας κύκλῳ τοῦ πύργου; Βλέπω, φημί, κυρία. Ὁ πύργος οὗτος ὑπὸ τούτων βαστάζεται κατ' ἐπιταγὴν τοῦ κυρίου. 3. ἄκουε νῦν τὰς ἐνεργείας αὐτῶν. ἡ μὲν πρώτη αὐτῶν, ἡ κρατοῦσα τὰς χεῖρας, Πίστις καλεῖται· διὰ ταύτης σῴζονται οἱ ἐκλεκτοὶ τοῦ θεοῦ. 4. ἡ δὲ ἑτέρα, ἡ περιεζωσμένη καὶ ἀνδριζομένη, Ἐγκράτεια καλεῖται· αὕτη θυγάτηρ ἐστὶν τῆς Πίστεως. ὃς ἂν οὖν ἀκολουθήσῃ αὐτῇ, μακάριος γίνεται ἐν τῇ ζωῇ αὐτοῦ, ὅτι πάντων τῶν πονηρῶν ἔργων ἀφέξεται, πιστεύων ὅτι, ἐὰν ἀφέξηται[1] πάσης ἐπιθυμίας πονηρᾶς, κληρονομήσει[2] ζωὴν αἰώνιον. 5. Αἱ δὲ ἕτεραι, κυρία, τίνες εἰσίν; Θυγατέρες ἀλλήλων εἰσίν   καλοῦνται δὲ ἡ μὲν Ἁπλότης, ἡ δὲ Ἐπιστήμη, ἡ δὲ Ἀκακία, ἡ δὲ Σεμνότης, ἡ δὲ Ἀγάπη. ὅταν οὖν τὰ ἔργα τῆς μητρὸς αὐτῶν πάντα ποιήσῃς, δύνασαι ζῆσαι. 6. Ἤθελον, φημί, γνῶναι, κυρία, τίς τίνα δύναμιν ἔχει αὐτῶν. Ἄκουε, φησίν, τὰς δυνάμεις, ἃς ἔχουσιν. 7 κρατοῦνται δὲ ὑπ' ἀλλήλων αἱ δυνάμεις αὐτῶν καὶ ἀκολουθοῦσιν ἀλλήλαις, καθὼς καὶ γεγεννημέναι εἰσίν. ἐκ τῆς Πίστεως γεννᾶται Ἐγκράτεια, ἐκ τῆς Ἐγκρατείας Ἁπλότης, ἐκ τῆς Ἁπλότητος Ἀκακία, ἐκ τῆς Ἀκακίας

---

[1] πιστεύων ὅτι ἐὰν ἀφέξηται ALE, καὶ ℵ.
[2] καὶ κληρονομήσει ℵ.

VIII

1. WHEN, therefore, I ceased asking her all these
things, she said to me: "Would you like to see
something else?" I was anxious to see it, and
rejoiced greatly at the prospect. 2. She looked at
me and smiled and said to me: "Do you see seven
women round the tower?" "Yes," I said; "I see
them." "This tower is being supported by them
according to the commandment of the Lord. 3.
Hear now their qualities. The first of them who
is clasping her hands is called Faith. Through her
the chosen of God are saved. 4. The second, who is
girded and looks like a man, is called Continence ;
she is the daughter of Faith. Whosoever then shall
follow her becomes blessed in his life, because he
will abstain from all evil deeds, believing that if he
refrains from every evil lust he will inherit eternal
life." 5. "But who are the others, Lady?" "They
are daughters one of the other, and their names are
Simplicity, Knowledge, Innocence, Reverence, and
Love. When therefore you perform all the deeds of
their mother, you can live." 6. "I would like,
Lady," said I, "to know what are their several
powers." [1] "Listen," she said, "to the powers which
they have. 7. Their powers are supported one by
the other, and they follow one another according to
their birth. From Faith is born Continence, from
Continence Simplicity, from Simplicity Innocence,

The vision of the seven women

The explanation

The powers of the Virtues

---

[1] Here also (cf. Vision III. iv. 3) 'powers' probably is
almost equivalent to 'meaning' or 'signification.'

Σεμνότης, ἐκ τῆς Σεμνότητος Ἐπιστήμη, ἐκ τῆς Ἐπιστήμης Ἀγάπη. τούτων οὖν τὰ ἔργα ἁγνὰ καὶ σεμνὰ καὶ θεῖά ἐστιν. 8. ὃς ἂν οὖν δουλεύσῃ ταύταις καὶ ἰσχύσῃ κρατῆσαι τῶν ἔργων αὐτῶν, ἐν τῷ πύργῳ ἕξει τὴν κατοίκησιν μετὰ τῶν ἁγίων τοῦ θεοῦ. 9. ἐπηρώτων δὲ αὐτὴν περὶ τῶν καιρῶν, εἰ ἤδη συντέλειά ἐστιν. ἡ δὲ ἀνέκραγε φωνῇ μεγάλῃ λέγουσα· Ἀσύνετε ἄνθρωπε, οὐχ ὁρᾷς τὸν πύργον ἔτι οἰκοδομούμενον; ὡς ἐὰν οὖν συντελεσθῇ ὁ πύργος οἰκοδομούμενος, ἔχει τέλος. ἀλλὰ ταχὺ ἐποικοδομηθήσεται. μηκέτι με ἐπερώτα μηδέν· ἀρκετή σοι ἡ ὑπόμνησις αὕτη καὶ τοῖς ἁγίοις καὶ ἡ ἀνακαίνωσις τῶν πνευμάτων ὑμῶν. 10. ἀλλ᾽ οὐ σοὶ μόνῳ ταῦτα ἀπεκαλύφθη, ἀλλ᾽ ἵνα πᾶσιν δηλώσῃς αὐτά, 11. μετὰ τρεῖς ἡμέρας, νοῆσαί σε γὰρ δεῖ πρῶτον. ἐντέλλομαι δέ σοι πρῶτον,[1] Ἑρμᾶ, τὰ ῥήματα ταῦτα, ἅ σοι μέλλω λέγειν, λαλῆσαι αὐτὰ πάντα εἰς τὰ ὦτα τῶν ἁγίων, ἵνα ἀκούσαντες αὐτὰ καὶ ποιήσαντες καθαρισθῶσιν ἀπὸ τῶν πονηριῶν αὐτῶν καὶ σὺ δὲ μετ᾽ αὐτῶν.

IX

1. Ἀκούσατέ μου, τέκνα· ἐγὼ ὑμᾶς ἐξέθρεψα ἐν πολλῇ ἁπλότητι καὶ ἀκακίᾳ καὶ σεμνότητι διὰ τὸ ἔλεος τοῦ κυρίου τοῦ ἐφ᾽ ὑμᾶς στάξαντος τὴν δικαιοσύνην, ἵνα δικαιωθῆτε καὶ ἁγιασθῆτε ἀπὸ πάσης πονηρίας καὶ ἀπὸ πάσης σκολιότητος· ὑμεῖς δὲ οὐ θέλετε παῆναι ἀπὸ τῆς πονηρίας ὑμῶν.

---

[1] ἐντέλλομαι δέ σοι πρῶτον om ℵ L₁.

from Innocence Reverence, from Reverence Knowledge, from Knowledge Love. Their works therefore are pure and reverent and godly. 8. Whosoever then serves them, and has the strength to lay hold of their works, shall have his dwelling in the tower with the saints of God." 9. And I began to ask her The end about the times, if the end were yet. But she cried out with a loud voice saying, "Foolish man, do you not see the tower still being built? Whenever therefore the building of the tower has been finished, the end comes. But it will quickly be built up; ask me nothing more. This reminder and the renewal of your spirits is sufficient for you and for the saints. 10. But the revelation was not for you alone, but for you to explain it to them all, 11. after three days, for you must understand it first. But I charge you first, Hermas, with these words, which I am going to say to you, to speak them all into the ears of the saints, that they may hear them and do them and be cleansed from their wickedness, and you with them.

IX

1. "LISTEN to me, children; I brought you up in The charge great simplicity and innocence and reverence by the of the Church mercy of God, who instilled righteousness into you that you should be justified and sanctified from all wickedness and all crookedness. But you do not wish to cease from your wickedness. 2. Now, there-

I Thess. 5, 13

Rom. 15, 17
cf. Acts 20, 35

Jam. 5, 4

Mt. 23, 6
Mc. 12, 39
Lc. 11, 43 ;
20, 46

Ps. 47, 2 etc.

2. νῦν οὖν ἀκούσατέ μου καὶ εἰρηνεύετε ἐν ἑαυτοῖς καὶ ἐπισκέπτεσθε ἀλλήλους καὶ ἀντιλαμβάνεσθε ἀλλήλων, καὶ μὴ μόνοι τὰ κτίσματα τοῦ θεοῦ μεταλαμβάνετε ἐκ καταχύματος, ἀλλὰ μεταδίδοτε καὶ τοῖς ὑστερουμένοις· 3. οἱ μὲν γὰρ ἀπὸ τῶν πολλῶν ἐδεσμάτων ἀσθένειαν τῇ σαρκὶ αὐτῶν ἐπισπῶνται καὶ λυμαίνονται τὴν σάρκα αὐτῶν· τῶν δὲ μὴ ἐχόντων ἐδέσματα λυμαίνεται ἡ σὰρξ αὐτῶν διὰ τὸ μὴ ἔχειν τὸ ἀρκετὸν τῆς τροφῆς, καὶ διαφθείρεται τὸ σῶμα αὐτῶν. 4. αὕτη οὖν ἡ ἀσυνκρασία βλαβερὰ ὑμῖν τοῖς ἔχουσι καὶ μὴ μεταδιδοῦσιν τοῖς ὑστερουμένοις. 5. βλέπετε τὴν κρίσιν τὴν ἐπερχομένην. οἱ ὑπερέχοντες οὖν ἐκζητεῖτε τοὺς πεινῶντας, ἕως οὔπω ὁ πύργος ἐτελέσθη· μετὰ γὰρ τὸ τελεσθῆναι τὸν πύργον θελήσετε ἀγαθοποιεῖν, καὶ οὐχ ἕξετε τόπον. 6. βλέπετε οὖν ὑμεῖς οἱ γαυριώμενοι[1] ἐν τῷ πλούτῳ ὑμῶν, μήποτε στενάξουσιν οἱ ὑστερούμενοι καὶ ὁ στεναγμὸς αὐτῶν ἀναβήσεται πρὸς τὸν κύριον καὶ ἐκκλεισθήσεσθε μετὰ τῶν ἀγαθῶν ὑμῶν ἔξω τῆς θύρας τοῦ πύργου. 7. νῦν οὖν ὑμῖν λέγω τοῖς προηγουμένοις τῆς ἐκκλησίας καὶ τοῖς πρωτοκαθεδρίταις· μὴ γίνεσθε ὅμοιοι τοῖς φαρμακοῖς. οἱ φαρμακοὶ μὲν οὖν τὰ φάρμακα ἑαυτῶν εἰς τὰς πυξίδας βαστάζουσιν, ὑμεῖς δὲ τὸ φάρμακον ὑμῶν καὶ τὸν ἰὸν εἰς τὴν καρδίαν. 8. ἐνεσκιρωμένοι ἐστὲ καὶ οὐ θέλετε καθαρίσαι τὰς καρδίας ὑμῶν καὶ συνκεράσαι ὑμῶν[2] τὴν φρόνησιν ἐπὶ τὸ αὐτὸ ἐν καθαρᾷ καρδίᾳ, ἵνα σχῆτε ἔλεος παρὰ τοῦ βασιλέως τοῦ μεγάλου. 9. βλέπετε οὖν, τέκνα,

---

[1] γαυριώμενοι א*, γαυρούμενοι אc, γαυριῶντες A.
[2] συνκεράσαι ὑμῶν om. א*.

fore, listen to me and 'be at peace among your-selves' and regard one another and 'help one another' and do not take a superabundant share of the creatures of God for yourselves, but give also a part to those who lack. 3. For some are contracting illness in the flesh by too much eating, and are injuring their flesh, and the flesh of the others who have nothing to eat is being injured by their not having sufficient food and their body is being destroyed. 4. So this lack of sharing is harmful to you who are rich, and do not share with the poor. 5. Consider the judgment which is coming. Let therefore they who have over-abundance seek out those who are hungry, so long as the tower is not yet finished ; for when the tower has been finished you will wish to do good, and will have no opportunity. 6. See to it then, you who rejoice in your wealth, that the destitute may not groan, and their groans go up to the Lord, and you with your goods be shut outside the door of the tower. 7. Therefore I speak now to the leaders of the Church and to those ' who take the chief seats.' Be not like the sorcerers, for sorcerers carry their charms in boxes, but you carry your charms and poison in your hearts. 8. You are hardened, and will not cleanse your hearts, and mix your wisdom together in a pure heart that you may find mercy by 'the great King.' 9. See to it,

51

μήποτε αὗται αἱ διχοστασίαι[1] ἀποστερήσουσιν
τὴν ζωὴν ὑμῶν. 10. πῶς ὑμεῖς παιδεύειν θέλετε
τοὺς ἐκλεκτοὺς κυρίου, αὐτοὶ μὴ ἔχοντες παιδείαν; παιδεύετε οὖν ἀλλήλους καὶ εἰρηνεύετε
ἐν αὑτοῖς ἵνα κἀγὼ κατέναντι τοῦ πατρὸς ἱλαρὰ
σταθεῖσα λόγον ἀποδῶ ὑπὲρ ὑμῶν πάντων τῷ
κυρίῳ.[2]

Thess. 5,
3

X

1. Ὅτε οὖν ἐπαύσατο μετ᾽ ἐμοῦ λαλοῦσα,
ἦλθον οἱ ἓξ νεανίσκοι οἱ οἰκοδομοῦντες καὶ
ἀπήνεγκαν αὐτὴν πρὸς τὸν πύργον, καὶ ἄλλοι
τέσσαρες ἦραν τὸ συμψέλιον καὶ ἀπήνεγκαν
καὶ αὐτὸ πρὸς τὸν πύργον. τούτων τὸ πρόσωπον οὐκ εἶδον, ὅτι ἀπεστραμμένοι ἦσαν.
2. ὑπάγουσαν δὲ[3] αὐτὴν ἠρώτων, ἵνα μοι ἀπο-
καλύψῃ περὶ τῶν τριῶν μορφῶν, ἐν αἷς μοι
ἐνεφανίσθη. ἀποκριθεῖσά μοι λέγει· Περὶ τούτων
ἕτερον δεῖ σε ἐπερωτῆσαι, ἵνα σοι ἀποκαλυφθῇ.
3. ὤφθη δέ μοι, ἀδελφοί, τῇ μὲν πρώτῃ ὁράσει τῇ
περυσινῇ λίαν πρεσβυτέρα καὶ ἐν καθέδρᾳ
καθημένη. 4. τῇ δὲ ἑτέρᾳ ὁράσει τὴν μὲν
ὄψιν νεωτέραν εἶχεν, τὴν δὲ σάρκα καὶ τὰς
τρίχας πρεσβυτέρας, καὶ ἑστηκυῖά μοι ἐλάλει·
ἱλαρωτέρα δὲ ἦν ἢ τὸ πρότερον.[4] 5. τῇ δὲ τρίτῃ
ὁράσει ὅλη νεωτέρα καὶ κάλλει ἐκπρεπεστάτη,
μόνας δὲ τὰς τρίχας πρεσβυτέρας εἶχεν· ἱλαρὰ δὲ
εἰς τέλος ἦν καὶ ἐπὶ συμψελίου καθημένη. 6. περὶ

---

[1] διχοστασίαι ℵ* A, διχοστασίαι ὑμῶν ℵc LE.
[2] τῷ κυρίῳ L₁E, τῷ κυρίῳ ἡμῶν ℵ, τῷ κυρίῳ ὑμῶν AL₂.
[3] δὲ ℵc AL₂, om. ℵ L₁.
[4] ἢ τὸ πρότερον ALE, τὸ πρόσωπον ℵ.

therefore, children, that these disagreements do not rob you of your life. 10. How will you correct the chosen of the Lord if you yourselves suffer no correction? Correct therefore one another and 'be at peace among yourselves,' that I also may stand joyfully before the Father, and give an account of you all to the Lord."

X

1. WHEN therefore she ceased speaking with me, the six young men who were building came and took her away to the tower, and four others took up the couch and bore it away also to the tower. I did not see their faces because they were turned away. 2. But as she was going I asked her to give me a revelation concerning the three forms in which she had appeared to me. She answered me and said, "Concerning these things you must ask some one else to reveal them to you." 3. Now she had appeared to me, brethren, in the first vision in the former year as very old and sitting on a chair. 4. But in the second vision her face was younger, but her body and hair were old and she spoke with me standing; but she was more joyful than the first time. 5. But in the third vision she was quite young and exceeding beautiful and only her hair was old; and she was quite joyful, and sat on a couch. 6. I was very unhappy about this, and

The departure of the ancient lady

53

τούτων περίλυπος ἤμην λίαν τοῦ γνῶναί με τὴν
ἀποκάλυψιν ταύτην, καὶ βλέπω τὴν πρεσβυτέραν ἐν ὁράματι τῆς νυκτὸς λέγουσάν μοι. Πᾶσα
ἐρώτησις ταπεινοφροσύνης χρῄζει. νήστευσον
οὖν, καὶ λήμψῃ ὃ αἰτεῖς παρὰ τοῦ κυρίου.
7. ἐνήστευσα οὖν μίαν ἡμέραν, καὶ αὐτῇ τῇ νυκτί
μοι ὤφθη νεανίσκος καὶ λέγει μοι· Τί σὺ ὑπὸ
χεῖρα αἰτεῖς ἀποκαλύψεις ἐν δεήσει; βλέπε,
μήποτε πολλὰ αἰτούμενος βλάψῃς σου τὴν
σάρκα. 8. ἀρκοῦσίν σοι αἱ ἀποκαλύψεις αὗται.[1]
μήτι δύνῃ ἰσχυροτέρας ἀποκαλύψεις ὧν ἑώρακας
ἰδεῖν; 9. ἀποκριθεὶς αὐτῷ λέγω· Κύριε, τοῦτο
μόνον αἰτοῦμαι, περὶ τῶν τριῶν μορφῶν τῆς
πρεσβυτέρας ἵνα ἀποκάλυψις ὁλοτελὴς γένηται.
ἀποκριθεὶς μοι λέγει· Μέχρι τίνος ἀσύνετοί ἐστε;
ἀλλ' αἱ διψυχίαι ὑμῶν ἀσυνέτους ὑμᾶς ποιοῦσιν
καὶ τὸ μὴ ἔχειν τὴν καρδίαν ὑμῶν πρὸς τὸν
κύριον. 10. ἀποκριθεὶς αὐτῷ πάλιν εἶπον· Ἀλλ'
ἀπὸ σοῦ, κύριε, ἀκριβέστερον αὐτὰ γνωσόμεθα.

XI

1. Ἄκουε, φησίν, περὶ τῶν μορφῶν[2] ὧν
ἐπιζητεῖς. 2. τῇ μὲν πρώτῃ ὁράσει διατί πρεσβυτέρα ὤφθη σοι καὶ ἐπὶ καθέδραν καθημένη; ὅτι
τὸ πνεῦμα ὑμῶν πρεσβύτερον καὶ ἤδη μεμαραμ-
μένον καὶ μὴ ἔχον δύναμιν ἀπὸ τῶν μαλακιῶν
ὑμῶν καὶ διψυχιῶν· 3. ὥσπερ γὰρ οἱ πρεσβύ-
τεροι, μηκέτι ἔχοντες ἐλπίδα τοῦ ἀνανεῶσαι, οὐδὲν

---

[1] ἀρκοῦσίν . . . . αὗται om. ℵ.
[2] μορφῶν ℵ* LE, τριῶν μορφῶν ℵᶜ A.

wished to understand this revelation, and in a vision
of the night I saw the ancient lady saying to me,
" Every request needs humility : fast therefore and
you shall receive what you ask from the Lord." 7.
So I fasted one day and in the same night a young The young
man appeared to me and said to me, " Why do you man
ask constantly for revelations in your prayer ? Take
care lest by your many requests you injure your
flesh. 8. These revelations are sufficient for you.
Can you see mightier revelations than you have
seen ? " 9. I answered and said to him, " Sir, I
only ask you that there may be a complete revelation
concerning the three forms of the ancient lady."
He answered and said to me, " How long are you
foolish ? You are made foolish by your double-
mindedness and because your heart is not turned to
the Lord." 10. I answered and said again to him,
" But from you, sir, we shall know them more
accurately."

XI

1. " LISTEN," he said, " concerning the forms The three
which you are asking about. 2. Why did she appear forms of
to you in the first vision as old and seated on a lady
chair ? Because your [1] spirit is old and already fading
away, and has no power through your weakness and
double-mindedness. 3. For just as old people, who
have no longer any hope of becoming young again,

[1] This ' your ' is plural, in contrast to the ' you ' in the
preceding sentence, which is singular.

ἄλλο προσδοκῶσιν εἰ μὴ τὴν κοίμησιν αὐτῶν,
οὕτως καὶ ὑμεῖς μαλακισθέντες ἀπὸ τῶν βιωτικῶν
πραγμάτων παρεδώκατε ἑαυτοὺς εἰς τὰς ἀκηδίας
καὶ οὐκ ἐπερίψατε ἑαυτῶν τὰς μερίμνας ἐπὶ τὸν
κύριον· ἀλλὰ ἐθραύσθη ὑμῶν ἡ διάνοια καὶ ἐπα-
λαιώθητε ταῖς λύπαις ὑμῶν. 4. Διατί οὖν ἐν
καθέδρᾳ ἐκάθητο, ἤθελον γνῶναι, κύριε. Ὅτι
πᾶς ἀσθενὴς εἰς καθέδραν καθέζεται διὰ τὴν
ἀσθένειαν αὐτοῦ, ἵνα συνκρατηθῇ ἡ ἀσθένεια τοῦ
σώματος αὐτοῦ. ἔχεις τὸν τύπον τῆς πρώτης
ὁράσεως.

Ps. 54, 23;
1 Pet. 5, 7

XII

1. Τῇ δὲ δευτέρᾳ ὁράσει εἶδες αὐτὴν ἑστηκυῖαν
καὶ τὴν ὄψιν νεωτέραν ἔχουσαν καὶ ἱλαρωτέραν
παρὰ τὸ πρότερον, τὴν δὲ σάρκα καὶ τὰς τρίχας
πρεσβυτέρας. ἄκουε, φησίν, καὶ ταύτην τὴν
παραβολήν· 2. ὅταν πρεσβύτερός τις, ἤδη ἀφηλ-
πικὼς ἑαυτὸν διὰ τὴν ἀσθένειαν αὐτοῦ καὶ τὴν
πτωχότητα, οὐδὲν ἕτερον προσδέχεται εἰ μὴ τὴν
ἐσχάτην ἡμέραν τῆς ζωῆς αὐτοῦ· εἶτα ἐξαίφνης
κατελείφθη αὐτῷ κληρονομία, ἀκούσας δὲ ἐξηγέρθη
καὶ περιχαρὴς γενόμενος ἐνεδύσατο τὴν ἰσχύν·
καὶ οὐκέτι ἀνάκειται, ἀλλὰ ἔστηκεν, καὶ ἀνανεοῦται
αὐτοῦ τὸ πνεῦμα τὸ ἤδη ἐφθαρμένον ἀπὸ τῶν
προτέρων αὐτοῦ πράξεων, καὶ οὐκέτι κάθηται,
ἀλλὰ ἀνδρίζεται· οὕτως καὶ ὑμεῖς, ἀκούσαντες
τὴν ἀποκάλυψιν, ἣν ὑμῖν ὁ κύριος ἀπεκάλυψεν,[1]
3. ὅτι ἐσπλαγχνίσθη ἐφ' ὑμᾶς, καὶ ἀνενεώσατο τὰ
πνεύματα ὑμῶν καὶ ἀπέθεσθε τὰς μαλακίας ὑμῶν,

[1] ἣν ... ἀπεκάλυψεν om. ℵ.

look for nothing except their last sleep, so also you, who have been weakened by the occupations of this life, have given yourself up to worry, and have not 'cast your cares upon the Lord.' But your mind was broken, and you grew old in your sorrows." 4. "Why, then, I should like to know, did she sit in a chair, sir?" "Because every sick person sits in a chair because of his sickness, that the weakness of the body may find support. Here you have the type of the first vision.

XII

1. "But in the second vision you saw her standing, and with a more youthful and more cheerful countenance than the former time, but with the body and hair of old age. Listen," he said, "also to this parable. 2. When anyone is old, he already despairs of himself by reason of his weakness and poverty, and expects nothing except the last day of his life. Then an inheritance was suddenly left him, and he heard it, and rose up and was very glad and put on his strength; and he no longer lies down but stands up, and his spirit which was already destroyed by his former deeds is renewed, and he no longer sits still, but takes courage. So also did you, when you heard the revelation, which the Lord revealed to you, 3. that he had mercy upon you, and renewed your spirit; and you put aside your weakness, and strength came to you, and you were made

καὶ προσῆλθεν ὑμῖν ἰσχυρότης καὶ ἐνεδυναμώθητε
ἐν τῇ πίστει, καὶ ἰδὼν ὁ κύριος τὴν ἰσχυροποίησιν
ὑμῶν ἐχάρη· καὶ διὰ τοῦτο ἐδήλωσεν ὑμῖν τὴν
οἰκοδομὴν τοῦ πύργου καὶ ἕτερα δηλώσει, ἐὰν ἐξ
ὅλης καρδίας εἰρηνεύετε ἐν ἑαυτοῖς.

XIII

1. Τῇ δὲ τρίτῃ ὁράσει εἶδες αὐτὴν νεωτέραν καὶ
καλὴν καὶ ἱλαρὰν καὶ καλὴν τὴν μορφὴν αὐτῆς·
2. ὡς ἐὰν γάρ τινι λυπουμένῳ ἔλθῃ ἀγγελία
ἀγαθή τις, εὐθὺς ἐπελάθετο τῶν προτέρων λυπῶν
καὶ οὐδὲν ἄλλο προσδέχεται εἰ μὴ τὴν ἀγγελίαν,
ἣν ἤκουσεν, καὶ ἰσχυροποιεῖται λοιπὸν εἰς τὸ
ἀγαθὸν καὶ ἀνανεοῦται αὐτοῦ τὸ πνεῦμα διὰ τὴν
χαράν, ἣν ἔλαβεν· οὕτως καὶ ὑμεῖς ἀνανέωσιν
εἰλήφατε τῶν πνευμάτων ὑμῶν ἰδόντες ταῦτα τὰ
ἀγαθά. 3. καὶ ὅτι ἐπὶ συμψελίου εἶδες καθη-
μένην, ἰσχυρὰ ἡ θέσις, ὅτι τέσσαρας πόδας ἔχει
τὸ συμψέλιον καὶ ἰσχυρῶς ἕστηκεν· καὶ γὰρ ὁ
κόσμος διὰ τεσσάρων στοιχείων κρατεῖται. 4. οἱ
οὖν μετανοήσαντες ὁλοτελῶς νέοι ἔσονται καὶ
τεθεμελιωμένοι, οἱ ἐξ ὅλης καρδίας μετανοήσαντες.
ἀπέχεις ὁλοτελῆ τὴν ἀποκάλυψιν· μηκέτι μηδὲν
αἰτήσῃς περὶ ἀποκαλύψεως,[1] ἐάν τι δὲ δέῃ,
ἀποκαλυφθήσεταί σοι.

[1] περὶ ἀποκαλύψεως AL₁E, om. ℵ L₂.

mighty in faith, and the Lord saw that you had been made strong and he rejoiced. And for this reason he showed you the building of the tower, and he will show you other things if you 'remain at peace among yourselves' with all your heart.

XIII

1. "But in the third vision you saw her young and beautiful and joyful and her appearance was beautiful. 2. For just as if some good news come to one who is in grief, he straightway forgets his former sorrow, and thinks of nothing but the news which he has heard, and for the future is strengthened to do good, and his spirit is renewed because of the joy which he has received; so you also have received the renewal of your spirits by seeing these good things. 3. And in that you saw her sitting on a couch, the position is secure, for a couch has four feet and stands securely, for even the world is controlled by four elements. 4. They, therefore, who have repented shall completely recover their youth and be well founded, because they have repented with all their heart. You have the revelation completed; no longer ask anything about the revelation, but if anything be needed it shall be revealed to you."

Ὅρασις δ.

I

1. Ἣν εἶδον, ἀδελφοί, μετὰ ἡμέρας εἴκοσι τῆς προτέρας ὁράσεως τῆς γενομένης, εἰς τύπον τῆς θλίψεως τῆς ἐπερχομένης.[1] 2. ὑπῆγον εἰς ἀγρὸν τῇ ὁδῷ τῇ καμπανῇ. ἀπὸ τῆς ὁδοῦ τῆς δημοσίας ἐστὶν ὡσεὶ στάδια δέκα· ῥᾳδίως δὲ ὁδεύεται ὁ τόπος. 3. μόνος οὖν περιπατῶν ἀξιῶ τὸν κύριον, ἵνα τὰς ἀποκαλύψεις καὶ τὰ ὁράματα, ἅ μοι ἔδειξεν διὰ τῆς ἁγίας Ἐκκλησίας αὐτοῦ, τελειώσῃ, ἵνα με ἰσχυροποιήσῃ καὶ δῷ τὴν μετάνοιαν τοῖς δούλοις αὐτοῦ τοῖς ἐσκανδαλισμένοις, ἵνα δοξασθῇ τὸ ὄνομα αὐτοῦ τὸ μέγα καὶ ἔνδοξον, ὅτι με ἄξιον ἡγήσατο τοῦ δεῖξαί μοι τὰ θαυμάσια αὐτοῦ. 4. καὶ δοξάζοντός μου καὶ εὐχαριστοῦντος αὐτῷ, ὡς ἦχος φωνῆς μοι ἀπεκρίθη· Μὴ διψυχήσεις, Ἑρμᾶ. ἐν ἐμαυτῷ ἠρξάμην διαλογίζεσθαι καὶ λέγειν· Ἐγὼ τί ἔχω διψυχῆσαι, οὕτω τεθεμελιωμένος ὑπὸ τοῦ κυρίου καὶ ἰδὼν ἔνδοξα πράγματα; 5. καὶ προσέβην[2] μικρόν, ἀδελφοί, καὶ ἰδού, βλέπω κονιορτὸν ὡς εἰς τὸν οὐρανὸν καὶ ἠρξάμην λέγειν ἐν ἐμαυτῷ· Μήποτε κτήνη ἔρχονται καὶ κονιορτὸν ἐγείρουσιν; οὕτω δὲ ἦν ἀπ᾽ ἐμοῦ ὡς ἀπὸ σταδίου. 6. γινομένου μείζονος καὶ μείζονος κονιορτοῦ ὑπενόησα εἶναί τι θεῖον· μικρὸν ἐξέλαμψεν ὁ ἥλιος καὶ ἰδού, βλέπω θηρίον μέγιστον ὡσεὶ κῆτός τι, καὶ ἐκ τοῦ στόματος αὐτοῦ ἀκρίδες πύριναι ἐξεπορεύοντο· ἦν δὲ τὸ θηρίον τῷ μήκει

Ps. 86, 9. 12; 99, 3

---

[1] εἰς τύπον . . . ἐπερχομένης AL₁E, om. א (L₂).
[2] προσέβην א L₂, προέβην AL₁E.

Vision 4

I

1. The fourth vision which I saw, brethren, The vision of the Leviathan twenty days after the former vision, was a type of the persecution which is to come. 2. I was going into the country by the Via Campana. The place is about ten furlongs from the public road, and is easily reached. 3. As I walked by myself I besought the Lord to complete the revelations and visions which he had shown me by his holy Church, to make me strong and give repentance to his servants who had been offended, 'to glorify his' great and glorious 'name' because he had thought me worthy to show me his wonders. 4. And while I was glorifying him and giving him thanks an answer came to me as an echo of my voice, "Do not be double-minded, Hermas." I began to reason in myself, and to say, "In what ways can I be double-minded after being given such a foundation by the Lord, and having seen his glorious deeds?" 5. And I approached a little further, brethren, and behold, I saw dust reaching as it were up to heaven, and I began to say to myself, Are cattle coming and raising dust? and it was about a furlong away from me. 6. When the dust grew greater and greater I supposed that it was some portent. The sun shone out a little, and lo! I saw a great beast like some Leviathan, and fiery locusts were going out of his mouth. The beast was in size about a hundred feet

ὡσεὶ ποδῶν ρ', τὴν δὲ κεφαλὴν εἶχεν ὡσεὶ
κεράμου. 7. καὶ ἠρξάμην κλαίειν καὶ ἐρωτᾶν
τὸν κύριον, ἵνα με λυτρώσηται ἐξ αὐτοῦ· καὶ
ἐπανεμνήσθην τοῦ ῥήματος οὗ ἀκηκόειν· Μὴ
διψυχήσεις, Ἑρμᾶ. 8. ἐνδυσάμενος οὖν, ἀδελφοί,
τὴν πίστιν τοῦ κυρίου καὶ μνησθεὶς ὧν ἐδίδαξέν
με μεγαλείων, θαρσήσας εἰς τὸ θηρίον ἐμαυτὸν
ἔδωκα. οὕτω δὲ ἤρχετο τὸ θηρίον ῥοίζῳ, ὥστε
δύνασθαι αὐτὸ πόλιν λυμᾶναι. 9. ἔρχομαι ἐγγὺς
αὐτοῦ, καὶ τὸ τηλικοῦτο κῆτος ἐκτείνει ἑαυτὸ
χαμαὶ καὶ οὐδὲν εἰ μὴ τὴν γλῶσσαν προέβαλλεν
καὶ ὅλως οὐκ ἐκινήθη, μέχρις ὅτε παρῆλθον αὐτό·
10. εἶχεν δὲ τὸ θηρίον ἐπὶ τῆς κεφαλῆς χρώματα
τέσσαρα· μέλαν, εἶτα πυροειδὲς καὶ αἱματῶδες,
εἶτα χρυσοῦν, εἶτα λευκόν.

II

1. Μετὰ δὲ τὸ παρελθεῖν με τὸ θηρίον καὶ
προελθεῖν ὡσεὶ πόδας λ', ἰδού, ὑπαντᾷ μοι παρθένος κεκοσμημένη ὡς ἐκ νυμφῶνος ἐκπορευομένη,
ὅλη ἐν λευκοῖς καὶ ὑποδήμασιν λευκοῖς, κατακεκα-
λυμμένη ἕως τοῦ μετώπου, ἐν μίτρᾳ δὲ ἦν ἡ
κατακάλυψις αὐτῆς· εἶχεν δὲ τὰς τρίχας αὐτῆς
λευκάς. 2. ἔγνων ἐγὼ ἐκ τῶν προτέρων ὁραμάτων,
ὅτι ἡ Ἐκκλησία ἐστίν, καὶ ἱλαρώτερος ἐγενόμην.
ἀσπάζεταί με λέγουσα· Χαῖρε σύ, ἄνθρωπε. καὶ
ἐγὼ αὐτὴν ἀντησπασάμην· Κυρία, χαῖρε. 3. ἀποκριθεῖσά μοι λέγει· Οὐδέν σοι ἀπήντησεν; λέγω
αὐτῇ· Κυρία, τηλικοῦτο θηρίον, δυνάμενον λαοὺς
διαφθεῖραι· ἀλλὰ τῇ δυνάμει τοῦ κυρίου καὶ τῇ

Ps. 19, 5;
Rev. 21, 2

and its head was like a piece of pottery. 7. And I began to weep and to pray the Lord to rescue me from it, and I remembered the word which I had heard, " Do not be double-minded, Hermas." 8. Thus, brethren, being clothed in the faith of the Lord and remembering the great things which he had taught me, I took courage and faced the beast. And as the beast came on with a rush it was as though it could destroy a city. 9. I came near to it, and the Leviathan for all its size stretched itself out on the ground, **and** put forth nothing except its tongue, and did not move at all until I had passed it by. 10. And the beast had on its head four colours, black, then the colour of flame and blood, then golden, then white.

II

1. After I had passed the beast by and had gone The ancient lady about thirty feet further, lo! a maiden met me, 'adorned as if coming forth from the bridal chamber,' all in white and with white sandals, veiled to the forehead, and a turban for a head-dress, but her hair was white. 2. I recognised from the former visions that it was the Church, and I rejoiced the more. She greeted me saying, "Hail, O man," and I greeted her in return, "Hail, Lady." 3. She answered me and said, " Did nothing meet you?" I said to her, " Yes, Lady, such a beast as could destroy nations, but by the power of the Lord, and by his great

πολυσπλαγχνία αὐτοῦ ἐξέφυγον αὐτό. 4. Καλῶς
ἐξέφυγες, φησίν, ὅτι τὴν μέριμνάν σου ἐπὶ τὸν
θεὸν ἐπέριψας καὶ τὴν καρδίαν σου ἤνοιξας πρὸς
τὸν κύριον, πιστεύσας, ὅτι δι᾽ οὐδενὸς δύνῃ σωθῆναι εἰ μὴ διὰ τοῦ μεγάλου[1] καὶ ἐνδόξου ὀνόματος.
διὰ τοῦτο ὁ κύριος ἀπέστειλεν τὸν ἄγγελον αὐτοῦ
τὸν ἐπὶ τῶν θηρίων ὄντα, οὗ τὸ ὄνομά ἐστιν
Θεγρί, καὶ ἐνέφραξεν τὸ στόμα αὐτοῦ, ἵνα μή
σε λυμάνῃ. μεγάλην θλῖψιν ἐκπέφευγας διὰ τὴν
πίστιν σου καὶ ὅτι τηλικοῦτο θηρίον ἰδὼν οὐκ
ἐδιψύχησας· 5. ὕπαγε οὖν καὶ ἐξήγησαι τοῖς
ἐκλεκτοῖς τοῦ κυρίου τὰ μεγαλεῖα αὐτοῦ καὶ εἰπὲ
αὐτοῖς, ὅτι τὸ θηρίον τοῦτο τύπος ἐστὶν θλίψεως
τῆς μελλούσης τῆς μεγάλης· ἐὰν οὖν προετοι-
μάσησθε καὶ μετανοήσητε ἐξ ὅλης καρδίας ὑμῶν
πρὸς τὸν κύριον, δυνήσεσθε ἐκφυγεῖν αὐτήν, ἐὰν
ἡ καρδία ὑμῶν γένηται καθαρὰ καὶ ἄμωμος καὶ
τὰς λοιπὰς τῆς ζωῆς ἡμέρας ὑμῶν δουλεύσητε τῷ
κυρίῳ ἀμέμπτως. ἐπιρίψατε τὰς μερίμνας ὑμῶν
ἐπὶ τὸν κύριον, καὶ αὐτὸς κατορθώσει αὐτάς.
6. πιστεύσατε τῷ κυρίῳ, οἱ δίψυχοι, ὅτι πάντα
δύναται καὶ ἀποστρέφει τὴν ὀργὴν αὐτοῦ ἀφ᾽
ὑμῶν καὶ ἐξαποστέλλει μάστιγας ὑμῖν τοῖς διψύχοις. οὐαὶ τοῖς ἀκούσασιν τὰ ῥήματα ταῦτα
καὶ παρακούσασιν· αἱρετώτερον ἦν αὐτοῖς τὸ μὴ
γεννηθῆναι.

Ps. 55, 22
Ps. 62, 7
Acts 4, 12

Dan. 6, 22 ;
cf. Heb. 11,
33

Ps. 55, 22

Mt. 26, 24 ;
Mk. 14, 21

---

[1] μεγάλου ALE, ἁγίου ἀγγέλου ℵ.

mercy, I escaped it." 4. "You did well to escape it," she said, "because you cast your care upon God, and opened your heart to the Lord, believing that salvation can be found through nothing save through the great and glorious name. Therefore the Lord sent his angel, whose name is Thegri,[1] who is over the beast, 'and shut his mouth that he should not hurt you.' You have escaped great tribulation through your faith, and because you were not double-minded when you saw so great a beast. 5. Go then and tell the Lord's elect ones of his great deeds, and tell them that this beast is a type of the great persecution which is to come. If then you are prepared beforehand, and repent with all your hearts towards the Lord, you will be able to escape it, if your heart be made pure and blameless, and you serve the Lord blamelessly for the rest of the days of your life. 'Cast your cares upon the Lord' and he will put them straight. 6. Believe on the Lord, you who are double-minded, that he can do all things, and turns his wrath away from you, and sends scourges on you who are double-minded. Woe to those who hear these words and disobey ; it were better for them not to have been born."

The explanation of the Leviathan

[1] No other mention of this Angel is found in Jewish or Christian literature, and no suitable meaning has been suggested for Thegri. Dr. Rendel Harris suggests Segri as an emendation, connecting it with the Hebrew word meaning ' to shut ' (sagar), found in Dan. 6, 22.

III

1. Ἠρώτησα αὐτὴν περὶ τῶν τεσσάρων χρω-
μάτων ὧν εἶχεν τὸ θηρίον εἰς τὴν κεφαλήν. ἡ δὲ
ἀποκριθεῖσά μοι λέγει· Πάλιν περίεργος εἶ περὶ
τοιούτων πραγμάτων. Ναί, φημί, κυρία· γνώρισόν μοι, τί ἐστιν ταῦτα. 2. Ἄκουε, φησίν· τὸ
μὲν μέλαν οὗτος ὁ κόσμος ἐστίν, ἐν ᾧ κατοικεῖτε·
3. τὸ δὲ πυροειδὲς καὶ αἱματῶδες, ὅτι δεῖ τὸν
κόσμον τοῦτον δι' αἵματος καὶ πυρὸς ἀπόλλυσθαι·
4. τὸ δὲ χρυσοῦν μέρος ὑμεῖς ἐστε οἱ ἐκφυ-
γόντες τὸν κόσμον τοῦτον. ὥσπερ γὰρ τὸ
χρυσίον δοκιμάζεται διὰ τοῦ πυρὸς καὶ εὔχρηστον γίνεται, οὕτως καὶ ὑμεῖς δοκιμάζεσθε οἱ
κατοικοῦντες ἐν αὐτοῖς.[1] οἱ οὖν μείναντες καὶ
πυρωθέντες ὑπ' αὐτῶν καθαρισθήσεσθε. ὥσπερ
τὸ χρυσίον ἀποβάλλει τὴν σκωρίαν αὐτοῦ, οὕτω
καὶ ὑμεῖς ἀποβαλεῖτε πᾶσαν λύπην καὶ στενοχωρίαν, καὶ καθαρισθήσεσθε καὶ χρήσιμοι ἔσεσθε
εἰς τὴν οἰκοδομὴν τοῦ πύργου. 5. τὸ δὲ λευκὸν
μέρος ὁ αἰὼν ὁ ἐπερχόμενός ἐστιν, ἐν ᾧ κατοικήσουσιν οἱ ἐκλεκτοὶ τοῦ θεοῦ· ὅτι ἄσπιλοι καὶ
καθαροὶ ἔσονται οἱ ἐκλελεγμένοι ὑπὸ τοῦ θεοῦ[2]
εἰς ζωὴν αἰώνιον. 6. σὺ οὖν μὴ διαλίπῃς λαλῶν
εἰς τὰ ὦτα τῶν ἁγίων. ἔχετε καὶ τὸν τύπον τῆς
θλίψεως τῆς ἐρχομένης μεγάλης. ἐὰν δὲ ὑμεῖς
θελήσητε, οὐδὲν ἔσται. μνημονεύετε τὰ προ-
γεγραμμένα. 7. ταῦτα εἴπασα ἀπῆλθεν, καὶ οὐκ
εἶδον, ποίῳ τόπῳ ἀπῆλθεν·[3] νέφος[4] γὰρ ἐγένετο·
κἀγὼ ἐπεστράφην εἰς τὰ ὀπίσω φοβηθείς, δοκῶν
ὅτι τὸ θηρίον ἔρχεται.

II Pet. 2, 20

I Pet. 1, 7;
cf. Ecclus.
2, 5;
Prov. 17, 3;
Job 23, 10

---

[1] ἐν αὐτοῖς אL, ἐν αὐτῷ AE. [2] ὅτι ἄσπιλοι . . . θεοῦ om. א.
[3] καὶ οὐκ . . . ἀπῆλθεν om. א. [4] νέφος א L₂, ψόφος AL₁E.

III

1. I ASKED her concerning the four colours which the beast had on its head. She answered and said to me, "Are you again curious about such matters?" "Yes," I said, "Lady, let me know what they are." 2. "Listen," she said, "the black is this world, in which you are living; 3. the colour of fire and blood means that this world must be destroyed by blood and fire. 4. The golden part is you, who have fled from this world, for even as gold is ' tried in the fire ' and becomes valuable, so also you who live among them,[1] are being tried. Those then who remain and pass through the flames shall be purified by them. Even as the gold puts away its dross, so also you will put away all sorrow and tribulation, and will be made pure and become useful for the building of the tower. 5. But the white part is the world to come, in which the elect of God shall dwell, for those who have been chosen by God for eternal life will be without spot and pure. 6. Therefore do not cease to speak to the ears of the saints. You have also the type of the great persecution to come, but if you will it shall be nothing. Remember what was written before." 7. When she had said this she went away, and I did not see to what place she departed, for there was a cloud, and I turned backwards in fear, thinking that the beast was coming.

The four colours on the Leviathan

[1] The "them" means "fire and blood"; but the construction of the sentence is awkward.

Ἀποκάλυψις ε΄.[1]

1. Προσευξαμένου μου ἐν τῷ οἴκῳ καὶ καθίσαντος εἰς τὴν κλίνην εἰσῆλθεν ἀνήρ τις ἔνδοξος τῇ ὄψει, σχήματι ποιμενικῷ, περικείμενος δέρμα αἴγειον λευκὸν καὶ πήραν ἔχων ἐπὶ τῶν ὤμων καὶ ῥάβδον εἰς τὴν χεῖρα. καὶ ἠσπάσατό με, κἀγὼ ἀντησπασάμην αὐτόν. 2. καὶ εὐθὺς παρεκάθισέν μοι καὶ λέγει μοι· Ἀπεστάλην ὑπὸ τοῦ σεμνοτάτου ἀγγέλου, ἵνα μετὰ σοῦ οἰκήσω τὰς λοιπὰς ἡμέρας τῆς ζωῆς σου. 3. ἔδοξα ἐγώ, ὅτι πάρεστιν ἐκπειράζων με, καὶ λέγω αὐτῷ· Σὺ γὰρ τίς εἶ; ἐγὼ γάρ, φημί, γινώσκω, ᾧ παρεδόθην. λέγει μοι· Οὐκ ἐπιγινώσκεις με; Οὔ, φημί. Ἐγώ, φησίν, εἰμὶ ὁ ποιμήν, ᾧ παρεδόθης. 4. ἔτι λαλοῦντος αὐτοῦ ἠλλοιώθη ἡ ἰδέα αὐτοῦ, καὶ ἐπέγνων αὐτόν, ὅτι ἐκεῖνος ἦν, ᾧ παρεδόθην, καὶ εὐθὺς συνεχύθην καὶ φόβος με ἔλαβεν καὶ ὅλος συνεκόπην ἀπὸ τῆς λύπης, ὅτι οὕτως αὐτῷ ἀπεκρίθην πονηρῶς καὶ ἀφρόνως. 5. ὁ δὲ ἀποκριθείς μοι λέγει· Μὴ συγχύννου, ἀλλὰ ἰσχυροποιοῦ ἐν ταῖς ἐντολαῖς μου αἷς σοι μέλλω ἐντέλλεσθαι. ἀπεστάλην γάρ, φησίν, ἵνα ἃ εἶδες πρότερον πάντα σοι πάλιν δείξω, αὐτὰ τὰ κεφάλαια τὰ ὄντα ὑμῖν σύμφορα. πρῶτον πάντων τὰς ἐντολάς μου γράψον καὶ τὰς παραβολάς· τὰ δὲ ἕτερα, καθώς σοι δείξω, οὕτως γράψεις· διὰ τοῦτο, φησίν, ἐντέλλομαί σοι πρῶτον γράψαι τὰς ἐντολὰς καὶ παραβολάς, ἵνα ὑπὸ χεῖρα ἀναγινώσκῃς

---

[1] Ἀποκάλυψις ε΄ א, ὅρασις ε΄ AE, incipiunt Pastoris mandata duodecim L₂, visio quinta initium Pastoris L₁.

The Fifth Revelation[1]

1. WHILE I was praying at home and sitting on The coming of the shepherd my bed, there entered a man glorious to look on, in the dress of a shepherd, covered with a white goat-skin, with a bag on his shoulders and a staff in his hand. And he greeted me, and I greeted him back. 2. And at once he sat down by me, and said to me, "I have been sent by the most reverend angel to dwell with you the rest of the days of your life." 3. I thought he was come tempting me, and said to him, "Yes, but who are you? for," I said, "I know to whom I was handed over." He said to me, "Do you not recognise me?" "No," I said. "I," said he, "am the shepherd to whom you were handed over."[2] 4. While he was still speaking, his appear-ance changed, and I recognised him, that it was he to whom I was handed over; and at once I was confounded, and fear seized me, and I was quite over-come with sorrow that I had answered him so basely and foolishly. 5. But he answered me and said, "Be not confounded, but be strong in my command-ments which I am going to command you. For I was sent," said he, "to show you again all the things which you saw before, for they are the main points which are helpful to you. First of all write my commandments and the parables; but the rest you shall write as I shall show you. This is the reason," said he, "that I command you to write first the commandments and parables, that you may read

[1] This section is clearly intended as an introduction to the Mandates, but it is always quoted as the Fifth Vision.
[2] There is no mention of this in the preceding Visions.

αὐτὰς καὶ δυνηθῇς φυλάξαι αὐτάς. 6. ἔγραψα
οὖν τὰς ἐντολὰς καὶ παραβολάς, καθὼς ἐνετείλατό
μοι. 7. ἐὰν οὖν ἀκούσαντες αὐτὰς φυλάξητε καὶ
ἐν αὐταῖς πορευθῆτε καὶ ἐργάσησθε αὐτὰς ἐν
καθαρᾷ καρδίᾳ, ἀπολήμψεσθε ἀπὸ τοῦ κυρίου,
ὅσα ἐπηγγείλατο ὑμῖν· ἐὰν δὲ ἀκούσαντες μὴ
μετανοήσητε, ἀλλ᾽ ἔτι προσθῆτε ταῖς ἁμαρτίαις
ὑμῶν, ἀπολήμψεσθε παρὰ τοῦ κυρίου τὰ ἐναντία.
ταῦτά μοι πάντα οὕτως γράψαι ὁ ποιμὴν ἐνετείλατο, ὁ ἄγγελος τῆς μετανοίας.

Ἐντολὴ α΄.

Eph. 3, 9
II Macc. 7,
28;
cf. Wisd. 1,
14

1. Πρῶτον πάντων πίστευσον, ὅτι εἷς ἐστὶν ὁ
θεός, ὁ τὰ πάντα κτίσας καὶ καταρτίσας καὶ
ποιήσας ἐκ τοῦ μὴ ὄντος εἰς τὸ εἶναι τὰ πάντα καὶ
πάντα χωρῶν, μόνος δὲ ἀχώρητος ὤν. 2. πίστευσον οὖν αὐτῷ καὶ φοβήθητι αὐτόν, φοβηθεὶς δὲ
ἐγκράτευσαι. ταῦτα φύλασσε, καὶ ἀποβαλεῖς
πᾶσαν πονηρίαν ἀπὸ σεαυτοῦ καὶ ἐνδύσῃ πᾶσαν
ἀρετὴν δικαιοσύνης καὶ ζήσῃ τῷ θεῷ, ἐὰν φυλάξῃς
τὴν ἐντολὴν ταύτην.

Ἐντολὴ β΄.

1. Λέγει μοι· Ἁπλότητα ἔχε καὶ ἄκακος γίνου,
καὶ ἔσῃ ὡς τὰ νήπια τὰ μὴ γινώσκοντα τὴν πονηρίαν τὴν ἀπολλύουσαν τὴν ζωὴν τῶν ἀνθρώπων.
2. πρῶτον μὲν μηδενὸς καταλάλει μηδὲ ἡδέως ἄκουε
Jam. 4, 11 καταλαλοῦντος· εἰ δὲ μή, καὶ σὺ ὁ ἀκούων ἔνοχος ἔσῃ
τῆς ἁμαρτίας τοῦ καταλαλοῦντος, ἐὰν πιστεύσῃς
τῇ καταλαλιᾷ ᾗ ἂν ἀκούσῃς· πιστεύσας γὰρ [1] καὶ
_____
[1] γάρ AE(L₁) Ath. Ant. om. אL₂.

them out at once, and be able to keep them." 6. So I wrote the commandments and parables as he commanded me. 7. If then you hear and keep them, and walk in them, and do them with a pure heart, you shall receive from the Lord all that he promised you, but if you hear them and do not repent, but continue to add to your sins, you shall receive the contrary from the Lord. All these things the shepherd commanded me to write thus, for he was the angel of repentance.

MANDATE 1

1. FIRST of all believe that God is one, ' who made all things and perfected them, and made all things to be out of that which was not,' and contains all things, and is himself alone uncontained. 2. Believe then in him, and fear him, and in your fear be continent. Keep these things, and you shall cast away from yourself all wickedness, and shall put on every virtue of righteousness, and shall live to God, if you keep this commandment.

Belief in God

MANDATE 2

1. HE said to me: "Have simplicity and be innocent and you shall be as the children who do not know the wickedness that destroys the life of men. 2. In the first place, speak evil of no one, and do not listen gladly to him who speaks evil. Otherwise you also by listening share in the sin of him who speaks evil, if you believe in the evil-speaking

Simplicity

σὺ αὐτὸς ἕξεις κατὰ τοῦ ἀδελφοῦ σου· οὕτως
οὖν ἔνοχος ἔσῃ τῆς ἁμαρτίας τοῦ καταλαλοῦντος.
3. πονηρὰ ἡ καταλαλιά· ἀκατάστατον δαιμόνιόν
ἐστιν, μηδέποτε εἰρηνεῦον, ἀλλὰ πάντοτε ἐν
διχοστασίαις κατοικοῦν. ἀπέχου οὖν ἀπ᾽ αὐτοῦ,
καὶ εὐθηνίαν πάντοτε ἕξεις[1] μετὰ πάντων. 4.
ἔνδυσαι δὲ τὴν σεμνότητα, ἐν ᾗ οὐδὲν πρόσκομμά
ἐστιν πονηρόν, ἀλλὰ πάντα ὁμαλὰ καὶ ἱλαρά.
ἐργάζου τὸ ἀγαθὸν καὶ ἐκ τῶν κόπων σου ὧν ὁ
θεὸς δίδωσίν σοι πᾶσιν ὑστερουμένοις δίδου
ἁπλῶς, μὴ διστάζων, τίνι δῷς ἢ τίνι μὴ δῷς.
πᾶσιν δίδου· πᾶσιν γὰρ ὁ θεὸς δίδοσθαι θέλει
ἐκ τῶν ἰδίων δωρημάτων. 5. οἱ οὖν λαμβάνοντες
ἀποδώσουσιν λόγον τῷ θεῷ, διατί ἔλαβον καὶ
εἰς τί· οἱ μὲν γὰρ λαμβάνοντες θλιβόμενοι
οὐ δικασθήσονται, οἱ δὲ ἐν ὑποκρίσει λαμβάνοντες τίσουσιν δίκην. 6. ὁ οὖν διδοὺς ἀθῶός
ἐστιν· ὡς γὰρ ἔλαβεν παρὰ τοῦ κυρίου τὴν
διακονίαν τελέσαι, ἁπλῶς αὐτὴν ἐτέλεσεν, μηθὲν
διακρίνων, τίνι δῷ ἢ μὴ δῷ. ἐγένετο οὖν ἡ δια-
κονία αὕτη ἁπλῶς τελεσθεῖσα ἔνδοξος παρὰ τῷ
θεῷ. ὁ οὖν οὕτως ἁπλῶς διακονῶν τῷ θεῷ
ζήσεται.[2] 7. φύλασσε οὖν τὴν ἐντολὴν ταύτην,
ὥς σοι λελάληκα, ἵνα ἡ μετάνοιά σου καὶ τοῦ
οἴκου σου . ἐν ἁπλότητι εὑρεθῇ, καὶ ἀκακία[3]
καθαρὰ καὶ ἀμίαντος.

[1] ἕξεις אᶜAL₂E Ath., ἴχεις אL₁.
[2] From here to the end of this Mandate א is missing except the end of the last word (-αντος).
[3] ἀκακία A (probably, but the MS is almost illegible), ἡ καρδία edd. the versions are all paraphrastic, but "cor" is found in L₁.

which you hear. For by believing you yourself also will have somewhat against your brother; thus therefore, you will share the sin of the speaker of evil. 3. Evil-speaking is wicked; it is a restless devil, never making peace, but always living in strife. Refrain from it then, and you shall have well-being at all times with all men. 4. And put on reverence, in which is no evil stumbling-block, but all is smooth and joyful. Do good, and of all your toil which God gives you, give in simplicity to all who need, not doubting to whom you shall give and to whom not: give to all, for to all God wishes gifts to be made of his own bounties. 5. Those then who receive shall render an account to God why they received it and for what. For those who accepted through distress shall not be punished, but those who accepted in hypocrisy shall pay the penalty.[1] 6. He therefore who gives is innocent; for as he received from the Lord the fulfilment of this ministry, he fulfilled it in simplicity, not doubting to whom he should give or not give. Therefore this ministry fulfilled in simplicity was honourable before God. He therefore who serves in simplicity shall live to God. 7. Keep therefore this commandment as I have told you, that your repentance and that of your family may be found to be in simplicity, and that your innocence may be " pure and without stain."

Evil-speaking

---

[1] This series of precepts is also found in the Didache (i. 5) and is there quoted as being "according to the commandment" (ἐντολή—the same word as Hermas uses for the commandments or Mandates of the Shepherd).

Ἐντολὴ γ΄.

1. Πάλιν μοι λέγει· Ἀλήθειαν ἀγάπα καὶ πᾶσα ἀλήθεια ἐκ τοῦ στόματός σου ἐκπορευέσθω, ἵνα τὸ πνεῦμα, ὃ ὁ θεὸς κατῴκισεν ἐν τῇ σαρκὶ ταύτῃ, ἀληθὲς εὑρεθῇ παρὰ πᾶσιν ἀνθρώποις, καὶ οὕτως δοξασθήσεται ὁ κύριος ὁ ἐν σοὶ κατοικῶν, ὅτι ὁ κύριος ἀληθινὸς ἐν παντὶ ῥήματι καὶ οὐδὲν παρ᾽ αὐτῷ ψεῦδος. 2. οἱ οὖν ψευδόμενοι ἀθετοῦσι τὸν κύριον καὶ γίνονται[1] ἀποστερηταὶ τοῦ κυρίου, μὴ παραδιδόντες αὐτῷ τὴν παρακαταθήκην, ἣν ἔλαβον. ἔλαβον γὰρ παρ᾽ αὐτοῦ πνεῦμα ἄψευστον. τοῦτο ἐὰν ψευδὲς ἀποδώσωσιν, ἐμίαναν τὴν ἐντολὴν τοῦ κυρίου καὶ ἐγένοντο ἀποστερηταί. 3. ταῦτα οὖν ἀκούσας ἐγὼ ἔκλαυσα λίαν· ἰδὼν δέ με κλαίοντα λέγει· Τί κλαίεις; Ὅτι, φημί, κύριε, οὐκ οἶδα, εἰ δύναμαι σωθῆναι. Διατί; φησίν. Οὐδέπω γάρ, φημί, κύριε, ἐν τῇ ἐμῇ ζωῇ ἀληθὲς ἐλάλησα ῥῆμα, ἀλλὰ πάντοτε πανούργως ἐλάλησα[2] μετὰ πάντων καὶ τὸ ψεῦδός μου ἀληθὲς ἐπέδειξα παρὰ πᾶσιν ἀνθρώποις· καὶ οὐδέποτέ μοι οὐδεὶς ἀντεῖπεν, ἀλλ᾽ ἐπιστεύθη τῷ λόγῳ μου. πῶς οὖν, φημί, κύριε, δύναμαι ζῆσαι ταῦτα πράξας; 4. Σὺ μέν, φησί, καλῶς καὶ ἀληθῶς φρονεῖς· ἔδει γάρ σε ὡς θεοῦ δοῦλον ἐν ἀληθείᾳ πορεύεσθαι, καὶ πονηρὰν συνείδησιν μετὰ τοῦ πνεύματος τῆς ἀληθείας μὴ κατοικεῖν μηδὲ λύπην ἐπάγειν τῷ πνεύματι τῷ σεμνῷ καὶ ἀληθεῖ. Οὐδέποτε, φημί, κύριε,

I Joh. 2, 27

II Tim. 1, 14

[1] From here to the last words of the Mandate (-τάτου ψεύσματος ζήσεται τῷ θεῷ) ℵ is missing.
[2] ἐλάλησα A, ἔζησα EL.

74

MANDATE 3

1. AGAIN he said to me, "Love truth : and let all Truth truth proceed from your mouth, that the spirit which God has made to dwell in this flesh may be found true by all men, and the Lord who dwells in you shall thus be glorified, for the Lord is true in every word and with him there is no lie. 2. They therefore who lie set the Lord at nought, and become defrauders of the Lord, not restoring to him the deposit which they received. For they received from him a spirit free from lies. If they return this as a lying spirit, they have defiled the commandment of the Lord and have robbed him." 3. When therefore I heard this I wept much, and when he saw me weeping he said, "Why do you weep ? " " Because, sir," said I, " I do not know if I can be saved." " Why ? " said he. " Because, sir," said I, " I have never yet in my life spoken a true word, but have ever spoken deceitfully with all men, and gave out that my lie was true among all, and no one ever contradicted me but believed my word. How then, sir," said I, " can I live after having done this ? " 4. " Your thought," said he, " is good and true ; for you ought to have walked in truth as God's servant, and an evil conscience ought not to dwell with the spirit of truth, nor ought grief to come on a spirit which is holy and true." " Never, sir," said I, " have I accurately understood[1] such words."

---

[1] The literal meaning of the Greek is "heard," but the meaning is clearly much more nearly "understood."

τοιαῦτα ῥήματα ἀκριβῶς ἤκουσα. 5. Νῦν οὖν,
φησίν, ἀκούεις· φύλασσε αὐτά, ἵνα καὶ τὰ
πρότερον ἃ ἐλάλησας ψευδὴ ἐν ταῖς πραγματείαις
σου, τούτων εὑρεθέντων ἀληθινῶν, κἀκεῖνα πιστὰ
γένηται· δύναται γὰρ κἀκεῖνα πιστὰ γενέσθαι.
ἐὰν ταῦτα φυλάξῃς καὶ ἀπὸ τοῦ νῦν πᾶσαν
ἀλήθειαν λαλήσῃς, δυνήσῃ σεαυτῷ ζωὴν περι-
ποιήσασθαι· καὶ ὃς ἂν ἀκούσῃ τὴν ἐντολὴν
ταύτην καὶ ἀπέξεται[1] τοῦ πονηροτάτου ψεύσματος ζήσεται τῷ θεῷ.

Ἐντολὴ δ'.

I

1. Ἐντέλλομαί σοι, φησίν, φυλάσσειν τὴν
ἁγνείαν, καὶ μὴ ἀναβαινέτω σου ἐπὶ τὴν καρδίαν
περὶ γυναικὸς ἀλλοτρίας ἢ περὶ πορνείας[2] τινὸς ἢ
περὶ τοιούτων τινῶν ὁμοιωμάτων πονηρῶν. τοῦτο
γὰρ ποιῶν μεγάλην ἁμαρτίαν ἐργάζῃ. τῆς δὲ
σῆς μνημονεύων πάντοτε γυναικὸς οὐδέποτε
διαμαρτήσεις. 2. ἐὰν γὰρ αὕτη ἡ ἐνθύμησις ἐπὶ
τὴν καρδίαν σου ἀναβῇ, διαμαρτήσεις, καὶ ἐὰν
ἕτερα οὕτως πονηρά,[3] ἁμαρτίαν ἐργάζῃ· ἡ γὰρ
ἐνθύμησις αὕτη θεοῦ δούλῳ ἁμαρτία μεγάλη ἐστίν·
ἐὰν δέ τις ἐργάσηται τὸ ἔργον τὸ πονηρὸν τοῦτο,
θάνατον ἑαυτῷ κατεργάζεται. 3. βλέπε οὖν σύ·

---

[1] ἀπέξεται A, but ℵ probably read ἀπέχηται as χη can be
read at the place where the word ought to be.

[2] πορνείας ℵcLE Ath., πονηρίας ℵ*A.

[3] καὶ ἐὰν . . . ἁμαρτίαν ℵ, καὶ ἐὰν ἑτέρως ὡσαύτως πονηρὰν
ἐνθυμήσῃ πονηρά A. The versions paraphrase.

5. "Now then," said he, "you do understand them. Keep them that your former lies in your business may themselves become trustworthy now that these have been found true. For it is possible for those also to become trustworthy.[1] If you keep these things and from henceforth keep the whole truth, you can obtain life for yourself; and whoever shall hear this commandment, and abstain from the sin of lying shall live to God."

MANDATE 4

I

1. "I COMMAND you," he said, "to keep purity and Purity let not any thought come into your heart about another man's wife, or about fornication or any such wicked things; for by doing this you do great sin. But if you always remember your own wife you will never sin. 2. For if this desire enter your heart you will sin, and if you do other such-like wicked things you commit sin. For this desire is a great sin for the servant of God. And if any man commit this wicked deed he works death for himself. 3. See to it then, abstain from this desire, for where holiness

[1] The meaning is obscure, but it appears to be that Hermas having made untrue statements in the course of business must try so to act that his statements will be justified in fact; for instance, if he had made extravagant promises he must fulfil them.

THE APOSTOLIC FATHERS

ἀπέχου ἀπὸ τῆς ἐνθυμήσεως ταύτης· ὅπου γὰρ
σεμνότης κατοικεῖ, ἐκεῖ ἀνομία οὐκ ὀφείλει ἀναβαίνειν ἐπὶ καρδίαν ἀνδρὸς δικαίου. 4. λέγω
αὐτῷ· Κύριε, ἐπίτρεψόν μοι ὀλίγα ἐπερωτῆσαί σε.
Λέγε, φησίν. Κύριε, φημί, εἰ γυναῖκα ἔχῃ τις πιστὴν
ἐν κυρίῳ καὶ ταύτην εὕρῃ ἐν μοιχείᾳ τινί, ἆρα
ἁμαρτάνει ὁ ἀνὴρ συνζῶν μετ᾽ αὐτῆς; 5. Ἄχρι
τῆς ἀγνοίας, φησίν, οὐχ ἁμαρτάνει· ἐὰν δὲ γνῷ ὁ
ἀνὴρ τὴν ἁμαρτίαν αὐτῆς καὶ μὴ μετανοήσῃ ἡ γυνή,
ἀλλ᾽ ἐπιμένῃ τῇ πορνείᾳ αὐτῆς καὶ συνζῇ ὁ ἀνὴρ
μετ᾽ αὐτῆς, ἔνοχος γίνεται τῆς ἁμαρτίας αὐτῆς καὶ
κοινωνὸς τῆς μοιχείας αὐτῆς. 6. Τί οὖν, φημί,
κύριε, ποιήσῃ ὁ ἀνήρ, ἐὰν ἐπιμείνῃ τῷ πάθει
τούτῳ ἡ γυνή; Ἀπολυσάτω, φησίν, αὐτὴν καὶ ὁ
ἀνὴρ ἐφ᾽ ἑαυτῷ μενέτω· ἐὰν δὲ ἀπολύσας τὴν
γυναῖκα ἑτέραν γαμήσῃ, καὶ αὐτὸς μοιχᾶται. 7.
Ἐὰν οὖν, φημί, κύριε, μετὰ τὸ ἀπολυθῆναι τὴν
γυναῖκα μετανοήσῃ ἡ γυνὴ καὶ θελήσῃ ἐπὶ τὸν
ἑαυτῆς ἄνδρα ὑποστρέψαι, οὐ παραδεχθήσεται;
8. Καὶ μήν, φησίν, ἐὰν μὴ παραδέξηται αὐτὴν ὁ
ἀνήρ, ἁμαρτάνει καὶ μεγάλην ἁμαρτίαν ἑαυτῷ
ἐπισπᾶται, ἀλλὰ δεῖ παραδεχθῆναι τὸν ἡμαρτηκότα καὶ μετανοοῦντα, μὴ ἐπὶ πολὺ δέ· τοῖς γὰρ
δούλοις τοῦ θεοῦ μετάνοιά ἐστιν μία. διὰ τὴν
μετάνοιαν οὖν οὐκ ὀφείλει γαμεῖν ὁ ἀνήρ. αὕτη ἡ

Mk. 10, 11;
Mt. 5, 32;
19, 9;
cf. I Cor. 7,
11

78

lives, lawlessness ought not to enter the heart of a righteous man." 4. I said to him, "Sir, allow me to ask you a few questions." "Say on," said he. "Sir," said I, "if a man have a wife faithful in the Lord, and he finds her out in some adultery, does the husband sin if he lives with her?" 5. "So long as he is ignorant," said he, "he does not sin, but if the husband knows her sin, and the wife does not repent, but remains in her fornication, and the husband go on living with her, he becomes a partaker of her sin, and shares in her adultery." 6. "What then," said I, "sir, shall the husband do if the wife remain in this disposition?" "Let him put her away," he said, "and let the husband remain by himself. But 'if he put his wife away and marry another he also commits adultery himself.'" 7. "If then," said I, "sir, after the wife be put away she repent, and wish to return to her own husband, shall she not be received?" 8. "Yes," said he; "if the husband do not receive her he sins and covers himself with great sin; but it is necessary to receive the sinner who repents, but not often, for the servants of God have but one repentance. Therefore, for the sake of repentance the husband ought not to marry.[1]

Man and wife

---

[1] This mandate is really explaining the practical problem which arose from the conflict between the Christian precept against divorce (Mt. 10, 11 f.) and the equally early precept against having intercourse with immoral persons. As the inserted clause "except for the cause of fornication" in the Matthaean version of Mk. 10, 11 f. (Mt. 19, 9; cf. Mt. 5, 32 and Lc. 16, 18) shows, the latter precept was regarded as more important, and immoral wives were put away, but Hermas and other writers always maintained that this was

πρᾶξις ἐπὶ γυναικὶ καὶ ἀνδρὶ κεῖται. 9. οὐ μόνον,
φησίν, μοιχεία ἐστίν, ἐάν τις τὴν σάρκα αὐτοῦ
μιάνῃ, ἀλλὰ καὶ ὃς ἂν τὰ ὁμοιώματα ποιῇ τοῖς
ἔθνεσιν, μοιχᾶται. ὥστε καὶ ἐν τοῖς τοιούτοις
ἔργοις ἐὰν ἐμμένῃ τις καὶ μὴ μετανοῇ, ἀπέχου ἀπ’
αὐτοῦ καὶ μὴ συνζῆθι αὐτῷ· εἰ δὲ μή, καὶ σὺ
μέτοχος εἶ τῆς ἁμαρτίας αὐτοῦ. 10. διὰ τοῦτο
προσετάγη ὑμῖν ἐφ’ ἑαυτοῖς μένειν, εἴτε ἀνὴρ εἴτε
γυνή· δύναται γὰρ ἐν τοῖς τοιούτοις μετάνοια
εἶναι. 11. ἐγὼ οὖν, φησίν, οὐ δίδωμι ἀφορμήν,
ἵνα αὕτη ἡ πρᾶξις οὕτως συντελῆται,[1] ἀλλὰ εἰς τὸ
μηκέτι ἁμαρτάνειν τὸν ἡμαρτηκότα. περὶ δὲ τῆς
προτέρας ἁμαρτίας αὐτοῦ ἔστιν ὁ δυνάμενος ἴασιν
δοῦναι·[2] αὐτὸς γάρ ἐστιν ὁ ἔχων πάντων τὴν
ἐξουσίαν.

II

1. Ἠρώτησα δὲ αὐτὸν πάλιν λέγων· Ἐπεὶ ὁ
κύριος ἄξιόν με ἡγήσατο, ἵνα μετ’ ἐμοῦ πάντοτε
κατοικῇς, ὀλίγα μου ῥήματα ἔτι ἀνάσχου, ἐπεὶ οὐ
συνίω οὐδὲν καὶ ἡ καρδία μου πεπώρωται ἀπὸ τῶν
προτέρων μου πράξεων· συνέτισόν με, ὅτι λίαν
ἄφρων εἰμὶ καὶ ὅλως οὐθὲν νοῶ. 2. ἀποκριθεὶς
μοι λέγει· Ἐγώ, φησίν, ἐπὶ τῆς μετανοίας εἰμὶ καὶ
πᾶσιν τοῖς μετανοοῦσιν σύνεσιν δίδωμι. ἢ οὐ

Mk. 6, 52

---

[1] συντελῆται ℵᶜA, συντελέσηται ℵ*.
[2] ὁ δυνάμενος ἴασιν δοῦναι om. ℵ*.

This is the course of action for wife and husband. 9. Not only," said he, " is it adultery if a man defile his flesh, but whosoever acts as do the heathen is also guilty of adultery, so that if anyone continue in such practices, and repent not, depart from him and do not live with him, otherwise you are also a sharer in his sin. 10. For this reason it was enjoined on you to live by yourselves, whether husband or wife, for in such cases repentance is possible. 11. I, therefore," said he, " am not giving an opportunity to laxity that this business be thus concluded, but in order that he who has sinned sin no more,[1] and for his former sin there is one who can give healing, for he it is who has the power over all."

II

1. AND I asked him again, saying : " If the Lord has thought me worthy for you always to live with me, suffer yet a few words of mine, since I have no understanding and my heart has been hardened by my former deeds ; give me understanding, for I am very foolish and have absolutely no understanding." 2. He answered me and said, " I am set over repentance, and I give understanding to all those

not strictly divorce, as the innocent party was not free to re-marry in order to give the other the opportunity of repenting and of returning.

[1] Hermas is guarding against the imputation that he is lowering the standard of morality. This accusation was actually brought against him later by Tertullian.

δοκεῖ σοι, φησίν, αὐτὸ τοῦτο τὸ μετανοῆσαι σύνεσιν εἶναι; τὸ μετανοῆσαι, φησίν, σύνεσίς ἐστιν
μεγάλη· συνίει γὰρ ὁ ἁμαρτήσας,[1] ὅτι πεποίηκεν
τὸ πονηρὸν ἔμπροσθεν τοῦ κυρίου, καὶ ἀναβαίνει
ἐπὶ τὴν καρδίαν αὐτοῦ ἡ πρᾶξις, ἣν ἔπραξεν, καὶ
μετανοεῖ καὶ οὐκέτι ἐργάζεται τὸ πονηρόν, ἀλλὰ
τὸ ἀγαθὸν πολυτελῶς ἐργάζεται καὶ ταπεινοῖ τὴν
ἑαυτοῦ ψυχὴν καὶ βασανίζει, ὅτι ἥμαρτεν.
βλέπεις οὖν, ὅτι ἡ μετάνοια σύνεσίς ἐστιν μεγάλη.
3. Διὰ τοῦτο οὖν, φημί, κύριε, ἐξακριβάζομαι
παρὰ σοῦ πάντα· πρῶτον μέν,[2] ὅτι ἁμαρτωλός
εἰμι, ἵνα γνῶ, ποῖα ἔργα ἐργαζόμενος ζήσομαι, ὅτι
πολλαί μου εἰσὶν αἱ ἁμαρτίαι καὶ ποικίλαι. 4.
Ζήσῃ, φησίν, ἐὰν τὰς ἐντολάς μου φυλάξῃς καὶ
πορευθῇς ἐν αὐταῖς· καὶ ὃς ἂν ἀκούσας τὰς
ἐντολὰς ταύτας φυλάξῃ, ζήσεται τῷ θεῷ.

Judg. 2, 11;
3, 12; 4, 1;
10, 6; 13, 1;
I Sam. 15,
19 etc.

III

1. Ἔτι, φημί, κύριε, προσθήσω τοῦ ἐπερωτῆσαι.
Λέγε, φησίν. Ἤκουσα, φημί, κύριε, παρά τινων
διδασκάλων, ὅτι ἑτέρα μετάνοια οὐκ ἔστιν εἰ μὴ
ἐκείνη, ὅτε εἰς ὕδωρ κατέβημεν καὶ ἐλάβομεν
ἄφεσιν ἁμαρτιῶν ἡμῶν τῶν προτέρων. 2. λέγει
μοι· Καλῶς ἤκουσας· οὕτω γὰρ ἔχει. ἔδει γὰρ
τὸν[3] εἰληφότα ἄφεσιν ἁμαρτιῶν μηκέτι ἁμαρτάνειν,
ἀλλ' ἐν ἁγνείᾳ κατοικεῖν. 3. ἐπεὶ δὲ πάντα
ἐξακριβάζῃ, καὶ τοῦτό σοι δηλώσω, μὴ διδοὺς
ἀφορμὴν τοῖς μέλλουσι πιστεύειν ἢ τοῖς νῦν

[1] ὁ ἁμαρτήσας ALE, ὁ ἀνὴρ ὁ ἁμαρτήσας ℵ.
[2] From here to Mand. IV. 3, 4 (καρδιογνώστης) ℵ is missing.
[3] τὸν Clem., τινα A.

who repent. Or do you not think," said he, " that
this very repentance is itself understanding? To
repent," said he, "is great understanding. For the
sinner understands that he 'has done wickedly
before the Lord,' and the deed which he wrought
comes into his heart, and he repents and no longer
does wickedly, but does good abundantly, and
humbles his soul and punishes it because he sinned.
You see, therefore, that repentance is great understanding." 3. " For this reason then, sir," said I,
" I enquire accurately from you as to all things.
First, because I am a sinner, that I may know what
I must do to live, because my sins are many and
manifold." 4. "You shall live," he said, "if you
keep my commandments and walk in them, and
whosoever shall hear and keep these commandments
shall live to God."

III

1. " I WILL yet, sir," said I, " continue to ask." Repentance
" Say on," said he. " I have heard, sir," said I, " from for sin after
baptism
some teachers[1] that there is no second repentance
beyond the one given when we went down into
the water and received remission of our former sins."
2. He said to me, " You have heard correctly, for
that is so. For he who has received remission of
sin ought never to sin again, but to live in purity.
3. But since you ask accurately concerning all things,
I will explain this also to you without giving an
excuse to those who in the future shall believe or to

---

[1] Possibly a reference to Heb. 6, 4 ff.

πιστεύσασιν εἰς τὸν κύριον. οἱ γὰρ νῦν πιστεύσαντες ἢ μέλλοντες πιστεύειν μετάνοιαν ἁμαρτιῶν
οὐκ ἔχουσιν, ἄφεσιν δὲ ἔχουσι τῶν προτέρων
ἁμαρτιῶν αὐτῶν. 4. τοῖς οὖν κληθεῖσι πρὸ τούτων τῶν ἡμερῶν ἔθηκεν ὁ κύριος μετάνοιαν· καρδιογνώστης γὰρ ὢν ὁ κύριος καὶ πάντα προγινώσκων
ἔγνω τὴν ἀσθένειαν τῶν ἀνθρώπων καὶ τὴν
πολυπλοκίαν τοῦ διαβόλου, ὅτι ποιήσει τι κακὸν
τοῖς δούλοις τοῦ θεοῦ καὶ πονηρεύσεται εἰς αὐτούς.
5. πολύσπλαγχνος οὖν ὢν ὁ κύριος ἐσπλαγχνίσθη
ἐπὶ τὴν ποίησιν αὐτοῦ καὶ ἔθηκεν τὴν μετάνοιαν
ταύτην, καὶ ἐμοὶ ἡ ἐξουσία τῆς μετανοίας ταύτης
ἐδόθη. 6. ἀλλὰ ἐγώ σοι λέγω, φησί[1]· μετὰ τὴν
κλῆσιν ἐκείνην τὴν μεγάλην καὶ σεμνὴν ἐάν τις
ἐκπειρασθεὶς ὑπὸ τοῦ διαβόλου ἁμαρτήσῃ, μίαν
μετάνοιαν ἔχει· ἐὰν δὲ ὑπὸ χεῖρα ἁμαρτάνῃ καὶ
μετανοήσῃ,[2] ἀσύμφορόν ἐστι τῷ ἀνθρώπῳ τῷ
τοιούτῳ· δυσκόλως γὰρ ζήσεται. 7. λέγω αὐτῷ·
Ἐξωοποιήθην ταῦτα παρὰ σοῦ ἀκούσας οὕτως
ἀκριβῶς· οἶδα γὰρ ὅτι, ἐὰν μηκέτι προσθήσω
ταῖς ἁμαρτίαις μου, σωθήσομαι. Σωθήσῃ, φησίν,
καὶ πάντες, ὅσοι ἐὰν ταῦτα ποιήσωσιν.

IV

1. Ἠρώτησα αὐτὸν πάλιν λέγων· Κύριε, ἐπεὶ
ἅπαξ ἀνέχῃ μου, ἔτι μοι καὶ τοῦτο δήλωσον.
Λέγε, φησίν. Ἐὰν γυνή, φημί, κύριε, ἢ πάλιν
ἀνήρ τις κοιμηθῇ καὶ γαμήσῃ τις ἐξ αὐτῶν, μήτι

I Cor. 7, 38-40

---

[1] With the φη of φησί the extant leaves of ℵ come to an
end. [2] μετανοήσῃ E (L), οὐ μετανοήσῃ A.

those who have already believed on the Lord. For those who have already believed or shall believe in the future, have no repentance of sins, but have remission of their former sin. 4. For those, then, who were called before these days, did the Lord appoint repentance, for the Lord knows the heart, and knowing all things beforehand he knew the weakness of man and the subtlety of the devil, that he will do some evil to the servants of God, and will do them mischief. 5. The Lord, therefore, being merciful, had mercy on his creation, and established this repentance, and to me was the control of this repentance given. 6. But I tell you," said he, "after that great and holy calling, if a man be tempted by the devil and sin, he has one repentance, but if he sin and repent repeatedly it is unprofitable for such a man, for scarcely shall he live." 7. I said to him, "I attained life when I heard these things thus accurately from you, for I know that if I do not again add to my sins I shall be saved." "You shall be saved," said he, "and all who do these things."

IV

1. I ASKED him again, saying, "Sir, since you for once endure me explain this also to me." "Say on," said he. "If, sir," said I, "a wife, or on the other hand a husband, die, and the survivor marry, does

Second marriages

ἁμαρτάνει ὁ γαμῶν; 2. Οὐχ ἁμαρτάνει, φησίν·
ἐὰν δὲ ἐφ᾽ ἑαυτῷ μείνῃ τις, περισσοτέραν ἑαυτῷ
τιμὴν καὶ μεγάλην δόξαν περιποιεῖται πρὸς τὸν
κύριον· ἐὰν δὲ καὶ γαμήσῃ, οὐχ ἁμαρτάνει. 3.
τήρει οὖν τὴν ἁγνείαν καὶ τὴν σεμνότητα, καὶ ζήσῃ
τῷ θεῷ. ταῦτά σοι ὅσα λαλῶ καὶ μέλλω λαλεῖν,
φύλασσε ἀπὸ τοῦ νῦν, ἀφ᾽ ἧς μοι παρεδόθης
ἡμέρας, καὶ εἰς τὸν οἶκόν σου κατοικήσω. 4. τοῖς
δὲ προτέροις σου παραπτώμασιν ἄφεσις ἔσται, ἐὰν
τὰς ἐντολάς μου φυλάξῃς· καὶ πᾶσι δὲ ἄφεσις
ἔσται, ἐὰν τὰς ἐντολάς μου ταύτας φυλάξωσι καὶ
πορευθῶσιν ἐν τῇ ἁγνότητι ταύτῃ.

Ἐντολὴ ε΄.

I

1. Μακρόθυμος, φησί, γίνου καὶ συνετός, καὶ
πάντων τῶν πονηρῶν ἔργων κατακυριεύσεις καὶ
ἐργάσῃ πᾶσαν δικαιοσύνην. 2. ἐὰν γὰρ μακρόθυμος ἔσῃ, τὸ πνεῦμα τὸ ἅγιον τὸ κατοικοῦν
ἐν σοὶ καθαρὸν ἔσται, μὴ ἐπισκοτούμενον ὑπὸ
ἑτέρου πονηροῦ πνεύματος, ἀλλ᾽ ἐν εὐρυχώρῳ
κατοικοῦν ἀγαλλιάσεται καὶ εὐφρανθήσεται μετὰ
τοῦ σκεύους, ἐν ᾧ κατοικεῖ, καὶ [1] λειτουργήσει
τῷ θεῷ ἐν ἱλαρότητι πολλῇ, ἔχον τὴν εὐθηνίαν
ἐν ἑαυτῷ. 3. ἐὰν δὲ ὀξυχολία τις προσέλθῃ,
εὐθὺς τὸ πνεῦμα τὸ ἅγιον, τρυφερὸν ὄν, στενο-

---

[1] καί EL Ant., before μετά A.

the one who marries commit sin ? " 2. " He does not sin," said he, " but if he remain single he gains for himself more exceeding honour and great glory with the Lord, but even if he marry he does not sin. 3. Preserve therefore purity and holiness, and you shall live to God. Keep from henceforth, from the day on which you were handed over to me, these things which I tell you and shall tell you, and I will dwell in your house. 4. And for your former transgression there shall be remission if you keep my commandments, and all men shall obtain a remission, if they keep these commandments of mine and walk in this purity."

MANDATE 5

I

1. " BE," said he, " long-suffering[1] and prudent and you shall have power over all evil deeds and shalt do all righteousness. 2. For if you are courageous the Holy Spirit which dwells in you will be pure, not obscured by another evil spirit, but will dwell at large and rejoice and be glad with the body in which it dwells, and will serve God in great cheerfulness, having well-being in itself. 3. But if any ill temper enter, at once the Holy Spirit, which is delicate, is oppressed, finding the place impure, and

Long-suffering

Against ill temper

---

[1] The translation of μακροθυμία and ὀξυχολία is difficult. Μακροθυμία is a little more than " long suffering " and almost equals courage. ὀξυχολία is a rare word, literally " quickness to wrath," but this phrase does not convey in English the bad sense which Hermas obviously implies.

χωρεῖται, μὴ ἔχον τὸν τόπον καθαρόν, καὶ ζητεῖ
ἀποστῆναι ἐκ τοῦ τόπου· πνίγεται γὰρ ὑπὸ τοῦ
πονηροῦ πνεύματος, μὴ ἔχον τόπον λειτουργῆσαι
τῷ κυρίῳ, καθὼς βούλεται, μιαινόμενον ὑπὸ
τῆς ὀξυχολίας. ἐν γὰρ τῇ μακροθυμίᾳ ὁ κύριος
κατοικεῖ, ἐν δὲ τῇ ὀξυχολίᾳ ὁ διάβολος. 4. ἀμφότερα οὖν τὰ πνεύματα ἐπὶ τὸ αὐτὸ κατοικοῦντα,
ἀσύμφορόν ἐστιν καὶ πονηρὸν τῷ ἀνθρώπῳ ἐκείνῳ,
ἐν ᾧ κατοικοῦσιν. 5. ἐὰν γὰρ λάβῃς ἀψινθίου
μικρὸν λίαν καὶ εἰς κεράμιον μέλιτος ἐπιχέῃς, οὐχὶ
ὅλον τὸ μέλι ἀφανίζεται, καὶ τοσοῦτον μέλι ὑπὸ
τοῦ ἐλαχίστου ἀψινθίου ἀπόλλυται καὶ ἀπόλλυσι
τὴν γλυκύτητα τοῦ μέλιτος, καὶ οὐκέτι τὴν αὐτὴν
χάριν ἔχει παρὰ τῷ δεσπότῃ, ὅτι ἐπικράνθη καὶ
τὴν χρῆσιν αὐτοῦ ἀπώλεσεν; ἐὰν δὲ εἰς τὸ μέλι
μὴ βληθῇ τὸ ἀψίνθιον, γλυκὺ εὑρίσκεται τὸ μέλι
καὶ εὔχρηστον γίνεται τῷ δεσπότῃ αὐτοῦ.[1] 6.
βλέπεις ὅτι ἡ μακροθυμία γλυκυτάτη ἐστὶν
ὑπὲρ τὸ μέλι καὶ εὔχρηστός ἐστι τῷ κυρίῳ, καὶ
ἐν αὐτῇ κατοικεῖ. ἡ δὲ ὀξυχολία πικρὰ καὶ
ἄχρηστός ἐστιν. ἐὰν οὖν μιγῇ ἡ ὀξυχολία τῇ
μακροθυμίᾳ, μιαίνεται ἡ μακροθυμία καὶ οὐκέτι
εὔχρηστός ἐστι τῷ θεῷ ἡ ἔντευξις αὐτῆς. 7.
Ἤθελον, φημί, κύριε, γνῶναι τὴν ἐνέργειαν τῆς
ὀξυχολίας, ἵνα φυλάξωμαι ἀπ᾽ αὐτῆς. Καὶ μήν,

---

[1] The text of this passage is reconstructed thus by the
editors from LE Ant. A reads ἀφανίζεται, καὶ πικρὸν γίνεται
καὶ ἀπολλύει τὴν γλυκύτητα τοῦ μέλιτος καὶ οὐκέτι τὴν αὐτὴν
χάριν ἔκει παρὰ τῷ δεσπότῃ ὅτι ἐπικράνθη καὶ τὴν χρῆσιν αὐτοῦ
ἀπώλεσεν, ἐὰν δὲ ἐπὶ τὸ ἀψίνθιον μὴ βληθῇ μέλι, οὐδὲ ἐπὶ τὸ
ἀψίνθιον μὴ βληθῇ μέλι οὐδὲ εὔχρηστον γίνεται τῷ δεσπότῃ αὐτοῦ.
This of course is hopelessly corrupt, but it seems to point to
a shorter text.

seeks to depart out of the place, for it is choked by the evil spirit, having no room to serve the Lord as it will, but is contaminated by the bitterness. For the Lord dwells in long-suffering and the devil dwells in ill temper. 4. If therefore, both spirits dwell in the same place it is unprofitable and evil for that man in whom they dwell. 5. For if you take a little wormwood, and pour into it a jar of honey, is not the whole honey spoilt? And a great quantity of honey is ruined by a very little wormwood, and it spoils the sweetness of the honey, and it has no longer the same favour with the master, because it has been mixed and he has lost its use. But if no wormwood be put into the honey, the honey is found to be sweet, and becomes valuable to the master. 6. You see that long suffering is very sweet, surpassing honey, and is valuable to the Lord and he dwells in it. But ill temper is bitter and useless. If, therefore, ill temper be mixed with courage, the courage is defiled, and its intercession is no longer valuable before God." 7. "I would like, sir," said I, "to know the working of ill temper, that I may be preserved from it." "Indeed," said he, "if you do not keep

φησίν, ἐὰν μὴ φυλάξῃ ἀπ' αὐτῆς σὺ καὶ ὁ οἶκός
σου, ἀπώλεσάς σου τὴν πᾶσαν ἐλπίδα. ἀλλὰ
φύλαξαι ἀπ' αὐτῆς· ἐγὼ γὰρ μετὰ σοῦ εἰμι. καὶ
πάντες δὲ ἀφέξονται ἀπ' αὐτῆς, ὅσοι ἂν μετανοήσωσιν ἐξ ὅλης τῆς καρδίας αὐτῶν· μετ' αὐτῶν γὰρ
ἔσομαι καὶ συντηρήσω αὐτούς· ἐδικαιώθησαν γὰρ
πάντες ὑπὸ τοῦ σεμνοτάτου ἀγγέλου.

II

1. Ἄκουε νῦν, φησί, τὴν ἐνέργειαν τῆς ὀξυχολίας, πῶς πονηρά ἐστι, καὶ πῶς τοὺς δούλους
μου[1] καταστρέφει τῇ ἑαυτῆς ἐνεργείᾳ καὶ πῶς
ἀποπλανᾷ αὐτοὺς ἀπὸ τῆς δικαιοσύνης. οὐκ
ἀποπλανᾷ δὲ τοὺς πλήρεις ὄντας ἐν τῇ πίστει
οὐδὲ ἐνεργῆσαι δύναται εἰς αὐτούς, ὅτι ἡ δύναμις
μου[1] μετ' αὐτῶν ἐστιν· ἀποπλανᾷ δὲ τοὺς
ἀποκένους καὶ διψύχους ὄντας. 2. ὅταν δὲ ἴδῃ
τοὺς τοιούτους ἀνθρώπους εὐσταθοῦντας, παρεμ-
βάλλει ἑαυτὴν εἰς τὴν καρδίαν τοῦ ἀνθρώπου
ἐκείνου, καὶ ἐκ τοῦ μηδενὸς ὁ ἀνὴρ ἢ ἡ γυνὴ ἐν
πικρίᾳ γίνεται ἕνεκεν βιωτικῶν πραγμάτων ἢ
περὶ ἐδεσμάτων ἢ μικρολογίας τινὸς ἢ περὶ φίλου
τινὸς[2] ἢ περὶ δόσεως ἢ λήψεως ἢ περὶ τοιούτων
μωρῶν πραγμάτων· ταῦτα γὰρ πάντα μωρά ἐστι
καὶ κενὰ καὶ ἄφρονα καὶ ἀσύμφορα τοῖς δούλοις
τοῦ θεοῦ. 3. ἡ δὲ μακροθυμία μεγάλη ἐστὶ
καὶ ἰσχυρὰ καὶ δύναμιν ἔχουσα καὶ στιβαρὰν
καὶ εὐθηνουμένην ἐν πλατυσμῷ μεγάλῳ, ἱλαρά,

---

[1] μου A, τοῦ κυρίου L₂, (E) τοῦ θεοῦ L₁.
[2] ἢ περὶ φίλου τινός om. A.

from it, both you and your house, you have destroyed
all your hope. But keep from it, for I am with you.
And all shall refrain from it, who repent with all
their heart ; for I will be with them, and will preserve
them, for all have been made righteous by the most
revered angel.

II

1. " HEAR, then," said he, " the working of ill
temper, and how evil it is and how it destroys the
servants of God by its working, and how it leads
them astray from righteousness. But it does not
lead astray those who are filled with faith, nor
can it work evil to them, because my power is
with them, but it leads astray those who are vain
and are double-minded. 2. And when it sees such
men in tranquillity, it forces its way into the heart of
that man, and the man or woman is made bitter out
of nothing, because of daily business or of food or
some trifle, or about some friend, or about giving or
receiving, or about some such foolish matters. For
all these things are foolish and vain and meaningless, and unprofitable to the servants of God. 3. But
long-suffering is great and mighty and has steadfast
power and prospers in great breadth, is joyful,
glad, without care, 'glorifying the Lord at every

Tob. 4, 19 ἀγαλλιωμένη, ἀμέριμνος οὖσα, δοξάζουσα τὸν
κύριον ἐν παντὶ καιρῷ, μηδὲν ἐν ἑαυτῇ ἔχουσα
πικρόν, παραμένουσα διὰ παντὸς πραεῖα καὶ
ἡσύχιος· αὕτη οὖν ἡ μακροθυμία κατοικεῖ μετὰ
τῶν τὴν πίστιν ἐχόντων ὁλόκληρον. 4. ἡ δὲ ὀξυχολία πρῶτον μὲν μωρά ἐστιν, ἐλαφρά τε καὶ
ἄφρων. εἶτα ἐκ τῆς ἀφροσύνης γίνεται πικρία, ἐκ
δὲ τῆς πικρίας θυμός, ἐκ δὲ τοῦ θυμοῦ ὀργή, ἐκ δὲ
τῆς ὀργῆς μῆνις· εἶτα ἡ μῆνις αὕτη ἐκ τοσούτων
κακῶν συνισταμένη γίνεται ἁμαρτία μεγάλη καὶ
ἀνίατος. 5. ὅταν γὰρ ταῦτα τὰ πνεύματα ἐν ἑνὶ ἀγ-
γείῳ κατοικῇ, οὗ καὶ τὸ πνεῦμα τὸ ἅγιον κατοικεῖ,
οὐ χωρεῖ τὸ ἄγγος ἐκεῖνο, ἀλλ᾽ ὑπερπλεονάζει. 6.
τὸ τρυφερὸν οὖν πνεῦμα, μὴ ἔχον συνήθειαν μετὰ
πονηροῦ πνεύματος κατοικεῖν μηδὲ μετὰ σκλη-
ρότητος, ἀποχωρεῖ ἀπὸ τοῦ ἀνθρώπου τοῦ τοιού-
του καὶ ζητεῖ κατοικεῖν μετὰ πραότητος καὶ
ἡσυχίας. 7. εἶτα ὅταν ἀποστῇ ἀπὸ τοῦ ἀνθρώπου ἐκείνου, οὗ κατοικεῖ, γίνεται ὁ ἄνθρωπος
ἐκεῖνος κενὸς ἀπὸ τοῦ πνεύματος τοῦ δικαίου, καὶ
τὸ λοιπὸν πεπληρωμένος τοῖς πνεύμασι τοῖς
πονηροῖς ἀκαταστατεῖ ἐν πάσῃ πράξει αὐτοῦ,
περισπώμενος ὧδε κἀκεῖσε ἀπὸ τῶν πνευμάτων
τῶν πονηρῶν, καὶ ὅλως ἀποτυφλοῦται ἀπὸ τῆς
διανοίας τῆς ἀγαθῆς. οὕτως οὖν συμβαίνει πᾶσι
τοῖς ὀξυχόλοις. 8. ἀπέχου οὖν ἀπὸ τῆς ὀξυχολίας, τοῦ πονηροτάτου πνεύματος· ἔνδυσαι δὲ
τὴν μακροθυμίαν καὶ ἀντίστα τῇ ὀξυχολίᾳ καὶ
τῇ πικρίᾳ, καὶ ἔσῃ εὑρισκόμενος μετὰ τῆς σεμνότητος τῆς ἠγαπημένης ὑπὸ τοῦ κυρίου. βλέπε
οὖν μήποτε παρενθυμηθῇς τὴν ἐντολὴν ταύτην·
ἐὰν γὰρ ταύτης τῆς ἐντολῆς κυριεύσῃς, καὶ τὰς

time,' has nothing bitter in itself, but remains ever meek and gentle. Therefore this long-suffering dwells with those who have faith in perfectness. 4. But ill temper is first foolish, frivolous, and silly ; then from silliness comes bitterness, from bitterness wrath, from wrath rage, and from rage fury; then fury, being compounded of such great evils, becomes great and inexpiable sin. 5. For when these spirits dwell in one vessel, where also the Holy Spirit dwells, there is no room in that vessel, but it is over-crowded. 6. Therefore the delicate spirit which is unaccustomed to dwell with an evil spirit, or with hardness, departs from such a man, and seeks to dwell with gentleness and quietness. 7. Then, when it departs from that man where it was dwelling, that man becomes empty of the righteous spirit, and for the future is filled with the evil spirits, and is disorderly in all his actions, being dragged here and there by the evil spirits, and is wholly blinded from goodness of thought. Thus, then, it happens with all who are ill tempered. 8. Abstain then from ill temper, that most evil spirit, but put on long suffering and withstand ill temper, and be found with the holiness which is beloved of the Lord. See then that you forget not this commandment, for if you master this commandment you will also be able to

λοιπὰς ἐντολὰς δυνήσῃ φυλάξαι, ἅς σοι μέλλω
ἐντέλλεσθαι. ἰσχυροῦ ἐν αὐταῖς καὶ ἐνδυναμοῦ,
καὶ πάντες ἐνδυναμούσθωσαν, ὅσοι ἐὰν θέλωσιν
ἐν αὐταῖς πορεύεσθαι.

Ἐντολὴ ϛʹ

I

1. Ἐνετειλάμην σοι, φησίν, ἐν τῇ πρώτῃ ἐντολῇ,
ἵνα φυλάξῃς τὴν πίστιν καὶ τὸν φόβον καὶ τὴν
ἐγκράτειαν. Ναί, φημί, κύριε. Ἀλλὰ νῦν θέλω
σοι, φησίν, δηλῶσαι καὶ τὰς δυνάμεις αὐτῶν, ἵνα
νοήσῃς τίς αὐτῶν τίνα δύναμιν ἔχει καὶ ἐνέργειαν·
διπλαῖ γάρ εἰσιν αἱ ἐνέργειαι αὐτῶν. κεῖνται
οὖν ἐπὶ δικαίῳ καὶ ἀδίκῳ· 2. σὺ οὖν πίστευε
τῷ δικαίῳ, τῷ δὲ ἀδίκῳ μὴ πιστεύσῃς· τὸ γὰρ
δίκαιον ὀρθὴν ὁδὸν ἔχει, τὸ δὲ ἄδικον στρεβλήν.
ἀλλὰ σὺ τῇ ὀρθῇ ὁδῷ πορεύου καὶ ὁμαλῇ, τὴν
δὲ στρεβλὴν ἔασον. 3. ἡ γὰρ στρεβλὴ ὁδὸς
τρίβους οὐκ ἔχει, ἀλλ' ἀνοδίας καὶ προσκόμματα
πολλὰ καὶ τραχεῖά ἐστι καὶ ἀκανθώδης. βλαβερὰ οὖν ἐστι τοῖς ἐν αὐτῇ πορευομένοις. 4. οἱ
δὲ τῇ ὀρθῇ ὁδῷ πορευόμενοι ὁμαλῶς περιπατοῦσι
καὶ ἀπροσκόπως· οὔτε γὰρ τραχεῖά ἐστιν οὔτε
ἀκανθώδης. βλέπεις οὖν, ὅτι συμφορώτερόν ἐστι
ταύτῃ τῇ ὁδῷ πορεύεσθαι. 5. Ἀρέσκει μοι, φημί,
κύριε, ταύτῃ τῇ ὁδῷ πορεύεσθαι. Πορεύσῃ, φησί,
καὶ ὃς ἂν ἐξ ὅλης καρδίας ἐπιστρέψῃ πρὸς κύριον,
πορεύσεται ἐν αὐτῇ.

Jer. 24, 7;
Joel 2, 12

keep the other commandments which I am going to give you. Be strong in them and strengthen yourself, and let all strengthen themselves who wish to walk in them.

MANDATE 6

I

1. "I COMMANDED you," said he, "in the first commandment to keep faith and fear and continence." "Yes, sir," said I. "But now I wish," said he, "to explain also their qualities that you may understand what is the quality of each and its working, for their working is of two sorts. They relate, then, to the righteous and to the unrighteous : 2. do you therefore believe the righteous, but do not believe the unrighteous. For that which is righteous has a straight path, but that which is unrighteous a crooked path. But do you walk in the straight path, but leave the crooked path alone. 3. For the crooked path has no road, but rough ground and many stumbling-blocks, and is steep and thorny. It is therefore harmful to those who walk in it. 4. But those who go in the straight path walk smoothly and without stumbling, for it is neither rough nor thorny. You see, then, that it is better to walk in this path." 5. "It pleases me, sir," said I, "to walk in this path." "You shall do so," said he, "and whoever 'turns to the Lord with all his heart' shall walk in it.

Expansion of the first Mandate

95

II

1. Ἄκουε νῦν, φησί, περὶ τῆς πίστεως. δύο εἰσὶν ἄγγελοι μετὰ τοῦ ἀνθρώπου, εἷς τῆς δικαιοσύνης καὶ εἷς τῆς πονηρίας. 2. Πῶς οὖν, φημί, κύριε, γνώσομαι τὰς αὐτῶν ἐνεργείας, ὅτι ἀμφότεροι ἄγγελοι μετ' ἐμοῦ κατοικοῦσιν; 3. Ἄκουε, φησί, καὶ συνιεῖς αὐτάς.[1] ὁ μὲν τῆς δικαιοσύνης ἄγγελος τρυφερός ἐστι καὶ αἰσχυντηρὸς καὶ πραῢς καὶ ἡσύχιος· ὅταν οὖν οὗτος ἐπὶ τὴν καρδίαν σου ἀναβῇ, εὐθέως λαλεῖ μετὰ σοῦ περὶ δικαιοσύνης, περὶ ἁγνείας, περὶ σεμνότητος καὶ περὶ αὐταρκείας καὶ περὶ παντὸς ἔργου δικαίου καὶ περὶ πάσης ἀρετῆς ἐνδόξου. ταῦτα πάντα ὅταν εἰς τὴν καρδίαν σου ἀναβῇ[2], γίνωσκε, ὅτι ὁ ἄγγελος τῆς δικαιοσύνης μετὰ σοῦ ἐστί. ταῦτα οὖν ἐστι τὰ ἔργα τοῦ ἀγγέλου τῆς δικαιοσύνης. τούτῳ οὖν πίστευε καὶ τοῖς ἔργοις αὐτοῦ. 4. ὅρα οὖν[3] καὶ τοῦ ἀγγέλου τῆς πονηρίας τὰ ἔργα. πρῶτον πάντων ὀξύχολός ἐστι καὶ πικρὸς καὶ ἄφρων,[4] καὶ τὰ ἔργα αὐτοῦ πονηρά, καταστρέφοντα τοὺς δούλους τοῦ θεοῦ· ὅταν οὖν οὗτος ἐπὶ τὴν καρδίαν σου ἀναβῇ, γνῶθι αὐτὸν ἀπὸ τῶν ἔργων αὐτοῦ.

Mt. 7, 16 5. Πῶς, φημί, κύριε, νοήσω αὐτόν, οὐκ ἐπίσταμαι. Ἄκουε, φησίν. ὅταν ὀξυχολία σοί τις προσπέσῃ ἢ πικρία, γίνωσκε, ὅτι αὐτός ἐστιν ἐν σοί· εἶτα ἐπιθυμία πράξεων πολλῶν καὶ πολυτέλειαι

---

[1] συνιεῖς αὐτάς A, σύνιε L, om E.
[2] εὐθέως λαλεῖ . . . ἀναβῇ (with some variations) LE Ath. Ant., om. A.   [3] οὖν A Ath., νῦν L(E).
[4] πικρὸς καὶ ἄφρων L Ath. Ant., om. A.

96

II

1. " HEAR now," said he, "concerning faith. There Faith are two angels with man, one of righteousness and one of wickedness." 2. " How then, sir," said I, " shall I know their workings, because both angels dwell with me?" "Listen," said he, " and understand them. The angel of righteousness is delicate and modest and meek and gentle. When, then, he comes into your heart he at once speaks with you of righteousness, of purity, of reverence, of self-control, of every righteous deed, and of all glorious virtue. When all these things come into your heart, know that the angel of righteousness is with you. These things, then, are the deeds of the angel of righteousness. Therefore believe him and his works. 4. Now see also the works of the angel of wickedness. First of all, he is ill tempered, and bitter, and foolish, and his deeds are evil, casting down the servants of God. Whenever therefore he comes into your heart, know him from his works." 5. " I do not understand, sir," said I, " how to perceive him." "Listen," said he. " When ill temper or bitterness come upon you, know that he is in you. Next the desire of many deeds and the luxury of

THE APOSTOLIC FATHERS

ἐδεσμάτων πολλῶν καὶ μεθυσμάτων καὶ κραι-
παλῶν πολλῶν καὶ ποικίλων τροφῶν καὶ οὐ
δεόντων καὶ ἐπιθυμίαι γυναικῶν καὶ πλεονεξιῶν
καὶ ὑπερηφανία πολλή τις καὶ ἀλαζονεία καὶ ὅσα
τούτοις παραπλήσιά ἐστι καὶ ὅμοια· ταῦτα οὖν
ὅταν ἐπὶ τὴν καρδίαν σου ἀναβῇ, γίνωσκε, ὅτι ὁ
ἄγγελος τῆς πονηρίας ἐστὶν ἐν σοί. 6. σὺ οὖν
ἐπιγνοὺς τὰ ἔργα αὐτοῦ ἀπόστα ἀπ᾽ αὐτοῦ,
μηδὲν [1] αὐτῷ πίστευε, ὅτι τὰ ἔργα αὐτοῦ πονηρά
εἰσι καὶ ἀσύμποφα τοῖς δούλοις τοῦ θεοῦ. ἔχεις
οὖν ἀμφοτέρων τῶν ἀγγέλων τὰς ἐνεργείας· σύνιε
αὐτὰς καὶ πίστευε τῷ ἀγγέλῳ τῆς δικαιοσύνης·
7. ἀπὸ δὲ τοῦ ἀγγέλου τῆς πονηρίας ἀπόστηθι,
ὅτι ἡ διδαχὴ αὐτοῦ πονηρά ἐστι παντὶ ἔργῳ· ἐὰν
γὰρ ᾖ τις πιστὸς ἀνὴρ καὶ ἡ ἐνθύμησις τοῦ
ἀγγέλου τούτου ἀναβῇ ἐπὶ τὴν καρδίαν αὐτοῦ, δεῖ
τὸν ἄνδρα ἐκεῖνον ἢ τὴν γυναῖκα ἐξαμαρτῆσαί τι.
8. ἐὰν δὲ πάλιν πονηρότατός τις ᾖ ἀνὴρ ἢ γυνὴ
καὶ ἀναβῇ ἐπὶ τὴν καρδίαν αὐτοῦ τὰ ἔργα τοῦ
ἀγγέλου τῆς δικαιοσύνης, ἐξ ἀνάγκης δεῖ αὐτὸν
ἀγαθόν τι ποιῆσαι. 9. βλέπεις οὖν, φησίν, ὅτι
καλόν ἐστι τῷ ἀγγέλῳ τῆς δικαιοσύνης ἀκολουθεῖν,
τῷ δὲ ἀγγέλῳ τῆς πονηρίας ἀποτάξασθαι. 10.
τὰ μὲν περὶ τῆς πίστεως αὕτη ἡ ἐντολὴ δηλοῖ, ἵνα
τοῖς ἔργοις τοῦ ἀγγέλου τῆς δικαιοσύνης πιστεύσῃς, καὶ ἐργασάμενος αὐτὰ ζήσῃ τῷ θεῷ.
πίστευε δέ, ὅτι τὰ ἔργα τοῦ ἀγγέλου τῆς πονηρίας
χαλεπά ἐστι· μὴ ἐργαζόμενος οὖν αὐτὰ ζήσῃ τῷ
θεῷ.

[1] μηδὲ AE, καὶ μηδὲν Ath., L.

much eating and drinking, and many feasts, and
various and unnecessary foods, and the desire of
women, and covetousness and haughtiness, and pride,
and whatsoever things are akin and like to these,—
when, therefore, these things come into your heart,
know that the angel of wickedness is with you.
6. When, therefore, you know his deeds, keep from
him, and do not trust him, because his deeds
are evil and unprofitable for the servants of God.
You have, therefore, the workings of both the
angels. Understand them and believe the angel of
righteousness, 7. but keep from the angel of wickedness because his teaching is evil in every act. For
though a man be faithful, if the thought of that
angel rise in his heart, it must be that that man
or woman commit some sin. 8. But again, though
a man or woman be very evil, if there rise in
his heart the deeds of the angel of righteousness, it
must needs be that he do some good act. 9. You
see, therefore," said he, " that it is good to follow the
angel of righteousness, but to keep away from
the angel of wickedness. 10. This commandment
makes plain the things of the faith, that you may
believe the works of the angel of righteousness, and
by doing them live to God. But believe that the
works of the angel of wickedness are bad : by not
doing them, therefore, you shall live to God."

Ἐντολὴ ζ

1. Φοβήθητι, φησί, τὸν κύριον καὶ φύλασσε τὰς

Eccles. 12,13 ἐντολὰς αὐτοῦ. φυλάσσων οὖν τὰς ἐντολὰς τοῦ θεοῦ ἔσῃ δυνατὸς ἐν πάσῃ πράξει, καὶ ἡ πρᾶξίς σου ἀσύγκριτος ἔσται. φοβούμενος γὰρ τὸν κύριον πάντα καλῶς ἐργάσῃ· οὗτος δέ ἐστιν ὁ φόβος, ὃν δεῖ σε φοβηθῆναι, καὶ σωθῆναι.[1] **2.** τὸν δὲ διάβολον μὴ φοβηθῇς· φοβούμενος γὰρ τὸν κύριον κατακυριεύσεις τοῦ διαβόλου, ὅτι δύναμις ἐν αὐτῷ οὐκ ἔστιν. ἐν ᾧ δὲ δύναμις οὐκ ἔστιν,[2] οὐδὲ φόβος· ἐν ᾧ δὲ δύναμις ἡ ἔνδοξος, καὶ φόβος ἐν αὐτῷ. πᾶς γὰρ ὁ δύναμιν ἔχων φόβον ἔχει· ὁ δὲ μὴ ἔχων δύναμιν ὑπὸ πάντων καταφρονεῖται. **3.** φοβήθητι δὲ τὰ ἔργα τοῦ διαβόλου, ὅτι πονηρά ἐστι. φοβούμενος οὖν τὸν κύριον[3] οὐκ ἐργάσῃ αὐτά, ἀλλ᾽ ἀφέξῃ ἀπ᾽ αὐτῶν. **4.** δισσοὶ οὖν εἰσιν οἱ φόβοι· ἐὰν γὰρ θέλῃς τὸ πονηρὸν ἐργάσασθαι, φοβοῦ τὸν κύριον, καὶ οὐκ ἐργάσῃ αὐτό· ἐὰν δὲ θέλῃς πάλιν τὸ ἀγαθὸν ἐργάσασθαι, φοβοῦ τὸν κύριον, καὶ ἐργάσῃ αὐτό. ὥστε ὁ φόβος τοῦ κυρίου ἰσχυρός ἐστι καὶ μέγας καὶ ἔνδοξος. φοβήθητι οὖν τὸν κύριον, καὶ ζήσῃ αὐτῷ· καὶ ὅσοι ἂν φοβηθῶσιν αὐτὸν καὶ τηρήσωσι[4] τὰς ἐντολὰς αὐτοῦ, ζήσονται τῷ θεῷ. **5.** Διατί, φημί, κύριε, εἶπας περὶ τῶν τηρούντων τὰς ἐντολὰς αὐτοῦ· Ζήσονται τῷ θεῷ; Ὅτι, φησίν, πᾶσα ἡ κτίσις φοβεῖται τὸν κύριον τὰς δὲ ἐντολὰς αὐτοῦ οὐ φυλάσσει. τῶν οὖν

---

[1] σωθῆναι A, σωθήσῃ L₂ Ant.

[2] ἐν ᾧ . . . ἔστιν om. (E) L₂ Ath.

[3] κύριον A, add. φοβηθήσῃ τὰ ἔργα τοῦ διαβόλου καί Ant. (L₁), L₂ omits the whole clause.

[4] καὶ τηρήσωσι E Ant., τῶν φυλασσόντων A.

Mandate 7

1. " ' Fear,' " said he, " ' the Lord and keep his Fear commandments.' By keeping, therefore, the commandments of God you shall be strong in every act, and your conduct shall be beyond compare. For by fearing the Lord you shall do all things well, and this is the fear with which you must fear and be saved. 2. But the devil do not fear, for by fearing the Lord you have power over the devil because there is no might in him. But where there is no might, neither is there fear. But where there is glorious might, there is also fear. For everyone who has might gains fear. But he who has not might is despised by all. 3. But fear the works of the devil, because they are evil. If therefore, you fear the Lord you shall not do them, but depart from them. 4. There are therefore two sorts of fear. For if you wish to do that which is evil, fear the Lord and you shall not do it. But, on the other hand, if you wish to do that which is good, fear the Lord, and you shall do it. So that the fear of the Lord is mighty and great and glorious. Therefore fear the Lord and you shall live in him. And whosoever shall fear him and keep his commandments, shall live to God." 5. "Wherefore, sir," said I, "did you say of those who keep his commandments, 'they shall live to God'?" "Because," said he, "the whole creation fears the Lord, but it does not keep his commandments. Those, therefore

φοβουμένων αὐτὸν καὶ φυλασσόντων τὰς ἐντολὰς
αὐτοῦ, ἐκείνων ἡ ζωή ἐστι παρὰ τῷ θεῷ· τῶν δὲ
μὴ φυλασσόντων τὰς ἐντολὰς αὐτοῦ, οὐδὲ ζωὴ ἐν
αὐτῷ.

Ἐντολὴ η′

1. Εἶπόν σοι, φησίν, ὅτι τὰ κτίσματα τοῦ θεοῦ
διπλᾶ ἐστι· καὶ γὰρ ἡ ἐγκράτεια διπλῆ ἐστιν.
ἐπί τινων γὰρ δεῖ ἐγκρατεύεσθαι, ἐπί τινων δὲ οὐ
δεῖ· 2. Γνώρισόν μοι, φημί, κύριε, ἐπὶ τίνων δεῖ
ἐγκρατεύεσθαι, ἐπὶ τίνων δὲ οὐ δεῖ. Ἄκουε, φησί.
τὸ πονηρὸν ἐγκρατεύου καὶ μὴ ποίει αὐτό· τὸ δὲ
ἀγαθὸν μὴ ἐγκρατεύου, ἀλλὰ ποίει αὐτό. ἐὰν
γὰρ ἐγκρατεύσῃ τὸ ἀγαθὸν μὴ ποιεῖν, ἁμαρτίαν
μεγάλην ἐργάζῃ·[1] ἐὰν δὲ ἐγκρατεύσῃ τὸ πονηρὸν
μὴ ποιεῖν, δικαιοσύνην μεγάλην ἐργάζῃ. ἐγκράτευσαι οὖν ἀπὸ πονηρίας πάσης ἐργαζόμενος τὸ
ἀγαθόν. 3. Ποταπαί, φημί, κύριε, εἰσὶν αἱ πονηρίαι, ἀφ' ὧν ἡμᾶς δεῖ ἐγκρατεύεσθαι; Ἄκουε,
φησίν· ἀπὸ μοιχείας καὶ πορνείας, ἀπὸ μεθύσ-
ματος ἀνομίας, ἀπὸ τρυφῆς πονηρᾶς, ἀπὸ
ἐδεσμάτων πολλῶν καὶ πολυτελείας πλούτου καὶ
καυχήσεως καὶ ὑψηλοφροσύνης καὶ ὑπερηφανίας
καὶ ἀπὸ ψεύσματος καὶ καταλαλιᾶς καὶ ὑποκρί-
σεως, μνησικακίας καὶ πάσης βλασφημίας. 4.
ταῦτα τὰ ἔργα πάντων πονηρότατά εἰσιν
ἐν τῇ ζωῇ τῶν ἀνθρώπων. ἀπὸ τούτων οὖν
τῶν ἔργων δεῖ ἐγκρατεύεσθαι τὸν δοῦλον τοῦ
θεοῦ· ὁ γὰρ μὴ ἐγκρατευόμενος ἀπὸ τούτων οὐ
δύναται ζῆσαι τῷ θεῷ. ἄκουε οὖν καὶ τὰ

---

[1] ἐὰν γὰρ . . . ἐργάζῃ EL, om. A.

who fear him and observe his commandments,—it is they who have life with God. But as for those who do not observe his commandments, neither have they life in him.

MANDATE 8

1. "I TOLD you," said he, "that the creatures of God are two-fold, and temperance is also two-fold. For from some things we must refrain and from some things not." 2. "Let me know, sir," said I, "from what we must refrain and from what not." "Listen," said he. "Refrain from evil, and do not do it, but do not refrain from good, but do it. For if you refrain from doing good, you do great sin; but if you refrain from doing evil, you do great righteousness. Refrain therefore from all evil, and do good." 3. "What, sir," said I, "are the wickednesses from which we must refrain?" "Listen," said he. "From adultery and fornication, from the lawlessness of drunkenness, from evil luxury, from much eating, and extravagance of wealth, and boastfulness and haughtiness and pride, and from lying and evil speaking and hypocrisy, malice and all blasphemy. 4. These deeds are the wickedest of all in the life of men. The servant of God must therefore refrain from these deeds. For he who does not refrain from these cannot live to God. Hear therefore what

Temperance

103

ἀκόλουθα τούτων, 5. Ἔτι γάρ, φημί, κύριε,
πονηρὰ ἔργα ἐστί; Καί γε πολλά, φησίν, ἔστιν,
ἀφ᾽ ὧν δεῖ τὸν δοῦλον τοῦ θεοῦ ἐγκρατεύεσθαι·
κλέμμα, ψεῦδος, ἀποστέρησις, ψευδομαρτυρία,
πλεονεξία, ἐπιθυμία πονηρά, ἀπάτη, κενοδοξία,
ἀλαζονεία καὶ ὅσα τούτοις ὅμοιά εἰσιν. 6. οὐ
δοκεῖ σοι ταῦτα πονηρὰ εἶναι; καὶ λίαν πονηρά,
φημί,[1] τοῖς δούλοις τοῦ θεοῦ. τούτων πάντων δεῖ
ἐγκρατεύεσθαι τὸν δουλεύοντα τῷ θεῷ. ἐγκράτευσαι οὖν ἀπὸ πάντων τούτων, ἵνα ζήσῃ τῷ θεῷ καὶ
ἐγγραφήσῃ μετὰ τῶν ἐγκρατευομένων αὐτά. ὧν
μὲν οὖν δεῖ σε ἐγκρατεύεσθαι, ταῦτά ἐστιν. 7. ἃ
δὲ δεῖ σε μὴ ἐγκρατεύεσθαι, φησίν, ἀλλὰ ποιεῖν,
ἄκουε. τὸ ἀγαθὸν μὴ ἐγκρατεύου, ἀλλὰ ποίει
αὐτό. 8. Καὶ τῶν ἀγαθῶν μοι, φημί, κύριε,
δήλωσον τὴν δύναμιν, ἵνα πορευθῶ ἐν αὐτοῖς καὶ
δουλεύσω αὐτοῖς, ἵνα ἐργασάμενος αὐτὰ δυνηθῶ
σωθῆναι. Ἄκουε, φησί, καὶ τῶν ἀγαθῶν τὰ ἔργα,
ἅ σε δεῖ ἐργάζεσθαι καὶ μὴ ἐγκρατεύεσθαι. 9.
πρῶτον πάντων πίστις, φόβος κυρίου, ἀγάπη,
ὁμόνοια, ῥήματα δικαιοσύνης, ἀλήθεια, ὑπομονή·
τούτων ἀγαθώτερον οὐδέν ἐστιν ἐν τῇ ζωῇ τῶν
ἀνθρώπων. ταῦτα ἐάν τις φυλάσσῃ καὶ μὴ
ἐγκρατεύηται ἀπ᾽ αὐτῶν, μακάριος γίνεται ἐν τῇ
ζωῇ αὐτοῦ. 10. εἶτα τούτων τὰ ἀκόλουθα
ἄκουσον· χήραις ὑπηρετεῖν, ὀρφανοὺς καὶ ὑστερου-
μένους ἐπισκέπτεσθαι, ἐξ ἀναγκῶν λυτροῦσθαι
τοὺς δούλους τοῦ θεοῦ, φιλόξενον εἶναι (ἐν γὰρ τῇ
φιλοξενίᾳ εὑρίσκεται ἀγαθοποίησίς ποτε), μηδενὶ
ἀντιτάσσεσθαι, ἡσύχιον εἶναι, ἐνδεέστερον γίνε-
σθαι πάντων ἀνθρώπων, πρεσβύτας σέβεσθαι,

[1] φημί A, φησί L₂, om. E.

follows on these things." 5. "But, sir," said I, "are there still other evil deeds?" "Yes," said he, "there are many from which the servant of God must refrain. Theft, lying, robbery, false witness, coveteousness, evil desire, deceit, vain-glory, pride, and whatever is like to these. 6. Do you not think that these are wicked?" "Yes, very wicked," said I, "for the servants of God." "From all these he who is serving God must refrain. Refrain, therefore from all these, that you may live to God and be enrolled with those who refrain from them. These then are the things from which you must refrain. 7. But now hear the things from which you must not refrain but do them," said he. "Do not refrain from that which is good, but do it." 8. "And explain to me, sir," said I, "the power of the things which are good, that I may walk in them and serve them, that by doing them I may be saved." "Listen, then," said he, "to the deeds of goodness, which you must do and not refrain from them. 9. First of all, faith, fear of God, love and harmony, words of righteousness, truth, patience; than these there is nothing better in the life of man. If any man keep these things and do not refrain from them, he becomes blessed in his life. 10. Next hear the things which follow: To minister to widows, to look after orphans and the destitute, to redeem from distress the servants of God, to be hospitable, for in hospitality may be found the practice of good, to resist none, to be gentle, to be poorer than all men, to reverence the aged, to practise justice, to preserve

δικαιοσύνην ἀσκεῖν, ἀδελφότητα συντηρεῖν, ὕβριν
ὑποφέρειν, μακρόθυμον εἶναι, μνησικακίαν μὴ
ἔχειν, κάμνοντας τῇ ψυχῇ παρακαλεῖν, ἐσκανδα-
λισμένους ἀπὸ τῆς πίστεως μὴ ἀποβάλλεσθαι,
ἀλλ' ἐπιστρέφειν καὶ εὐθύμους ποιεῖν, ἁμαρτά-
νοντας νουθετεῖν, χρεώστας μὴ θλίβειν καὶ ἐνδεεῖς,
καὶ εἴ τινα τούτοις ὅμοιά ἐστι. 11. δοκεῖ σοι,
φησί, ταῦτα ἀγαθὰ εἶναι; Τί γάρ, φημί, κύριε,
τούτων ἀγαθώτερον; Πορεύου οὖν, φησίν, ἐν αὐτοῖς
καὶ μὴ ἐγκρατεύου ἀπ' αὐτῶν, καὶ ζήσῃ τῷ θεῷ.
12. φύλασσε οὖν τὴν ἐντολὴν ταύτην· ἐὰν τὸ
ἀγαθὸν ποιῇς καὶ μὴ ἐγκρατεύσῃ ἀπ' αὐτοῦ, ζήσῃ
τῷ θεῷ, καὶ πάντες ζήσονται τῷ θεῷ οἱ οὕτω
ποιοῦντες. καὶ πάλιν ἐὰν τὸ πονηρὸν μὴ ποιῇς
καὶ ἐγκρατεύσῃ ἀπ' αὐτοῦ, ζήσῃ τῷ θεῷ, καὶ
πάντες ζήσονται τῷ θεῷ, ὅσοι ἐὰν ταύτας τὰς
ἐντολὰς φυλάξωσι καὶ πορευθῶσιν ἐν αὐταῖς.

Ἐντολὴ θ'.

1. Λέγει μοι· Ἆρον ἀπὸ σεαυτοῦ τὴν διψυχίαν
καὶ μὲν ὅλως διψυχήσῃς αἰτήσασθαί τι παρὰ τοῦ
θεοῦ, λέγων ἐν σεαυτῷ ὅτι πῶς δύναμαι αἰτή-
σασθαι παρὰ τοῦ κυρίου καὶ λαβεῖν, ἡμαρτηκὼς
τοσαῦτα εἰς αὐτόν; 2. μὴ διαλογίζου ταῦτα, ἀλλ'
ἐξ ὅλης τῆς καρδίας σου ἐπίστρεψον ἐπὶ τὸν
κύριον καὶ αἰτοῦ παρ' αὐτοῦ ἀδιστάκτως, καὶ
γνώσῃ τὴν πολλὴν εὐσπλαγχνίαν αὐτοῦ, ὅτι οὐ
μή σε ἐγκαταλίπῃ, ἀλλὰ τὸ αἴτημα τῆς ψυχῆς σου
πληροφορήσει. 3. οὐκ ἔστι γὰρ ὁ θεὸς ὡς οἱ
ἄνθρωποι μνησικακοῦντες, ἀλλ' αὐτὸς ἀμνησίκακος

Jer. 24, 7;
Joel 2, 12

brotherhood, to submit to insult, to be brave, to bear no malice, to comfort those who are oppressed in spirit, not to cast aside those who are offended in the faith, but to convert them and give them courage, to reprove sinners, not to oppress poor debtors, and whatever is like to these things. 11. Do you not think," said he, " that these things are good?" "Yes, sir, "said I, " for what is better than these things?" " Walk then," said he, " in them, and do not refrain from them, and you shall live to God. 12. Keep therefore this commandment. If you do good, and do not refrain from it, you shall live to God, and all who act so shall live to God. And again, if you do not do that which is wicked, and refrain from it, you shall live to God, and all shall live to God who keep these commandments and walk in them."

MANDATE 9

1. AND he said to me : " Remove from yourself double-mindedness, and be not at all double-minded about asking anything from God, saying in yourself, How can I ask anything from the Lord and receive it after having sinned so greatly against him? 2. Do not have these thoughts but 'turn to the Lord with all your heart,' and ask from him without doubting, and you shall know his great mercifulness, that he will not desert you, but will fulfil the petition of your soul. 3. For God is not as men who

Against double-mindedness

ἐστι καὶ σπλαγχνίζεται ἐπὶ τὴν ποίησιν αὐτοῦ.
4. σὺ οὖν καθάρισόν σου τὴν καρδίαν ἀπὸ πάντων
τῶν ματαιωμάτων τοῦ αἰῶνος τούτου καὶ τῶν
προειρημένων σοι ῥημάτων καὶ αἰτοῦ παρὰ τοῦ
κυρίου, καὶ ἀπολήψῃ πάντα καὶ ἀπὸ πάντων τῶν
αἰτημάτων σου ἀνυστέρητος ἔσῃ, ἐὰν ἀδιστάκτως
αἰτήσῃς παρὰ τοῦ κυρίου. 5. ἐὰν δὲ διστάσῃς ἐν
τῇ καρδίᾳ σου, οὐδὲν οὐ μὴ λήψῃ τῶν αἰτημάτων
σου. οἱ γὰρ διστάζοντες εἰς τὸν θεόν, οὗτοί εἰσιν
οἱ δίψυχοι καὶ οὐδὲν ὅλως ἐπιτυγχάνουσι τῶν
αἰτημάτων αὐτῶν. 6. οἱ δὲ ὁλοτελεῖς ὄντες ἐν τῇ

Ps. 2, 12;
etc.
πίστει πάντα αἰτοῦνται πεποιθότες ἐπὶ τὸν κύριον
καὶ λαμβάνουσιν, ὅτι ἀδιστάκτως αἰτοῦνται, μηδὲν
cf. Jac. 1, 8
διψυχοῦντες. πᾶς γὰρ δίψυχος ἀνήρ, ἐὰν μὴ
μετανοήσῃ, δυσκόλως σωθήσεται. 7. καθάρισον
οὖν τὴν καρδίαν σου ἀπὸ τῆς διψυχίας, ἔνδυσαι
δὲ τὴν πίστιν, ὅτι ἰσχυρά ἐστι, καὶ πίστευε τῷ
θεῷ, ὅτι πάντα τὰ αἰτήματά σου ἃ αἰτεῖς λήψῃ,
καὶ ἐὰν αἰτησάμενός ποτε παρὰ τοῦ κυρίου αἴτημά
τι βραδύτερον λαμβάνῃς, μὴ διψυχήσῃς, ὅτι ταχὺ
οὐκ ἔλαβες τὸ αἴτημα τῆς ψυχῆς σου· πάντως
γὰρ διὰ πειρασμόν τινα ἢ παράπτωμά τι, ὃ σὺ
ἀγνοεῖς, βραδύτερον λαμβάνεις τὸ αἴτημά σου.
8. σὺ οὖν μὴ διαλίπῃς αἰτούμενος τὸ αἴτημα τῆς
ψυχῆς σου, καὶ λήψῃ αὐτό· ἐὰν δὲ ἐκκακήσῃς καὶ
διψυχήσῃς αἰτούμενος, σεαυτὸν αἰτιῶ καὶ μὴ τὸν
διδόντα σοι. 9. βλέπε τὴν διψυχίαν ταύτην·
πονηρὰ γάρ ἐστι καὶ ἀσύνετος καὶ πολλοὺς
ἐκριζοῖ ἀπὸ τῆς πίστεως καί γε λίαν πιστοὺς καὶ
ἰσχυρούς. καὶ γὰρ αὕτη ἡ διψυχία θυγάτηρ[1] ἐστὶ

---

[1] ἀδελφή Α.

bear malice, but is himself without malice, and has mercy on that which he made. 4. Therefore purify your heart from all the vanities of this world, and from the words which were spoken to you beforehand, and ask from the Lord, and you shall receive all things, and shall not fail to obtain any of your petitions, if you ask from the Lord without doubting. 5. But if you doubt in your heart, you shall receive none of your petitions. For those who have doubts towards God, these are the double-minded, and they shall not in any wise obtain any of their petitions. 6. But they who are perfect. in faith ask for all things, 'trusting in the Lord,' and they receive them, because they ask without doubting, and are double-minded in nothing. For every double-minded man, unless he repent, shall with difficulty be saved. 7. Therefore purify your heart from double-mindedness, but put on faith, because it is mighty, and believe God, that you shall obtain all your requests which you make. And if ever you make any petition from the Lord, and receive it but slowly, do not be double-minded because you have not received the request of your soul speedily, for in every case it is because of some temptation or some transgression, of which you are ignorant, that you receive your request slowly. 8. Do not therefore cease from making the request of your soul, and you shall receive it. But if you grow weary, and are double-minded in your request, blame yourself and not him who gives to you. 9. Consider this double-mindedness; for it is wicked and foolish, and uproots many from the faith, yes, even those who are very faithful and strong. For this double-minded-

τοῦ διαβόλου καὶ λίαν πονηρεύεται εἰς τοὺς
δούλους τοῦ θεοῦ. 10. καταφρόνησον οὖν τῆς
διψυχίας καὶ κατακυρίευσον αὐτῆς ἐν παντὶ
πράγματι, ἐνδυσάμενος τὴν πίστιν τὴν ἰσχυρὰν
καὶ δυνατήν· ἡ γὰρ πίστις πάντα ἐπαγγέλλεται,
πάντα τελειοῖ, ἡ δὲ διψυχία μὴ καταπιστεύουσα
ἑαυτῇ πάντων ἀποτυγχάνει τῶν ἔργων αὐτῆς ὧν
πράσσει. 11. βλέπεις οὖν, φησίν, ὅτι ἡ πίστις
ἄνωθέν ἐστι παρὰ τοῦ κυρίου καὶ ἔχει δύναμιν
μεγάλην· ἡ δὲ διψυχία ἐπίγειον πνεῦμά ἐστι παρὰ
τοῦ διαβόλου, δύναμιν μὴ ἔχουσα. 12. σὺ οὖν
δούλευε τῇ ἐχούσῃ δύναμιν τῇ πίστει καὶ ἀπὸ τῆς
διψυχίας ἀπόσχου τῆς μὴ ἐχούσης δύναμιν, καὶ
ζήσῃ τῷ θεῷ, καὶ πάντες ζήσονται τῷ θεῷ οἱ ταῦτα
φρονοῦντες.[1]

Ἐντολὴ ιʹ

I

1. Ἆρον ἀπὸ σεαυτοῦ, φησί, τὴν λύπην· καὶ
γὰρ αὕτη ἀδελφή ἐστι τῆς διψυχίας καὶ τῆς
ὀξυχολίας. 2. Πῶς, φημί, κύριε, ἀδελφή ἐστι
τούτων; ἄλλο γάρ μοι δοκεῖ εἶναι ὀξυχολία καὶ
ἄλλο διψυχία καὶ ἄλλο λύπη. Ἀσύνετος εἶ
ἄνθρωπε, φησί, καὶ[2] οὐ νοεῖς, ὅτι ἡ λύπη
πάντων τῶν πνευμάτων πονηροτέρα ἐστὶ καὶ
δεινοτάτη τοῖς δούλοις τοῦ θεοῦ καὶ παρὰ πάντα
τὰ πνεύματα καταφθείρει τὸν ἄνθρωπον καὶ

---

[1] φρονοῦντες L₂ Ath., φρονήσαντες AL₁(E).
[2] φησί, καί om. A.

ness is the daughter of the devil, and commits much wickedness against the servants of God. 10. Despise therefore double-mindedness. and master it in every act, putting on the faith which is strong and powerful. For faith promises all things, perfects all things. But the double-mindedness which has no full faith in itself fails in all deeds which it undertakes. 11. You see, then," said he, "that faith is from above, from the Lord, and has great power ; but double-mindedness is an earthly spirit, from the devil, and has no power. Do you, therefore, serve the faith which has power, and refrain from the double-mindedness which has no power, and you shall live to God, and all who have this mind shall live to God.

Mandate 10

I

1. "Put away," said he, "grief from yourself, for Grief this also is a sister of double-mindedness and bitterness." 2. "How, sir," I said, "is she their sister, for it seems to me that bitterness is one thing and double-mindedness is another, and grief another?" "You are foolish, O man," he said, "and do not understand that grief is more evil than all the spirits, and is most terrible to the servants of God, and corrupts man beyond all the spirits, and wears

ἐκτρίβει τὸ πνεῦμα τὸ ἅγιον καὶ πάλιν σώζει;
3. Ἐγώ, φημί, κύριε, ἀσύνετός εἰμι καὶ οὐ συνίω
τὰς παραβολὰς ταύτας. πῶς γὰρ δύναται ἐκτρί-
βειν καὶ πάλιν σώζειν, οὐ νοῶ. 4. Ἄκουε,
φησίν· οἱ μηδέποτε ἐρευνήσαντες περὶ τῆς ἀληθείας μηδὲ ἐπιζητήσαντες περὶ τῆς θεότητος,
πιστεύσαντες δὲ μόνον, ἐμπεφυρμένοι δὲ πραγματείαις καὶ πλούτῳ καὶ φιλίαις ἐθνικαῖς καὶ
ἄλλαις πολλαῖς πραγματείαις τοῦ αἰῶνος τούτου·
ὅσοι οὖν τούτοις πρόσκεινται, οὐ νοοῦσι τὰς
παραβολὰς τῆς θεότητος· ἐπισκοτοῦνται γὰρ
ὑπὸ τούτων τῶν πράξεων καὶ καταφθείρονται
καὶ γίνονται κεχερσωμένοι. 5. καθὼς οἱ ἀμπε-
λῶνες οἱ καλοί, ὅταν ἀμελείας τύχωσι, χερσοῦνται
ἀπὸ τῶν ἀκανθῶν καὶ βοτανῶν ποικίλων, οὕτως
οἱ ἄνθρωποι οἱ πιστεύσαντες καὶ εἰς ταύτας τὰς
πράξεις τὰς πολλὰς ἐμπίπτοντες τὰς προειρη-
μένας, ἀποπλανῶνται ἀπὸ τῆς διανοίας αὐτῶν,
καὶ οὐδὲν ὅλως νοοῦσι περὶ δικαιοσύνης, ἀλλὰ
καὶ ὅταν ἀκούσωσι περὶ θεότητος καὶ ἀληθείας,
ὁ νοῦς αὐτῶν περὶ τὴν πρᾶξιν αὐτῶν καταγίνεται,
καὶ οὐδὲν ὅλως νοοῦσιν. 6. οἱ δὲ φόβον ἔχοντες
θεοῦ καὶ ἐρευνῶντες περὶ θεότητος καὶ ἀληθείας
καὶ τὴν καρδίαν ἔχοντες πρὸς τὸν κύριον, πάντα
τὰ λεγόμενα αὐτοῖς τάχιον νοοῦσι καὶ συνίουσιν,[1]
ὅτι ἔχουσι τὸν φόβον τοῦ κυρίου ἐν ἑαυτοῖς· ὅπου
γὰρ ὁ κύριος κατοικεῖ, ἐκεῖ καὶ σύνεσις πολλή.
κολλήθητι οὖν τῷ κυρίῳ, καὶ πάντα συνήσεις καὶ
νοήσεις.

Ps. 111, 10;
Prov. 1, 7;
etc.

Ecclus. 2, 3

---

[1] τάχιον νοοῦσι καὶ συνίουσι Ath (LE), ταχύνουσι καὶ νοοῦσι A.

out the Holy Spirit—and again saves us." 3. "Yes, sir," said I, "I am a foolish man, and do not understand these parables, for how it can wear out and again save, I do not understand." 4. "Listen," he said, "those who have never inquired concerning the truth, nor made search concerning the Godhead, but only have faith, and are mixed up with business and riches, and heathen friendships, and many other occupations of this world,—such as are intent on these, do not understand the parables of the Godhead; for they are darkened by these deeds, and are corrupted and become sterile. 5. Just as good vineyards when they meet with neglect, are made barren by the thorns and various weeds, so men, who have believed, and fall into these many occupations, which have been mentioned above, are deceived in their understanding, and understand nothing completely about righteousness. But even when they listen concerning the Godhead and truth their mind is taken up with their business, and they understand nothing properly. 6. But they who have the fear of God, and inquire concerning the Godhead and truth, and have their heart towards the Lord, perceive quickly and understand all that is said to them, because they have the fear of the Lord in themselves; for where the Lord dwells, there also is great understanding. 'Cleave therefore to the Lord,' and you shall understand and perceive all things.

II

1. Ἄκουε οὖν, φησίν, ἀνόητε, πῶς ἡ λύπη ἐκτρίβει τὸ πνεῦμα τὸ ἅγιον καὶ πάλιν σώζει· 2. ὅταν ὁ δίψυχος ἐπιβάληται πρᾶξίν τινα καὶ ταύτης ἀποτύχῃ διὰ τὴν διψυχίαν αὐτοῦ, ἡ λύπη αὕτη εἰσπορεύεται εἰς τὸν ἄνθρωπον καὶ λυπεῖ τὸ πνεῦμα τὸ ἅγιον καὶ ἐκτρίβει αὐτό. 3. εἶτα πάλιν ἡ ὀξυχολία ὅταν κολληθῇ τῷ ἀνθρώπῳ περὶ πράγματός τινος, καὶ λίαν πικρανθῇ, πάλιν ἡ λύπη εἰσπορεύεται εἰς τὴν καρδίαν τοῦ ἀνθρώπου τοῦ ὀξυχολήσαντος, καὶ λυπεῖται ἐπὶ τῇ πράξει αὐτοῦ ᾗ ἔπραξε καὶ μετανοεῖ, ὅτι πονηρὸν εἰργάσατο. 4. αὕτη οὖν ἡ λύπη δοκεῖ σωτηρίαν ἔχειν, ὅτι τὸ πονηρὸν πράξας μετενόησεν. ἀμφότεραι οὖν αἱ πράξεις λυποῦσι τὸ πνεῦμα· ἡ μὲν διψυχία, ὅτι οὐκ ἐπέτυχε τῆς πράξεως αὐτῆς, ἡ δὲ ὀξυχολία λυπεῖ τὸ πνεῦμα, ὅτι ἔπραξε τὸ πονηρόν. ἀμφότερα οὖν λυπηρά ἐστι τῷ πνεύματι τῷ ἁγίῳ, ἡ Eph. 4, 30 διψυχία καὶ ἡ ὀξυχολία. 5. ἆρον οὖν ἀπὸ σεαυτοῦ τὴν λύπην καὶ μὴ θλῖβε τὸ πνεῦμα τὸ ἅγιον τὸ ἐν σοὶ κατοικοῦν, μήποτε ἐντεύξηται τῷ θεῷ[1] καὶ ἀποστῇ ἀπὸ σοῦ. 6. τὸ γὰρ πνεῦμα τοῦ θεοῦ τὸ δοθὲν εἰς τὴν σάρκα ταύτην λύπην οὐχ ὑποφέρει οὐδὲ στενοχωρίαν.

III

1. Ἔνδυσαι οὖν τὴν ἱλαρότητα, τὴν πάντοτε ἔχουσαν χάριν παρὰ τῷ θεῷ καὶ εὐπρόσδεκτον

[1] τῷ θεῷ EL Ath.[2] Ant., κατὰ σοῦ A, κατὰ σοῦ τοῦ θεοῦ Ath.[1]

114

II

1. " HEAR, now," said he, " foolish man, how grief Grief and the Holy Spirit
wears out the Holy Spirit, and again brings salvation.
2. When the double-minded undertakes any work,
and fails in it because of his double-mindedness,
this grief enters into the man, and grieves the Holy
Spirit and wears it out. 3. Then again, when for
any matter ill temper cleave to a man, and he
become exceedingly bitter, again grief enters into
the heart of the ill tempered man, and he
is grieved at the act which he did, and repents
because he did wickedly. 4. Therefore this grief
seems to bring salvation, because he repented of
having done wickedly. Therefore both deeds
grieve the Spirit ; double-mindedness, because he
did not obtain his purpose, and ill temper grieves the
Spirit, because he acted wickedly. Both, therefore,
are grievous to the Holy Spirit, double-mindedness
and ill temper. 5. Put therefore away from yourself
grief, and do not oppress the Holy Spirit which
dwells in you, lest it beseech God,[1] and it depart
from you. 6. For the Spirit of God which is
given to this flesh endures neither grief nor
oppression.

III

1. " PUT on, therefore, joyfulness, which always Joyfulness
has favour with God and is acceptable to him, and

---

[1] Apparently the meaning is 'beseech God to allow it to
depart from the man in whom it is.' This is brought out in
the variants of A and Ath.

115

THE APOSTOLIC FATHERS

οὖσαν αὐτῷ, καὶ ἐντρύφα ἐν αὐτῇ. πᾶς γὰρ
ἱλαρὸς ἀνὴρ ἀγαθὰ ἐργάζεται καὶ ἀγαθὰ φρονεῖ
καὶ καταφρονεῖ τῆς λύπης. 2. ὁ δὲ λυπηρὸς ἀνὴρ
πάντοτε πονηρεύεται· πρῶτον μὲν πονηρεύεται,
ὅτι λυπεῖ τὸ πνεῦμα τὸ ἅγιον τὸ δοθὲν τῷ ἀνθρώπῳ
ἱλαρόν· δεύτερον δὲ λυπῶν τὸ πνεῦμα τὸ ἅγιον ἀνο-
μίαν ἐργάζεται, μὴ ἐντυγχάνων μηδὲ ἐξομολογού-
μενος τῷ κυρίῳ. Πάντοτε γὰρ λυπηροῦ ἀνδρὸς ἡ
ἔντευξις οὐκ ἔχει δύναμιν τοῦ ἀναβῆναι ἐπὶ τὸ
θυσιαστήριον τοῦ θεοῦ. 3. Διατί, φημί, οὐκ
ἀναβαίνει ἐπὶ τὸ θυσιαστήριον ἡ ἔντευξις τοῦ
λυπουμένου; Ὅτι, φησίν, ἡ λύπη ἐγκάθηται εἰς
τὴν καρδίαν αὐτοῦ. μεμιγμένη οὖν ἡ λύπη μετὰ
τῆς ἐντεύξεως οὐκ ἀφίησι τὴν ἔντευξιν ἀναβῆναι
καθαρὰν ἐπὶ τὸ θυσιαστήριον. ὥσπερ γὰρ ὄξος
καὶ οἶνος μεμιγμένα ἐπὶ τὸ αὐτὸ τὴν αὐτὴν ἡδονὴν
οὐκ ἔχουσιν, οὕτω καὶ ἡ λύπη μεμιγμένη μετὰ
τοῦ ἁγίου πνεύματος τὴν αὐτὴν ἔντευξιν οὐκ ἔχει.
4. καθάρισον οὖν σεαυτὸν ἀπὸ τῆς λύπης τῆς
πονηρᾶς ταύτης, καὶ ζήσῃ τῷ θεῷ· καὶ πάντες
ζήσονται τῷ θεῷ, ὅσοι ἂν ἀποβάλωσιν ἀφ' ἑαυτῶν
τὴν λύπην καὶ ἐνδύσωνται πᾶσαν ἱλαρότητα.

Ἐντολὴ ιαʹ

1. Ἔδειξέ μοι ἐπὶ συμψελλίου καθημένους
ἀνθρώπους καὶ ἕτερον ἄνθρωπον καθήμενον ἐπὶ
καθέδραν, καὶ λέγει μοι· Βλέπεις τοὺς ἐπὶ τοῦ
συμψελλίου καθημένους; Βλέπω, φημί, κύριε.
Οὗτοι, φησί, πιστοί εἰσι, καὶ ὁ καθήμενος ἐπὶ τὴν
καθέδραν ψευδοπροφήτης ἐστίν, ὃς ἀπόλλυσι

116

flourish in it; for every joyful man does good deeds, and has good thoughts, and despises grief. 2. But the mournful man always does wickedly. First of all he does wickedly because he grieves the Holy Spirit, which is given to man in joyfulness, and secondly he grieves the Holy Spirit by doing wickedly, not praying nor confessing to the Lord. For the intercession of the mournful man has nowhere power to ascend to the altar of God." 3. "Why," said I, "does not the intercession of the mournful man ascend to the altar?" "Because," said he, "grief sits in his heart. Therefore, the grief which is mixed with his intercession does not permit the intercession to ascend in purity to the altar. For just as vinegar mixed with wine has not the same agreeableness, so also grief mixed with the Holy Spirit, has not the same power of intercession. 4. Therefore purify yourself from this wicked grief, and you shall live to God, and all shall live to God who cast away from themselves grief, and put on all joyfulness."

MANDATE 11

1. HE showed me men sitting on a bench,[1] and another man sitting on a chair, and he said to me: "Do you see the men sitting on the bench?" "Yes, sir," said I; "I see them." "They," said he, "are faithful, and he who is sitting on the chair is a false prophet, who is corrupting the understanding

False and true prophets

---

[1] συμψέλλιον cannot be here translated by the same word as in Vis. III. i. 4. Here it is the 'bench' of the learner as opposed to the 'chair' of the teacher.

117

τὴν διάνοιαν τῶν δούλων τοῦ θεοῦ· τῶν διψύχων
δὲ ἀπόλλυσιν, οὐ τῶν πιστῶν. 2. οὗτοι οὖν οἱ
δίψυχοι ὡς ἐπὶ μάντιν ἔρχονται καὶ ἐπερωτῶσιν
αὐτόν, τί ἄρα ἔσται αὐτοῖς· κἀκεῖνος ὁ ψευδοπροφήτης, μηδεμίαν ἔχων ἐν ἑαυτῷ δύναμιν
πνεύματος θείου, λαλεῖ μετ᾽ αὐτῶν κατὰ τὰ
ἐπερωτήματα αὐτῶν καὶ κατὰ τὰς ἐπιθυμίας
τῆς πονηρίας αὐτῶν καὶ πληροῖ τὰς ψυχὰς
αὐτῶν, καθὼς αὐτοὶ βούλωνται. 3. αὐτὸς γὰρ
κενὸς ὢν κενὰ καὶ ἀποκρίνεται κενοῖς· ὃ γὰρ ἐὰν
ἐπερωτηθῇ, πρὸς τὸ κένωμα τοῦ ἀνθρώπου
ἀποκρίνεται. τινὰ δὲ καὶ ῥήματα ἀληθῆ λαλεῖ·
ὁ γὰρ διάβολος πληροῖ αὐτὸν τῷ αὐτοῦ πνεύματι,
εἴ τινα δυνήσεται ῥῆξαι τῶν δικαίων. 4. ὅσοι
οὖν ἰσχυροί εἰσιν ἐν τῇ πίστει τοῦ κυρίου, ἐνδεδυμένοι τὴν ἀλήθειαν, τοῖς τοιούτοις πνεύμασιν
οὐ κολλῶνται, ἀλλ᾽ ἀπέχονται ἀπ᾽ αὐτῶν· ὅσοι
δὲ δίψυχοί εἰσι καὶ πυκνῶς μετανοοῦσι, μαντεύ-
ονται ὡς καὶ τὰ ἔθνη καὶ ἑαυτοῖς μείζονα ἁμαρτίαν
ἐπιφέρουσιν εἰδωλολατροῦντες· ὁ γὰρ ἐπερωτῶν
ψευδοπροφήτην περὶ πράξεώς τινος εἰδωλολάτρης
ἐστὶ καὶ κενὸς ἀπὸ τῆς ἀληθείας καὶ ἄφρων.
5. πᾶν γὰρ πνεῦμα ἀπὸ θεοῦ δοθὲν οὐκ ἐπερωτᾶται,
Cf. Jam.3,15 ἀλλὰ ἔχον τὴν δύναμιν τῆς θεότητος ἀφ᾽ ἑαυτοῦ
λαλεῖ πάντα, ὅτι ἄνωθέν ἐστιν ἀπὸ τῆς δυνάμεως
τοῦ θείου πνεύματος. 6. τὸ δὲ πνεῦμα τὸ ἐπε-
ρωτώμενον καὶ λαλοῦν κατὰ τὰς ἐπιθυμίας τῶν
ἀνθρώπων ἐπίγειόν ἐστι καὶ ἐλαφρόν, δύναμιν μὴ
ἔχον· καὶ ὅλως οὐ λαλεῖ, ἐὰν μὴ ἐπερωτηθῇ.
7. Πῶς οὖν, φημί, κύριε, ἄνθρωπος γνώσεται, τίς
αὐτῶν προφήτης καὶ τίς ψευδοπροφήτης ἐστίν;
Ἄκουε, φησί, περὶ ἀμφοτέρων τῶν προφητῶν· καὶ

of the servants of God. He corrupts the understanding of the double-minded, not of the faithful.
2. Therefore these double-minded men come to him
as to a wizard, and ask him concerning their future ;
and that false prophet, having no power of the
Divine Spirit in himself, speaks with them according
to their requests, and according to the desires of
their wickedness, and fills their souls, as they themselves wish. 3. For he is empty and makes empty
answers to empty men ; for whatever question is put
he answers according to the emptiness of the man.
But he also speaks some true words, for the devil
fills him with his spirit, to see if he can break any of
the righteous. 4. Therefore, as many as are strong
in the faith of the Lord, and have put on the truth,
do not cleave to such spirits, but refrain from them.
But as many as are double-minded, and constantly
repent, practise soothsaying, like the heathen, and
bring greater shame upon themselves by their
idolatry. For he who asks a false prophet concerning any act is an idolator, and empty of the truth
and foolish. 5. For every spirit which is given from
God is not asked questions, but has the power of the
Godhead and speaks all things of itself, because it is
from above, from the power of the Divine spirit.
6. But the spirit which is questioned and speaks
according to the lusts of man is earthly and light,
and has no power, and it does not speak at all unless
it be questioned." 7. " How, then," said I, " sir,
shall a man know which of them is a true prophet
and which a false prophet ? " " Listen," said he,
" concerning both the prophets, and as I shall tell

ὥς σοι μέλλω λέγειν, οὕτω δοκιμάσεις τὸν προφήτην καὶ τὸν ψευδοπροφήτην. ἀπὸ τῆς ζωῆς δοκίμαζε τὸν ἄνθρωπον τὸν ἔχοντα τὸ πνεῦμα τὸ
θεῖον. 8. πρῶτον μὲν ὁ ἔχων τὸ πνεῦμα τὸ
ἄνωθεν[1] πραΰς ἐστι καὶ ἡσύχιος καὶ ταπεινόφρων
καὶ ἀπεχόμενος ἀπὸ πάσης πονηρίας καὶ ἐπιθυμίας ματαίας τοῦ αἰῶνος τούτου καὶ ἑαυτὸν
ἐνδεέστερον ποιεῖ πάντων τῶν ἀνθρώπων καὶ
οὐδενὶ οὐδὲν ἀποκρίνεται ἐπερωτώμενος, οὐδὲ κατα-
μόνας λαλεῖ, οὐδὲ ὅταν θέλῃ ἄνθρωπος λαλεῖν,
λαλεῖ τὸ πνεῦμα τὸ ἅγιον, ἀλλὰ τότε λαλεῖ, ὅταν
θελήσῃ αὐτὸν ὁ θεὸς λαλῆσαι. 9. ὅταν οὖν ἔλθῃ
ὁ ἄνθρωπος ὁ ἔχων τὸ πνεῦμα τὸ θεῖον εἰς συναγωγὴν ἀνδρῶν δικαίων τῶν ἐχόντων πίστιν θείου
πνεύματος καὶ ἔντευξις γένηται πρὸς τὸν θεὸν τῆς
συναγωγῆς τῶν ἀνδρῶν ἐκείνων, τότε ὁ ἄγγελος
τοῦ προφητικοῦ πνεύματος[2] ὁ κείμενος πρὸς αὐτὸν
πληροῖ τὸν ἄνθρωπον, καὶ πληρωθεὶς ὁ ἄνθρωπος
τῷ πνεύματι τῷ ἁγίῳ λαλεῖ εἰς τὸ πλῆθος, καθὼς
ὁ κύριος βούλεται. 10. οὕτως οὖν φανερὸν ἔσται
τὸ πνεῦμα τῆς θεότητος. ὅση οὖν περὶ τοῦ
πνεύματος τῆς θεότητος τοῦ κυρίου ἡ δύναμις
αὕτη. 11. ἄκουε νῦν, φησί, περὶ τοῦ πνεύματος
τοῦ ἐπιγείου καὶ κενοῦ καὶ δύναμιν μὴ ἔχοντος,
ἀλλὰ ὄντος μωροῦ. 12. πρῶτον μὲν ὁ ἄνθρωπος
ἐκεῖνος ὁ δοκῶν πνεῦμα ἔχειν ὑψοῖ ἑαυτὸν καὶ
θέλει πρωτοκαθεδρίαν ἔχειν, καὶ εὐθὺς ἰταμός ἐστι
καὶ ἀναιδὴς καὶ πολύλαλος καὶ ἐν τρυφαῖς
πολλαῖς ἀναστρεφόμενος καὶ ἐν ἑτέραις πολλαῖς

---

[1] τὸ ἄνωθεν AL₁, τὸ θεῖαν τὸ ἄνωθεν EL₂.
[2] τοῦ προφητικοῦ πνεύματος L₂E₁, τοῦ προφητοῦ A, nuntius
sanctus divinitatis (ἄγγελος ἅγιος θεότητος).

you, so you shall judge the true prophet and the false prophet. Test the man who has the Divine Spirit by his life. 8. In the first place, he who has the spirit which is from above, is meek and gentle, and lowly-minded, and refrains from all wickedness and evil desire of this world, and makes himself poorer than all men, and gives no answers to anyone when he is consulted, nor does he speak by himself (for the Holy Spirit does not speak when a man wishes to speak), but he speaks at that time when God wishes him to speak. 9. Therefore, when the man who has the Divine Spirit comes into a meeting of righteous men who have the faith of the Divine Spirit, and intercession is made to God from the assembly of those men, then the angel of the prophetic spirit rests on him and fills the man, and the man, being filled with the Holy Spirit, speaks to the congregation as the Lord wills. 10. Thus, then, the Spirit of the Godhead will be plain. Such, then, is the power of the Lord concerning the Spirit of the Godhead. 11. Listen, now," said he, "concerning the spirit which is earthly, and empty, and has no power, but is foolish.. 12. In the first place, that man who seems to have a spirit exalts himself and wishes to have the first place, and he is instantly impudent and shameless and talkative, and lives in great luxury and in many other deceits, and accepts

ἀπάταις καὶ μισθοὺς λαμβάνων τῆς προφητείας
αὐτοῦ· ἐὰν δὲ μὴ λάβῃ, οὐ προφητεύει. δύναται οὖν
πνεῦμα θεῖον μισθοὺς λαμβάνειν καὶ προφητεύειν;
οὐκ ἐνδέχεται τοῦτο ποιεῖν θεοῦ προφήτην, ἀλλὰ
τῶν τοιούτων προφητῶν ἐπίγειόν ἐστι τὸ πνεῦμα.
13. εἶτα ὅλως εἰς συναγωγὴν ἀνδρῶν δικαίων οὐκ
ἐγγίζει, ἀλλ᾿ ἀποφεύγει αὐτούς· κολλᾶται δὲ τοῖς
διψύχοις καὶ κενοῖς καὶ κατὰ γωνίαν αὐτοῖς
προφητεύει καὶ ἀπατᾷ αὐτοὺς λαλῶν κατὰ τὰς
ἐπιθυμίας αὐτῶν πάντα κενῶς· κενοῖς γὰρ καὶ
ἀποκρίνεται· τὸ γὰρ κενὸν σκεῦος μετὰ τῶν κενῶν
συντιθέμενον οὐ θραύεται, ἀλλὰ συμφωνοῦσιν
ἀλλήλοις.   14. ὅταν δὲ ἔλθῃ εἰς συναγωγὴν
πλήρη ἀνδρῶν δικαίων ἐχόντων πνεῦμα θεότητος
καὶ ἔντευξις ἀπ᾿ αὐτῶν γένηται, κενοῦται ὁ
ἄνθρωπος ἐκεῖνος, καὶ τὸ πνεῦμα τὸ ἐπίγειον ἀπὸ
τοῦ φόβου φεύγει ἀπ᾿ αὐτοῦ, καὶ κωφοῦται ὁ
ἄνθρωπος ἐκεῖνος καὶ ὅλως συνθραύεται, μηδὲν
δυνάμενος λαλῆσαι.   15. ἐὰν γὰρ εἰς ἀποθήκην
στιβάσῃς οἶνον ἢ ἔλαιον καὶ ἐν αὐτοῖς θῇς
κεράμιον κενόν, καὶ πάλιν ἀποστιβάσαι θελήσῃς
τὴν ἀποθήκην, τὸ κεράμιον ἐκεῖνο, ὃ ἔθηκας κενόν,
κενὸν καὶ εὑρήσεις· οὕτω καὶ οἱ προφῆται οἱ κενοὶ
ὅταν ἔλθωσιν εἰς πνεύματα δικαίων, ὁποῖοι ἦλθον,
τοιοῦτοι καὶ εὑρίσκονται.   16. ἔχεις ἀμφοτέρων
τῶν προφητῶν τὴν ζωήν. δοκίμαζε οὖν ἀπὸ τῶν
ἔργων καὶ τῆς ζωῆς τὸν ἄνθρωπον τὸν λέγοντα
ἑαυτὸν πνευματοφόρον εἶναι.   17. σὺ δὲ πίστευε
τῷ πνεύματι τῷ ἐρχομένῳ ἀπὸ τοῦ θεοῦ καὶ
ἔχοντι δύναμιν· τῷ δὲ πνεύματι τῷ ἐπιγείῳ καὶ
κενῷ μηδὲν πίστευε, ὅτι ἐν αὐτῷ δύναμις οὐκ
ἔστιν· ἀπὸ τοῦ διαβόλου γὰρ ἔρχεται.   18. ἄκου-

rewards for his prophecy, and if he does not receive them he does not prophesy. Is it then possible for a Divine Spirit to accept rewards and prophesy? It is not possible for a prophet of God to do this, but the spirit of such prophets is of the earth. 13. Next, on no account does he come near to an assembly of righteous men, but shuns them. But he cleaves to the double-minded and empty, and prophesies to them in a corner, and deceives them by empty speech about everything according to their lusts, for he is also answering the empty. For an empty vessel which is put with others that are empty is not broken, but they match one another. 14. But when he comes into a meeting full of righteous men, who have a spirit of the God-head, and intercession is made by them, that man is made empty, and the earthly spirit flees from him in fear, and that man is made dumb and is altogether broken up, being able to say nothing. 15. For if you stack wine or oil in a cellar, and put among them an empty jar, and again wish to unstack the cellar, the jar which you put in empty you will find still empty. So also the prophets who are empty, when they come to the spirits of just men, are found out to be such as when they came. 16. You have the life of both the prophets. Test, then, from his life and deeds, the man who says that he is inspired. 17. But believe yourself in the Spirit which comes from God and has power, but have no faith in the spirit which is from the earth and empty, because there is no power in it, for it comes from the devil. 18. Hear, then, the parable which I will tell you.

σον οὖν¹ τὴν παραβολήν, ἣν μέλλω σοι λέγειν·
λάβε λίθον καὶ βάλε εἰς τὸν οὐρανόν, ἴδε, εἰ
δύνασαι ἅψασθαι αὐτοῦ· ἢ πάλιν λάβε σίφωνα
ὕδατος καὶ σιφώνισον εἰς τὸν οὐρανόν, ἴδε, εἰ
δύνασαι τρυπῆσαι τὸν οὐρανόν. 19. Πῶς, φημί,
κύριε, δύναται ταῦτα γενέσθαι; ἀδύνατα γὰρ
ἀμφότερα ταῦτα εἴρηκας. Ὡς ταῦτα οὖν, φησίν,
ἀδύνατά ἐστιν, οὕτω καὶ τὰ πνεύματα τὰ ἐπίγεια
ἀδύνατά ἐστι καὶ ἀδρανῆ. 20. λάβε οὖν² τὴν
δύναμιν τὴν ἄνωθεν ἐρχομένην· ἡ χάλαζα ἐλά-
χιστόν ἐστι κοκκάριον, καὶ ὅταν ἐπιπέσῃ ἐπὶ
κεφαλὴν ἀνθρώπου, πῶς πόνον παρέχει; ἢ πάλιν
λάβε σταγόνα, ἢ ἀπὸ τοῦ κεράμου πίπτει χαμαὶ
καὶ τρυπᾷ τὸν λίθον. 21. βλέπεις οὖν, ὅτι τὰ
ἄνωθεν ἐλάχιστα πίπτοντα ἐπὶ τὴν γῆν μεγάλην
δύναμιν ἔχει· οὕτω καὶ τὸ πνεῦμα τὸ θεῖον ἄνωθεν
ἐρχόμενον δυνατόν ἐστι· τούτῳ οὖν τῷ πνεύματι
πίστευε, ἀπὸ δὲ τοῦ ἑτέρου ἀπέχου.

Ἐντολὴ ιβ΄.

I

1. Λέγει μοι· Ἆρον ἀπὸ σεαυτοῦ πᾶσαν ἐπιθυμίαν πονηράν, ἔνδυσαι δὲ τὴν ἐπιθυμίαν τὴν
ἀγαθὴν καὶ σεμνήν· ἐνδεδυμένος γὰρ τὴν ἐπιθυμίαν ταύτην μισήσεις τὴν πονηρὰν ἐπιθυμίαν καὶ
χαλιναγωγήσεις αὐτήν, καθὼς βούλει. 2. ἀγρία
γάρ ἐστιν ἡ ἐπιθυμία ἡ πονηρὰ καὶ δυσκόλως
ἡμεροῦται. φοβερὰ γάρ ἐστι καὶ λίαν τῇ ἀγριό-

¹ οὖν L (ergo) E (now), om. A.
² οὖν A, νῦν L (E is confused).

124

Take a stone and throw it up to Heaven and see if you can touch it; or take a syringe[1] and squirt it towards the sky, and see if you can make a hole in the Heavens." 19. "How, sir," said I, "can these things be? For both these things which you have spoken of are impossible." "Even," said he, "as these are impossible, so also are the earthly spirits without power and feeble. 20. Take now the power which comes from above. The hail is a very little grain, and when it falls on man's head, how it hurts! Or, again, take a drop which falls on the ground from the roof, and makes a hole in stone. 21. You see, then, that the smallest things which come from above and fall on the earth have great power; so also the Divine Spirit which comes from above is powerful. Have faith, then, in this Spirit, but refrain from the other."

MANDATE 12

I

1. He said to me, "Put away from yourself every Desire evil desire, but put on the desire which is good and holy; for by putting on this desire you will hate the wicked desire, and will curb it as you will. 2. For the wicked desire is cruel and hard to tame, for it is fearful, and destroys men greatly in its cruelty, but

[1] The syringe or hand pump used for cleaning and watering the vines in the Italian vineyards.

τητι αὐτῆς δαπανᾷ τοὺς ἀνθρώπους· μάλιστα δὲ
ἐὰν ἐμπέσῃ εἰς αὐτὴν δοῦλος θεοῦ καὶ μὴ ᾖ
συνετός, δαπανᾶται ὑπ᾽ αὐτῆς δεινῶς· δαπανᾷ δὲ
τοὺς τοιούτους τοὺς μὴ ἔχοντας ἔνδυμα τῆς
ἐπιθυμίας τῆς ἀγαθῆς, ἀλλὰ ἐμπεφυρμένους
τῷ αἰῶνι τούτῳ· τούτους οὖν παραδίδωσιν εἰς
θάνατον. 3. Ποῖα, φημί, κύριε, ἔργα ἐστὶν τῆς
ἐπιθυμίας τῆς πονηρᾶς τὰ παραδιδόντα τοὺς
ἀνθρώπους εἰς θάνατον; γνώρισόν μοι, ἵνα ἀφέ-
ξωμαι ἀπ᾽ αὐτῶν. Ἄκουσον, φησίν,[1] ἐν ποίοις
ἔργοις θανατοῖ ἡ ἐπιθυμία ἡ πονηρὰ τοὺς δούλους
τοῦ θεοῦ.

II

1. Πάντων προέχουσα ἐπιθυμία γυναικὸς ἀλλοτρίας ἢ ἀνδρὸς καὶ πολυτελείας πλούτου καὶ
ἐδεσμάτων πολλῶν ματαίων καὶ μεθυσμάτων καὶ
ἑτέρων τρυφῶν πολλῶν καὶ μωρῶν· πᾶσα γὰρ
τρυφὴ μωρά ἐστι καὶ κενὴ τοῖς δούλοις τοῦ θεοῦ.
2. αὗται οὖν αἱ ἐπιθυμίαι πονηραί εἰσι, θανατοῦ-
σαι τοὺς δούλους τοῦ θεοῦ· αὕτη γὰρ ἡ ἐπιθυμία
ἡ πονηρὰ τοῦ διαβόλου θυγάτηρ ἐστίν. ἀπέχεσθαι
οὖν δεῖ ἀπὸ τῶν ἐπιθυμιῶν τῶν πονηρῶν, ἵνα
ἀποσχόμενοι ζήσητε τῷ θεῷ. 3. ὅσοι δὲ ἂν κατα-
κυριευθῶσιν ὑπ᾽ αὐτῶν καὶ μὴ ἀντισταθῶσιν
αὐταῖς, ἀποθανοῦνται εἰς τέλος· θανατώδεις γάρ
εἰσιν αἱ ἐπιθυμίαι[2] αὗται. 4. σὺ δὲ ἔνδυσαι τὴν
ἐπιθυμίαν τῆς δικαιοσύνης, καὶ καθοπλισάμενος
τὸν φόβον τοῦ κυρίου ἀντίστηθι αὐταῖς· ὁ γὰρ
φόβος τοῦ θεοῦ κατοικεῖ ἐν τῇ ἐπιθυμίᾳ τῇ ἀγαθῇ.

Cf. Eph. 6,
13 ff.

---

[1] φησίν om. A.   [2] ἐπιθυμίαι εἰς τέλος A.

especially if a servant of God fall into it, and be not prudent, he is terribly destroyed by it. But it destroys such as have not the good desire as a covering, but are mixed with this world; these then it delivers to death." 3. "What, sir," said I, "are the deeds of the wicked desire, which deliver men to death? Let me know that I may refrain from them." "Listen," said he, "by what deeds the evil desire brings to death the servants of God.

II

1. "Before all is desire for the wife or husband of another, and of extravagance of wealth, and much needless food and drink, and many other foolish luxuries. For all luxury is foolish and vain for the servants of God. 2. These desires then are wicked, and bring the servants of God to death, for this desire is the wicked daughter of the devil. It is necessary therefore, to refrain from the wicked desires, that by refraining you may live to God. 3. But as many as are overcome by them, and do not resist them, shall perish finally, for these desires are deadly. 4. But put on the desire of righteousness, and resist them, being armed with the fear of the Lord. For the fear of God dwells in the desire which is good. If the evil desire see you armed

Carnal desires

127

Jam. 4, 7

ἡ ἐπιθυμία ἡ πονηρὰ ἐὰν ἴδῃ σε καθωπλισμένον τῷ φόβῳ τοῦ θεοῦ καὶ ἀνθεστηκότα αὐτῇ, φεύξεται ἀπὸ σοῦ μακρὰν καὶ οὐκέτι σοι ὀφθήσεται φοβουμένη τὰ ὅπλα σου. 5. σὺ οὖν νικήσας καὶ[1] στεφανωθεὶς κατ᾿ αὐτῆς ἐλθὲ πρὸς τὴν ἐπιθυμίαν τῆς δικαιοσύνης, καὶ παραδοὺς αὐτῇ τὸ νῖκος, ὃ ἔλαβες, δούλευσον αὐτῇ, καθὼς αὐτὴ βούλεται. ἐὰν δουλεύσῃς τῇ ἐπιθυμίᾳ τῇ ἀγαθῇ καὶ ὑποταγῇς αὐτῇ, δυνήσῃ τῆς ἐπιθυμίας τῆς πονηρᾶς κατακυριεῦσαι καὶ ὑποτάξαι αὐτήν, καθὼς βούλει.

III

1. Ἤθελον, φημί, κύριε, γνῶναι, ποίοις τρόποις με δεῖ δουλεῦσαι τῇ ἐπιθυμίᾳ τῇ ἀγαθῇ. Ἄκουε, φησίν· ἔργασαι δικαιοσύνην καὶ ἀρετήν, ἀλήθειαν καὶ φόβον κυρίου, πίστιν καὶ πραότητα καὶ ὅσα τούτοις ὅμοιά ἐστιν ἀγαθά. ταῦτα ἐργαζόμενος εὐάρεστος ἔσῃ δοῦλος τοῦ θεοῦ καὶ ζήσῃ αὐτῷ· καὶ πᾶς, ὃς ἂν δουλεύσῃ τῇ ἐπιθυμίᾳ τῇ ἀγαθῇ, ζήσεται τῷ θεῷ. 2. συνετέλεσεν οὖν τὰς ἐντολὰς τὰς δώδεκα καὶ λέγει μοι· Ἔχεις τὰς ἐντολὰς ταύτας· πορεύου ἐν αὐταῖς καὶ τοὺς ἀκούοντας παρακάλει, ἵνα ἡ μετάνοια αὐτῶν καθαρὰ γένηται τὰς λοιπὰς ἡμέρας τῆς ζωῆς αὐτῶν. 3. τὴν διακονίαν ταύτην, ἥν σοι δίδωμι, ἐκτέλει ἐπιμελῶς, καὶ πολὺ ἐργάσῃ· εὑρήσεις γὰρ χάριν ἐν τοῖς μέλλουσι μετανοεῖν, καὶ πεισ-

Ps. 15, 2

---

[1] νικήσας καὶ om A. (The exact words are of course doubtful, but LE both imply some such phrase before στεφανωθείς. Hollenberg and Funk read νῖκος λαβών to correspond with τὸ νῖκος ὃ ἔλαβες.)

with the fear of God, and resisting it, it will flee far
from you and will no longer be seen by you, for fear
of your weapons. 5. Do you, therefore, conquer
it, and come in triumph over it to the desire of
righteousness, and giving up to it the victory which
you have gained, serve it as it wishes. If you serve
the good desire, and submit to it, you will be able to
overcome the wicked desire, and subdue it as you
wish."

III

1. " I WOULD like, sir," said I, " to know in what
way I must serve the good desire." "Listen," said
he, "'work righteousness' and virtue, and fear of the
Lord, faith and meekness, and whatever good things
are like to these. For by working these you will be
a well-pleasing servant of God, and shall live to him,
and whoever shall serve the good desire, shall live to
God." 2. So he finished the twelve commandments, Conclusion
and said to me : " You have these commandments ; of Mandates
walk in them, and exhort those who hear that their
repentance may be pure for the rest of the days of
their life. 3. Fulfil carefully this ministry which I
give you, and work much in it, for you will find
favour with those who are about to repent, and they

θήσονταί σου τοῖς ῥήμασιν· ἐγὼ γὰρ μετὰ σοῦ
ἔσομαι καὶ ἀναγκάσω αὐτοὺς πεισθῆναί σοι[1].
Ps. 19, 8;
104, 15
4. Λέγω αὐτῷ· Κύριε, αἱ ἐντολαὶ αὗται μεγάλαι
καὶ καλαὶ καὶ ἔνδοξοί εἰσι καὶ δυνάμεναι εὐφρᾶναι
καρδίαν ἀνθρώπου τοῦ δυναμένου τηρῆσαι αὐτάς.
οὐκ οἶδα δέ, εἰ δύνανται αἱ ἐντολαὶ αὗται ὑπὸ
ἀνθρώπου φυλαχθῆναι, διότι σκληραί εἰσι λίαν.
5. ἀποκριθεὶς λέγει μοι· Ἐὰν σὺ σεαυτῷ προθῇς,
ὅτι δύνανται φυλαχθῆναι, εὐκόλως αὐτὰς φυλάξεις
καὶ οὐκ ἔσονται σκληραί· ἐὰν δὲ ἐπὶ τὴν καρδίαν
σου ἤδη ἀναβῇ μὴ δύνασθαι αὐτὰς ὑπὸ ἀνθρώπου
φυλαχθῆναι, οὐ φυλάξεις αὐτάς. 6. νῦν δέ σοι
λέγω· ἐὰν ταύτας μὴ φυλάξῃς, ἀλλὰ παρενθυμηθῇς, οὐχ ἕξεις σωτηρίαν οὔτε τὰ τέκνα σου οὔτε
ὁ οἶκός σου. ἐπεὶ ἤδη σεαυτῷ κέκρικας τοῦ μὴ
δύνασθαι τὰς ἐντολὰς ταύτας ὑπὸ ἀνθρώπου
φυλαχθῆναι.

IV

1. Καὶ ταῦτά μοι λίαν ὀργίλως ἐλάλησεν, ὥστε
με συγχυθῆναι καὶ λίαν αὐτὸν φοβηθῆναι· ἡ
μορφὴ γὰρ αὐτοῦ ἠλλοιώθη, ὥστε μὴ δύνασθαι
ἄνθρωπον ὑπενεγκεῖν τὴν ὀργὴν αὐτοῦ.[2] 2. ἰδὼν
δέ με τεταραγμένον ὅλον καὶ συγκεχυμένον ἤρξατό
μοι ἐπιεικέστερον καὶ ἱλαρώτερον λαλεῖν καὶ
λέγει· Ἄφρον, ἀσύνετε καὶ δίψυχε, οὐ νοεῖς τὴν
δόξαν τοῦ θεοῦ, πῶς μεγάλη ἐστὶ καὶ ἰσχυρὰ καὶ

---

[1] There are some indications that in some recensions the
Similitudes began here. A inserts ἀρχή before the next
paragraph and E inserts *initium similitudinum*.

[2] A inserts here σὺ συνέκλεισας φῶς καὶ ἐχώρισας τὸ σκότος
ἀπ᾿ ἀλλήλων, ἐθεμελίωσας τὴν γῆν, καὶ ἔκτισας καρποὺς παντα-

will obey your words, for I will be with you, and will
force them to be persuaded by you." 4. I said
to him, "Sir, these commandments are great and
beautiful and glorious, and 'able to make glad the
heart of man' if he be able to keep them. But I do
not know if these commandments can be kept by
man, because they are very hard." 5. He answered
and said to me, "If you set it before yourself that
they can be kept you will easily keep them, and
they will not be difficult; but if it already comes
into your heart that they cannot be kept by man,
you will not keep them. 6. But now I say to you, if
you do not keep them, but neglect them, you shall
not have salvation, nor your children, nor your house,
because you have already judged for yourself that
these commandments cannot be kept by man."

IV

1. AND he spoke these things to me very angrily,
so that I was confounded, and greatly afraid of him,
for his appearance was changed so that a man could
not endure his wrath. 2. But when he saw me quite
disturbed and confused he began to speak to me
more gently and cheerfully, and said : "Foolish one
without understanding and double-minded, do you
not understand the glory of God, how great and

δαπούς, ἥλιον, σελήνην, ἄστρων ἐναρμόνιον κίνησιν, ζῷα πτερωτά,
τετράποδα, ἑρπετά, ἔνυδρα, ἄγριά τε καὶ τὰ τούτοις παραπλησιά-
ζοντα, καὶ τούτων ἁπάντων ἔκτισας δεσπότην τὸν ἄνθρωπον.
Apparently a pious comment inserted in the text by mistake.

Ps. 8, 7 θαυμαστή, ὅτι ἔκτισε τὸν κόσμον ἕνεκα τοῦ
ἀνθρώπου καὶ πᾶσαν τὴν κτίσιν αὐτοῦ ὑπέταξε
τῷ ἀνθρώπῳ καὶ τὴν ἐξουσίαν πᾶσαν ἔδωκεν αὐτῷ
τοῦ κατακυριεύειν τῶν ὑπὸ τὸν οὐρανὸν πάντων;
3. εἰ οὖν, φησίν, πάντων ὁ ἄνθρωπος κύριός ἐστι
τῶν κτισμάτων τοῦ θεοῦ καὶ πάντων κατακυριεύει,
οὐ δύναται καὶ τούτων τῶν ἐντολῶν κατακυριεῦσαι; δύναται, φησί, πάντων καὶ πασῶν τῶν
ἐντολῶν τούτων κατακυριεῦσαι ὁ ἄνθρωπος ὁ
ἔχων τὸν κύριον ἐν τῇ καρδίᾳ αὐτοῦ. 4. οἱ δὲ
ἐπὶ τοῖς χείλεσιν ἔχοντες τὸν κύριον, τὴν δὲ
καρδίαν αὐτῶν πεπωρωμένην καὶ μακρὰν ὄντες
ἀπὸ τοῦ κυρίου, ἐκείνοις αἱ ἐντολαὶ αὗται σκληραί
εἰσι καὶ δύσβατοι. 5. θέσθε οὖν ὑμεῖς, οἱ κενοὶ
καὶ ἐλαφροὶ ὄντες ἐν τῇ πίστει, τὸν κύριον ὑμῶν
εἰς τὴν καρδίαν, καὶ γνώσεσθε, ὅτι οὐδέν ἐστιν
εὐκοπώτερον τῶν ἐντολῶν τούτων οὔτε γλυκύτερον
οὔτε ἡμερώτερον. 6. ἐπιστράφητε ὑμεῖς οἱ ταῖς
ἐντολαῖς πορευόμενοι τοῦ διαβόλου, ταῖς δυσκόλοις
καὶ πικραῖς καὶ ἀγρίαις καὶ ἀσελγέσι, καὶ μὴ
φοβήθητε τὸν διάβολον, ὅτι ἐν αὐτῷ δύναμις οὐκ
ἔστιν καθ' ὑμῶν· 7. ἐγὼ γὰρ ἔσομαι μεθ' ὑμῶν,
ὁ ἄγγελος τῆς μετανοίας ὁ κατακυριεύων αὐτοῦ.
ὁ διάβολος μόνον φόβον ἔχει, ὁ δὲ φόβος αὐτοῦ
τόνον οὐκ ἔχει· μὴ φοβήθητε οὖν αὐτόν, καὶ φεύξεται ἀφ' ὑμῶν.

V

1. Λέγω αὐτῷ· Κύριε, ἄκουσόν μου ὀλίγων
ῥημάτων. Λέγε, φησίν, ὃ βούλει. Ὁ μὲν ἄνθρωπος, φημί, κύριε, πρόθυμός ἐστι τὰς ἐντολὰς

mighty and wonderful it is, because 'he created the world' for man's sake, and subdued all his creation to man, and gave him all power, to master all things under heaven? 3. If, then," said he, "man is the lord of all the creatures of God, and masters them, is it not possible to master these commandments also? The man," said he, "who has the Lord in his heart, is able to master all things and all these commandments. 4. But those who have the Lord on their lips, but their heart is hardened, and they are far from the Lord, for them these commandments are hard, and difficult to walk in. 5. Do you, therefore, who are empty and light in the faith, put the Lord into your heart, and you shall know that nothing is easier or sweeter or more gentle than these commandments. 6. Be converted, you who walk in the commandments of the devil, which are difficult and bitter and cruel and foul, and do not fear the devil, for there is no power in him against you. 7. For I, the angel of repentance who masters him, will be with you. The devil can only cause fear, but fear of him has no force. Therefore do not fear him and he will fly from you."

V

1. I SAID to him "Sir, listen to a few words from me." "Say what you will," he said. "Sir," said I, "man desires to keep the commandments of God,

133

THE APOSTOLIC FATHERS

τοῦ θεοῦ φυλάσσειν, καὶ οὐδείς ἐστιν ὁ μὴ αἰτούμενος παρὰ τοῦ κυρίου, ἵνα ἐνδυναμωθῇ ἐν ταῖς
ἐντολαῖς αὐτοῦ καὶ ὑποταγῇ αὐταῖς· ἀλλ' ὁ
διάβολος σκληρός ἐστι καὶ καταδυναστεύει αὐτῶν.
2. Οὐ δύναται, φησί, καταδυναστεύειν τῶν δούλων
τοῦ θεοῦ τῶν ἐξ ὅλης καρδίας ἐλπιζόντων ἐπ'
αὐτόν. δύναται ὁ διάβολος ἀντιπαλαῖσαι, κατα-
παλαῖσαι δὲ οὐ δύναται. ἐὰν οὖν ἀντισταθῆτε
αὐτῷ, νικηθεὶς φεύξεται ἀφ' ὑμῶν κατῃσχυμμένος.
ὅσοι δέ, φησίν, ἀπόκενοί εἰσι, φοβοῦνται τὸν διάβολον ὡς δύναμιν ἔχοντα. 3. ὅταν ὁ ἄνθρωπος
κεράμια ἱκανώτατα γεμίσῃ οἴνου καλοῦ καὶ ἐν
τοῖς κεραμίοις ἐκείνοις ὀλίγα ἀπόκενα ᾖ, ἔρχεται
ἐπὶ τὰ κεράμια καὶ οὐ κατανοεῖ τὰ πλήρη· οἶδε
γάρ, ὅτι πλήρη εἰσί· κατανοεῖ δὲ τὰ ἀπόκενα,
φοβούμενος, μήποτε ὤξισαν· ταχὺ γὰρ τὰ ἀπόκενα κεράμια ὀξίζουσι, καὶ ἀπόλλυται ἡ ἡδονὴ
τοῦ οἴνου. 4. οὕτω καὶ ὁ διάβολος ἔρχεται ἐπὶ
πάντας τοὺς δούλους τοῦ θεοῦ ἐκπειράζων αὐτούς.
ὅσοι οὖν πλήρεις εἰσὶν ἐν τῇ πίστει, ἀνθεστήκασιν
αὐτῷ ἰσχυρῶς, κἀκεῖνος ἀποχωρεῖ ἀπ' αὐτῶν μὴ
ἔχων τόπον, ποῦ εἰσέλθῃ. ἔρχεται οὖν τότε πρὸς
τοὺς ἀποκένους καὶ ἔχων τόπον εἰσπορεύεται εἰς
αὐτούς, καὶ ὃ δὲ βούλεται ἐν αὐτοῖς ἐργάζεται,
καὶ γίνονται αὐτῷ ὑπόδουλοι.

VI

1. Ἐγὼ δὲ ὑμῖν λέγω, ὁ ἄγγελος τῆς μετανοίας·
μὴ φοβήθητε τὸν διάβολον. ἀπεστάλην γάρ,
φησί, μεθ' ὑμῶν εἶναι τῶν μετανοούντων ἐξ ὅλης

and there is none that does not pray to the Lord,
that he may be made strong in his commandments,
and submit to them. But the devil is hard, and
oppresses them." 2. "He cannot," said he, "oppress the servants of the Lord who hope in him with
all their heart. The devil can wrestle with them,
but he cannot throw them down. If then you 'resist
him' he will be conquered and 'fly from you' in shame.
But as many," said he, "as are empty fear the devil
as though he had power. 3. When a man fills
very many pots with good wine, and among those
pots a few are half empty, he comes to the pots, and
does not consider those which are full, for he knows
that they are full, but he looks at those which are
half empty, fearing that they have gone sour, for
empty pots quickly go sour, and the flavour of the
wine is spoilt. 4. So also the devil comes to all the
servants of God, tempting them ; as many therefore as are full of faith withstand him power-
fully, and he departs from them, having no room
by which to enter. Then, therefore, he comes
to those who are half empty and finding room he
enters into them, and does what he will in them, and
they become his servants.

VI

1. "BUT I, the angel of repentance, say to you, Do
not fear the devil. For I was sent," said he, "to
be with you who repent with all your heart, and

135

καρδίας αὐτῶν καὶ ἰσχυροποιῆσαι αὐτοὺς ἐν τῇ
πίστει. 2. πιστεύσατε οὖν τῷ θεῷ ὑμεῖς οἱ διὰ
τὰς ἁμαρτίας ὑμῶν ἀπεγνωκότες τὴν ζωὴν ὑμῶν
καὶ προστιθέντες ἁμαρτίαις καὶ καταβαρύνοντες
τὴν ζωὴν ὑμῶν, ὅτι, ἐὰν ἐπιστραφῆτε πρὸς τὸν
κύριον ἐξ ὅλης τῆς καρδίας ὑμῶν καὶ ἐργάσησθε
τὴν δικαιοσύνην, τὰς λοιπὰς ἡμέρας τῆς ζωῆς
ὑμῶν καὶ δουλεύσητε αὐτῷ ὀρθῶς κατὰ τὸ θέλημα
αὐτοῦ, ποιήσει ἴασιν τοῖς προτέροις ὑμῶν ἁμαρ-
τήμασι καὶ ἕξετε δύναμιν τοῦ κατακυριεῦσαι τῶν
ἔργων τοῦ διαβόλου. τὴν δὲ ἀπειλὴν τοῦ διαβόλου ὅλως μὴ φοβήθητε· ἄτονος γάρ ἐστιν
ὥσπερ νεκροῦ νεῦρα. 3. ἀκούσατε οὖν μου καὶ
φοβήθητε τὸν πάντα δυνάμενον, σῶσαι καὶ
ἀπολέσαι, καὶ τηρεῖτε τὰς ἐντολὰς ταύτας, καὶ
ζήσεσθε τῷ θεῷ. 4. λέγω αὐτῷ· Κύριε, νῦν
ἐνεδυναμώθην ἐν πᾶσι τοῖς δικαιώμασι τοῦ
κυρίου, ὅτι σὺ μετ' ἐμοῦ εἶ· καὶ οἶδα, ὅτι συγ-
κόψεις τὴν δύναμιν τοῦ διαβόλου πᾶσαν καὶ
ἡμεῖς αὐτοῦ κατακυριεύσομεν καὶ κατισχύσομεν
πάντων τῶν ἔργων αὐτοῦ. καὶ ἐλπίζω, κύριε,
δύνασθαί με τὰς ἐντολὰς ταύτας, ἃς ἐντέταλσαι,
τοῦ κυρίου ἐνδυναμοῦντος φυλάξαι. 5. Φυλάξεις, φησίν, ἐὰν ἡ καρδία σου καθαρὰ γένηται
πρὸς κύριον· καὶ πάντες δὲ φυλάξουσιν, ὅσοι
ἂν καθαρίσωσιν ἑαυτῶν τὰς καρδίας ἀπὸ τῶν
ματαίων ἐπιθυμιῶν τοῦ αἰῶνος τούτου, καὶ ζήσονται τῷ θεῷ.

Jer. 24, 7;
Joel 2, 12
Ps. 15, 2

Jam. 4, 12

to strengthen you in the faith. 2. Believe, therefore, in God, though you have renounced your life through your sins, and have added to your sins, and have made your life heavy, that if you 'turn to the Lord with all your heart, and do righteousness' for the rest of the days of your life, and serve him in uprightness, according to his will, he will heal your former sins, and you shall have power to master the works of the devil. But do not fear the threat of the devil at all, for he is powerless as the sinews of a dead man. 3. Listen, therefore, to me, and fear him who has all power, 'to save and to destroy,' and keep these commandments, and you shall live to God." 4. I said to him : "Sir, now I have received power in all the ordinances of the Lord, because you are with me, and I know that you will break down all the power of the devil, and we shall master him, and have power against all his deeds. And I hope, sir, that I shall now be able to keep these commandments which you have commanded, the Lord giving me strength." 5. "You shall keep them," said he, " if your heart be pure towards the Lord, and all who ever purify their hearts from the vain desires of this world shall keep them, and shall live to God."

ΠΑΡΑΒΟΛΑΙ [1] ΑΣ ΕΛΑΛΗΣΕ ΜΕΤ' ΕΜΟΥ

1. Λέγει μοι· Οἴδατε, φησίν, ὅτι ἐπὶ ξένης κατοικεῖτε ὑμεῖς οἱ δοῦλοι τοῦ θεοῦ· ἡ γὰρ πόλις ὑμῶν μακράν ἐστιν ἀπὸ τῆς πόλεως ταύτης· εἰ οὖν οἴδατε, φησί, τὴν πόλιν ὑμῶν, ἐν ᾗ μέλλετε κατοικεῖν, τί ὧδε ὑμεῖς ἑτοιμάζετε ἀγροὺς καὶ παρατάξεις πολυτελεῖς καὶ οἰκοδομὰς καὶ οἰκήματα μάταια; 2. ταῦτα οὖν ὁ ἑτοιμάζων εἰς ταύτην τὴν πόλιν οὐ δύναται [2] ἐπανακάμψαι εἰς τὴν ἰδίαν πόλιν. 3. ἄφρον καὶ δίψυχε καὶ ταλαίπωρε ἄνθρωπε, οὐ νοεῖς, ὅτι ταῦτα πάντα ἀλλότριά εἰσι καὶ ὑπ' ἐξουσίαν ἑτέρου εἰσίν; ἐρεῖ γὰρ ὁ κύριος τῆς πόλεως ταύτης· Οὐ θέλω σε κατοικεῖν εἰς τὴν πόλιν μου, ἀλλ' ἔξελθε ἐκ τῆς πόλεως ταύτης, ὅτι τοῖς νόμοις μου οὐ χρᾶσαι. 4. σὺ οὖν ἔχων ἀγροὺς καὶ οἰκήσεις καὶ ἑτέρας ὑπάρξεις πολλάς, ἐκβαλλόμενος ὑπ' αὐτοῦ τί ποιήσεις σου τὸν ἀγρὸν καὶ τὴν οἰκίαν καὶ τὰ λοιπά, ὅσα ἡτοίμασας σεαυτῷ; λέγει γάρ σοι δικαίως ὁ κύριος τῆς χώρας ταύτης· Ἢ τοῖς νόμοις μου χρῶ ἢ ἐκχώρει ἐκ τῆς χώρας μου. 5. σὺ οὖν τί μέλλεις ποιεῖν, ἔχων νόμον ἐν τῇ σῇ πόλει; ἕνεκεν τῶν ἀγρῶν σου καὶ τῆς λοιπῆς ὑπάρξεως τὸν νόμον σου πάντως ἀπαρνήσῃ καὶ πορεύσῃ τῷ νόμῳ τῆς πόλεως ταύτης; βλέπε,

[1] Translated *Similitudines* in L, hence the custom of quoting this section of the Shepherd as the "Similitudes."

[2] δύναται A, cogitat L, vult E. (LE perhaps represent προσδοκᾷ).

THE PARABLES WHICH HE SPOKE
WITH ME

1. HE said to me, "You know that you, as the servants of God, are living in a strange country,[1] for your city is far from this city. If then you know your city, in which you are going to dwell, why do you here prepare lands and costly establishments and buildings and vain dwellings? 2. He therefore, who prepares these things for this city, is not able to return to his own city. 3. O foolish and double-hearted and wretched man, do you not understand that all these things are foreign to you, and are under the power of another? For the Lord of this city will say: ' I do not wish you to dwell in my city, but go out from this city, because you do not use my law.' 4. If then you have fields and dwellings, and many other possessions, when you are cast out by him, what will you do with your land and house, and all the other things which you have prepared for yourself? For the lord of this country justly says to you, 'Either use my law or go out from my country.' 5. What then are you going to do, seeing that you have a law in your own city? Will you because of your fields and other possessions altogether deny your law, and walk in the law of

Christians are strangers in the world

---

[1] The idea of the conflict of interests between earthly and heavenly citizenship is common in early Christian literature. Cf. Heb. 13, 14. "For here have we no continuing city, but we seek one to come."

μὴ ἀσύμφορόν ἐστιν ἀπαρνῆσαι τὸν νόμον σου·
ἐὰν γὰρ ἐπανακάμψαι θελήσῃς εἰς τὴν πόλιν σου,
οὐ μὴ παραδεχθήσῃ, ὅτι ἀπηρνήσω τὸν νόμον
τῆς πόλεώς σου, καὶ ἐκκλεισθήσῃ ἀπ' αὐτῆς.
6. βλέπε οὖν σύ· ὡς ἐπὶ ξένης κατοικῶν μηδὲν
πλέον ἑτοίμαζε σεαυτῷ εἰ μὴ τὴν αὐτάρκειαν
τὴν ἀρκετήν σοι, καὶ ἕτοιμος γίνου, ἵνα, ὅταν
θέλῃ ὁ δεσπότης τῆς πόλεως ταύτης ἐκβαλεῖν σε
ἀντιταξάμενον τῷ νόμῳ αὐτοῦ, ἐξέλθῃς ἐκ τῆς
πόλεως αὐτοῦ καὶ ἀπέλθῃς ἐν τῇ πόλει σου καὶ
τῷ σῷ νόμῳ χρήσῃ ἀνυβρίστως ἀγαλλιώμενος.[1]
7. βλέπετε οὖν ὑμεῖς οἱ δουλεύοντες τῷ κυρίῳ καὶ
ἔχοντες αὐτὸν εἰς τὴν καρδίαν· ἐργάζεσθε τὰ
Ps. 103, 18   ἔργα τοῦ θεοῦ μνημονεύοντες τῶν ἐντολῶν αὐτοῦ
καὶ τῶν ἐπαγγελιῶν ὧν ἐπηγγείλατο, καὶ πιστεύσατε αὐτῷ, ὅτι ποιήσει αὐτάς, ἐὰν αἱ ἐντολαὶ
αὐτοῦ φυλαχθῶσιν. 8. ἀντὶ ἀγρῶν οὖν ἀγορά-
ζετε ψυχὰς θλιβομένας, καθά τις δυνατός ἐστι,
Jam. 1, 27   καὶ χήρας καὶ ὀρφανοὺς ἐπισκέπτεσθε καὶ μὴ
παραβλέπετε αὐτούς, καὶ τὸν πλοῦτον ὑμῶν καὶ
τὰς παρατάξεις πάσας εἰς τοιούτους ἀγροὺς καὶ
οἰκίας δαπανᾶτε, ἃς ἐλάβετε παρὰ τοῦ θεοῦ.
9. εἰς τοῦτο γὰρ ἐπλούτισεν ὑμᾶς ὁ δεσπότης, ἵνα
ταύτας τὰς διακονίας τελέσητε αὐτῷ· πολὺ
βέλτιόν ἐστι τοιούτους ἀγροὺς ἀγοράζειν καὶ
κτήματα καὶ οἴκους, οὓς εὑρήσεις ἐν τῇ πόλει σου,
ὅταν ἐπιδημήσῃς εἰς αὐτήν.   10. αὕτη ἡ πολυ-
τέλεια καλὴ καὶ ἱερά, λύπην μὴ ἔχουσα μηδὲ
φόβον, ἔχουσα δὲ χαράν. τὴν οὖν πολυτέλειαν
τῶν ἐθνῶν μὴ πράσσετε· ἀσύμφορον γάρ ἐστιν

[1] ἀνυβρίστως ἀγαλλιώμενος LE, ἀνυβρίστως καὶ ἀγαλλιωμένος.
A.

this city? Take heed that it be not unprofitable to deny your law, for if you wish to return back to your city, you will not be received, because you have denied the law of your city, and you will be excluded from it. 6. Take heed, then, make no further preparations for yourself beyond a sufficient competence for yourself, as though you were living in a foreign country, and be ready in order that, whenever the master of this city wishes to expel you for resisting his law, you may go out from his city, and depart to your own city, and joyfully follow your own law suffering no harm.[1] 7. Take heed, then, you who serve the Lord and have him in your heart. Do the deeds of God, 'remembering his commandments,' and the promises which he made, and believe him that he will perform them if his commandments be observed. 8. Therefore instead of lands, purchase afflicted souls, as each is able, 'and look after widows and orphans,' and do not despise them, and spend your wealth and all your establishments for such fields and houses as you have received from God. 9. For, for this reason did the Master make you rich, that you should fulfil these ministries for him. It is far better to purchase such lands and houses, as you will find in your own city, when you go to it. 10. This wealth is beautiful and joyful, and has neither grief nor fear, but has joy. Follow therefore not after the wealth of the heathen, for it

---

[1] ἀνυβρίστως is either active or passive : it may qualify ἀγαλλιώμενος, "in decorous joy," "joy unmixed with ὕβρις."

ὑμῖν τοῖς δούλοις τοῦ θεοῦ. 11. τὴν δὲ ἰδίαν
πολυτέλειαν πράσσετε, ἐν ᾗ δύνασθε χαρῆναι,
καὶ μὴ παραχαράσσετε μηδὲ τοῦ ἀλλοτρίου
ἅψησθε μηδὲ ἐπιθυμεῖτε αὐτοῦ· πονηρὸν γάρ
ἐστιν ἀλλοτρίων ἐπιθυμεῖν. τὸ δὲ σὸν ἔργον
ἐργάζου, καὶ σωθήσῃ.

Ἄλλη παραβολή

1. Περιπατοῦντός μου εἰς τὸν ἀγρὸν καὶ κατα-
νοοῦντος πτελέαν καὶ ἄμπελον καὶ διακρίνοντος
περὶ αὐτῶν καὶ τῶν καρπῶν αὐτῶν, φανεροῦταί
μοι ὁ ποιμὴν καὶ λέγει· Τί σὺ ἐν ἑαυτῷ ζητεῖς
περὶ τῆς πτελέας καὶ τῆς ἀμπέλου; Συζητῶ,
φημί, κύριε,[1] ὅτι εὐπρεπέσταταί εἰσιν ἀλλήλαις.
2. Ταῦτα τὰ δύο δένδρα, φησίν, εἰς τύπον κεῖνται
τοῖς δούλοις τοῦ θεοῦ. Ἤθελον, φημί, γνῶναι
τὸν τύπον τῶν δένδρων τούτων ὧν λέγεις. Βλέπεις, φησί, τὴν πτελέαν καὶ τὴν ἄμπελον;
Βλέπω, φημί, κύριε. 3. Ἡ ἄμπελος, φησίν,
αὕτη καρπὸν φέρει, ἡ δὲ πτελέα ξύλον ἄκαρπόν
ἐστιν· ἀλλ' ἡ ἄμπελος αὕτη ἐὰν μὴ ἀναβῇ ἐπὶ
τὴν πτελέαν, οὐ δύναται καρποφορῆσαι πολὺ
ἐρριμμένη χαμαί, καὶ ὃν φέρει καρπόν, σεσηπότα
φέρει μὴ κρεμαμένη ἐπὶ τῆς πτελέας, ὅταν οὖν
ἐπιρριφῇ ἡ ἄμπελος ἐπὶ τὴν πτελέαν, καὶ παρ'
ἑαυτῆς φέρει καρπὸν καὶ παρὰ τῆς πτελέας.
4. βλέπεις οὖν, ὅτι καὶ ἡ πτελέα πολὺν
καρπὸν δίδωσιν, οὐκ ἐλάσσονα τῆς ἀμπέλου,
μᾶλλον δὲ καὶ πλείονα. Πῶς, φημί, κύριε,

[1] κύριε LE, om. A.

is unprofitable to you, who are the servants of God. 11. Follow your own wealth, in which you can rejoice, and do not counterfeit nor touch that which is another's, nor desire it, for it is wicked to desire that which is another's, but do your own work and you shall be saved."

ANOTHER PARABLE (II)

1. WHILE I was walking in the country I noticed an elm and a vine, and was considering them and their fruits, when the shepherd appeared to me and said : "What are you considering in yourself about the elm and vine ?" "I am considering, sir," said I, "that they are very well suited to one another." 2. "These two trees," said he " are put as a type for the servants of God." "I should like," said I, "to know the type of the trees of which you speak." "You see," said he, "the vine and the elm." "Yes, sir," said I, " I see them." 3. "This vine," said he, "bears fruit, but the elm is a sterile tree. But this vine, if it do not grow upon the elm, cannot bear much fruit, because it is spread on the ground, and the fruit which it bears, it bears rotten, when it is not hanging on the elm. When, therefore, the vine is attached to the elm, it bears fruit from itself and from the elm. 4. You see then that the elm gives much fruit, not less than the vine, but rather more." " How, sir," said I, " does it bear more ?" "Be-

Rich and poor like a vine and elm

πλείονα; [1] Ὅτι, φησίν, ἡ ἄμπελος κρεμαμένη
ἐπὶ τὴν πτελέαν τὸν καρπὸν πολὺν καὶ καλὸν
δίδωσιν, ἐρριμμένη δὲ χαμαὶ [2] ὀλίγον καὶ σαπρὸν
φέρει. αὕτη οὖν ἡ παραβολὴ εἰς τοὺς δούλους
τοῦ θεοῦ κεῖται, εἰς πτωχὸν καὶ πλούσιον.
5. Πῶς, φημί, κύριε, γνώρισον μοι. Ἄκουε,
φησίν· ὁ μὲν πλούσιος ἔχει χρήματα, τὰ δὲ πρὸς
τὸν κύριον πτωχεύει, περισπώμενος περὶ τὸν
πλοῦτον ἑαυτοῦ, καὶ λίαν μικρὰν ἔχει τὴν ἔντευξιν
καὶ τὴν ἐξομολόγησιν πρὸς τὸν κύριον, καὶ ἣν
ἔχει, βληχρὰν καὶ μικρὰν καὶ ἄλλην [3] μὴ ἔχουσαν
δύναμιν. ὅταν οὖν ἐπαναπάῃ ἐπὶ τὸν πένητα ὁ
πλούσιος καὶ χορηγήσῃ αὐτῷ τὰ δέοντα, πιστεύει,
ὅτι ἐὰν ἐργάσηται εἰς τὸν πένητα δυνηθήσεται τὸν
μισθὸν εὑρεῖν παρὰ τῷ θεῷ· ὅτι ὁ πένης πλούσιός
ἐστιν ἐν τῇ ἐντεύξει καὶ ἐν τῇ ἐξομολογήσει καὶ
δύναμιν μεγάλην ἔχει παρὰ τῷ θεῷ ἡ ἔντευξις
αὐτοῦ. ἐπιχορηγεῖ οὖν ὁ πλούσιος τῷ πένητι πάντα
ἀδιστάκτως. 6. ὁ πένης δὲ ἐπιχορηγούμενος ὑπὸ
τοῦ πλουσίου ἐντυγχάνει τῷ θεῷ εὐχαριστῶν
αὐτῷ, ὑπὲρ τοῦ διδόντος αὐτῷ· κἀκεῖνος ἔτι ἐπι-
σπουδάζει περὶ τοῦ πένητος, ἵνα ἀδιάλειπτος γένηται ἐν τῇ ζωῇ αὐτοῦ· οἶδε γάρ, ὅτι ἡ τοῦ πένητος
ἔντευξις προσδεκτή ἐστι καὶ πλουσία πρὸς κύριον.
7. ἀμφότεροι οὖν τὸ ἔργον τελοῦσιν· ὁ μὲν πένης
ἐργάζεται τῇ ἐντεύξει, ἐν ᾗ πλουτεῖ, ἣν ἔλαβεν
παρὰ τοῦ κυρίου· ταύτην ἀποδίδωσι τῷ κυρίῳ τῷ
ἐπιχορηγοῦντι αὐτῷ. καὶ ὁ πλούσιος ὡσαύτως

---

[1] πῶς . . . πλείονα LE, om. A.
[2] χαμαὶ om. Pᵒˣʸ.
[3] ἄλλην conjectured from Pᵒˣʸ (ἀ . . ην), ἀνοῦ (= ἀνθρώπου) A.

cause," said he, "the vine, when it hangs on the elm, gives much beautiful fruit, but when it is lying on the ground, it bears but little fruit and rotten. This parable, therefore, applies to the servants of God, to the poor and the rich." 5. "How, sir?" said I, "let me know." "Listen," said he. "The rich man has much wealth, but he is poor as touching the Lord, being busied about his riches, and his intercession and confession towards the Lord is very small, and that which he has is weak and small, and has no other power. But when the rich man rests upon the poor, and gives him what he needs, he believes that what he does to the poor man can find a reward with God, because the poor is rich in intercession and confession, and his intercession has great power with God. The rich man, therefore, helps the poor in all things without doubting. 6. But the poor man, being helped by the rich, makes intercession to God, giving him thanks, for him who gave to him, and the rich man is still zealous for the poor man, that he fail not in his life, for he knows that the intercession of the poor is acceptable and rich toward the Lord. 7. Therefore the two together complete the work, for the poor works in the intercession in which he is rich, which he received from the Lord : this he pays to the Lord who helps him.

τὸ πλοῦτος, ὃ ἔλαβεν παρὰ τοῦ κυρίου, ἀδιστάκτως παρέχεται τῷ πένητι. καὶ τοῦτο ἔργον
μέγα ἐστὶ καὶ δεκτὸν παρὰ τῷ θεῷ, ὅτι συνῆκεν
ἐπὶ τῷ πλούτῳ αὐτοῦ καὶ εἰργάσατο εἰς τὸν
πένητα ἐκ τῶν δωρημάτων τοῦ κυρίου καὶ
ἐτέλεσε τὴν διακονίαν ὀρθῶς. 8. παρὰ τοῖς
οὖν ἀνθρώποις ἡ πτελέα δοκεῖ καρπὸν μὴ φέρειν,
καὶ οὐκ οἴδασιν οὐδὲ νοοῦσιν, ὅτι, ὅταν ἀβροχία
γένηται, ἡ πτελέα ἔχουσα ὕδωρ τρέφει τὴν
ἄμπελον καὶ ἡ ἄμπελος ἀδιάλειπτον ἔχουσα
τὸ ὕδωρ διπλοῦν τὸν καρπὸν ἀποδίδωσι, καὶ
ὑπὲρ ἑαυτῆς καὶ ὑπὲρ τῆς πτελέας. οὕτως καὶ
οἱ πένητες ὑπὲρ τῶν πλουσίων ἐντυγχάνοντες
πρὸς τὸν κύριον πληροφοροῦσι τὸ πλοῦτος
αὐτῶν, καὶ πάλιν οἱ πλούσιοι χορηγοῦντες τοῖς
πένησι τὰ δέοντα πληροφοροῦσι τὰς εὐχὰς[1]
αὐτῶν. 9. γίνονται οὖν ἀμφότεροι κοινωνοὶ τοῦ
ἔργου τοῦ δικαίου. ταῦτα οὖν ὁ ποιῶν οὐκ
ἐγκαταλειφθήσεται ὑπὸ τοῦ θεοῦ, ἀλλ᾽ ἔσται
γεγραμμένος εἰς τὰς βίβλους τῶν ζώντων.
10. μακάριοι οἱ ἔχοντες καὶ συνιέντες, ὅτι παρὰ
τοῦ κυρίου πλουτίζονται, ὁ γὰρ συνίων τοῦτο
δυνήσεται καὶ διακονῆσαί τι ἀγαθόν.

Ἄλλη παραβολή

1. Ἔδειξέ μοι δένδρα πολλὰ μὴ ἔχοντα φύλλα,
ἀλλ᾽ ὡσεὶ ξηρὰ ἐδόκει μοι εἶναι· ὅμοια γὰρ ἦν
πάντα. καὶ λέγει μοι· Βλέπεις τὰ δένδρα ταῦτα;

---

[1] εὐχάς is a conjecture; ψυχάς AL₂, L₁E paraphrase and
clearly could not understand the Greek.

And the rich man likewise provides the poor, without hesitating, with the wealth which he received from the Lord ; and this work is great and acceptable with God, because he has understanding in his wealth, and has wrought for the poor man from the gifts of the Lord, and fulfilled his ministry rightly.   8. Among men, therefore, the elm appears as if it bore no fruit, and they do not know nor understand that if there is drought the elm which has water nourishes the vine, and the vine, having water continuously, gives double fruit, both for itself and for the elm. So also the poor, interceding with the Lord for the rich, complement[1] their wealth, and again, the rich helping the poor with their necessities complement their prayers.   9. Both, therefore, share in the righteous work. Therefore he who does these things shall not be deserted by God, but shall be inscribed in the books of the living.   10. Blessed are they who are wealthy and understand that their riches are from the Lord, for he who understands this will also be able to do some good service.

ANOTHER PARABLE (III)

1. He showed me many trees, without leaves, which appeared to me to be as if dry, for they were all alike. And he said to me : " Do you see these

---

[1] The idea in πληροφοροῦσι is that of filling up that which is lacking,—a ὑστέρημα.

Βλέπω, φημί, κύριε, ὅμοια ὄντα καὶ ξηρά. ἀπο
κριθείς μοι λέγει· Ταῦτα τὰ δένδρα, ἃ βλέπεις, οἱ
κατοικοῦντές εἰσιν ἐν τῷ αἰῶνι τούτῳ. 2. Διατί οὖν,
φημί, κύριε, ὡσεὶ ξηρά εἰσι καὶ ὅμοια; Ὅτι,
φησίν, οὔτε οἱ δίκαιοι φαίνονται οὔτε οἱ ἁμαρτωλοὶ ἐν τῷ αἰῶνι τούτῳ, ἀλλ' ὅμοιοί εἰσιν· ὁ γὰρ
αἰὼν οὗτος τοῖς δικαίοις χειμών ἐστι, καὶ οὐ
φαίνονται μετὰ τῶν ἁμαρτωλῶν κατοικοῦντες.
3. ὥσπερ γὰρ ἐν τῷ χειμῶνι τὰ δένδρα ἀποβε-
βληκότα τὰ φύλλα ὅμοιά εἰσι καὶ οὐ φαίνονται
τὰ ξηρὰ ποῖά εἰσιν ἢ τὰ ζῶντα, οὕτως ἐν τῷ αἰῶνι
τούτῳ οὐ φαίνονται οὔτε οἱ δίκαιοι οὔτε οἱ ἁμαρτωλοί, ἀλλὰ πάντες ὅμοιοί εἰσιν.

Ἄλλη παραβολή

1. Ἔδειξέ μοι πάλιν δένδρα πολλά, ἃ μὲν βλαστῶντα, ἃ δὲ ξηρά, καὶ λέγει μοι· Βλέπεις, φησί, τὰ
δένδρα ταῦτα; Βλέπω, φημί, κύριε, τὰ μὲν βλαστῶντα τὰ δὲ ξηρά. 2. Ταῦτα, φησί, τὰ δένδρα τὰ
βλαστῶντα οἱ δίκαιοί εἰσιν οἱ μέλλοντες κατοικεῖν
εἰς τὸν αἰῶνα τὸν ἐρχόμενον· ὁ γὰρ αἰὼν ὁ ἐρχό-
μενος θερεία ἐστὶ τοῖς δικαίοις, τοῖς δὲ ἁμαρτωλοῖς
χειμών. ὅταν οὖν ἐπιλάμψῃ τὸ ἔλεος τοῦ κυρίου,
τότε φανερωθήσονται οἱ δουλεύοντες τῷ θεῷ, καὶ
πάντες φανερωθήσονται. 3. ὥσπερ γὰρ τῷ θέρει
ἑνὸς ἑκάστου δένδρου οἱ καρποὶ φανεροῦνται
καὶ ἐπιγινώσκονται ποταποί εἰσιν, οὕτω καὶ τῶν
δικαίων οἱ καρποὶ φανεροὶ ἔσονται καὶ γνωσθήσ-
ονται πάντες εὐθαλεῖς ὄντες ἐν τῷ αἰῶνι ἐκείνῳ.
4. τὰ δὲ ἔθνη καὶ οἱ ἁμαρτωλοί, ἃ εἶδες τὰ δένδρα

trees?" "Yes, sir," said I, "and I see that they are all alike and dry." And he answered me and said: "These trees which you see are they who dwell in this world." 2. "Why, then," said I, "sir, are they as it were dry and all alike?" "Because," said he, "in this world, neither righteous nor sinners are apparent, but are all alike. For this world is winter for the righteous and they are not apparent, though they are living with sinners. 3. For just as in the winter the trees which have shed their leaves are alike, and it is not apparent which are dry and which are alive, so in this world neither the righteous nor the sinners are apparent, but all are alike."

Another Parable (IV)

1. He showed me again many trees, some budding and some withered, and said to me, "Do you see," said he, "these trees." "I see them, sir," said I, "some budding and some withered." 2. "These trees," said he, "which are budding are the righteous, who are destined to live in the world to come; for the world to come is summer for the righteous, but winter for the sinners. When therefore the mercy of the Lord shall shine, then the servants of God shall be made plain and all men shall be made apparent. 3 For, just as in the summer the fruit of each individual tree is made plain, and they are recognised for what they are, so also the fruit of the righteous will be plain, and they will all be known, by blossoming in that world. 4. But the heathen and the sinners—the withered

The budding and withered trees

149

τὰ ξηρά, τοιοῦτοι εὑρεθήσονται ξηροὶ καὶ ἄκαρποι
ἐν ἐκείνῳ τῷ αἰῶνι καὶ ὡς ξύλα κατακαυθήσονται
καὶ φανεροὶ ἔσονται, ὅτι ἡ πρᾶξις αὐτῶν
πονηρὰ γέγονεν ἐν τῇ ζωῇ αὐτῶν. οἱ μὲν γὰρ
ἁμαρτωλοὶ καυθήσονται, ὅτι ἥμαρτον καὶ οὐ
μετενόησαν· τὰ δὲ ἔθνη καυθήσονται, ὅτι οὐκ
ἔγνωσαν τὸν κτίσαντα αὐτούς. 5. σὺ οὖν καρπο-
φόρησον, ἵνα ἐν τῷ θέρει ἐκείνῳ γνωσθῇ σου ὁ
καρπός· ἀπέχου δὲ ἀπὸ πολλῶν πράξεων καὶ οὐδὲν
διαμαρτήσεις. οἱ γὰρ τὰ πολλὰ πράσσοντες πολλὰ
καὶ ἁμαρτάνουσι, περισπώμενοι περὶ τὰς πράξεις
αὐτῶν καὶ μηδὲν[1] δουλεύοντες τῷ κυρίῳ ἑαυτῶν.
6. πῶς οὖν, φησίν, ὁ τοιοῦτος δύναταί τι αἰτή-
σασθαι παρὰ τοῦ κυρίου καὶ λαβεῖν, μὴ δουλεύων
τῷ κυρίῳ; οἱ δουλεύοντες αὐτῷ, ἐκεῖνοι λήψονται
τὰ αἰτήματα αὐτῶν. οἱ δὲ μὴ δουλεύοντες τῷ
κυρίῳ, ἐκεῖνοι οὐδὲν λήψονται. 7. ἐὰν δὲ μίαν
τις πρᾶξιν ἐργάσηται, δύναται καὶ τῷ κυρίῳ
δουλεῦσαι· οὐ γὰρ διαφθαρήσεται ἡ διάνοια
αὐτοῦ ἀπὸ τοῦ κυρίου, ἀλλὰ δουλεύσει αὐτῷ
ἔχων τὴν διάνοιαν αὐτοῦ καθαράν. 8. ταῦτα οὖν
ἐὰν ποιήσῃς, δύνασαι καρποφορῆσαι εἰς τὸν
αἰῶνα τὸν ἐρχόμενον· καὶ ὃς ἂν ταῦτα ποιήσῃ,
καρποφορήσει.

Ἄλλη παραβολή

I

1. Νηστεύων καὶ καθήμενος εἰς ὄρος τι κα
εὐχαριστῶν τῷ κυρίῳ περὶ πάντων ὧν ἐποίησε

[1] μηδέν A, μηδέ L.

trees which you saw—will be found to be such, dried and fruitless in that world, and they shall be burnt up like wood and shall be made manifest, because their conduct was wicked in their lives. For the sinners shall be burnt, because they sinned and did not repent, and the heathen shall be burnt, because they did not know their Creator. 5. Be therefore fruitful, that your fruit may be known in that summer. But abstain from much business, and you will do no sin. For those who do much business also sin much, being engrossed in their business, and serving their Lord in nothing. 6. How then," said he, " can such a one pray for anything from the Lord and receive it, when he does not serve the Lord ? " They who serve him,—they shall receive their requests. But they who do not serve the Lord,—they shall receive nothing. 7. But if anyone be occupied with but one business, he can serve the Lord also. For his understanding is not corrupted away from the Lord, but he will serve him with a pure mind. 8. If, therefore, you do this, you can bear fruit for the world to come. And whoever does this shall bear fruit."

ANOTHER PARABLE (V)

I

1. WHILE I was fasting, and sitting on a certain Fasting mountain, and thanking the Lord for all that he had

μετ᾽ ἐμοῦ, βλέπω τὸν ποιμένα παρακαθήμενόν μοι καὶ λέγοντα· Τί ὀρθρινὸς ὧδε ἐλήλυθας; Ὅτι, φημί, κύριε, στατίωνα ἔχω. 2. Τί, φησίν, ἐστὶ στατίων; Νηστεύω, φημί, κύριε. Νηστεία δὲ, φησί, τί ἐστιν αὕτη, ἣν νηστεύετε; Ὡς εἰώθειν, φημί, κύριε, οὕτω νηστεύω. 3. Οὐκ οἴδατε, φησί, νηστεύειν τῷ κυρίῳ, οὐδέ ἐστιν νηστεία αὕτη ἡ ἀνωφελής, ἣν νηστεύετε αὐτῷ. Διατί, φημί, κύριε, τοῦτο λέγεις; Λέγω σοι, φησίν, ὅτι οὐκ ἔστιν αὕτη νηστεία, ἣν δοκεῖτε νηστεύειν· ἀλλ᾽ ἐγώ σε διδάξω, τί ἐστι νηστεία δεκτὴ καὶ πλήρης τῷ κυρίῳ.[1] Ἄκουε, φησίν. 4. ὁ θεὸς οὐ βούλεται τοιαύτην νηστείαν ματαίαν· οὕτω γὰρ νηστεύων τῷ θεῷ οὐδὲν ἐργάσῃ τῇ δικαιοσύνῃ. νήστευσον δὲ τῷ θεῷ νηστείαν τοιαύτην· 5. μηδὲν πονηρεύσῃ ἐν τῇ ζωῇ σου, ἀλλὰ δούλευσον τῷ κυρίῳ ἐν καθαρᾷ καρδίᾳ· τήρησον τὰς ἐντολὰς αὐτοῦ πορευόμενος ἐν τοῖς προστάγμασιν αὐτοῦ καὶ μηδεμία ἐπιθυμία πονηρὰ ἀναβήτω ἐν τῇ καρδίᾳ σου· πίστευσον δὲ τῷ θεῷ, ὅτι, ἐὰν ταῦτα ἐργάσῃ καὶ φοβηθῇς αὐτὸν καὶ ἐγκρατεύσῃ ἀπὸ παντὸς πονηροῦ πράγματος, ζήσῃ τῷ θεῷ· καὶ ταῦτα ἐὰν ἐργάσῃ, μεγάλην νηστείαν ποιήσεις καὶ δεκτὴν τῷ θεῷ.

Mt. 19, 17

---

[1] κυρίῳ AEL₂, κυρίῳ. Ναί, φημί, κύριε, μακάριόν με ποιήσεις ἐὰν γνῷ τὴν νηστείαν τὴν δεκτὴν τῷ θεῷ HL₂.

done with me, I saw the shepherd sitting by me, and saying: "Why have you come here so early?" "Because, sir," said I, "I have a station."[1] 2. "What," said he, "is a station." "I am fasting, sir," said I. "But," said he, "what is this fast, which you are fasting?" "I am fasting, sir," said I, "as I have been accustomed." 3. "You do not know," said he, "how to fast to the Lord, and this useless fast which you are fasting to him is not a fast?" "Why, sir," said I, "do you say this?" "I tell you," said he, "that this fast which you think to fast is nothing, but I will teach you what is a fast, acceptable and complete to the Lord. Listen," he said: 4. "God does not wish such a vain fast. For if you thus fast to God you do nothing for righteousness. But fast to God in this way: 5. do nothing evil in your life, but serve the Lord with a pure heart; 'keep his commandments' and walk in his ordinances, and let no evil desire arise in your heart, but believe in God, that if you do these things and fear him, and refrain from every wicked act, you shall live to God; and if you do this you will fulfil a great fast and one acceptable to God.

[1] 'Station' is not found elsewhere in Greek writers but is used in Latin writers in the sense of a fixed time for fasting (e.g. cf. Tertullian de orat. 19, de jejun. 1, 10, etc.). It is apparently one of the many terms taken from military language 'statio de militari exemplo nomen accepit, nam et militia dei sumus' says Tertullian.

II

1. Ἄκουε τὴν παραβολήν, ἣν μέλλω σοι λέγειν, ἀνήκουσαν τῇ νηστείᾳ. 2. εἶχέ τις ἀγρὸν καὶ δούλους πολλοὺς καὶ μέρος τι τοῦ ἀγροῦ ἐφύτευσεν ἀμπελῶνα· καὶ ἐκλεξάμενος δοῦλόν τινα πιστὸν καὶ εὐάρεστον ἔντιμον,[1] προσεκαλέσατο αὐτὸν καὶ λέγει αὐτῷ· Λάβε τὸν ἀμπελῶνα τοῦτον, ὃν ἐφύτευσα, καὶ χαράκωσον αὐτόν, ἕως ἔρχομαι, καὶ ἕτερον δὲ μὴ ποιήσῃς τῷ ἀμπελῶνι· καὶ ταύτην μου τὴν ἐντολὴν φύλαξον, καὶ ἐλεύθερος ἔσῃ παρ᾽ ἐμοί. ἐξῆλθε δε ὁ δεσπότης τοῦ δούλου εἰς τὴν ἀποδημίαν. 3. ἐξελθόντος δὲ αὐτοῦ ἔλαβεν ὁ δοῦλος καὶ ἐχαράκωσε τὸν ἀμπελῶνα. καὶ τελέσας τὴν χαράκωσιν τοῦ ἀμπελῶνος εἶδε τὸν ἀμπελῶνα βοτανῶν πλήρη ὄντα. 4. ἐν ἑαυτῷ οὖν ἐλογίσατο λέγων· Ταύτην τὴν ἐντολὴν τοῦ κυρίου τετέλεκα· σκάψω λοιπὸν τὸν ἀμπελῶνα τοῦτον, καὶ ἔσται εὐπρεπέστερος ἐσκαμμένος, καὶ βοτάνας μὴ ἔχων δώσει καρπὸν πλείονα, μὴ πνιγόμενος ὑπὸ τῶν βοτανῶν. λαβὼν ἔσκαψε τὸν ἀμπελῶνα καὶ πάσας τὰς βοτάνας τὰς οὔσας ἐν τῷ ἀμπελῶνι ἐξέτιλλε. καὶ ἐγένετο ὁ ἀμπελὼν ἐκεῖνος εὐπρεπέστατος καὶ εὐθαλής, μὴ ἔχων βοτάνας πνιγούσας αὐτόν. 5. μετὰ χρόνον ἦλθεν ὁ δεσπότης τοῦ δούλου καὶ τοῦ ἀγροῦ καὶ εἰσῆλθεν εἰς τὸν ἀμπελῶνα. καὶ ἰδὼν τὸν ἀμπελῶνα κεχαρακωμένον εὐπρεπῶς, ἔτι δὲ καὶ ἐσκαμ-

---

[1] There is probably something missing in the text : L₁ reads deinde peregre profectus elegit servum etc., EL₂ paraphrase the whole, but insert the phrase peregre afuturus, or its equivalent.

II

1. "LISTEN to the Parable which I am going to tell you concerning Fasting. 2. A certain man had a field, and many servants, and on part of the field he planted a vineyard. And he chose out a certain servant, who was faithful, in good esteem and honour with him, and he called him and said to him : " Take this vineyard which I have planted, and fence it until I come, and do nothing more to the vineyard. And follow this order of mine and you shall have your freedom from me. And the master of the servant went abroad. 3. Now when he had gone the servant took and fenced the vineyard, and when he had finished the fencing of the vineyard he saw that the vineyard was full of weeds. 4. Therefore he reasoned in himself, saying : I have finished this order of the Lord ; I will next dig this vineyard, and it will be better when it is dug, and having no weeds will yield more fruit, not being choked by the weeds. He took and dug the vineyard, and pulled out all the weeds which were in the vineyard. And that vineyard became very beautiful and fertile with no weeds to choke it. 5. After a time the master of the servant and the field came, and entered into the vineyard, and seeing the vineyard beautifully fenced, and moreover dug, and all the weeds pulled up and

The parable of Fasting

THE APOSTOLIC FATHERS

μένον καὶ πάσας τὰς βοτάνας ἐκτετιλμένας καὶ
εὐθαλεῖς οὔσας τὰς ἀμπέλους, ἐχάρη λίαν ἐπὶ τοῖς
ἔργοις τοῦ δούλου. 6. προσκαλεσάμενος οὖν τὸν
υἱὸν αὐτοῦ τὸν ἀγαπητόν, ὃν εἶχε κληρονόμον,
καὶ τοὺς φίλους, οὓς εἶχε συμβούλους, λέγει
αὐτοῖς, ὅσα ἐνετείλατο τῷ δούλῳ αὐτοῦ καὶ ὅσα
εὖρε γεγονότα. κἀκεῖνοι συνεχάρησαν τῷ δούλῳ
ἐπὶ τῇ μαρτυρίᾳ ᾗ ἐμαρτύρησεν αὐτῷ ὁ δεσπότης.
7. καὶ λέγει αὐτοῖς· Ἐγὼ τῷ δούλῳ τούτῳ ἐλευ-
θερίαν ἐπηγγειλάμην,[1] ἐάν μου τὴν ἐντολὴν
φυλάξῃ, ἣν ἐνετειλάμην αὐτῷ· ἐφύλαξε δέ μου
τὴν ἐντολὴν καὶ προσέθηκε τῷ ἀμπελῶνι ἔργον
καλόν, καὶ ἐμοὶ λίαν ἤρεσεν. ἀντὶ τούτου οὖν τοῦ
ἔργου οὗ εἰργάσατο θέλω αὐτὸν συγκληρονόμον
τῷ υἱῷ μου ποιῆσαι, ὅτι τὸ καλὸν φρονήσας
οὐ παρενεθυμήθη, ἀλλ' ἐτέλεσεν αὐτό. 8. ταύτῃ
τῇ γνώμῃ ὁ υἱὸς τοῦ δεσπότου συνηυδόκησεν
αὐτῷ, ἵνα συγκληρονόμος γένηται ὁ δοῦλος τῷ
υἱῷ. 9. μετὰ ἡμέρας ὀλίγας δεῖπνον ἐποίησεν[2]
καὶ ἔπεμψεν αὐτῷ ἐκ τοῦ δείπνου ἐδέσματα
πολλά. λαβὼν δὲ ὁ δοῦλος τὰ ἐδέσματα τὰ
πεμφθέντα αὐτῷ παρὰ τοῦ δεσπότου τὰ ἀρκοῦντα
αὐτῷ ἦρε, τὰ λοιπὰ δὲ τοῖς συνδούλοις αὐτοῦ
διέδωκεν. 10. οἱ δὲ σύνδουλοι αὐτοῦ λαβόντες
τὰ ἐδέσματα ἐχάρησαν καὶ ἤρξαντο εὔχεσθαι
ὑπὲρ αὐτοῦ, ἵνα χάριν μείζονα εὕρῃ παρὰ τῷ
δεσπότῃ, ὅτι οὕτως ἐχρήσατο αὐτοῖς. 11. ταῦτα
πάντα τὰ γεγονότα ὁ δεσπότης αὐτοῦ ἤκουσε

---

[1] ἐπηγγειλάμην A, Hilgenfeld and others emend to
ἐνετειλάμην.
[2] ἐποίησεν A, L adds paterfamilias which the editors
usually accept and translate οἰκοδεσπότης.

156

vines fertile, he was greatly pleased at the acts of the servant. 6. So he called his beloved son, whom he had as heir, and his friends whom he had as counsellors, and told them what he had ordered his servant, and what he had found accomplished. And they congratulated the servant on the character which the master gave him. 7. And he said to them : I promised this servant his freedom if he kept the orders which I gave him. Now he has kept my orders, and has added good work in the vineyard, and greatly pleased me. So in reward for this work which he has done I wish to make him joint heir with my son, because, when he had a good thought he did not put it on one side, but carried it out. 8. The son of the master agreed with this plan, that the servant should be joint heir with the son. 9. After a few days he made a feast and sent to him much food from the feast. But the servant took the food which was sent to him by the master, kept what was sufficient for himself, and distributed the rest to his fellow-servants. 10. And his fellow-servants were glad when they received the food, and began to pray for him, that he might find greater favour with his master, because he had treated them thus. 11. His master heard all these events, and again rejoiced

καὶ πάλιν λίαν ἐχάρη ἐπὶ τῇ πράξει αὐτοῦ.
συγκαλεσάμενος πάλιν τοὺς φίλους ὁ δεσπότης
καὶ τὸν υἱὸν αὐτοῦ ἀπήγγειλεν αὐτοῖς τὴν πρᾶξιν
αὐτοῦ, ἣν ἔπραξεν ἐπὶ τοῖς ἐδέσμασιν αὐτοῦ οἷς
ἔλαβεν· οἱ δὲ ἔτι μᾶλλον συνευδόκησαν γενέσθαι
τὸν δοῦλον συγκληρονόμον τῷ υἱῷ αὐτοῦ.

III

1. Λέγω· Κύριε, ἐγὼ ταύτας τὰς παραβολὰς
οὐ γινώσκω οὐδὲ δύναμαι νοῆσαι, ἐὰν μή μοι
ἐπιλύσῃς αὐτάς. 2. Πάντα σοι ἐπιλύσω, φησί,
καὶ ὅσα ἂν λαλήσω μετὰ σοῦ. 3. δείξω σοι
τὰς ἐντολὰς αὐτοῦ[1] ἐὰν δέ τι ἀγαθὸν ποιήσῃς
ἐκτὸς τῆς ἐντολῆς τοῦ θεοῦ, σεαυτῷ περιποιήσῃ
δόξαν περισσοτέραν καὶ ἔσῃ ἐνδοξότερος παρὰ
τῷ θεῷ οὗ ἔμελλες εἶναι. ἐὰν οὖν φυλάσσων
τὰς ἐντολὰς τοῦ θεοῦ προσθῇς καὶ τὰς λει-
τουργίας ταύτας, χαρήσῃ, ἐὰν τηρήσῃς αὐτὰς
κατὰ τὴν ἐμὴν ἐντολήν. 4. λέγω αὐτῷ· Κύριε,
ὃ ἐάν μοι ἐντείλῃ, φυλάξω αὐτό· οἶδα γάρ, ὅτι
σὺ μετ᾽ ἐμοῦ εἶ. Ἔσομαι, φησί, μετὰ σοῦ, ὅτι
τοιαύτην προθυμίαν ἔχεις τῆς ἀγαθοποιήσεως,
καὶ μετὰ πάντων δὲ ἔσομαι, φησίν, ὅσοι ταύτην
τὴν προθυμίαν ἔχουσιν. 5. ἡ νηστεία αὕτη, φησί,
τηρουμένων τῶν ἐντολῶν τοῦ κυρίου, λίαν καλή
ἐστιν. οὕτως οὖν φυλάξεις τὴν νηστείαν ταύτην,
ἣν μέλλεις τηρεῖν· 6. πρῶτον πάντων φύλαξαι

---

[1] τὰς ἐντολὰς αὐτοῦ. A, mandata domini custodi et eris
probatus et scriberis in numero eorum qui custodivit
mandata eius L₁(L₂E) which the editors usually accept and
re-translate into Greek.

greatly at his conduct. The master again assembled his friends and his son and reported to them what he had done with the food which he had received, and they were still more pleased that the servant should be made joint heir with his son."

III

1. I SAID : " Sir, I do not know these parables and I cannot understand them if you do not explain them to me." 2. " I will explain everything to you," he said, " and everything that I talk with you. 3. I will show you his commandments and if you do anything good, beyond the commandment of God, you will gain for yourself greater glory, and shall be more honourable with God than you were destined to be. If then, you keep the commandments of God, and add these services also, you shall rejoice, if you keep them according to my commandment." 4. I said to him : " Sir, I will keep whatever you command me, for I know that you are with me." " I will be with you," said he, " because you have such zeal for doing good, and I will be with all, said he, who have this zeal. 5. This fast," said he, " if the commandments of the Lord are kept, is very good. You shall therefore keep this fast, which you are going to observe in this way : 6. First of all, keep from every

The application of the parable to Fasting

ἀπὸ παντὸς ῥήματος πονηροῦ καὶ πάσης ἐπιθυμίας
πονηρᾶς καὶ καθάρισόν σου τὴν καρδίαν ἀπὸ
πάντων τῶν ματαιωμάτων τοῦ αἰῶνος τούτου.
ἐὰν ταῦτα φυλάξῃς, ἔσται σοι αὕτη ἡ νηστεία
τελεία.   7. οὕτω δὲ ποιήσεις· συντελέσας τὰ
γεγραμμένα, ἐν ἐκείνῃ τῇ ἡμέρᾳ ᾗ νηστεύεις μηδὲν
γεύσῃ εἰ μὴ ἄρτον καὶ ὕδωρ, καὶ ἐκ τῶν ἐδεσμάτων
σου ὧν ἔμελλες τρώγειν συμψηφίσας τὴν ποσό-
τητα τῆς δαπάνης ἐκείνης τῆς ἡμέρας ἧς ἔμελλες
ποιεῖν, δώσεις αὐτὸ χήρᾳ ἢ ὀρφανῷ ἢ ὑστερουμένῳ,
καὶ οὕτω ταπεινοφρονήσεις, ἵν᾽ ἐκ τῆς ταπεινοφροσύνης σου ὁ εἰληφὼς ἐμπλήσῃ τὴν ἑαυτοῦ ψυχὴν
καὶ εὔξηται ὑπὲρ σοῦ πρὸς τὸν κύριον.   8. ἐὰν
οὖν οὕτω τελέσῃς τὴν νηστείαν, ὥς σοι ἐνετειλάμην, ἔσται ἡ θυσία σου δεκτὴ παρὰ τῷ θεῷ,[1] καὶ
ἔγγραφος ἔσται ἡ νηστεία αὕτη, καὶ ἡ λειτουργία
οὕτως ἐργαζομένη καλὴ καὶ ἱλαρά ἐστι καὶ εὐπρός-
δεκτος τῷ κυρίῳ.   9. ταῦτα οὕτω τηρήσεις σὺ
μετὰ τῶν τέκνων σου καὶ ὅλου τοῦ οἴκου σου·
τηρήσας δὲ αὐτὰ μακάριος ἔσῃ· καὶ ὅσοι ἂν
ἀκούσαντες αὐτὰ τηρήσωσι, μακάριοι ἔσονται, καὶ
ὅσα ἂν αἰτήσωνται παρὰ τοῦ κυρίου λήψονται.

Ecclus. 32, 9
(Vulg. 35. 9);
Philipp. 4,
18, cf. Is. 56,
7 ; etc.

IV

1. Ἐδεήθην αὐτοῦ πολλά, ἵνα μοι δηλώσῃ τὴν
παραβολὴν τοῦ ἀγροῦ καὶ τοῦ δεσπότου καὶ τοῦ
ἀμπελῶνος καὶ τοῦ δούλου τοῦ χαρακώσαντος τὸν
ἀμπελῶνα καὶ τῶν χαράκων καὶ τῶν βοτανῶν
τῶν ἐκτετιλμένων ἐκ τοῦ ἀμπελῶνος καὶ τοῦ υἱοῦ

[1] θεῷ A Ant., κυρίῳ L Ath.

evil word, and from every evil desire and purify your heart from all the vanities of this world. If you keep these things, this fast shall be perfect for you. 7. And you shall do thus: After completing what has been written, in that day on which you fast you shall taste nothing except bread and water, and you shall reckon the price of the expense for that day which you are going to keep, of the foods which you would have eaten, and you shall give it to a widow or an orphan or to some one destitute, and you shall thus be humble-minded that through your humility he who receives it may fill his soul and pray to the Lord for you. 8. If then you thus fulfil the fast as I commanded you, your ' sacrifice shall be acceptable to God,' and this fast shall be written down to your credit, and the service which is thus done is good and joyful and acceptable to the Lord. 9. You shall therefore keep these things thus with your children and all your house, and if you keep them you shall be blessed, and all who hear them and keep them shall be blessed and shall obtain from the Lord whatever they ask."

IV.

1. I BESOUGHT him much to explain to me the parable of the field and the master and the vineyard and the servant who fenced the vineyard, and the fences, and the weeds which were pulled up from the vineyard, and the son, and the friends the counsellors.

The application of the parable as to the servant

καὶ τῶν φίλων τῶν συμβούλων· συνῆκα γάρ, ὅτι
παραβολή τίς ἐστι ταῦτα πάντα. 2. ὁ δὲ ἀποκριθείς μοι εἶπεν· Αὐθάδης εἶ λίαν εἰς τὸ ἐπερωτᾶν.
οὐκ ὀφείλεις, φησίν, ἐπερωτᾶν οὐδὲν ὅλως· ἐὰν
γάρ σοι δέῃ δηλωθῆναι, δηλωθήσεται. λέγω
αὐτῷ· Κύριε, ὅσα ἄν μοι δείξῃς καὶ μὴ δηλώσῃς,
μάτην ἔσομαι ἑωρακὼς αὐτὰ καὶ μὴ νοῶν, τί ἐστιν·
ὡσαύτως καὶ ἐάν μοι παραβολὰς λαλήσῃς καὶ μὴ
ἐπιλύσῃς μοι αὐτάς, εἰς μάτην ἔσομαι ἀκηκοώς τι
παρὰ σοῦ. 3. ὁ δὲ πάλιν ἀπεκρίθη μοι λέγων·
Ὃς ἄν, φησί, δοῦλος ᾖ τοῦ θεοῦ καὶ ἔχῃ τὸν
κύριον ἑαυτοῦ ἐν τῇ καρδίᾳ, αἰτεῖται παρ' αὐτοῦ
σύνεσιν καὶ λαμβάνει καὶ πᾶσαν παραβολὴν
ἐπιλύει, καὶ γνωστὰ αὐτῷ γίνονται τὰ ῥήματα
τοῦ κυρίου τὰ λεγόμενα διὰ παραβολῶν· ὅσοι δὲ
βληχροί εἰσι καὶ ἀργοὶ πρὸς τὴν ἔντευξιν, ἐκεῖνοι
διστάζουσιν αἰτεῖσθαι παρὰ τοῦ κυρίου· 4. ὁ δὲ
κύριος πολυεύσπλαγχνός ἐστι καὶ πᾶσι τοῖς
αἰτουμένοις παρ' αὐτοῦ ἀδιαλείπτως δίδωσι. σὺ
δὲ ἐνδεδυναμωμένος ὑπὸ τοῦ ἁγίου ἀγγέλου καὶ
εἰληφὼς παρ' αὐτοῦ τοιαύτην ἔντευξιν καὶ μὴ ὢν
ἀργός, διατί οὐκ αἰτῇ παρὰ τοῦ κυρίου σύνεσιν
καὶ λαμβάνεις παρ' αὐτοῦ; 5. λέγω αὐτῷ· Κύριε,
ἐγὼ ἔχων σὲ μεθ' ἑαυτοῦ ἀνάγκην ἔχω σὲ
αἰτεῖσθαι καὶ σὲ ἐπερωτᾶν· σὺ γάρ μοι δεικνύεις
πάντα καὶ λαλεῖς μετ' ἐμοῦ· εἰ δὲ ἄτερ σου
ἔβλεπον ἢ ἤκουον αὐτά, ἠρώτων ἂν τὸν κύριον, ἵνα
μοι δηλωθῇ.

For I understood that all these things are a parable.
2. He answered and said to me: " You are very importunate with asking. You ought not," he said, " to
ask at all, for if it be necessary for it to be explained
to you it will be explained." I said to him: " Sir,
whatever you show me and do not explain I shall have
seen in vain, and not understand what it is. So likewise if you speak parables to me and do not interpret them to me, I shall have heard something from
you in vain." 3. He answered and said to me again:
" Whoever," said he, " is God's servant, and has his
Lord in his heart, seeks understanding from him and
receives it, and he interprets every parable, and the
sayings of the Lord which were spoken through
parables are made known to him. But as many as
are weak and idle in prayer, those hesitate to ask
from the Lord. 4. But the Lord is very merciful
and gives unceasingly to all who ask from him.
But you, since you have been given power by the
Holy Angel, and received from him such intercession and are not idle, wherefore do you not seek
understanding from the Lord and receive it from
him?" 5. I said to him: " Sir, when I have you
with me I needs must ask you and enquire of
you, for you show me all things and talk with
me, but if I had seen or heard them without
you, I should have asked the Lord that it might
be explained to me."

V

1. Εἰπόν σοι, φησί, καὶ ἄρτι, ὅτι πανοῦργος εἶ καὶ αὐθάδης, ἐπερωτῶν τὰς ἐπιλύσεις τῶν παραβολῶν. ἐπειδὴ δὲ οὕτω παράμονος εἶ, ἐπιλύσω σοι τὴν παραβολὴν τοῦ ἀγροῦ καὶ τῶν λοιπῶν τῶν ἀκολούθων πάντων, ἵνα γνωστὰ πᾶσι ποιήσῃς αὐτά. ἄκουε νῦν, φησί, καὶ σύνιε αὐτά. 2. ὁ ἀγρὸς ὁ κόσμος οὗτός ἐστιν· ὁ δὲ κύριος τοῦ ἀγροῦ ὁ κτίσας τὰ πάντα καὶ ἀπαρτίσας αὐτὰ καὶ δυναμώσας·[1] ὁ δὲ δοῦλος ὁ υἱὸς τοῦ θεοῦ ἐστιν· αἱ δὲ ἄμπελοι ὁ λαὸς οὗτός ἐστιν, ὃν αὐτὸς ἐφύτευσεν· 3. οἱ δὲ χάρακες οἱ ἅγιοι ἄγγελοί εἰσι τοῦ κυρίου οἱ συγκρατοῦντες τὸν λαὸν αὐτοῦ· αἱ δὲ βοτάναι αἱ ἐκτετιλμέναι ἐκ τοῦ ἀμπελῶνος ἀνομίαι εἰσὶ τῶν δούλων τοῦ θεοῦ· τὰ δὲ ἐδέσματα, ἃ ἔπεμψεν αὐτῷ ἐκ τοῦ δείπνου, αἱ ἐντολαί εἰσιν, ἃς ἔδωκε τῷ λαῷ αὐτοῦ διὰ τοῦ υἱοῦ αὐτοῦ· οἱ δὲ φίλοι καὶ σύμβουλοι οἱ ἅγιοι ἄγγελοι οἱ πρῶτοι κτισθέντες· ἡ δὲ ἀποδημία τοῦ δεσπότου ὁ χρόνος ὁ περισσεύων εἰς τὴν παρουσίαν αὐτοῦ. 4. λέγω αὐτῷ· Κύριε, μεγάλως καὶ θαυμαστῶς πάντα ἐστὶ καὶ ἐνδόξως πάντα ἔχει. μὴ οὖν, φημί, ἐγὼ ἠδυνάμην ταῦτα νοῆσαι; οὐδὲ ἕτερος τῶν ἀνθρώπων, κἂν λίαν συνετὸς ᾖ τις, οὐ δύναται νοῆσαι αὐτά. ἔτι, φημί, κύριε, δήλωσόν μοι, ὃ μέλλω σε ἐπερωτᾶν. 5. Λέγε, φησίν, εἴ τι βούλει. Διατί, φημί, κύριε, ὁ υἱὸς τοῦ θεοῦ εἰς δούλου τρόπον κεῖται ἐν τῇ παραβολῇ;

Mt. 13, 38
Eph. 3, 9
Cf. Ps. 68, 28

---

[1] L₁ adds filius autem spiritus sanctus est. Cf. Sim. ix. 1. 1, 'ἐκεῖνο γὰρ τὸ πνεῦμα ὁ υἱὸς τοῦ θεοῦ ἐστιν.'

V

1. "I TOLD you," said he, "just now, that you The further application are obstinate and importunate in asking for the explanations of the parable. But since you are so persistent I will explain to you the parable of the field and all the other consequences of it, that you may make them known to everyone. Listen, now," he said, "and understand it. 2. 'The field is this world,' and the Lord of the field is 'He who created everything' and perfected it and gave it strength. And the servant is the Son of God,[1] and the vines are this people which he planted. 3. And the fences are the holy Angels of the Lord who support his people. And the weeds which are pulled up out of the vineyard are iniquities of the servants of God. And the food which he sent to him from the supper is the commandments which he gave to his people through his Son, and the friends and counsellors are the holy Angels who were first created. And the absence of the Master[2] is the time which remains before his coming." 4. I said to him: "Sir, all is great and wonderful and all is glorious. How then," said I, "could I understand it? Nor is there any other man, however understanding he may be, who can understand it. Moreover, sir," said I, "explain to me what I am going to ask you." 5. "Say," said he, "what you wish." "Why," said I, "sir, is the Son of God in the parable given the form of a servant?"

[1] With the text given it must be noted that the Son in the parable (Sim. v. ii. 6.) remains unexplained.

[2] The absence of the Master is not mentioned in the text of the parable; but see the critical note on Sim. v. 2, 2.

VI

1. Ἄκουε, φησίν· εἰς δούλου τρόπον οὐ[2] κεῖται ὁ υἱὸς τοῦ θεοῦ, ἀλλ' εἰς ἐξουσίαν μεγάλην κεῖται καὶ κυριότητα. Πῶς, φημί, κύριε, οὐ νοῶ. 2. Ὅτι, φησίν, ὁ θεὸς τὸν ἀμπελῶνα ἐφύτευσε, τοῦτ' ἔστι τὸν λαὸν ἔκτισε καὶ παρέδωκε τῷ υἱῷ αὐτοῦ· καὶ ὁ υἱὸς κατέστησε τοὺς ἀγγέλους ἐπ' αὐτοὺς τοῦ συντηρεῖν αὐτούς· καὶ αὐτὸς τὰς ἁμαρτίας αὐτῶν ἐκαθάρισε πολλὰ κοπιάσας καὶ πολλοὺς κόπους ἠντληκώς· οὐδεὶς γὰρ ἀμπελὼν δύναται σκαφῆναι ἄτερ κόπου ἢ μόχθου. 3. αὐτὸς οὖν καθαρίσας τὰς ἁμαρτίας τοῦ λαοῦ ἔδειξεν αὐτοῖς τὰς τρίβους τῆς ζωῆς, δοὺς αὐτοῖς τὸν νόμον, ὃν ἔλαβε παρὰ τοῦ πατρὸς αὐτοῦ.[2] 4. ὅτι δὲ ὁ κύριος σύμβουλον ἔλαβε τὸν υἱὸν αὐτοῦ καὶ τοὺς ἐνδόξους ἀγγέλους περὶ τῆς κληρονομίας τοῦ δούλου, ἄκουε· 5. τὸ πνεῦμα τὸ ἅγιον τὸ προόν, τὸ κτίσαν πᾶσαν τὴν κτίσιν, κατῴκισεν ὁ θεὸς εἰς σάρκα, ἣν ἠβούλετο· αὕτη οὖν ἡ σάρξ, ἐν ᾗ κατῴκησε τὸ πνεῦμα τὸ ἅγιον, ἐδούλευσε τῷ πνεύματι καλῶς ἐν σεμνότητι καὶ ἁγνείᾳ πορευθεῖσα, μηδὲν ὅλως μιάνασα τὸ πνεῦμα. 6. πολιτευσαμένην οὖν αὐτὴν καλῶς καὶ ἁγνῶς καὶ συγκοπιάσασαν τῷ πνεύματι καὶ συνεργήσασαν ἐν παντὶ πράγματι, ἰσχυρῶς καὶ ἀνδρείως ἀναστραφεῖσαν, μετὰ τοῦ πνεύματος τοῦ ἁγίου εἵλατο κοινωνόν· ἤρεσε γὰρ[3] ἡ

Ps. 15, 11 ;
Prov. 16, 17

Joh. 10, 18 ;
12, 49. 50 ;
14, 31
15, 10

---

[1] οὐ LE, om. A.

[2] L adds vides inquit dominum eum esse populi accepta a patre suo omni potestate, which the Editors are inclined to accept.   [3] ἤρεσε A, ἤρεσε τῷ θεῷ (or τῷ Κυρίῳ) L₁L₂.

VI

1. " LISTEN," said he: "The Son of God is not The son of God as given the form of a servant, but is given great servant power and lordship." "How, sir?" said I, "I do not understand." 2. "Because God planted the vineyard," said he, "that is, created the people, and gave it over to his Son. And the Son appointed the angels over them to keep them. And he himself cleansed their sins, labouring much and undergoing much toil. For no vineyard can be dug without toil or labour. 3. When, therefore, he had cleansed the sins of the people, he showed them the ways of life, and gave them the law which he 'received from his Father.' 4. But listen why the Lord took his Son and the glorious angels as counsellors concerning the heritage of the servant. 5. The Holy Spirit which pre-exists, which created all creation, did God make to dwell in the flesh which he willed. Therefore this flesh, in which the Holy Spirit dwelled, served the Spirit well, walking in holiness and purity, and did not in any way defile the spirit. 6. When, therefore, it had lived nobly and purely, and had laboured with the Spirit, and worked with it in every deed, behaving with power and bravery, he chose it as companion with the Holy Spirit[1]; for the conduct

---

[1] The meaning is apparently that the flesh (i.e. the human being?), in which the Spirit had been incarnate, was elevated to be the companion, for the future, of the Father and of the Son who is the Spirit.

πορεία τῆς σαρκὸς ταύτης, ὅτι οὐκ ἐμιάνθη
ἐπὶ τῆς γῆς ἔχουσα τὸ πνεῦμα τὸ ἅγιον.
7. σύμβουλον οὖν ἔλαβε τὸν υἱὸν καὶ τοὺς
ἀγγέλους τοὺς ἐνδόξους, ἵνα καὶ ἡ σὰρξ αὕτη,
δουλεύσασα τῷ πνεύματι ἀμέμπτως, σχῇ τόπον
τινὰ κατασκηνώσεως καὶ μὴ δόξῃ τὸν μισθὸν
τῆς δουλείας αὐτῆς ἀπολωλεκέναι· πᾶσα γὰρ
σὰρξ ἀπολήψεται μισθὸν[1] ἡ εὑρεθεῖσα ἀμίαντος
καὶ ἄσπιλος, ἐν ᾗ τὸ πνεῦμα τὸ ἅγιον κατῴκησεν.
8. ἔχεις καὶ ταύτης τῆς παραβολῆς τὴν ἐπίλυσιν.

VII

1. Ηὐφράνθην, φημί, κύριε, ταύτην τὴν ἐπίλυσιν ἀκούσας. Ἄκουε νῦν, φησί· τὴν σάρκα σου
ταύτην φύλασσε καθαρὰν καὶ ἀμίαντον, ἵνα
τὸ πνεῦμα τὸ κατοικοῦν ἐν αὐτῇ μαρτυρήσῃ
αὐτῇ καὶ δικαιωθῇ σου ἡ σάρξ. 2. βλέπε,
μήποτε ἀναβῇ ἐπὶ τὴν καρδίαν σου τὴν σάρκα
σου ταύτην φθαρτὴν εἶναι καὶ παραχρήσῃ
αὐτῇ ἐν μιασμῷ τινί. ἐὰν μιάνῃς τὴν σάρκα σου,
μιανεῖς καὶ τὸ πνεῦμα τὸ ἅγιον· ἐὰν δὲ μιάνῃς τὴν
σάρκα,[2] οὐ ζήσῃ. 3. Εἰ δέ τις, φημί, κύριε,
γέγονεν ἄγνοια προτέρα, πρὶν ἀκουσθῶσι τὰ ῥήματα ταῦτα, πῶς σωθῇ ὁ ἄνθρωπος ὁ μιάνας τὴν
σάρκα αὐτοῦ; Περὶ τῶν προτέρων, φησίν, ἀγνοη-
μάτων τῷ θεῷ μόνῳ δυνατὸν ἴασιν δοῦναι, αὐτοῦ

---

[1] τῆς δουλείας . . . μισθόν om. A. The text is reconstructed
from L.
[2] σάρκα ALE, but the editors usually emend to τὸ πνεῦμα
in the supposed interests of the sense.

of this flesh pleased him, because it was not defiled while it was bearing the Holy Spirit on earth. 7. Therefore he took the Son and the glorious angels as counsellors, that this flesh also, having served the Spirit blamelessly, should have some place of sojourn, and not seem to have lost the reward of its service. For all flesh in which the Holy Spirit has dwelt shall receive a reward if it be found undefiled and spotless. 8. You have the explanation of this parable also."

VII

1. " I am glad, sir," said I, "to hear this explanation." "Listen, now," he said. "Guard this flesh of yours, pure and undefiled, that the spirit which dwells in it may bear it witness, and your flesh may be justified. 2. See to it, lest the idea enter your heart that this flesh of yours is mortal, and you abuse it in some defilement. For if you defile your flesh you defile also the Holy Spirit, and if you defile the flesh you shall not live." 3. "But, if, sir," said I, "there was any previous ignorance before these words were heard, how can the man who defiled his flesh be saved?" "For the former ignorances," said he, "it is possible for God

The practical conclusion

Mt. 28, 18 γάρ ἐστι πᾶσα ἐξουσία,[1] 4. ἐὰν τὸ λοιπὸν μὴ
μιάνῃς σου τὴν σάρκα μηδὲ τὸ πνεῦμα· ἀμφότερα
γὰρ κοινά ἐστι καὶ ἄτερ ἀλλήλων μιανθῆναι οὐ
δύναται. ἀμφότερα οὖν καθαρὰ φύλασσε, καὶ
ζήσῃ τῷ θεῷ.

Παραβολὴ ϛ′

I

1. Καθήμενος ἐν τῷ οἴκῳ μου καὶ δοξάζων τὸν
κύριον περὶ πάντων ὧν ἑωράκειν καὶ συζητῶν
Jam. 1, 21 περὶ τῶν ἐντολῶν, ὅτι καλαὶ καὶ δυναταὶ καὶ
ἱλαραὶ καὶ ἔνδοξοι καὶ δυνάμεναι σῶσαι ψυχὴν
Ps. 1, 1-2;
119, 1 ἀνθρώπου, ἔλεγον ἐν ἐμαυτῷ· Μακάριος ἔσομαι,
ἐὰν ταῖς ἐντολαῖς ταύταις πορευθῶ, καὶ ὃς ἂν
ταύταις πορευθῇ, μακάριος ἔσται. 2. ὡς ταῦτα
ἐν ἐμαυτῷ ἐλάλουν, βλέπω αὐτὸν ἐξαίφνης
παρακαθήμενόν μοι καὶ λέγοντα ταῦτα· Τί
διψυχεῖς περὶ τῶν ἐντολῶν ὧν σοι ἐνετειλάμην;
καλαί εἰσιν· ὅλως μὴ διψυχήσῃς, ἀλλ' ἔνδυσαι
τὴν πίστιν τοῦ κυρίου, καὶ ἐν αὐταῖς πορεύσῃ·
ἐγὼ γάρ σε ἐνδυναμώσω ἐν αὐταῖς. 3. αὗται αἱ
ἐντολαὶ σύμφοροί εἰσι τοῖς μέλλουσι μετανοεῖν·
ἐὰν γὰρ μὴ πορευθῶσιν ἐν αὐταῖς, εἰς μάτην ἐστὶν
ἡ μετάνοια αὐτῶν. 4. οἱ οὖν μετανοοῦντες ἀπο-
βάλλετε τὰς πονηρίας τοῦ αἰῶνος τούτου τὰς
ἐκτριβούσας ὑμᾶς· ἐνδυσάμενοι δὲ πᾶσαν ἀρετὴν

---

[1] L (A) add (with some variations) sed nunc custodi te, et
cum sit dominus omnipotens misericors, prioribus admissis
remedium dabit. The editors (probably rightly) usually
accept this addition.

alone to give healing, for 'he has all power,' 4. if, for the future, you defile neither the flesh nor the spirit; for both are in communion, and neither can be defiled without the other. Keep, therefore, both pure, and you shall live to God." [1]

PARABLE 6

I

1. WHILE I was seated in my house, and was glorifying the Lord for all that I had seen, and enquiring about the commandments because they were beautiful and joyful and glorious, and 'able to save the soul' of man, I said in myself: I shall be blessed if I 'walk in these commandments,' and whoever shall walk in them shall be blessed. 2. While I said this in myself I suddenly saw him seated by me, and saying this: "Why are you double-minded concerning the commandments which I commanded you? They are beautiful. Be not double-minded at all, but put on the faith of the Lord, and you shall walk in them, for I will strengthen you in them. 3. These commandments are helpful to those who are going to repent, for if they do not walk in them their repentance is in vain. 4. Do you, therefore, who repent, put away the wickednesses of this world which lead you astray, but if you put on all the virtue of righteous-

Intro-
duction

---

[1] This is directed against the Gnostic tendency to divide flesh and spirit, and to regard the acts of the flesh as unimportant. Against this the church insisted on purity of life now, and on the hope of a resurrection of the flesh hereafter.

171

δικαιοσύνης δυνήσεσθε τηρῆσαι τὰς ἐντολὰς ταύτας
καὶ μηκέτι προστιθέναι ταῖς ἁμαρτίαις ὑμῶν.[1]
πορεύεσθε οὖν ταῖς ἐντολαῖς μου ταύταις, καὶ
ζήσεσθε τῷ θεῷ. ταῦτα πάντα παρ' ἐμοῦ λελά-
ληται ὑμῖν. 5. καὶ μετὰ τὸ ταῦτα λαλῆσαι αὐτὸν
μετ' ἐμοῦ, λέγει μοι· Ἄγωμεν εἰς ἀγρόν, καὶ δείξω
σοι τοὺς ποιμένας τῶν προβάτων. Ἄγωμεν, φημί,
κύριε. καὶ ἤλθομεν εἴς τι πεδίον, καὶ δεικνύει μοι
ποιμένα νεανίσκον ἐνδεδυμένον σύνθεσιν ἱματίων τῷ
χρώματι κροκώδη. 6. ἔβοσκε δὲ πρόβατα πολλὰ
λίαν, καὶ τὰ πρόβατα ταῦτα ὡσεὶ τρυφῶντα ἦν
καὶ λίαν σπαταλῶντα καὶ ἱλαρὰ ἦν σκιρτῶντα
ὧδε κἀκεῖσε· καὶ αὐτὸς ὁ ποιμὴν πάνυ ἱλαρὸς ἦν
ἐπὶ τῷ ποιμνίῳ αὐτοῦ· καὶ αὐτὴ ἡ ἰδέα τοῦ
ποιμένος ἱλαρὰ ἦν λίαν, καὶ ἐν τοῖς προβάτοις
περιέτρεχε.

II

1. Καὶ λέγει μοι· Βλέπεις τὸν ποιμένα τοῦτον;
Βλέπω, φημί, κύριε. Οὗτος, φησίν, ἄγγελος τρυφῆς καὶ ἀπάτης ἐστίν. οὗτος ἐκτρίβει τὰς ψυχὰς
τῶν δούλων τοῦ θεοῦ καὶ καταστρέφει αὐτοὺς ἀπὸ
τῆς ἀληθείας, ἀπατῶν αὐτοὺς ταῖς ἐπιθυμίαις ταῖς
πονηραῖς, ἐν αἷς ἀπόλλυνται. 2. ἐπιλανθάνονται
γὰρ τῶν ἐντολῶν τοῦ θεοῦ τοῦ ζῶντος καὶ πορεύονται ἀπάταις καὶ τρυφαῖς ματαίαις καὶ ἀπόλλυνται ὑπὸ τοῦ ἀγγέλου τούτου, τινὰ μὲν εἰς
θάνατον, τινὰ δὲ εἰς καταφθοράν. 3. λέγω αὐτῷ

---

[1] L adds nihil ergo adicientes plurimum ex prioribus
recidetis.

ness, you shall be able to keep these commandments, and no longer add to your sins. Therefore walk in these commandments of mine, and you shall live to God. All these things have been spoken to you by me." 5. And after he spoke these things with me, he said to me: "Let us go into the country, and I will show you the shepherds of the sheep." "Let us go, sir," said I. And we came into a plain, and he showed me a young shepherd, clothed with a suit of garments of yellow colour. 6. And he was feeding very many sheep, and these sheep were well fed and very frisky, and were glad as they skipped here and there. And the shepherd himself was very joyful over his flock, and the face of the shepherd was very joyful, and he ran about among the sheep.

II

1. AND he said to me: "Do you see this shepherd?" "Yes, sir," said I, "I see him." "This," said he, "is the angel of luxury and deceit. He wears out the souls of the servants of God, and perverts them from the truth, deceiving them with evil desires in which they perish. 2. For they forget the commandments of the Living God, and walk in deceit and vain luxury, and are destroyed by this angel, some to death, and some to corruption." 3. I said to him: "Sir, I do not know what is ' to

THE APOSTOLIC FATHERS

Κύριε, οὐ γινώσκω ἐγώ, τί ἐστιν εἰς θάνατον καὶ τί εἰς καταφθοράν. Ἄκουε, φησίν· ἃ εἶδες πρόβατα ἱλαρὰ καὶ σκιρτῶντα, οὗτοί εἰσιν οἱ ἀπεσπασμένοι ἀπὸ τοῦ θεοῦ εἰς τέλος καὶ παραδεδωκότες ἑαυτοὺς ταῖς ἐπιθυμίαις τοῦ αἰῶνος τούτου. ἐν τούτοις οὖν μετάνοια ζωῆς οὐκ ἔστιν, ὅτι προσέθηκαν ταῖς ἁμαρτίαις αὐτῶν καὶ εἰς τὸ ὄνομα τοῦ θεοῦ ἐβλασφήμησαν. τῶν τοιούτων οὖν ὁ θάνατός ἐστιν. 4. ἃ δὲ εἶδες πρόβατα μὴ σκιρτῶντα, ἀλλ' ἐν τόπῳ ἑνὶ βοσκόμενα, οὗτοί εἰσιν οἱ παραδεδωκότες μὲν ἑαυτοὺς[1] ταῖς τρυφαῖς καὶ ἀπάταις, εἰς δὲ τὸν κύριον οὐδὲν ἐβλασφήμησαν· οὗτοι οὖν κατεφθαρμένοι εἰσὶν ἀπὸ τῆς ἀληθείας. ἐν τούτοις ἐλπίς ἐστι μετανοίας, ἐν ᾗ δύνανται ζῆσαι. ἡ καταφθορὰ οὖν ἐλπίδα ἔχει ἀνανεώσεώς τινος, ὁ δὲ θάνατος ἀπώλειαν ἔχει αἰώνιον. 5. πάλιν προέβην[2] μικρόν, καὶ δεικνύει μοι ποιμένα μέγαν ὡσεὶ ἄγριον τῇ ἰδέᾳ, περικείμενον δέρμα αἴγειον λευκόν, καὶ πήραν τινὰ εἶχεν ἐπὶ τῶν ὤμων καὶ ῥάβδον σκληρὰν λίαν καὶ ὄζους ἔχουσαν καὶ μάστιγα μεγάλην· καὶ τὸ βλέμμα εἶχε περίπικρον, ὥστε φοβηθῆναί με αὐτόν· τοιοῦτον εἶχε τὸ βλέμμα. 6. οὗτος οὖν ὁ ποιμὴν παρελάμβανε τὰ πρόβατα ἀπὸ τοῦ ποιμένος τοῦ νεανίσκου, ἐκεῖνα τὰ σπαταλῶντα καὶ τρυφῶντα, μὴ σκιρτῶντα δέ, καὶ ἔβαλεν αὐτὰ εἴς τινα τόπον κρημνώδη καὶ ἀκανθώδη καὶ τριβολώδη, ὥστε ἀπὸ τῶν ἀκανθῶν καὶ τριβόλων μὴ δύνασθαι ἐκπλέξαι τὰ πρόβατα, ἀλλ' ἐμπλέκεσθαι εἰς τὰς

[1] The preceding seven lines (ταῖς ἐπιθυμίαις .... ἑαυτοὺς) are omitted in A, but are found in Ath. LE, though with much minor variation. [2] προέβην AE, προεβήμεν L.

174

death,' and what is ' to corruption.' " " Listen," he
said, " the sheep which you see joyful and skipping,
these are those which have been torn away from
God completely, and have given themselves up to
the lusts of this world. For these, then, there is no
repentance of life, because they added to their sins
and blasphemed against the name of God. Such
men incur death. 4. But the sheep which you see
not skipping, but feeding in one place, these are
they who have given themselves up to luxury and
deceit, but have uttered no blasphemy against the
Lord. These then have been corrupted from the
truth ; in them there is hope of repentance, in which
they can live. Corruption, then, has hope of
some renewing, but death has eternal destruction."
5. Again I went on a little, and he showed me a The
great shepherd, as it were savage in appearance, Shepherd of
clothed in a white goat-skin, and he had a bag on Punishment
his shoulders, with a great staff, very hard and with
knots, and a great whip. And he looked very bitter
so that I was afraid of him, such a look had he.
6. This shepherd then was receiving the sheep from
the young shepherd ; that is to say, those who were
frisky and well-fed but not skipping, and put them
in a certain place precipitous and thorny and full of
thistles, so that the sheep could not disentangle
themselves from the thorns and thistles, but were

ἀκάνθας καὶ τριβόλους. 7. ταῦτα οὖν ἐμπεπλεγ-
μένα ἐβόσκοντο ἐν ταῖς ἀκάνθαις καὶ τριβόλοις
καὶ λίαν ἐταλαιπώρουν δαιρόμενα ὑπ' αὐτοῦ· καὶ
ὧδε κἀκεῖσε περιήλαυνεν αὐτὰ καὶ ἀνάπαυσιν
αὐτοῖς οὐκ ἐδίδου, καὶ ὅλως οὐκ εὐσταθοῦσαν τὰ
πρόβατα ἐκεῖνα.

III

1. Βλέπων οὖν αὐτὰ οὕτω μαστιγούμενα καὶ
ταλαιπωρούμενα ἐλυπούμην ἐπ' αὐτοῖς, ὅτι οὕτως
ἐβασανίζοντο καὶ ἀνοχὴν ὅλως οὐκ εἶχον. 2. λέγω
τῷ ποιμένι τῷ μετ' ἐμοῦ λαλοῦντι· Κύριε, τίς
ἐστιν οὗτος ὁ ποιμὴν ὁ οὕτως ἄσπλαγχνος καὶ
πικρὸς καὶ ὅλως μὴ σπλαγχνιζόμενος ἐπὶ τὰ
πρόβατα ταῦτα; Οὗτος, φησίν, ἐστὶν ὁ ἄγγελος
τῆς τιμωρίας· ἐκ δὲ τῶν ἀγγέλων τῶν δικαίων
ἐστί, κείμενος δὲ ἐπὶ τῆς τιμωρίας. 3. παρα-
λαμβάνει οὖν τοὺς ἀποπλανωμένους ἀπὸ τοῦ θεοῦ
καὶ πορευθέντας ταῖς ἐπιθυμίαις καὶ ἀπάταις τοῦ
αἰῶνος τούτου καὶ τιμωρεῖ αὐτούς, καθὼς ἄξιοί
εἰσι, δειναῖς καὶ ποικίλαις τιμωρίαις. 4. Ἤθελον, φημί, κύριε, γνῶναι τὰς ποικίλας ταύτας
τιμωρίας,[1] ποταπαί εἰσιν. Ἄκουε, φησί, τὰς
ποικίλας βασάνους καὶ τιμωρίας. βιωτικαί εἰσιν
αἱ βάσανοι· τιμωροῦνται γὰρ οἱ μὲν ζημίαις, οἱ δὲ
ὑστερήσεσιν, οἱ δὲ ἀσθενείαις ποικίλαις, οἱ δὲ
πάσῃ ἀκαταστασίᾳ, οἱ δὲ ὑβριζόμενοι ὑπὸ ἀναξ-
ίων καὶ ἑτέραις πολλαῖς πράξεσι πάσχοντες.
5. πολλοὶ γὰρ ἀκαταστατοῦντες ταῖς βουλαῖς

[1] τὰς ποικίλας ταύτας τιμωρίας L Ath., τὰς ποικίλας βασάνους
ταύτας τιμωρίας A(E).

caught in the thorns and thistles. 7. These then were being pastured all entangled in the thorns and thistles, and they were very wretched, being beaten by him, and he was driving them about here and there, and gave them no rest, and those sheep had no happy time at all.

III

1. When therefore I saw them thus beaten and miserable I grieved for them that they were being so tormented, and had no rest at all. 2. I said to the shepherd who was speaking with me : " Sir, who is this shepherd who is so pitiless and bitter, and has no compassion at all on these sheep ? " " This," said he, " is the angel of punishment. He is one of the righteous angels, but is set over punishment. 3. Therefore he receives those who have wandered away from God, and walked in the lusts and deceits of this world, and punishes them, as they deserve, with various terrible punishments." 4. " I should like, sir," said I, " to know these different punishments, of what kind they are." " Hear," said he, " the different tortures and punishments. The tortures befall them in this life, for some are punished with loss, others with deprivations, others with divers illnesses, others with all unsettlement, and others are insulted by the unworthy, and suffer many other things. 5. For many have been unsettled in their

177

αὐτῶν ἐπιβάλλονται πολλά, καὶ οὐδὲν αὐτοῖς
ὅλως προχωρεῖ. καὶ λέγουσιν ἑαυτοὺς μὴ εὐο-
δοῦσθαι ἐν ταῖς πράξεσιν αὐτῶν, καὶ οὐκ
ἀναβαίνει αὐτῶν ἐπὶ τὴν καρδίαν, ὅτι ἔπραξαν πονηρὰ ἔργα, ἀλλ' αἰτιῶνται τὸν κύριον. 6. ὅταν οὖν θλιβῶσι πάσῃ θλίψει, τότε
ἐμοὶ παραδίδονται εἰς ἀγαθὴν παιδείαν καὶ ἰσχυ-
Ps. 51, 10   ροποιοῦνται ἐν τῇ πίστει τοῦ κυρίου καὶ τὰς
λοιπὰς ἡμέρας τῆς ζωῆς αὐτῶν δουλεύουσι τῷ
κυρίῳ ἐν καθαρᾷ καρδίᾳ· ἐὰν δὲ μετανοήσωσι, τότε ἀναβαίνει ἐπὶ τὴν καρδίαν αὐτῶν τὰ ἔργα ἃ ἔπραξαν πονηρά, καὶ τότε
Ps. 7, 12;   δοξάζουσι τὸν θεόν, λέγοντες, ὅτι δίκαιος κριτής
Ps. 62, 12;   ἐστι καὶ δικαίως ἔπαθον ἕκαστος κατὰ τὰς
πράξεις αὐτοῦ· δουλεύουσι δὲ λοιπὸν τῷ κυρίῳ ἐν
καθαρᾷ καρδίᾳ[1] αὐτῶν καὶ εὐοδοῦνται ἐν πάσῃ
Mt. 21, 22;   πράξει αὐτῶν, λαμβάνοντες παρὰ τοῦ κυρίου
I Jo. 3, 22   πάντα, ὅσα ἂν αἰτῶνται· καὶ τότε δοξάζουσι τὸν
κύριον, ὅτι ἐμοὶ παρεδόθησαν, καὶ οὐκέτι οὐδὲν
πάσχουσι τῶν πονηρῶν.

IV

1. Λέγω αὐτῷ· Κύριε, ἔτι μοι τοῦτο δήλωσον.
Τί, φησίν, ἐπιζητεῖς; Εἰ ἄρα, φημί, κύριε, τὸν
αὐτὸν χρόνον βασανίζονται οἱ τρυφῶντες καὶ
ἀπατώμενοι, ὅσον τρυφῶσι καὶ ἀπατῶνται; λέγει
μοι· Τὸν αὐτὸν χρόνον βασανίζονται. 2. Ἐλάχιστον, φημί, κύριε, βασανίζονται·[2] ἔδει γάρ

---

[1] ἐὰν δὲ μετανοήσωσι . . . . καρδίᾳ L Ath., om. A.

[2] ἐλάχιστον, φημί, κύριε, βασανίζονται om. A. The Greek
is reconstructed from L.

counsels and try many things, and nothing goes well for them at all. And they say that they do not prosper in their undertaking, and it does not enter into their hearts that they have done wicked deeds, but they blame the Lord. 6. When, therefore, they have been afflicted with every affliction, then they are handed over to me, for good instruction, and are made strong in the faith of the Lord, and they serve the Lord the rest of the days of their life 'with a pure heart.' And if they repent, then it enters into their hearts, that the deeds which they did were evil, and then they glorify God saying that he is 'a righteous judge,' and that they suffered righteously, 'each according to his deeds,' and for the future they serve the Lord with a pure heart, and they prosper in all their deeds, 'receiving from the Lord all things, whatever they ask;' and then they glorify the Lord that they were handed over to me, and they no longer suffer any of the evils."

IV

1. I said to him: "Sir, tell me this also." "What more," said he, "do you ask?" "Whether, Sir," said I, "those who live in luxury and are deceived are punished for the same time as they live in luxury and deceit?" And he said to me: "Yes, they are punished the same time." 2. "Sir," said I, "they are punished a very short time, for those who live in

τοὺς οὕτω τρυφῶντας καὶ ἐπιλανθανομένους τοῦ
θεοῦ ἑπταπλασίως βασανίζεσθαι. 3. λέγει μοι·
Ἄφρων εἶ καὶ οὐ νοεῖς τῆς βασάνου τὴν δύναμιν.
Εἰ γὰρ ἐνόουν, φημί, κύριε, οὐκ ἂν ἐπηρώτων, ἵνα
μοι δηλώσῃς. Ἄκουε, φησίν, ἀμφοτέρων τὴν
δύναμιν. 4. τῆς τρυφῆς καὶ ἀπάτης ὁ χρόνος ὥρα
ἐστὶ μία· τῆς δὲ βασάνου ἡ ὥρα τριάκοντα ἡμερῶν
δύναμιν ἔχει. ἐὰν οὖν μίαν ἡμέραν τρυφήσῃ τις
καὶ ἀπατηθῇ, μίαν δὲ ἡμέραν βασανισθῇ, ὅλον
ἐνιαυτὸν ἰσχύει ἡ ἡμέρα τῆς βασάνου. ὅσας οὖν
ἡμέρας τρυφήσῃ τις, τοσούτους ἐνιαυτοὺς βασανίζεται. βλέπεις οὖν, φησίν, ὅτι τῆς τρυφῆς καὶ
ἀπάτης ὁ χρόνος ἐλάχιστός ἐστι, τῆς δὲ τιμωρίας
καὶ βασάνου πολύς.

V

1. Ἔτι, φημί, κύριε, οὐ νενόηκα ὅλως περὶ τοῦ
χρόνου τῆς ἀπάτης καὶ τρυφῆς καὶ βασάνου·
τηλαυγέστερόν μοι δήλωσον. 2. ἀποκριθείς μοι
λέγει· Ἡ ἀφροσύνη σου παράμονός ἐστι, καὶ οὐ
θέλεις σου τὴν καρδίαν καθαρίσαι καὶ δουλεύειν
τῷ θεῷ. βλέπε, φησί, μήποτε ὁ χρόνος πληρωθῇ
καὶ σὺ ἄφρων εὑρεθῇς. ἄκουε οὖν, φησί, καθὼς
βούλει, ἵνα νοήσῃς αὐτά. 3. ὁ τρυφῶν καὶ ἀπατώμενος μίαν ἡμέραν καὶ πράσσων, ἃ βούλεται,
πολλὴν ἀφροσύνην ἐνδέδυται καὶ οὐ νοεῖ τὴν πρᾶξιν,
ἣν ποιεῖ· εἰς τὴν αὔριον ἐπιλανθάνεται γάρ, τί πρὸ
μιᾶς ἔπραξεν· ἡ γὰρ τρυφὴ καὶ ἀπάτη μνήμας οὐκ
ἔχει διὰ τὴν ἀφροσύνην, ἣν ἐνδέδυται, ἡ δὲ τιμωρία
καὶ ἡ βάσανος ὅταν κολληθῇ τῷ ἀνθρώπῳ μίαν

such luxury and forget God, ought to be punished sevenfold." 3. He said to me : " You are foolish, and do not understand the power of punishment." " No," said I, " Sir, for if I had understood it, I should not have asked you to tell me." " Listen," said he, " to the power of both. 4. The time of luxury and deceit is one hour, but the hour of punishment has the power of thirty days. If, therefore, any man live in luxury and deceit for one day, and be punished one day, the day of punishment has the power of a whole year, for a man is punished as many years as he has lived days in luxury. You see, therefore," said he, " that the time of luxury and deceit is very short, but the time of punishment is long."

V

1. " Sir," said I, " I still do not at all understand about the time of deceit and luxury and torture ; explain it to me more clearly." 2. He answered and said to me : " Your foolishness is lasting, and you do not wish to purify your heart and to serve God. See to it," said he, " lest the time be fulfilled, and you be found still foolish. Listen, then," said he, " that you may understand it as you wish. 3. He who lives in luxury and deceit for a single day, and does what he likes, is clothed with great foolishness, and does not understand the deed which he is doing. For he forgets to-morrow what he did yesterday. For luxury and deceit have no memory, because of the foolishness which they have put on. But when punishment and torture cleave to a man for a single

ἡμέραν, μέχρις ἐνιαυτοῦ τιμωρεῖται καὶ βασανί-
ζεται· μνήμας γὰρ μεγάλας ἔχει ἡ τιμωρία καὶ ἡ
βάσανος. 4. βασανιζόμενος οὖν καὶ τιμωρού-
μενος ὅλον τὸν ἐνιαυτόν, μνημονεύει τότε τῆς
τρυφῆς καὶ ἀπάτης καὶ γινώσκει, ὅτι δι᾽ αὐτὰ
πάσχει τὰ πονηρά. πᾶς οὖν ἄνθρωπος ὁ τρυφῶν
καὶ ἀπατώμενος οὕτω βασανίζεται, ὅτι ἔχοντες
ζωὴν εἰς θάνατον ἑαυτοὺς παραδεδώκασι. 5. Ποῖαι,
φημί, κύριε, τρυφαί εἰσι βλαβεραί; Πᾶσα, φησί,
πρᾶξις τρυφή ἐστι τῷ ἀνθρώπῳ, ὃ ἐὰν ἡδέως
ποιῇ· καὶ γὰρ ὁ ὀξύχολος τῷ ἑαυτοῦ πάθει τὸ
ἱκανὸν ποιῶν τρυφᾷ· καὶ ὁ μοιχὸς καὶ ὁ μέθυσος
καὶ ὁ κατάλαλος καὶ ὁ ψεύστης καὶ ὁ πλεονέκτης
καὶ ὁ ἀποστερητὴς καὶ ὁ τούτοις τὰ ὅμοια
ποιῶν τῇ ἰδίᾳ νόσῳ τὸ ἱκανὸν ποιεῖ· τρυφᾷ οὖν
ἐπὶ τῇ πράξει αὐτοῦ. 6. αὗται πᾶσαι αἱ τρυφαὶ
βλαβεραί εἰσι τοῖς δούλοις τοῦ θεοῦ. διὰ ταύτας
οὖν τὰς ἀπάτας πάσχουσιν οἱ τιμωρούμενοι καὶ
βασανιζόμενοι. 7. εἰσὶν δὲ καὶ τρυφαὶ σώζουσαι
τοὺς ἀνθρώπους· πολλοὶ γὰρ ἀγαθὸν ἐργαζόμενοι
τρυφῶσι τῇ ἑαυτῶν ἡδονῇ φερόμενοι. αὕτη οὖν ἡ
τρυφὴ σύμφορός ἐστι τοῖς δούλοις τοῦ θεοῦ καὶ
ζωὴν περιποιεῖται τῷ ἀνθρώπῳ τῷ τοιούτῳ· αἱ δὲ
βλαβεραὶ τρυφαὶ αἱ προειρημέναι βασάνους καὶ
τιμωρίας αὐτοῖς περιποιοῦνται· ἐὰν δὲ ἐπιμένωσι
καὶ μὴ μετανοήσωσι, θάνατον ἑαυτοῖς περιποι-
οῦνται.

Παραβολὴ ζ΄

1. Μετὰ ἡμέρας ὀλίγας εἶδον αὐτὸν εἰς τὸ
πεδίον τὸ αὐτό, ὅπου καὶ τοὺς ποιμένας ἑωράκειν,

day, he is punished and tortured for a year, for punishment and torture have long memories. 4. Therefore, being tortured and punished for a whole year, he then remembers his luxury and deceit, and knows that he is suffering evil because of them. Therefore, all men who live in luxury and deceit are thus tortured, because though they have life, they have given themselves over to death." 5. "What sort of luxuries, Sir," said I, "are harmful?" "Every act which a man does with pleasure," said he, "is luxury, for even the ill-tempered man, by giving satisfaction to his own temper, lives luxuriously. And the adulterer and drunkard and evil-speaker and liar, and the covetous and the robber, and he who does such things as these gives satisfaction to his own disease; therefore he lives in luxury from his own acts. 6. All these luxuries are harmful to the servants of God. Those, therefore, who are punished and tortured suffer, because of these deceits. 7. But there are also luxuries which bring men salvation, for many who do good luxuriate and are carried away with their own pleasure. This luxury therefore is profitable to the servants of God, and brings life to such a man. But the harmful luxuries spoken of already bring them torture and punishment. But if they continue in them and do not repent, they procure death for themselves.

Parable 7

1. After a few days I saw him in the same plain, where I had also seen the shepherds, and he said to

καὶ λέγει μοι· Τί ἐπιζητεῖς; Πάρειμι, φημί, κύριε,
ἵνα τὸν ποιμένα τὸν τιμωρητὴν κελεύσῃς ἐκ τοῦ
οἴκου μου ἐξελθεῖν, ὅτι λίαν με θλίβει. Δεῖ σε,
φησί, θλιβῆναι· οὕτω γάρ, φησί, προσέταξεν ὁ
ἔνδοξος ἄγγελος τὰ περὶ σοῦ· θέλει γάρ σε
πειρασθῆναι. Τί γάρ, φημί, κύριε, ἐποίησα οὕτω
πονηρόν, ἵνα τῷ ἀγγέλῳ τούτῳ παραδοθῶ;
2. Ἄκουε, φησίν· αἱ μὲν ἁμαρτίαι σου πολλαί,
ἀλλ᾽ οὐ τοσαῦται, ὥστε τῷ ἀγγέλῳ τούτῳ παρα-
δοθῆναι· ἀλλ᾽ ὁ οἶκός σου μεγάλας ἀνομίας καὶ
ἁμαρτίας εἰργάσατο, καὶ παρεπικράνθη ὁ ἔνδοξος
ἄγγελος ἐπὶ τοῖς ἔργοις αὐτῶν καὶ διὰ τοῦτο
ἐκέλευσέ σε χρόνον τινὰ θλιβῆναι, ἵνα κἀκεῖνοι
μετανοήσωσι καὶ καθαρίσωσιν ἑαυτοὺς ἀπὸ πάσης
ἐπιθυμίας τοῦ αἰῶνος τούτου. ὅταν οὖν μετανοήσωσι καὶ καθαρισθῶσι, τότε ἀποστήσεται ἀπὸ
σοῦ[1] ὁ ἄγγελος τῆς τιμωρίας. 3. λέγω αὐτῷ·
Κύριε, εἰ ἐκεῖνοι τοιαῦτα εἰργάσαντο, ἵνα παρα-
πικρανθῇ ὁ ἔνδοξος ἄγγελος, τί ἐγὼ ἐποίησα;
Ἄλλως, φησίν, οὐ δύνανται ἐκεῖνοι θλιβῆναι,
ἐὰν μὴ σὺ ἡ κεφαλὴ τοῦ οἴκου θλιβῇς· σοῦ γὰρ
θλιβομένου ἐξ ἀνάγκης κἀκεῖνοι θλιβήσονται,
εὐσταθοῦντος δὲ σοῦ οὐδεμίαν δύνανται θλῖψιν
ἔχειν. 4. Ἀλλ᾽ ἰδού, φημί, κύριε, μετανενοήκασιν
ἐξ ὅλης καρδίας αὐτῶν. Οἶδα, φησί, κἀγώ, ὅτι
μετανενοήκασιν ἐξ ὅλης καρδίας αὐτῶν· τῶν
οὖν μετανοούντων εὐθὺς[2] δοκεῖς τὰς ἁμαρτίας
ἀφίεσθαι; οὐ παντελῶς· ἀλλὰ δεῖ τὸν μετανοοῦντα βασανίσαι τὴν ἑαυτοῦ ψυχὴν καὶ ταπεινο-
φρονῆσαι ἐν πάσῃ πράξει αὐτοῦ ἰσχυρῶς καὶ
θλιβῆναι ἐν πάσαις θίψεσι ποικίλαις· καὶ ἐὰν

---

[1] ἀπὸ σοῦ LE, om. A.　　　[2] εὐθύς LE, om. A.

me: "What more are you seeking?" "I have come here, Sir," said I, "in order that you may command the shepherd of punishment to depart from my house, because he afflicts me too much." "You must be afflicted," said he, "For thus," said he, "the glorious angel enjoined concerning you. For he wishes you to be tried." "Yes, Sir," said I, "but what have I done so wicked, that I should be handed over to this angel?" 2. "Listen," said he, "your sins are many, but not so great as that you should be handed over to this angel; but your family has done great iniquity and sin, and the glorious angel has become enraged at their deeds, and for this reason he commanded you to be afflicted for some time, that they also may repent and purify themselves from every lust of this world. When, therefore, they repent, and have been purified, then the angel of punishment will depart from you." 3. I said to him: "Sir, even if they have done such things that the glorious angel is enraged, what have I done?" "They cannot," said he, "be punished in any other way, than if you, the head of the house, be afflicted. For when you are afflicted, they also will necessarily be afflicted, but while you prosper, they cannot suffer any affliction." 4. "But see, Sir," said I, "they have repented with all their heart." "I know," said he, "myself also, that they have repented with all their heart; do you then think that the sins of those who repent are immediately forgiven? By no means; but he who repents must torture his own soul, and be humble in all his deeds and be afflicted with many divers afflictions. And if

The reason for the continued punishment of the penitent

ὑπενέγκῃ τὰς θλίψεις τὰς ἐπερχομένας αὐτῷ, πάντως σπλαγχνισθήσεται ὁ τὰ πάντα κτίσας καὶ
ἐνδυναμώσας καὶ ἰασίν τινα δώσει αὐτῷ· 5. καὶ
τοῦτο πάντως, ἐὰν ἴδῃ τὴν καρδίαν τοῦ μετανοοῦντος καθαρὰν [1] ἀπὸ παντὸς πονηροῦ πράγματος. σοὶ δὲ συμφέρον ἐστὶ καὶ τῷ οἴκῳ σου
νῦν θλιβῆναι. τί δέ σοι πολλὰ λέγω ; θλιβῆναί
σε δεῖ, καθὼς προσέταξεν ὁ ἄγγελος κυρίου
ἐκεῖνος, ὁ παραδιδούς σε ἐμοί· καὶ τοῦτο εὐχα-
ρίστει τῷ κυρίῳ, ὅτι ἄξιόν σε ἡγήσατο τοῦ
προδηλῶσαί σοι τὴν θλῖψιν, ἵνα προγνοὺς αὐτὴν
ὑπενέγκῃς ἰσχυρῶς. 6. λέγω αὐτῷ· Κύριε, σὺ
μετ᾽ ἐμοῦ γίνου, καὶ δυνήσομαι πᾶσαν θλῖψιν
ὑπενεγκεῖν. Ἐγώ, φησίν, ἔσομαι μετὰ σοῦ·
ἐρωτήσω δέ καὶ τὸν ἄγγελον τὸν τιμωρητήν, ἵνα
σε ἐλαφροτέρως θλίψῃ· ἀλλ᾽ ὀλίγον χρόνον
θλιβήσῃ καὶ πάλιν ἀποκατασταθήσῃ εἰς τὸν
οἶκόν σου. μόνον παράμεινον ταπεινοφρονῶν καὶ
λειτουργῶν τῷ κυρίῳ ἐν πάσῃ καθαρᾷ καρδίᾳ,
καὶ τὰ τέκνα σου καὶ ὁ οἶκός σου, καὶ πορεύου ἐν
ταῖς ἐντολαῖς μου αἷς σοι ἐντέλλομαι, καὶ δυνή-
σεταί σου ἡ μετάνοια ἰσχυρὰ καὶ καθαρὰ εἶναι·
7. καὶ ἐὰν ταύτας φυλάξῃς μετὰ τοῦ οἴκου σου,
ἀποστήσεται πᾶσα θλῖψις ἀπὸ σοῦ· καὶ ἀπὸ
πάντων δέ, φησίν, ἀποστήσεται θλῖψις. ὅσοι
ἐὰν ἐν ταῖς ἐντολαῖς μου ταύταις πορευθῶσιν.

Eph. 3, 9
Ps. 68, 28

[1] πάντως . . . καθαράν LE, πάντως τοῦ μετανοοῦντος καθαρῶς A

he endure the afflictions which come upon him he who 'created all things' and gave them power will have compassion in all ways upon him, and will give him some measure of healing; 5. and this in every case when he sees that the heart of the penitent is clean from every evil deed. But it is good for you and for your house, to suffer affliction now. But why do I say much to you? you must be afflicted, even as that angel of the Lord, who handed you over to me, ordained. And give the Lord thanks for this, because he deemed you worthy to show you the affliction beforehand, that in your foreknowledge you may endure it with strength." 6. I said to him: "Sir, do you be with me, and I shall be able to endure every affliction." "Yes," said he, "I will be with you, and I will also ask the angel of punishment to afflict you more lightly. But you shall be afflicted a little time and you shall be restored again to your house. Only continue humble and serving the Lord with a pure heart, both your children and your household, and walk in my commandments which I give you, and your repentance shall be able to be strong and pure. 7. And if you keep these commandments with your family all affliction shall depart from you. Yes," said he, "and affliction shall depart from all who walk in these my commandments."

THE APOSTOLIC FATHERS

Παραβολὴ η΄

I

1. Ἔδειξέ μοι ἰτέαν μεγάλην, σκεπάζουσαν πεδία καὶ ὄρη, καὶ ὑπὸ τὴν σκέπην τῆς ἰτέας πάντες ἐληλύθασιν οἱ κεκλημένοι ἐν ὀνόματι κυρίου. 2. εἱστήκει δὲ ἄγγελος κυρίου ἔνδοξος λίαν ὑψηλὸς παρὰ τὴν ἰτέαν, δρέπανον ἔχων μέγα, καὶ ἔκοπτε κλάδους ἀπὸ τῆς ἰτέας, καὶ ἐπεδίδου τῷ λαῷ τῷ σκεπαζομένῳ ὑπὸ τῆς ἰτέας· μικρὰ δὲ ῥαβδία ἐπεδίδου αὐτοῖς, ὡσεὶ πηχυαῖα. 3. μετὰ τὸ πάντας λαβεῖν τὰ ῥαβδία ἔθηκε τὸ δρέπανον ὁ ἄγγελος, καὶ τὸ δένδρον ἐκεῖνο ὑγιὲς ἦν, οἷον καὶ ἑωράκειν αὐτό. 4. ἐθαύμαζον δὲ ἐγὼ ἐν ἐμαυτῷ λέγων· Πῶς τοσούτων κλάδων κεκομμένων τὸ δένδρον ὑγιές ἐστι[1]; λέγει μοι ὁ ποιμήν· Μὴ θαύμαζε, εἰ τὸ δένδρον τοῦτο ὑγιὲς ἔμεινε τοσούτων κλάδων κοπέντων· ἐὰν[2] δέ, φησί, πάντα ἴδῃς, σοι δηλωθήσεται τὸ τί ἐστιν. 5. ὁ ἄγγελος ὁ ἐπιδεδωκὼς τῷ λαῷ τὰς ῥάβδους πάλιν ἀπῄτει αὐτούς· καὶ καθὼς ἔλαβον, οὕτω καὶ ἐκαλοῦντο πρὸς αὐτόν, καὶ εἷς ἕκαστος αὐτῶν ἀπεδίδου τὰς ῥάβδους. ἐλάμβανε δὲ ὁ ἄγγελος τοῦ κυρίου καὶ κατενόει αὐτάς. 6. παρά τινων ἐλάμβανε τὰς ῥάβδους ξηρὰς καὶ βεβρωμένας ὡς ὑπὸ σητός· ἐκέλευσεν ὁ ἄγγελος τοὺς τὰς τοιαύτας ῥάβδους ἐπιδεδωκότας χωρὶς ἱστάνεσθαι. 7. ἕτεροι δὲ ἐπεδίδοσαν ξηράς, ἀλλ᾿ οὐκ ἦσαν βεβρωμέναι ὑπὸ σητός· καὶ τούτους

[1] λέγων... ἐστι om. L and probably P[Berl].
[2] ἐὰν P[Berl], ἀφ᾿ ἧς A, LE paraphrases.

PARABLE 8

I

1. HE showed me a great willow, covering plains and mountains, and under the cover of the willow-tree all had come who were called by the name of the Lord. 2. And there stood an angel of the Lord, glorious and very tall, by the side of the willow, with a great pruning-hook, and he kept cutting branches from the willow, and gave them to the people who were in the shade of the willow, and he gave them little rods about a cubit long. 3. After they had all received the little sticks the angel put down the pruning-hook, and that tree remained as sound as when I first saw it. 4. And I wondered in myself saying: How is the tree sound, when so many branches have been cut off? The shepherd said to me: "Do not wonder that this tree has remained sound, though so many branches have been cut off; but if you see everything it will be made clear to you what it is." 5. The angel who had given the sticks to the people asked them back, and as they had received so also they were called to him, and each of them gave back the sticks. And the angel of the Lord took them and looked at them. 6. From some he received the sticks dried and, as it were, moth-eaten. The angel commanded those who had given up such sticks, to stand apart. 7. And others gave up dry sticks, but they were not moth-eaten, and these he commanded

189

ἐκέλευσε χωρὶς ἱστάνεσθαι.[1] 8. ἕτεροι δὲ ἐπεδίδουν
ἡμιξήρους· καὶ οὗτοι χωρὶς ἱστάνοντο. 9. ἕτεροι
δὲ ἐπεδίδουν τὰς ῥάβδους αὐτῶν ἡμιξήρους καὶ
σχισμὰς ἐχούσας· καὶ οὗτοι χωρὶς ἵσταντο.
10. ἕτεροι δὲ ἐπεδίδουν τὰς ῥάβδους αὐτῶν
χλωρὰς καὶ σχισμὰς ἐχούσας· καὶ οὗτοι χωρὶς
ἱστάνοντο.[2] 11. ἕτεροι δὲ ἐπεδίδουν τὰς ῥάβδους
τὸ ἥμισυ ξηρὸν καὶ τὸ ἥμισυ μέρος[3] χλωρόν· καὶ
οὗτοι χωρὶς ἱστάνοντο. 12. ἕτεροι δὲ προσέφερον
τὰς ῥάβδους αὐτῶν τὰ δύο μέρη τῆς ῥάβδου χλωρά,
τὸ δὲ τρίτον ξηρόν· καὶ οὗτοι χωρὶς ἱστάνοντο.
13. ἕτεροι δὲ ἐπεδίδουν τὰ δύο μέρη ξηρά, τὸ
δὲ τρίτον χλωρόν· καὶ οὗτοι χωρὶς ἱστάνοντο.
14. ἕτεροι δὲ ἐπεδίδουν τὰς ῥάβδους αὐτῶν παρὰ
μικρὸν ὅλας χλωράς, ἐλάχιστον δὲ τῶν ῥάβδων
αὐτῶν ξηρὸν ἦν, αὐτὸ τὸ ἄκρον· σχισμὰς δὲ
εἶχον ἐν αὐταῖς· καὶ οὗτοι χωρὶς ἵσταντο.
15. ἑτέρων δὲ ἦν ἐλάχιστον χλωρόν, τὰ δὲ λοιπὰ
τῶν ῥάβδων ξηρά· καὶ οὗτοι χωρὶς ἱστάνοντο.
16. ἕτεροι δὲ ἤρχοντο τὰς ῥάβδους χλωρὰς φέ-
ροντες ὡς ἔλαβον παρὰ τοῦ ἀγγέλου· τὸ δὲ πλεῖον
μέρος τοῦ ὄχλου τοιαύτας ῥάβδους ἐπεδίδουν. ὁ
δὲ ἄγγελος ἐπὶ τούτοις ἐχάρη λίαν· καὶ οὗτοι
χωρὶς ἱστάνοντο. 17. ἕτεροι δὲ ἐπεδίδουν τὰς
ῥάβδους αὐτῶν χλωρὰς καὶ παραφυάδας ἐχούσας·
καὶ οὗτοι χωρὶς ἵσταντο· καὶ ἐπὶ τούτοις ὁ ἄγγελος
λίαν ἐχάρη.[4] 18. ἕτεροι δὲ ἐπεδίδουν τὰς ῥάβδους
αὐτῶν χλωρὰς καὶ παραφυάδας ἐχούσας· αἱ δὲ

---

[1] ἱστάνεσθαι P[Bo1], ἵστασθαι A and so throughout this
section.
[2] ἕτεροι . . . ἵσταντο, om. AL₁.   [3] μέρος P[Berl], om. A.
[4] ἕτεροι . . . ἐχάρη, retranslated from LE, om. A.

to stand apart. 8. And others gave up sticks half dry, and these stood apart. 9. And others gave up their sticks half dry and with cracks, and these stood apart. 10. And others gave up their sticks, green and having cracks, and these stood apart. 11. And others gave up their sticks half dry and half green, and these stood apart. 12. And others brought two-thirds of the stick green, and one-third dry, and these stood apart. 13. And others gave up two-thirds dry, and one-third green, and these stood apart. 14. And others gave up their sticks almost wholly green, but a little of their sticks was dry, just the tip, and they had cracks in them, and these stood apart. 15. And of others there was very little green and the rest of the sticks was dry, and these stood apart. 16. And others came, bearing their sticks green, as they had received them from the angel, and the greater part of the multitude gave up such sticks, and the angel rejoiced greatly over these, and these stood apart. 17. And others gave up their sticks green and with buds, and these stood apart, and over these also the angel rejoiced greatly. 18. And others gave up their sticks green and with buds,

παραφυάδες αὐτῶν ὡσεὶ καρπόν τινα εἶχον· καὶ λίαν ἱλαροὶ ἦσαν οἱ ἄνθρωποι ἐκεῖνοι, ὧν αἱ ῥάβδοι τοιαῦται εὑρέθησαν· καὶ ὁ ἄγγελος ἐπὶ τούτοις ἠγαλλιᾶτο, καὶ ὁ ποιμὴν λίαν ἱλαρὸς ἦν ἐπὶ τούτοις.

II

1. Ἐκέλευσε δὲ ὁ ἄγγελος κυρίου στεφάνους ἐνεχθῆναι. καὶ ἐνέχθησαν στέφανοι ὡσεὶ ἐκ φοινίκων γεγονότες, καὶ ἐστεφάνωσε τοὺς ἄνδρας τοὺς ἐπιδεδωκότας τὰς ῥάβδους τὰς ἐχούσας τὰς παραφυάδας καὶ καρπόν τινα καὶ ἀπέλυσεν αὐτοὺς εἰς τὸν πύργον. 2. καὶ τοὺς ἄλλους δὲ ἀπέστειλεν εἰς τὸν πύργον, τοὺς τὰς ῥάβδους τὰς χλωρὰς ἐπιδεδωκότας καὶ παραφυάδας ἐχούσας, καρπὸν δὲ μὴ ἐχούσας τὰς παραφυάδας, δοὺς αὐτοῖς σφραγῖδας. 3. ἱματισμὸν δὲ τὸν αὐτὸν πάντες εἶχον λευκὸν ὡσεὶ χιόνα, οἱ πορευόμενοι εἰς τὸν πύργον. 4. καὶ τοὺς τὰς ῥάβδους ἐπιδεδωκότας χλωρὰς ὡς ἔλαβον ἀπέλυσε, δοὺς αὐτοῖς ἱματισμὸν καὶ σφραγῖδας. 5. μετὰ τὸ ταῦτα τελέσαι τὸν ἄγγελον λέγει τῷ ποιμένι· Ἐγὼ ὑπάγω· σὺ δὲ τούτους ἀπολύσεις εἰς τὰ τείχη, καθὼς ἄξιός ἐστί τις κατοικεῖν. κατανόησον δὲ τὰς ῥάβδους αὐτῶν ἐπιμελῶς καὶ οὕτως ἀπόλυσον· ἐπιμελῶς δὲ κατανόησον. βλέπε, μή τίς σε παρέλθῃ, φησίν, ἐὰν δὲ τίς σε παρέλθῃ, ἐγὼ αὐτοὺς ἐπὶ τὸ θυσιαστήριον δοκιμάσω. ταῦτα εἰπὼν τῷ ποιμένι ἀπῆλθε. 6. καὶ μετὰ τὸ ἀπελθεῖν τὸν ἄγγελον λέγει μοι ὁ ποιμήν· Λάβωμεν πάντων τὰς ῥάβδους καὶ φυτεύσωμεν αὐτάς, εἴ τινες ἐξ αὐτῶν δυνήσονται ζῆσαι.

and the buds had, as it were, some fruit. And those men whose sticks were found thus were very joyful, and the angel rejoiced and the shepherd was very joyful over them.

II

1. And the angel of the Lord commanded crowns to be brought, and crowns were brought, made, as it were, of palm leaves, and he crowned the men who had given up their sticks with buds and some fruit, and sent them away into the tower. 2. And he sent also the others into the tower who gave up their sticks green and with buds, but the buds without fruit, and he gave them seals. 3. And all who went into the tower had the same clothing, white as snow. 4. And he sent away those who had given up their sticks green, as they had received them, and gave them clothing and seals. 5. After the angel had finished this he said to the shepherd : "I am going away, but you shall send these within the walls, according as any is worthy to dwell there. But consider their sticks carefully and thus let them go, but look carefully. See to it that none pass you," he said, "but if anyone pass you, I will test them at the altar." When he had said this to the shepherd he departed. 6. And after the angel had departed the shepherd said to me: "Let us take the sticks of all of them, and plant them to see if some

The instructions of the angel to the Shepherd

λέγω αὐτῷ· Κύριε, τὰ ξηρὰ ταῦτα πῶς δύνανται
ζῆσαι; 7. ἀποκριθείς μοι λέγει· Τὸ δένδρον τοῦτο
ἰτέα ἐστὶ καὶ φιλόζωον τὸ γένος· ἐὰν οὖν φυτευ-
θῶσι καὶ μικρὰν ἰκμάδα λαμβάνωσιν αἱ ῥάβδοι,
ζήσονται πολλαὶ ἐξ αὐτῶν· εἶτα δὲ πειράσωμεν
καὶ ὕδωρ αὐταῖς παραχέειν. ἐάν τις αὐτῶν
δυνηθῇ ζῆσαι, συγχαρήσομαι αὐταῖς· ἐὰν δὲ μὴ
ζήσῃ, οὐχ εὑρεθήσομαι ἐγὼ ἀμελής. 8. ἐκέλευσε
δέ μοι ὁ ποιμὴν καλέσαι, καθώς τις αὐτῶν ἐστάθη.
ἦλθον τάγματα τάγματα καὶ ἐπεδίδουν τὰς ῥάβδους
τῷ ποιμένι· ἐλάμβανε δὲ ὁ ποιμὴν τὰς ῥάβδους καὶ
κατὰ τάγματα ἐφύτευσεν αὐτὰς καὶ μετὰ τὸ
φυτεῦσαι ὕδωρ αὐταῖς πολὺ παρέχεεν, ὥστε ἀπὸ
τοῦ ὕδατος μὴ φαίνεσθαι τὰς ῥάβδους. 9. καὶ
μετὰ τὸ ποτίσαι αὐτὸν τὰς ῥάβδους λέγει μοι·
Ἄγωμεν [1] καὶ μετ᾽ ὀλίγας ἡμέρας ἐπανέλθωμεν
καὶ ἐπισκεψώμεθα τὰς ῥάβδους πάσας· ὁ γὰρ

1 Tim. 2, 4

κτίσας τὸ δένδρον τοῦτο θέλει πάντας ζῆν τοὺς
λαβόντας ἐκ τοῦ δένδρου τούτου κλάδους. ἐλπίζω
δὲ κἀγώ, ὅτι λαβόντα τὰ ῥαβδία ταῦτα ἰκμάδα
καὶ ποτισθέντα ὕδατι ζήσονται τὸ πλεῖστον μέρος
αὐτῶν.

III

1. Λέγω αὐτῷ· Κύριε, τὸ δένδρον τοῦτο γνώρισόν μοι τί ἐστιν· ἀπορῦμαι γὰρ περὶ αὐτοῦ, ὅτι
τοσούτων κλάδων κοπέντων ὑγιές ἐστι τὸ δένδρον
καὶ οὐδὲν φαίνεται κεκομμένον ἀπ᾽ αὐτοῦ· ἐν τούτῳ
οὖν ἀπορῦμαι. 2. Ἄκουε, φησί· τὸ δένδρον
τοῦτο τὸ μέγα τὸ σκεπάζον πεδία καὶ ὄρη καὶ

[1] ἄγωμεν LE, om. A.

194

of them will be able to live." I said to him: " Sir, The treatment of the sticks by the shepherd
how can these dry things live?" 7. He answered
me, and said: " This tree is a willow, and is a
species tenacious of life. If then, the sticks be
planted and receive a little moisture, many of them
will live ; but next we must try them, and water
them. If any of them can live I shall rejoice with
them, and if they do not live I shall not be proved
careless." 8. And the shepherd commanded me to
call each of them as they stood. They came, rank
by rank, and gave up their sticks to the shepherd.
And the shepherd took the sticks amd planted them
in ranks, and after planting them, poured much
water round them, so that the sticks could not be
seen for the water. 9. And after he had watered the
sticks he said to me: " Let us go and come back
after a few days, and visit all the sticks, for he who
created this tree wishes all to live who received
branches from this tree. And I too have hope for
these sticks which have received moisture and been
watered, that the greater part of them will live."

III

1. I said to him : " Sir, tell me what this tree is. The explanation of the parable
For I am perplexed about it, that although so many
branches have been cut off, the tree is healthy, and
nothing seems to have been cut from it ; I am
perplexed at this." 2. " Listen," said he, " this
great tree, which covers plains and mountains and

πᾶσαν τὴν γῆν νόμος θεοῦ ἐστιν ὁ δοθεὶς εἰς ὅλον
τὸν κόσμον· ὁ δὲ νόμος οὗτος υἱὸς θεοῦ ἐστι
κηρυχθεὶς εἰς τὰ πέρατα τῆς γῆς· οἱ δὲ ὑπὸ τὴν
σκέπην λαοὶ ὄντες οἱ ἀκούσαντες τοῦ κηρύγματος
καὶ πιστεύσαντες εἰς αὐτόν· 3. ὁ δὲ ἄγγελος ὁ
μέγας καὶ ἔνδοξος Μιχαὴλ ὁ ἔχων τὴν ἐξουσίαν
τούτου τοῦ λαοῦ καὶ διακυβερνῶν αὐτούς·[1]
οὗτος γάρ ἐστιν ὁ διδοὺς αὐτοῖς τὸν νόμον εἰς τὰς
καρδίας τῶν πιστευόντων· ἐπισκέπτεται οὖν
αὐτούς, οἷς ἔδωκεν, εἰ ἄρα τετηρήκασιν αὐτόν.
4. βλέπεις δὲ ἑνὸς ἑκάστου τὰς ῥάβδους· αἱ γὰρ
ῥάβδοι ὁ νόμος ἐστί. βλέπεις οὖν πολλὰς ῥάβδους ἠχρειωμένας, γνώσῃ δὲ αὐτοὺς πάντας τοὺς
μὴ τηρήσαντας τὸν νόμον· καὶ ὄψει ἑνὸς ἑκάστου
τὴν κατοικίαν. 5. λέγω αὐτῷ· Κύριε, διατί οὓς
μὲν ἀπέλυσεν εἰς τὸν πύργον, οὓς δὲ σοὶ κατέ-
λειψεν; Ὅσοι, φησί, παρέβησαν τὸν νόμον, ὃν
ἔλαβον παρ᾿ αὐτοῦ, εἰς τὴν ἐμὴν ἐξουσίαν
κατέλιπεν αὐτοὺς εἰς μετάνοιαν· ὅσοι δὲ ἤδη
εὐηρέστησαν τῷ νόμῳ καὶ τετηρήκασιν αὐτόν, ὑπὸ
τὴν ἰδίαν ἐξουσίαν ἔχει αὐτούς. 6. Τίνες οὖν, φημί,
κύριε, εἰσὶν οἱ ἐστεφανωμένοι καὶ εἰς τὸν πύργον
ὑπάγοντες; Ὅσοι, φησίν, ἀντεπάλαισαν τῷ
διαβόλῳ καὶ ἐνίκησαν αὐτόν, ἐστεφανωμένοι
εἰσίν·[2] οὗτοί εἰσιν οἱ ὑπὲρ τοῦ νόμου παθόντες·
7. οἱ δὲ ἕτεροι καὶ αὐτοὶ χλωρὰς τὰς ῥάβδους
ἐπιδεδωκότες καὶ παραφυάδας ἐχούσας, καρπὸν δὲ
μὴ ἐχούσας οἱ ὑπὲρ τοῦ νόμου θλιβέντες, μὴ

---

[1] αὐτούς om. A.
[2] ὅσοι . . . εἰσίν retranslated from LE ; instead of ἐνίκησαν
editors usually read κατεπάλαισαν, but this is not justified by
the Latin (colluctati . . . vicerunt).

all the earth, is God's law which was given to all
the world. And this law is God's son preached to
the ends of the earth. And those who are under its
shade are nations which have heard the preaching
and have believed in it. 3. And the great and
glorious angel[1] is Michael, who has power over this
people and governs them; for this is he who put the
law into the hearts of those who believe. Therefore
he looks after those to whom he gave it to see if
they have really kept it. 4. But you see the sticks
of each one, for the sticks are the law. Therefore,
you see that many sticks have been made useless,
and you will understand, that they are all the men
who have not observed the law; and you will see the
dwelling of each one of them." 5. I said to him:
" Sir, why did he send some into the tower, and left
some to you?" "All those who have transgressed
against the law, which they received from him, he
left to my authority for repentance. But as many
as were already well-pleased with the law, and have
observed it, he keeps them under his own authority."
6. " Who then, Sir," said I, " are they who were
crowned and went into the tower?" " All those,"
said he, " who wrestled with the devil and conquered
him, have been crowned. These are they who
suffered for the law. 7. And the others who also gave
up their sticks green and having buds, but without
fruit, are they who were persecuted for the law, but

[1] But in Sim. ix. he is the Son of God. This together
with the identification of the Son with the Spirit in Sim. ix.
1 (cf. Sim. v. 5) makes it very hard to reconstruct the
Christology of Hermas. On the question of Michael see
W. Lueken's *Michael*, Göttingen, 1898.

THE APOSTOLIC FATHERS

παθόντες δὲ μηδὲ ἀρνησάμενοι τὸν νόμον αὐτῶν.
8. οἱ δὲ χλωρὰς ἐπιδεδωκότες, οἵας ἔλαβον, σεμνοὶ
καὶ δίκαιοι καὶ λίαν πορευθέντες ἐν καθαρᾷ καρδίᾳ
καὶ τὰς ἐντολὰς κυρίου πεφυλακότες. τὰ δὲ λοιπὰ
γνώσῃ, ὅταν κατανοήσω τὰς ῥάβδους ταύτας τὰς
πεφυτευμένας καὶ πεποτισμένας.

IV

1. Καὶ μετὰ ἡμέρας ὀλίγας ἤλθομεν εἰς τὸν
τόπον, καὶ ἐκάθισεν ὁ ποιμὴν εἰς τὸν τόπον τοῦ
ἀγγέλου, κἀγὼ παρεστάθην αὐτῷ. καὶ λέγει μοι·
Περίζωσαι ὠμόλινον καὶ[1] διακόνει μοι. περιεζω-
σάμην ὠμόλινον ἐκ σάκκου γεγονὸς καθαρόν.
2. ἰδὼν δέ με περιεζωσμένον καὶ ἕτοιμον ὄντα τοῦ
διακονεῖν αὐτῷ, Κάλει, φησί, τοὺς ἄνδρας, ὧν
εἰσὶν αἱ ῥάβδοι πεφυτευμέναι, κατὰ τὸ τάγμα, ὡς
τις ἔδωκε τὰς ῥάβδους. καὶ ἀπῆλθον εἰς τὸ πεδίον
καὶ ἐκάλεσα πάντας· καὶ ἔστησαν πάντες τάγματα
τάγματα.[2] 3. λέγει αὐτοῖς· Ἕκαστος τὰς ἰδίας
ῥάβδους ἐκτιλάτω καὶ φερέτω πρός με. 4. πρῶτοι ἐπέδωκαν οἱ τὰς ξηρὰς καὶ κεκομμένας
ἐσχηκότες, καὶ ὡς αὗται εὑρέθησαν ξηραὶ καὶ
κεκομμέναι, ἐκέλευσεν αὐτοὺς χωρὶς σταθῆναι.
5. εἶτα ἐπέδωκαν οἱ τὰς ξηρὰς καὶ μὴ κεκομμένας
ἔχοντες· τινὲς δὲ ἐξ αὐτῶν ἐπέδωκαν τὰς ῥάβδους

[1] καὶ διακόνει . . . ὠμόλινον om. A.
[2] τάγματα τάγματα emended in accordance with Sim. VIII.
ii. 8. A reads πάντα τὰ τάγματα: Funk emends to κατὰ
τάγματα.

198

did not suffer,[1] and did not deny their law.   8. And
those who gave them up green, as they received
them, are holy and righteous and have walked far
with a pure heart, and have kept the commandments
of the Lord.   And the rest you will know, when I
look at these sticks which have been planted and
watered."

IV

1. AND after a few days he came to the place, The con-
and the shepherd sat in the place of the angel, and of the
I stood by him, and he said to me; "Gird your- parable
self with a towel[2] and serve me."   And I girded
myself with a clean towel made of sackcloth.
2. And when he saw me girded and ready to serve
him he said : "Call the men whose sticks have
been planted, according to the order in which each
gave his stick."   And I went into the plain and
called all of them, and they all stood in their stations.
3. And he said to them : "Let each pull out his own
stick and bring it to me."   4. And they first gave
them up who had had them dry and cut, and they
were found to be still dry and cut, and he commanded them to stand apart.   5. Then they gave
them up who had them dry, but not cut, and some

---

[1] 'Suffer' means 'suffer a death of martyrdom,' and the
law means the Christian rule of life, not (as in the N.T.) the
Jewish Law.
[2] The exact meaning of ὠμόλινον is apparently 'made of
undressed flax,' but it came to mean merely a towel.

χλωράς, τινὲς δὲ ξηρὰς καὶ κεκομμένας ὡς ὑπὸ
σητός. τοὺς ἐπιδεδωκότας οὖν χλωρὰς ἐκέλευσε
χωρὶς σταθῆναι, τοὺς δὲ ξηρὰς καὶ κεκομμένας
ἐπιδεδωκότας ἐκέλευσε μετὰ τῶν πρώτων σταθῆναι. 6. εἶτα ἐπέδωκαν οἱ τὰς ἡμιξήρους καὶ
σχισμὰς ἐχούσας· καὶ πολλοὶ ἐξ αὐτῶν χλωρὰς
ἐπέδωκαν καὶ μὴ ἐχούσας σχισμάς· τινὲς δὲ
χλωρὰς καὶ παραφυάδας ἐχούσας καὶ εἰς τὰς
παραφυάδας καρπούς, οἵους εἶχον οἱ εἰς τὸν πύργον
πορευθέντες ἐστεφανωμένοι. τινὲς δὲ ἐπέδωκαν
ξηρὰς καὶ βεβρωμένας, τινὲς δὲ ξηρὰς καὶ ἀβρώ-
τους, τινὲς δὲ οἷαι ἦσαν ἡμίξηροι καὶ σχισμὰς
ἔχουσαι. ἐκέλευσεν αὐτοὺς ἕνα ἕκαστον χωρὶς
σταθῆναι, τοὺς μὲν πρὸς τὰ ἴδια τάγματα, τοὺς δὲ
χωρίς.

V

1. Εἶτα ἐπεδίδουν οἱ τὰς ῥάβδους χλωρὰς μὲν
ἔχοντες, σχισμὰς δὲ ἐχούσας· οὗτοι πάντες
χλωρὰς ἐπέδωκαν καὶ ἔστησαν εἰς τὸ ἴδιον τάγμα.
ἐχάρη δὲ ὁ ποιμὴν ἐπὶ τούτοις, ὅτι πάντες
ἠλλοιώθησαν καὶ ἀπέθεντο τὰς σχισμὰς αὐτῶν.
2. ἐπέδωκαν δὲ καὶ οἱ τὸ ἥμισυ χλωρόν, τὸ δὲ
ἥμισυ ξηρὸν ἔχοντες· τινῶν οὖν εὑρέθησαν αἱ
ῥάβδοι ὁλοτελῶς χλωραί,_τινῶν ἡμίξηροι, τινῶν
ξηραὶ καὶ βεβρωμέναι, τινῶν δὲ χλωραὶ καὶ
παραφυάδας ἔχουσαι· οὗτοι πάντες ἀπελύθησαν
ἕκαστος πρὸς τὸ τάγμα αὐτοῦ. 3. εἶτα ἐπέδωκαν
οἱ τὰ δύο μέρη χλωρὰ ἔχοντες, τὸ δὲ τρίτον ξηρόν.
πολλοὶ ἐξ αὐτῶν χλωρὰς ἐπέδωκαν, πολλοὶ δὲ

of them gave up their sticks green and some dry
and cut as it were by moth. Those then who gave
them up green he commanded to stand apart, and
those who had given them up dry and cut he
commanded to stand with the first ones. 6. Then
those gave them up who had them half dry and
cracked, and many of them gave them up green and
without cracks, and some green and with buds, and
with fruit on the buds, as those had had who
had gone crowned into the tower. But some gave
them up dry and moth-eaten, and some dry but not
eaten, and some remained half dry and with cracks.
And he commanded each of them to stand apart,
some in their own station and some apart.[1]

V

1. Next those gave up their sticks who had had
them green but with cracks, and these all gave them
up green and stood in their own station. And the
shepherd rejoiced over these that all were changed and
had lost their cracks. 2. And those also gave them
up who had had them half green and half dry. The
sticks of some of them were found quite green, of
some half dry, of some dry and moth-eaten, but of
some green and with buds. All these were sent each
to his own station. 3. Next those gave them up who
had two-thirds green and one-third dry ; many of

---

[1] This must mean that some were sent back to their
original place, others were moved aside. But the text is
obscure and probably corrupt.

ἡμιξήρους, ἕτεροι δὲ ξηρὰς καὶ βεβρωμένας·
οὗτοι πάντες ἔστησαν εἰς τὸ ἴδιον τάγμα.
4. εἶτα ἐπέδωκαν οἱ τὰ δύο μέρη ξηρὰ ἔχοντες,
τὸ δὲ τρίτον χλωρόν· πολλοὶ ἐξ αὐτῶν ἡμιξήρους
ἐπέδωκαν, τινὲς δὲ ξηρὰς καὶ βεβρωμένας, ἕτεροι
δὲ ἡμιξήρους, καὶ σχισμὰς ἐχούσας, ὀλίγοι δὲ
χλωράς· οὗτοι πάντες ἔστησαν εἰς τὸ ἴδιον
τάγμα.[1] 5. ἐπέδωκαν δὲ οἱ τὰς ῥάβδους αὐτῶν
χλωρὰς ἐσχηκότες, ἐλάχιστον δὲ ξηρὸν[2] καὶ
σχισμὰς ἐχούσας· ἐκ τούτων τινὲς χλωρὰς
ἐπέδωκαν, τινὲς δὲ χλωρὰς καὶ παραφυάδας·
ἀπῆλθον καὶ οὗτοι εἰς τὸ τάγμα αὐτῶν. 6. εἶτα
ἐπέδωκαν οἱ ἐλάχιστον ἔχοντες χλωρόν, τὰ δὲ
λοιπὰ μέρη ξηρά· τούτων αἱ ῥάβδοι εὑρέθησαν
τὸ πλεῖστον μέρος χλωραὶ καὶ παραφυάδας
ἔχουσαι καὶ καρπὸν ἐν ταῖς παραφύσι, καὶ
ἕτεραι χλωραὶ ὅλαι. ἐπὶ ταύταις ταῖς ῥάβδοις
ἐχάρη ὁ ποιμὴν λίαν μεγάλως, ὅτι οὕτως εὑρέθησαν. ἀπῆλθον δὲ οὗτοι ἕκαστος εἰς τὸ ἴδιον
τάγμα.

VI

1. Μετὰ τὸ παντων κατανοῆσαι τὰς ῥάβδους
τὸν ποιμένα λέγει μοι· Εἶπόν σοι, ὅτι τὸ δένδρον
τοῦτο φιλόζωόν ἐστι. βλέπεις, φησί, πόσοι
μετενόησαν καὶ ἐσώθησαν; Βλέπω, φημί, κύριε.
Ἵνα ἴδῃς, φησί, τὴν πολυευσπλαγχνίαν τοῦ
κυρίου, ὅτι μεγάλη καὶ ἔνδοξός ἐστι, καὶ ἔδωκε
πνεῦμα τοῖς ἀξίοις οὖσι μετανοίας. 2. Διατί
οὖν, φημί, κύριε, πάντες οὐ μετενόησαν; Ὧν

[1] εἶτα . . . τάγμα retranslated from LE, om. A.
[2] ξηρόν LE, om. A.

them gave them up green, but many half-dry, and
others dry and moth-eaten ; these all stood in their
own station.   4. Next they gave them up who had
had two-thirds dry, and one-third green.   Many
of them gave them up half-dry, and some dry and
moth-eaten and others half-dry and with cracks,
and a few green.   These all stood in their own
station.   5. And those gave up their sticks who had
had them green, but a very little dry and with
cracks.   Of these some gave them up green, and
some green and with buds.   These also went away
to their own station.   6. Next, those gave them up
who had had a very little green, but the rest dry.
Of these the sticks were found for the greatest
part green and with buds, and fruit on the buds,
and others quite green.   Over these sticks the
shepherd rejoiced greatly because they were found
thus.   And these went away each to his own station.

VI

1. AFTER the shepherd had looked at the sticks of The
them all, he said to me : " I told you that this tree further
is tenacious of life.   Do you see," said he, " how
many have repented and been saved ? "   " Yes, Sir,"
said I, " I see it."   " See then," said he, " the mercifulness of the Lord, that it is great and glorious, and
he has given his spirit to those who are worthy of
repentance."   2. " Why then, Sir," said I, "did not all

εἶδε, φησί, τὴν καρδίαν μέλλουσαν καθαρὰν γενέσθαι καὶ δουλεύειν αὐτῷ ἐξ ὅλης καρδίας, τούτοις ἔδωκε τὴν μετάνοιαν· ὧν δὲ εἶδε τὴν δολιότητα καὶ πονηρίαν, μελλόντων ἐν ὑποκρίσει μετανοεῖν, ἐκείνοις οὐκ ἔδωκε μετάνοιαν, μήποτε πάλιν βεβηλώσωσι τὸ ὄνομα αὐτοῦ. 3. λέγω αὐτῷ· Κύριε, νῦν οὖν μοι δήλωσον τοὺς τὰς ῥάβδους ἐπιδεδωκότας, ποταπός τις αὐτῶν ἐστί, καὶ τὴν τούτων κατοικίαν, ἵνα ἀκούσαντες οἱ πιστεύσαντες καὶ εἰληφότες τὴν σφραγῖδα καὶ τεθλακότες αὐτὴν καὶ μὴ τηρήσαντες ὑγιῆ, ἐπιγνόντες τὰ ἑαυτῶν ἔργα μενανοήσωσι, λαβόντες ὑπὸ σοῦ σφραγῖδα, καὶ δοξάσωσι .τὸν κύριον, ὅτι ἐσπλαγχνίσθη ἐπ᾽ αὐτοὺς καὶ ἀπέστειλέ σε τοῦ ἀνακαινίσαι τὰ πνεύματα αὐτῶν. 4. Ἄκουε, φησίν· ὧν αἱ ῥάβδοι ξηραὶ καὶ βεβρωμέναι ὑπὸ σητὸς εὑρέθησαν, οὗτοί εἰσιν οἱ ἀποστάται καὶ προδόται τῆς ἐκκλησίας καὶ βλασφημήσαντες

Jam. 2, 7 cf.
Gen. 48, 16 ;
etc.

ἐν ταῖς ἁμαρτίαις αὐτῶν τὸν κύριον, ἔτι δὲ καὶ ἐπαισχυνθέντες τὸ ὄνομα κυρίου τὸ ἐπικληθὲν ἐπ᾽ αὐτούς. οὗτοι οὖν εἰς τέλος ἀπώλοντο τῷ θεῷ. βλέπεις δέ, ὅτι οὐδὲ εἷς αὐτῶν μετενόησε, καίπερ ἀκούσαντες τὰ ῥήματα, ἃ ἐλάλησας αὐτοῖς, ἅ σοι ἐνετειλάμην· ἀπὸ τῶν τοιούτων ἡ ζωὴ ἀπέστη. 5. οἱ δὲ τὰς ξηρὰς καὶ ἀσήπτους ἐπιδεδωκότες, καὶ οὗτοι ἐγγὺς αὐτῶν· ἦσαν γὰρ ὑποκριταὶ καὶ διδαχὰς ξένας εἰσφέροντες καὶ ἐκστρέφοντες τοὺς δούλους τοῦ θεοῦ, μάλιστα δὲ τοὺς ἡμαρτηκότας, μὴ ἀφιέντες μετανοεῖν αὐτούς, ἀλλὰ ταῖς διδαχαῖς ταῖς μωραῖς πείθοντες αὐτούς. οὗτοι οὖν ἔχουσιν ἐλπίδα τοῦ μετανοῆσαι. 6. βλέπεις δὲ πολλοὺς ἐξ αὐτῶν καὶ μετανενοηκότας,

repent?" "He gave repentance to those," said he, "whose heart he saw would be pure, and would serve him with all their heart. But in whom he saw guile and wickedness, that they would repent with hypocrisy, to them he gave no repentance, lest they should again defile his name." 3. I said to him: "Sir, now therefore, explain to me those who gave up the sticks, what is the character of each and their dwelling, that when those hear who have believed and have received the seal, and have broken it, and have not kept it whole, they may recognize their own deeds, and repent, and receive a seal from you and glorify the Lord, that he had mercy on them, and sent you to renew their spirits." 4. "Listen," said he, "those whose sticks are dry and were found moth-eaten are the apostates and the betrayers of the Church, and blasphemers of the Lord in their sins; and moreover they were ashamed of 'the name of the Lord which was called over them.' These then have finally perished to God. And you see that not even one of them repented, although they heard the words which you spoke to them, which I commanded you; from such life is departed. 5. And they who gave up their sticks dry and not moth-eaten, these are also near them; for they were hypocrites, and introduced strange doctrines and corrupted the servants of God, and especially those who have sinned, not suffering them to repent, but persuading them with their foolish doctrines. These, then, have hope of repentance. 6. And you see that many of them have repented since I

ἀφ' ἧς ἐλάλησα[1] αὐτοῖς τὰς ἐντολάς μου· καὶ
ἔτι μετανοήσουσιν. ὅσοι δὲ οὐ μετανοήσουσιν,
ἀπώλεσαν τὴν ζωὴν αὐτῶν. ὅσοι δὲ μετενόησαν
ἐξ αὐτῶν, ἀγαθοὶ ἐγένοντο, καὶ ἐγένετο ἡ κατοικία
αὐτῶν εἰς τὰ τείχη τὰ πρῶτα· τινὲς δὲ καὶ εἰς τὸν
πύργον ἀνέβησαν. βλέπεις οὖν, φησίν, ὅτι ἡ
μετάνοια τῶν ἁμαρτιῶν ζωὴν ἔχει, τὸ δὲ μὴ
μετανοῆσαι θάνατον.

VII

1. Ὅσοι δὲ ἡμιξήρους ἐπέδωκαν καὶ ἐν αὐταῖς
σχισμὰς εἶχον, ἄκουε καὶ περὶ αὐτῶν. ὅσων
ἦσαν αἱ ῥάβδοι ἡμίξηροι,[2] δίψυχοί εἰσιν· οὔτε
γὰρ ζῶσιν οὔτε τεθνήκασιν. 2. οἱ δὲ ἡμιξήρους ἔχοντες καὶ ἐν αὐταῖς σχιτμάς, οὗτοι
καὶ δίψυχοι καὶ κατάλαλοί εἰσι καὶ μηδέποτε
εἰρηνεύοντες εἰς ἑαυτούς, ἀλλὰ διχοστατοῦντες
πάντοτε. ἀλλὰ καὶ τούτοις, φησίν, ἐπίκειται
μετάνοια. βλέπεις, φησί, τινὰς ἐξ αὐτῶν μετανενοηκότας. καὶ ἔτι, φησίν, ἐστὶν ἐν αὐτοῖς
ἐλπὶς μετανοίας.[3] 3. καὶ ὅσοι, φησίν, ἐξ αὐτῶν
μετανενοήκασι, τὴν κατοικίαν εἰς τὸν πύργον
ἕξουσιν·[4] ὅσοι δὲ ἐξ αὐτῶν βραδύτερον μετανενοήκασιν, εἰς τὰ τείχη κατοικήσουσιν· ὅσοι δὲ οὐ
μετανοοῦσιν, ἀλλ' ἐμμένουσι ταῖς πράξεσιν αὐτῶν,
θανάτῳ ἀποθανοῦνται. 4. οἱ δὲ χλωρὰς ἐπιδε-

I Thess. 5,
13

---

[1] ἐλάλησα A, ἐλάλησας L, 'nuntiatum est' E.
[2] ἡμίξηροι L₂E₁ κατὰ τὸ αὐτὸ ἡμίξηροι A, tantummodo
semiaridae L₁; κατὰ τὸ αὐτό seems meaningless, and may be a
misunderstood gloss taken into the text.
[3] καὶ ἔτι . . . μετανοίας om. L.   [4] ἕξουσιν A, ἔχουσιν LE.

told them my commandments; and they shall still repent. But as many as shall not repent have lost their lives. But as many of them as repented became good and their dwelling was within the first walls, and some of them even went up into the tower. You see then," said he, " that repentance of sins brings life, but not to repent brings death."

VII

1. "AND as many as gave them up half dry and had cracks in them; listen also, concerning them :— They, whose sticks were half dry are the double-minded, for they are neither alive nor dead. 2. And those who had them half dry and with cracks, these are double-minded and evil speakers, and are never 'at peace among themselves,' but are always making schisms; but repentance," said he, " waits also for these. You see," said he, " that some of them have repented, and there remains," said he, " still hope of repentance in them. 3. And as many of them," said he, " as have repented, shall have their dwellings in the tower, and as many of them as have repented more slowly, shall dwell on the walls. But as many as do not repent, but remain in their deeds, shall die the death. 4. And

δωκότες τὰς ῥάβδους αὐτῶν καὶ σχισμὰς ἐχούσας,
πάντοτε οὗτοι πιστοὶ καὶ ἀγαθοὶ ἐγένοντο,
ἔχοντες δὲ ζῆλόν τινα ἐν ἀλλήλοις περὶ
πρωτείων καὶ περὶ δόξης τινός· ἀλλὰ πάντες
οὗτοι μωροί εἰσιν, ἐν ἀλλήλοις ἔχοντες ζῆλον
περὶ πρωτείων. 5. ἀλλὰ καὶ οὗτοι ἀκούσαντες
τῶν ἐντολῶν μου, ἀγαθοὶ ὄντες, ἐκαθάρισαν
ἑαυτοὺς καὶ μετενόησαν ταχύ. ἐγένετο οὖν ἡ
κατοίκησις αὐτῶν εἰς τὸν πύργον· ἐὰν δέ τις
πάλιν ἐπιστρέψῃ εἰς τὴν διχοστασίαν, ἐκβλη-
θήσεται ἀπὸ τοῦ πύργου καὶ ἀπολέσει τὴν ζωὴν
αὐτοῦ. 6. ἡ ζωὴ πάντων ἐστὶ τῶν τὰς ἐντολὰς
τοῦ κυρίου φυλασσόντων· ἐν ταῖς ἐντολαῖς δὲ
περὶ πρωτείων ἢ περὶ δόξης τινος οὐκ ἔστιν, ἀλλὰ
περὶ μακροθυμίας καὶ περὶ ταπεινοφρονήσεως
ἀνδρός. ἐν τοῖς τοιούτοις οὖν ἡ ζωὴ τοῦ κυρίου
ἐν τοῖς διχοστάταις δὲ καὶ παρανόμοις θάνατος.

VIII

1. Οἱ δὲ ἐπιδεδωκότες τὰς ῥάβδους ἥμισυ μὲν
χλωράς, ἥμισυ δὲ ξηράς, οὗτοί εἰσιν οἱ ἐν ταῖς
πραγματείαις ἐμπεφυρμένοι καὶ μὴ κολλώμενοι
τοῖς ἁγίοις· διὰ τοῦτο τὸ ἥμισυ αὐτῶν ζῇ, τὸ δὲ
ἥμισυ νεκρόν ἐστι. 2. πολλοὶ οὖν ἀκούσαντές
μου τῶν ἐντολῶν μετενόησαν. ὅσοι γοῦν μετενόησαν, ἡ κατοικία αὐτῶν εἰς τὸν πύργον. τινὲς
δὲ αὐτῶν εἰς τέλος ἀπέστησαν. οὗτοι οὖν μετάνοιαν οὐκ ἔχουσιν· διὰ γὰρ τὰς πραγματείας
αὐτῶν ἐβλασφήμησαν τὸν κύριον καὶ ἀπηρνή-
σαντο. ἀπώλεσαν οὖν τὴν ζωὴν αὐτῶν διὰ τὴν

they who gave up their sticks green and with cracks, these were ever faithful and good, but had some jealousy among themselves over the first place and some question of reputation. But all these are foolish, who quarrel among themselves about the first place. 5. But these also, when they heard my commandments, because they were good, purified themselves and quickly repented; so their dwelling was in the tower. But if any of them turn again to schism he shall be cast out from the tower, and shall lose his life. 6. Life is for all those who keep the commandments of the Lord. And in the commandments there is nothing about the first place or any question of reputation, but about man's long-suffering and humility. Among such, then, is the life of the Lord, but among the schismatic and law-breakers there is death.

VIII

1. "But those who gave up their sticks half-green and half-dry these are those who are concerned with business and do not cleave to the saints; for this reason half of them is alive, and half is dead. 2. Many, then, of them, when they heard my commandments repented. As many, as repented, have their dwelling in the tower; but some of them were apostate to the end. These then have no repentance, for because of their business they blasphemed the Lord and denied him. So they lost their life because

πονηρίαν, ἣν ἔπραξαν. 3. πολλοὶ δὲ ἐξ αὐτῶν
ἐδιψύχησαν. οὗτοι ἔτι ἔχουσι μετάνοιαν, ἐὰν ταχὺ
μετανοήσωσι, καὶ ἔσται αὐτῶν ἡ κατοικία εἰς τὸν
πύργον· ἐὰν δὲ βραδύτερον μετανοήσωσι, κατοικήσουσιν εἰς τὰ τείχη· ἐὰν δὲ μὴ μετανοήσωσι, καὶ
αὐτοὶ ἀπώλεσαν τὴν ζωὴν αὐτῶν. 4. οἱ δὲ τὰ
δύο μέρη χλωρά, τὸ δὲ τρίτον ξηρὸν ἐπιδεδωκότες,
οὗτοί εἰσιν οἱ ἀρνησάμενοι ποικίλαις ἀρνήσεσι.
5. πολλοὶ οὖν μετενόησαν ἐξ αὐτῶν, καὶ ἀπῆλθον
εἰς τὸν πύργον κατοικεῖν· πολλοὶ δὲ ἀπέστησαν
εἰς τέλος τοῦ θεοῦ· οὗτοι τὸ ζῆν εἰς τέλος
ἀπώλεσαν. τινὲς δὲ ἐξ αὐτῶν ἐδιψύχησαν καὶ
ἐδιχοστάτησαν. τούτοις οὖν ἐστὶ μετάνοια, ἐὰν
ταχὺ μετανοήσωσι καὶ μὴ ἐπιμείνωσι ταῖς ἡδοναῖς
αὐτῶν· ἐὰν δὲ ἐπιμείνωσι ταῖς πράξεσιν αὐτῶν,
καὶ οὗτοι θάνατον ἑαυτοῖς κατεργάζονται.

IX

1. Οἱ δὲ ἐπιδεδωκότες τὰς ῥάβδους τὰ μὲν δύο
μέρη ξηρά, τὸ δὲ τρίτον χλωρόν, οὗτοί εἰσι πιστοὶ
μὲν γεγονότες, πλουτήσαντες δὲ καὶ γενόμενοι
ἔνδοξοι παρὰ τοῖς ἔθνεσιν· ὑπερηφανίαν μεγάλην
ἐνεδύσαντο καὶ ὑψηλόφρονες ἐγένοντο καὶ κατέ-
λιπον τὴν ἀλήθειαν καὶ οὐκ ἐκολλήθησαν τοῖς
δικαίοις, ἀλλὰ μετὰ τῶν ἐθνῶν συνέζησαν, καὶ αὕτη
ἡ ὁδὸς ἡδυτέρα αὐτοῖς ἐγένετο· ἀπὸ δὲ τοῦ θεοῦ
οὐκ ἀπέστησαν, ἀλλ' ἐνέμειναν τῇ πίστει, μὴ
ἐργαζόμενοι τὰ ἔργα τῆς πίστεως. 2. πολλοὶ οὖν
ἐξ αὐτῶν μετενόησαν, καὶ ἐγένετο ἡ κατοίκησις
αὐτῶν ἐν τῷ πύργῳ. 3. ἕτεροι δὲ εἰς τέλος μετὰ

of the wickedness which they wrought. 3. And many of them were double-minded. These have still repentance if they repent quickly, and their dwelling shall be in the tower, but if they repent more slowly they shall dwell on the walls. But if they do not repent they also have lost their life. 4. And those who gave up their sticks two-thirds green, and one-third dry, these are they who have denied with manifold denials. 5. Many of them therefore repented and went to live in the tower. But many of them were apostates from God to the end; these lost their life finally. And some of them were double-minded, and were schismatic, these then have repentance, if they repent quickly, and do not remain in their pleasures; but if they continue in their deeds, these also procure death for themselves.

IX

1. AND those who gave up their sticks two-thirds dry, and one-third green, these are they who were faithful, but became rich and in honour among the heathen; then they put on great haughtiness and became high-minded, and abandoned the truth, and did not cleave to the righteous, but lived together with the heathen, and this way pleased them better. But they were not apostates from God, but remained in the faith, without doing the works of the faith. 2. Many, then, of them repented, and their dwelling was in the tower. 3. But others lived to the end

τῶν ἐθνῶν συζῶντες καὶ φθειρόμενοι ταῖς κενοδο-
ξίαις τῶν ἐθνῶν ἀπέστησαν ἀπὸ τοῦ θεοῦ καὶ
ἔπραξαν τὰς πράξεις τῶν ἐθνῶν. οὗτοι μετὰ τῶν
ἐθνῶν ἐλογίσθησαν. 4. ἕτεροι δὲ ἐξ αὐτῶν
ἐδιψύχησαν μὴ ἐλπίζοντες σωθῆναι διὰ τὰς
πράξεις, ἃς ἔπραξαν· ἕτεροι δὲ ἐδιψύχησαν καὶ
σχίσματα ἐν ἑαυτοῖς ἐποίησαν. τούτοις οὖν τοῖς
διψυχήσασι διὰ τὰς πράξεις αὐτῶν μετάνοια ἔτι
ἐστίν· ἀλλ' ἡ μετάνοια αὐτῶν ταχινὴ ὀφείλει
εἶναι, ἵνα ἡ κατοικία αὐτῶν γένηται εἰς τὸν
πύργον τῶν δὲ μὴ μετανοούντων, ἀλλ' ἐπιμενόντων
ταῖς ἡδοναῖς, ὁ θάνατος ἐγγύς.

X

1. Οἱ δὲ τὰς ῥάβδους ἐπιδεδωκότες χλωράς,
αὐτὰ δὲ τὰ ἄκρα ξηρὰ καὶ σχισμὰς ἔχοντα, οὗτοι
πάντοτε ἀγαθοὶ καὶ πιστοὶ καὶ ἔνδοξοι παρὰ τῷ
θεῷ ἐγένοντο, ἐλάχιστον δὲ ἐξήμαρτον διὰ μικρὰς
ἐπιθυμίας καὶ μικρὰ κατ' ἀλλήλων ἔχοντες· ἀλλ'
ἀκούσαντές μου τῶν ῥημάτων τὸ πλεῖστον μέρος
ταχὺ μετενόησαν, καὶ ἐγένετο ἡ κατοικία αὐτῶν
εἰς τὸν πύργον. 2. τινὲς δὲ ἐξ αὐτῶν ἐδιψύχησαν,
τινὲς δὲ διψυχήσαντες διχοστασίαν μείζονα
ἐποίησαν. ἐν τούτοις οὖν ἔνεστι μετανοίας ἐλπίς,
ὅτι ἀγαθοὶ πάντοτε ἐγένοντο· δυσκόλως δέ τις
αὐτῶν ἀποθανεῖται. 3. οἱ δὲ τὰς ῥάβδους αὐτῶν
ξηρὰς ἐπιδεδωκότες, ἐλάχιστον δὲ χλωρὸν ἐχούσας,
οὗτοί εἰσιν οἱ πιστεύσαντες μόνον, τὰ δὲ ἔργα τῆς
ἀνομίας ἐργασάμενοι· οὐδέποτε δὲ ἀπὸ τοῦ θεοῦ
ἀπέστησαν καὶ τὸ ὄνομα ἡδέως ἐβάστασαν καὶ εἰς

with the heathen, and were corrupted by the vain-
glory of the heathen, and were apostates from God,
and did the deeds of the heathen. These were
reckoned with the heathen. 4. And others of them
were double-minded, not hoping to be saved,
because of the deeds which they had done. And
others were double-minded, and made schisms
among themselves. For these, then, who became
double-minded because of their deeds there is still
repentance, but their repentance must be speedy
that their dwelling may be within the tower. But
for those who do not repent, but remain in their
pleasures, death is near.

X

1. But those who gave up their sticks green, but
the tips were dry and had cracks, these were always
good and faithful and glorious before God, but they
sinned a little because of small lusts, and had small
quarrels with one another. But when they heard
my word the greater part repented quickly, and
their dwelling was in the tower. 2. But some of
them were double-minded, and some in their
double-mindedness made a greater schism. For
these then there is still hope of repentance, because
they were always good, and not easily shall any of
them die. 3. But those who gave up their sticks dry,
but with a little green, these are they who had
belief only but did the deeds of wickedness; but
they were never apostates from God, and they bore

τοὺς οἴκους αὐτῶν ἡδέως ὑπεδέξαντο τοὺς δούλους
τοῦ θεοῦ. ἀκούσαντες οὖν ταύτην τὴν μετάνοιαν
ἀδιστάκτως μετενόησαν, καὶ ἐργάζονται πᾶσαν
ἀρετὴν καὶ δικαιοσύνην. 4. τινὲς δὲ ἐξ αὐτῶν
καὶ φοβοῦνται,[1] γινώσκοντες τὰς πράξεις αὐτῶν,
ἃς ἔπραξαν. τούτων οὖν πάντων ἡ κατοικία εἰς τὸν
πύργον ἔσται.

XI

1. Καὶ μετὰ τὸ συντελέσαι αὐτὸν τὰς ἐπιλύσεις
πασῶν τῶν ῥάβδων λέγει μοι· Ὕπαγε καὶ πᾶσιν
λέγε, ἵνα μετανοήσωσιν, καὶ ζήσωνται τῷ θεῷ·
ὅτι ὁ κύριος ἔπεμψέ με σπλαγχνισθεὶς πᾶσι
δοῦναι τὴν μετάνοιαν, καίπερ τινῶν μὴ ὄντων
II Pet. 3, 9 ἀξίων διὰ τὰ ἔργα αὐτῶν· ἀλλὰ μακρόθυμος ὢν ὁ
κύριος θέλει τὴν κλῆσιν τὴν γενομένην διὰ τοῦ
υἱοῦ αὐτοῦ σώζεσθαι. 2. λέγω αὐτῷ· Κύριε,
ἐλπίζω, ὅτι πάντες ἀκούσαντες αὐτὰ μετανοή-
σουσι· πείθομαι γάρ, ὅτι εἷς ἕκαστος τὰ ἴδια ἔργα
ἐπιγνοὺς καὶ φοβηθεὶς τὸν θεὸν μετανοήσει.
3. ἀποκριθείς μοι λέγει· Ὅσοι, φησίν, ἐξ ὅλης
καρδίας αὐτῶν μετανοήσωσι καὶ[2] καθαρίσωσιν
ἑαυτοὺς ἀπὸ τῶν πονηριῶν αὐτῶν τῶν προειρημένων καὶ μηκέτι μηδὲν προσθῶσι ταῖς ἁμαρτίαις
αὐτῶν, λήψονται ἴασιν παρὰ τοῦ κυρίου τῶν
προτέρων ἁμαρτιῶν, ἐὰν μὴ διψυχήσωσιν ἐπὶ

---

[1] καὶ φοβοῦνται A, aliqui vero eorum morte obierunt et
libenter patiuntur L₁, alii vero compressi libenter patiuntur
L₂, et quidam ex iis seipsos afflixerunt E ; it is probable that
something has dropped out from the Greek. Funk suggests
καὶ [παθεῖν οὐ] φοβοῦνται.   [2] μετανοήσωσι καί I.E, om. A.

the name gladly, and they gladly received into their
houses the servants of God. When they heard, then,
of this repentance, they repented without doubting,
and are accomplishing all virtue and righteousness.
4. But some of them are also afraid, knowing the
deeds which they had done. All these, then, shall
have their dwelling in the tower."

XI

1. AND after he had finished the explanations of Conclusion
all the sticks he said to me: "Go and tell all
men to repent and live to God, for the Lord
sent me in his mercy to give repentance to all,
although some are not worthy because of their
deeds. But the Lord, being long-suffering, wishes
those who were called through his Son to be saved."
2. I said to him: "Sir, I hope that all who hear
them will repent. For I am persuaded that each
one who recognizes his own deeds and fears God will
repent." 3. "And he answered me and said: "As
many," said he, "as repent with all their hearts, and
purify themselves from the wickednesses which have
been mentioned before, and no longer add anything
to their sins, shall receive healing from the Lord for
their former sins, if they are not double-minded as

ταῖς ἐντολαῖς ταύταις, καὶ ζήσονται τῷ θεῷ.
ὅσοι δέ, φησίν, προσθῶσι ταῖς ἁμαρτίαις αὐτῶν
καὶ πορευθῶσιν ἐν ταῖς ἐπιθυμίαις τοῦ αἰῶνος
τούτου, θανάτῳ ἑαυτοὺς κατακρινοῦσιν.[1] 4. σὺ
δὲ πορεύου ἐν ταῖς ἐντολαῖς μου, καὶ ζήσῃ τῷ
θεῷ· καὶ ὅσοι ἂν πορευθῶσιν ἐν αὐταῖς καὶ
ἐργάσωνται ὀρθῶς, ζήσονται τῷ θεῷ.[2] 5. ταῦτά
μοι δείξας καὶ λαλήσας πάντα λέγει μοι· Τὰ δὲ
λοιπὰ ἐπιδείξω μετ' ὀλίγας ἡμέρας.

Παραβολὴ θ'

I

1. Μετὰ τὸ γράψαι με τὰς ἐντολὰς καὶ παραβολὰς τοῦ ποιμένος, τοῦ ἀγγέλου τῆς μετανοίας,
ἦλθε πρός με καὶ λέγει μοι· Θέλω σοι δεῖξαι, ὅσα
σοι ἔδειξε τὸ πνεῦμα τὸ ἅγιον τὸ λαλῆσαν μετὰ
σοῦ ἐν μορφῇ τῆς Ἐκκλησίας· ἐκεῖνο γὰρ τὸ
πνεῦμα ὁ · υἱὸς τοῦ θεοῦ ἐστιν. 2. ἐπειδὴ γὰρ
ἀσθενέστερος τῇ σαρκὶ ἦς, οὐκ ἐδηλώθη σοι δι'
ἀγγέλου. ὅτε οὖν ἐνεδυναμώθης διὰ τοῦ πνεύματος καὶ ἴσχυσας τῇ ἰσχύϊ σου, ὥστε δύνασθαί
σε καὶ ἄγγελον ἰδεῖν, τότε μὲν οὖν ἐφανερώθη σοι
διὰ τῆς Ἐκκλησίας ἡ οἰκοδομὴ τοῦ πύργου· καλῶς
καὶ σεμνῶς πάντα ὡς ὑπὸ παρθένου ἑώρακας.
νῦν δὲ ὑπὸ ἀγγέλου βλέπεις διὰ τοῦ αὐτοῦ μὲν
πνεύματος· 3. δεῖ δέ σε παρ' ἐμοῦ ἀκριβέστερον

---

[1] ὅσοι . . . κατακρινοῦσιν, retranslated from LE, om. A
(qui vero adiecerint, inquit, ad delicta sua et conversati fuerint
in desideriis saeculi huius, damnabunt se ad mortem L₁).

[2] τῷ θεῷ . . . τῷ θεῷ, retranslated from LE, om. A (et
vives deo, et quicumque ambulaverint in his, et ea recte
exercuerint, vivent deo L₂),

to these commandments, and they shall live to God. But as many," said he, "as add to their sins, and live in the lusts of this world shall condemn themselves to death. 4. But do you walk in my commandments and you shall live to God, and as many as walk in them and do rightly, shall live to God." 5. When he had showed me these things and had told me everything, he said to me : " And the rest I will show you after a few days."

PARABLE 9

I

1. After I had written the commandments and parables of the shepherd, the angel of repentance, he came to me and said to me : " I wish to show you what the Holy Spirit which spoke with you in the form of the Church showed you, for that Spirit is the Son of God. 2. For since you were too weak in the flesh, it was not shown you by an angel. But when you were strengthened by the spirit, and made strong in your strength, so that you could also see an angel, then the building of the tower was shown to you by the Church. You saw all things well and holily as if from a virgin.[1] But now you see them from an angel, yet through the same Spirit. 3. But

Intro-
duction

---

[1] The point is that the form of the vision was accommodated to Hermas' powers. It was at first sent in the form of a human being (the emphasis is on the humanity, not on the Virginity) and afterwards when he was stronger spiritually in the form of an angel.

πάντα μαθεῖν. εἰς τοῦτο γὰρ καὶ ἐδόθην ὑπὸ τοῦ
ἐνδόξου ἀγγέλου εἰς τὸν οἶκόν σου κατοικῆσαι,
ἵνα δυνατῶς πάντα ἴδῃς, μηδὲν δειλαινόμενος καὶ
ὡς τὸ πρότερον. 4. καὶ ἀπήγαγέ με εἰς τὴν
Ἀρκαδίαν, εἰς ὄρος τι μαστῶδες καὶ ἐκάθισέ με
ἐπὶ τὸ ἄκρον τοῦ ὄρους καὶ ἔδειξέ μοι πεδίον μέγα,
κύκλῳ δὲ τοῦ πεδίου ὄρη δώδεκα, ἄλλην καὶ ἄλλην
ἰδέαν ἔχοντα τὰ ὄρη. 5. τὸ πρῶτον ἦν μέλαν ὡς
ἀσβόλη· τὸ δὲ δεύτερον ψιλόν, βοτάνας μὴ ἔχον·
τὸ δὲ τρίτον ἀκανθῶν καὶ τριβόλων πλῆρες· 6. τὸ
δὲ τέταρτον βοτάνας ἔχον ἡμιξήρους, τὰ μὲν
ἐπάνω τῶν βοτανῶν χλωρά, τὰ δὲ πρὸς ταῖς
ῥίζαις ξηρά· τινὲς δὲ βοτάναι, ὅταν ὁ ἥλιος ἐπι-
κεκαύκει, ξηραὶ ἐγίνοντο·[1] 7. τὸ δὲ πέμπτον
ὄρος ἔχον βοτάνας χλωρὰς καὶ τραχὺ ὄν. τὸ δὲ
ἕκτον ὄρος σχισμῶν ὅλως ἔγεμεν, ὧν μὲν μικρῶν,
ὧν δὲ μεγάλων· εἶχον δὲ βοτάνας αἱ σχισμαί,
οὐ λίαν δὲ ἦσαν εὐθαλεῖς αἱ βοτάναι, μᾶλλον
δὲ ὡς μεμαραμμέναι ἦσαν. 8. τὸ δὲ ἕβδομον ὄρος
εἶχε βοτάνας ἱλαράς, καὶ ὅλον τὸ ὄρος εὐθηνοῦν
ἦν, καὶ πᾶν γένος κτηνῶν καὶ ὀρνέων ἐνέμοντο εἰς
τὸ ὄρος ἐκεῖνο· καὶ ὅσον ἐβόσκοντο τὰ κτήνη καὶ
τὰ πετεινά, μᾶλλον καὶ μᾶλλον αἱ βοτάναι τοῦ
ὄρους ἐκείνου ἔθαλλον. τὸ δὲ ὄγδοον ὄρος πηγῶν
πλῆρες ἦν, καὶ πᾶν γένος τῆς κτίσεως τοῦ κυρίου
ἐποτίζοντο ἐκ τῶν πηγῶν τοῦ ὄρους ἐκείνου. 9. τὸ
δὲ ἔννατον ὄρος ὅλως ὕδωρ οὐκ εἶχεν καὶ ὅλον
ἐρημῶδες ἦν. εἶχε δὲ ἐν αὐτῷ θηρία καὶ ἑρπετὰ
θανάσιμα διαφθείροντα ἀνθρώπους. τὸ δὲ δέκατον

---

[1] A adds τὸ δὲ ὄρος τραχὺ λίαν ἦν βοτάνας ἔχον ξηράς.

you must learn everything more accurately from me.
For, for this reason too, I was given by the glorious
angel, to live in your house, that you might see all
things with power and fear nothing, as you did for-
merly. 4. And he took me away to Arcadia,[1] to a *The vision of the Mountains*
breast-shaped mountain, and set me on top of the
mountain, and showed me a great plain and round
the plain twelve mountains, and each mountain had a
different appearance. 5. The first was black as pitch,
the second was bare without herbs, and the third was
full of thorns and thistles. 6. And the fourth had
half-dried herbage ; the tops of the herbs were green,
but the parts by the roots were dry. And some of
the herbs, when the sun had burnt them, were becoming dry. 7. And the fifth mountain had green
herbs and was steep. And the sixth mountain was
altogether full of cracks, some small and some great.
And the cracks had herbage, but the herbage was
not very flourishing, but rather as if it were fading.
8. And the seventh mountain had vigorous herbage,
and the whole mountain was flourishing, and all
kinds of cattle and birds were feeding on that
mountain. And the more the cattle and birds
were feeding, the more the herbage of that mountain
flourished. And the eighth mountain was full of
springs, and every kind of creature of the Lord was
given to drink from the springs of that mountain.
9. But the ninth mountain had no water at all, and
was quite desert. But it had in it wild beasts and
deadly reptiles destroying men. And the tenth moun-

[1] Arcadia is found in all the authorities ; but it plays no
further part in the story. Zahn emends to 'Aricia'; but
Aricia is a village, and Monte Cavo, which might be
intended, is not specially near to it

ὄρος εἶχε δένδρα μέγιστα καὶ ὅλον κατάσκιον
ἦν, καὶ ὑπὸ τὴν σκέπην τῶν δένδρων πρόβατα
κατέκειντο ἀναπαυόμενα καὶ μαρυκώμενα. 10. τὸ
δὲ ἑνδέκατον ὄρος λίαν σύνδενδρον ἦν, καὶ τὰ
δένδρα ἐκεῖνα κατάκαρπα ἦν, ἄλλοις καὶ ἄλλοις
καρποῖς κεκοσμημένα, ἵνα ἰδών τις αὐτὰ ἐπιθυμήσῃ φαγεῖν ἐκ τῶν καρπῶν αὐτῶν. τὸ δὲ
δωδέκατον ὄρος ὅλον ἦν λευκόν, καὶ ἡ πρόσοψις
αὐτοῦ ἱλαρὰ ἦν· καὶ εὐπρεπέστατον ἦν ἐν αὐτῷ
τὸ ὄρος.

II

1. Εἰς μέσον δὲ τοῦ πεδίου ἔδειξέ μοι πέτραν
μεγάλην λευκὴν ἐκ τοῦ πεδίου ἀναβεβηκυῖαν. ἡ
δὲ πέτρα ὑψηλοτέρα ἦν τῶν ὀρέων, τετράγωνος,
ὥστε δύνασθαι ὅλον τὸν κόσμον χωρῆσαι.
2. παλαιὰ δὲ ἦν ἡ πέτρα ἐκείνη, πύλην ἐκκε-
κομμένην ἔχουσα· ὡς πρόσφατος δὲ ἐδόκει μοι
εἶναι ἡ ἐκκόλαψις τῆς πύλης. ἡ δὲ πύλη οὕτως
ἔστιλβεν ὑπὲρ τὸν ἥλιον, ὥστε με θαυμάζειν ἐπὶ
τῇ λαμπηδόνι τῆς πύλης. 3. κύκλῳ δὲ τῆς πύλης
εἱστήκεισαν παρθένοι δώδεκα. αἱ οὖν τέσσαρες
αἱ εἰς τὰς γωνίας ἑστηκυῖαι ἐνδοξότεραί μοι
ἐδόκουν εἶναι· καὶ αἱ ἄλλαι δὲ ἔνδοξοι ἦσαν. εἱστήκεισαν δὲ εἰς τὰ τέσσαρα μέρη τῆς πύλης, ἀνὰ
μέσον αὐτῶν ἀνὰ δύο παρθένοι. 4. ἐνδεδυμέναι δὲ

tain had great trees and was full of shady places, and under the shade of the trees sheep were lying resting and ruminating. 10. And the eleventh mountain was full of trees and those trees had fruit, and were each adorned with different fruits, so that whoever saw them desired to eat of their fruits. And the twelfth mountain was all white, and its appearance was joyful, and the mountain was in itself very beautiful.

II

1. In the middle of the plain he showed me a great white rock, which had risen out of the plain, and the rock was higher than the hills, four-square, so that it could hold the whole world. 2. And that rock was old, and had a door hewn out of it. But it seemed to me that the cutting of the door was recent. And the door glistened so in the sun, that I marvelled at the brightness of the door. 3. And round the door there stood twelve maidens ; the four who stood at the corner, seemed to me to be the more glorious, but the others also were glorious, and they stood at the four parts of the door, each with two other maidens on each side.[1] 4. And they were clothed in linen mantles,

The great stone in the plain

The Maidens

---

[1] The arrangement meant is $\begin{pmatrix} A\,b\,b\,A \\ b \qquad b \\ b \qquad b \\ A\,b\,b\,A \end{pmatrix}$, so that the 'door' must have been a sort of porch, cut out of the rock, and the tower was built directly above it

ἦσαν λινοῦς χιτῶνας καὶ περιεζωσμέναι ἦσαν[1] εὐπρεπῶς, ἔξω τοὺς ὤμους ἔχουσαι τοὺς δεξιοὺς ὡς μέλλουσαι φορτίον τι βαστάζειν. οὕτως ἕτοιμοι ἦσαν· λίαν γὰρ ἱλαραὶ ἦσαν καὶ πρόθυμοι. 5. μετὰ τὸ ἰδεῖν με ταῦτα ἐθαύμαζον ἐν ἐμαυτῷ, ὅτι μεγάλα καὶ ἔνδοξα πράγματα βλέπω. καὶ πάλιν διηπόρουν ἐπὶ ταῖς παρθένοις, ὅτι τρυφεραὶ οὖσαι ἀνδρείως εἱστήκεισαν ὡς μέλλουσαι ὅλον τὸν οὐρανὸν βαστάζειν. 6. καὶ λέγει μοι ὁ ποιμήν· Τί ἐν σεαυτῷ διαλογίζῃ καὶ διαπορῇ καὶ σεαυτῷ λύπην ἐπισπάσαι; ὅσα γὰρ οὐ δύνασαι νοῆσαι, μὴ ἐπιχείρει, συνετὸς ὤν, ἀλλ᾽ ἐρώτα τὸν κύριον, ἵνα λαβὼν σύνεσιν νοῇς αὐτά. 7. τὰ ὀπίσω σου ἰδεῖν οὐ δύνῃ, τὰ δὲ ἔμπροσθέν σου βλέπεις. ἃ οὖν ἰδεῖν οὐ δύνασαι, ἔασον, καὶ μὴ στρέβλου σεαυτόν· ἃ δὲ βλέπεις, ἐκείνων κατακυρίευε καὶ περὶ τῶν λοιπῶν μὴ περιεργάζου· πάντα δέ σοι ἐγὼ δηλώσω, ὅσα ἄν σοι δείξω. ἔμβλεπε οὖν τοῖς λοιποῖς.

III

1. Εἶδον ἐξ ἄνδρας ἐληλυθότας ὑψηλοὺς καὶ ἐνδόξους καὶ ὁμοίους τῇ ἰδέᾳ· καὶ ἐκάλεσαν πλῆθός τι ἀνδρῶν. κἀκεῖνοι δὲ οἱ ἐληλυθότες ὑψηλοὶ ἦσαν ἄνδρες καὶ καλοὶ καὶ δυνατοί· καὶ ἐκέλευσαν αὐτοὺς οἱ ἐξ ἄνδρες οἰκοδομεῖν ἐπάνω τῆς πέτρας[2] πύργον τινά. ἦν δὲ θόρυβος τῶν ἀνδρῶν ἐκείνων μέγας τῶν ἐληλυθότων οἰκοδομεῖν τὸν πύργον ὧδε κἀκεῖσε περιτρε-

---

[1] ἦσαν P^{Amh}, om. A.
[2] πέτρας AE, πέτρας καὶ ἐπάνω τῆς πύλης L.

and were beautifully girded, and had their right shoulders outside, as if they were going to carry a load. Thus they were ready, for they were very joyful and eager. 5. After I had seen these things I wondered in myself, for I was seeing great and glorious things. And again I was perplexed at the maidens, that though they were so delicate, they stood bravely as though they would carry the whole heaven. 6. And the shepherd said to me : " Why do you reason in yourself and are perplexed, and give yourself sorrow ? For what things you cannot comprehend,—be prudent, do not attempt them, but ask the Lord that you may receive understanding and comprehend them. 7. What is behind you you cannot see, but you see what is before you. Let go what you cannot see, and do not trouble yourself. But what you see, master that, and do not be curious about the rest, and I will explain everything to you, whatever I show you. Look then at the rest.

III

1. I SAW six men who came, tall and glorious, and alike in appearance, and they summoned a multitude of men, and they too who came were tall men and beautiful and strong, and the six men commanded them to build a certain tower above the rock. And there was a great throng of those men who had come to build the tower,

The six men

χόντων κύκλῳ τῆς πύλης. 2. αἱ δὲ παρθένοι ἑστηκυῖαι κύκλῳ τῆς πύλης ἔλεγον τοῖς ἀνδράσι σπεύδειν τὸν πύργον οἰκοδομεῖσθαι· ἐκπεπετάκεισαν δὲ τὰς χεῖρας αἱ παρθένοι ὡς μέλλουσαί τι λαμβάνειν παρὰ τῶν ἀνδρῶν. 3. οἱ δὲ ἓξ ἄνδρες ἐκέλευον ἐκ βυθοῦ τινος λίθους ἀναβαίνειν καὶ ὑπάγειν εἰς τὴν οἰκοδομὴν τοῦ πύργου. ἀνέβησαν δὲ λίθοι δέκα τετράγωνοι λαμπροί, μὴ[1] λελατομημένοι. 4. οἱ δὲ ἓξ ἄνδρες ἐκάλουν τὰς παρθένους καὶ ἐκέλευσαν αὐτὰς τοὺς λίθους πάντας τοὺς μέλλοντας εἰς τὴν οἰκοδομὴν ὑπάγειν τοῦ πύργου βαστάζειν καὶ διαπυρεύεσθαι διὰ τῆς πύλης καὶ ἐπιδιδόναι τοῖς ἀνδράσι τοῖς μέλλουσιν οἰκοδομεῖν τὸν πύργον. 5. αἱ δὲ παρθένοι τοὺς δέκα λίθους τοὺς πρώτους τοὺς ἐκ τοῦ βυθοῦ ἀναβάντας ἐπετίθουν ἀλλήλαις καὶ κατὰ ἕνα λίθον ἐβάσταζον ὁμοῦ.

IV

1. Καθὼς δὲ ἐστάθησαν ὁμοῦ κύκλῳ τῆς πύλης, οὕτως ἐβάσταζον αἱ δοκοῦσαι δυναταὶ εἶναι καὶ ὑπὸ τὰς γωνίας τοῦ λίθου ὑποδεδυκυῖαι ἦσαν. αἱ δὲ ἄλλαι ἐκ τῶν πλευρῶν τοῦ λίθου ὑποδεδύκεισαν καὶ οὕτως ἐβάσταζον πάντας τοὺς λίθους· διὰ δὲ τῆς πύλης διέφερον αὐτούς, καθὼς ἐκελεύσθησαν, καὶ ἐπεδίδουν τοῖς ἀνδράσιν εἰς τὸν πύργον· ἐκεῖνοι δὲ ἔχοντες τοὺς λίθους ᾠκοδόμουν. 2. ἡ

---

[1] μή om. AEL, but the addition seems to be made necessary by the reference in Sim. ix. 5, 3, where these stones are described as μὴ λελατομημένοι.

running here and there round the tower. 2. And the maidens stood round the tower, and told the men to make speed with building the tower. And the maidens held out their hands as if they were going to take something from the men. 3. And the six men commanded stones to come up from a certain deep place, and to go into the building of the tower. And there came up ten square stones, beautiful and not hewn. 4. And the six men called the maidens and commanded them to take all the stones which were to come for the building of the tower, and to go through the gate, and give them to the men who were going to build the tower. 5. And the maidens put the ten stones, which first came out of the deep place, on one another, and they carried them together like a single stone.

The ten stones

IV

1. AND just as they had stood together round the gate, so the maidens who seemed to be strong were carrying, and they were stooping under the corners of the stone.[1] But the others were stooping by the sides of the stone, and so they were carrying all the stones. And they brought them through the gate as they had been commanded, and gave them to the men in the tower, and they took the stones and went on building. 2. Now, the building of the tower

The building of the tower stones by the maidens and the men

---

[1] The meaning is that the four maidens kept to their original formation, with the four strongest at the corners, and the others in the middle of each side of the stone which they carried.

THE APOSTOLIC FATHERS

οἰκοδομὴ δὲ τοῦ πύργου ἐγένετο ἐπὶ τὴν πέτραν
τὴν μεγάλην καὶ ἐπάνω τῆς πύλης. ἡρμόσθησαν
οὖν οἱ δέκα λίθοι ἐκεῖνοι καὶ ἐνέπλησαν¹ ὅλην τὴν
πετραν· καὶ ἐγένοντο ἐκεῖνοι¹ θεμέλιος τῆς οἰκοδομῆς τοῦ πύργου· ἡ δὲ πέτρα καὶ ἡ πύλη ἦν βασ-
τάζουσα ὅλον τὸν πύργον· 3. μετὰ δὲ τοὺς δέκα
λίθους ἄλλοι ἀνέβησαν ἐκ τοῦ βυθοῦ εἴκοσι² λίθοι·
καὶ οὗτοι ἡρμόσθησαν εἰς τὴν οἰκοδομὴν τοῦ
πύργου, βασταζόμενοι ὑπὸ τῶν παρθένων καθὼς
καὶ οἱ πρότεροι. μετὰ δὲ τούτους ἀνέβησαν λέ,
καὶ οὗτοι ὁμοίως ἡρμόσθησαν εἰς τὸν πύργον.
μετὰ δὲ τούτους ἕτεροι ἀνέβησαν λίθοι μ', καὶ
οὗτοι πάντες ἐβλήθησαν εἰς τὴν οἰκοδομὴν τοῦ
πύργου· ἐγένοντο οὖν στοῖχοι τέσσαρες ἐν τοῖς
θεμελίοις τοῦ πύργου.³ 4. καὶ ἐπαύσαντο ἐκ τοῦ
βυθοῦ ἀναβαίνοντες· ἐπαύσαντο δὲ καὶ οἱ οἰκοδομοῦντες μικρόν. καὶ πάλιν ἐπέταξαν οἱ ἓξ ἄνδρες
τῷ πλήθει τοῦ ὄχλου ἐκ τῶν ὀρέων παραφέρειν
λίθους εἰς τὴν οἰκοδομὴν τοῦ πύργου. 5. παρε-
φέροντο οὖν ἐκ πάντων τῶν ὀρέων χρόαις ποικίλαις
λελατομημένοι ὑπὸ τῶν ἀνδρῶν καὶ ἐπεδίδοντο
ταῖς παρθένοις· αἱ δὲ παρθένοι διέφερον αὐτοὺς
διὰ τῆς πύλης καὶ ἐπεδίδουν εἰς τὴν οἰκοδομὴν τοῦ
πύργου. καὶ ὅταν εἰς τὴν οἰκοδομὴν ἐτέθησαν οἱ
λίθοι οἱ ποικίλοι, ὅμοιοι ἐγένοντο λευκοὶ καὶ τὰς
χρόας τὰς ποικίλας ἤλλασσον. 6. τινὲς δὲ λίθοι
ἐπεδίδοντο ὑπὸ τῶν ἀνδρῶν εἰς τὴν οἰκοδομὴν καὶ
οὐκ ἐγίνοντο λαμπροί, ἀλλ' οἷοι ἐτέθησαν, τοιοῦτοι
καὶ εὑρέθησαν· οὐ γὰρ ἦσαν ὑπὸ τῶν παρθένων

¹ καὶ ἐνέπλησαν . . . ἐκεῖνοι retranslated from LE, om. A.
² κ' A, viginti quinque L, quindecim E.
³ ἐγένοντο . . . πύργου retranslated from LE, om. A.

was raised on the great rock, and above the gate. So those ten stones were fitted in, and they filled the whole rock. And they were the foundation of the building of the tower, and the rock and the gate were supporting the whole tower. 3. And after the ten stones, twenty other stones came up out of the deep place, and these were fitted into the building of the tower and were carried by the maidens like the former stones. And after these there came up thirty-five, and these likewise were fitted into the tower. And after these there came up forty other stones, and all these were placed into the building of the tower ; so there became four tiers in the foundations of the tower. 4. And they ceased to come up from the deep place, and the builders also stopped for a little. And again the six men commanded the mass of the multitude to bring stones for the building of the tower from the mountains. 5. Therefore there were brought from all the mountains stones of different colours, hewn out by the men, and they were given to the maidens, and the maidens carried them through the gate and gave them over for the building of the tower. And when the various stones were put into the building they became all alike white and changed their various colours. 6. But some stones were given by the men for the building, which did not become bright but proved to remain as they were when they were put in. For they had not been given by the maidens, and had

Marginal notes: The 20 stones · The 35 stones · The 40 stones · The second stage of the building

ἐπιδεδομένοι οὐδὲ διὰ τῆς πύλης παρενηνεγμένοι.
οὗτοι οὖν οἱ λίθοι ἀπρεπεῖς ἦσαν ἐν τῇ οἰκοδομῇ τοῦ
πύργου. 7. ἰδόντες δὲ οἱ ἒξ ἄνδρες τοὺς λίθους
τοὺς ἀπρεπεῖς ἐν τῇ οἰκοδομῇ ἐκέλευσαν αὐτοὺς
ἀρθῆναι καὶ ἀπαχθῆναι κάτω εἰς τὸν ἴδιον τόπον,
ὅθεν ἠνέχθησαν. 8. καὶ λέγουσι τοῖς ἀνδράσι
τοῖς παρεμφέρουσι τοὺς λίθους· Ὅλως ὑμεῖς μὴ
ἐπιδίδοτε εἰς τὴν οἰκοδομὴν λίθους· τίθετε δὲ
αὐτοὺς παρὰ τὸν πύργον, ἵνα αἱ παρθένοι διὰ τῆς
πύλης παρενέγκωσιν αὐτοὺς καὶ ἐπιδιδῶσιν εἰς
τὴν οἰκοδομήν. ἐὰν γάρ, φασί, διὰ τῶν χειρῶν
τῶν παρθένων τούτων μὴ παρενεχθῶσι διὰ τῆς
πύλης, τὰς χρόας αὐτῶν ἀλλάξαι οὐ δύνανται· μὴ
κοπιᾶτε οὖν, φασίν, εἰς μάτην.

V

1. Καὶ ἐτελέσθη τῇ ἡμέρᾳ ἐκείνῃ ἡ οἰκοδομή,
οὐκ ἀπετελέσθη δὲ ὁ πύργος· ἔμελλε γὰρ πάλιν
ἐποικοδομεῖσθαι· καὶ ἐγένετο ἀνοχὴ τῆς οἰκοδομῆς.
ἐκέλευσαν δὲ οἱ ἒξ ἄνδρες τοὺς οἰκοδομοῦντας
ἀναχωρῆσαι μικρὸν πάντας καὶ ἀναπαυθῆναι·
ταῖς δὲ παρθένοις ἐπέταξαν ἀπὸ τοῦ πύργου
μὴ ἀναχωρῆσαι. ἐδόκει δέ μοι τὰς παρθένους
καταλελεῖφθαι τοῦ φυλάσσειν τὸν πύργον.
2. μετὰ δὲ τὸ ἀναχωρῆσαι πάντας καὶ ἀναπαυ-
θῆναι λέγω τῷ ποιμένι· Τί ὅτι, φημί, κύριε, οὐ
συνετελέσθη ἡ οἰκοδομὴ τοῦ πύργου; Οὔπω,
φησί, δύναται ἀποτελεσθῆναι ὁ πύργος, ἐὰν
μὴ ἔλθη ὁ κύριος αὐτοῦ καὶ δοκιμάσῃ τὴν
οἰκοδομὴν ταύτην, ἵνα, ἐάν τινες λίθοι σαπροὶ

not been brought in through the door. Therefore these stones were unseemly in the building of the tower. 7. And when the six men saw the unseemly stones in the building they commanded them to be taken away and to be brought down to their own place, whence they had been taken. 8. And they said to the men who were bringing the stones in : "You must on no account put stones into the building, but put them by the side of the tower, that the maidens may bring them in through the gate, and give them over for the building. For if," said they, " they are not brought in by the hands of these maidens through the gate they cannot change their colours ; do not then," said they, " labour in vain."

V

1. AND on that day the building was finished, but The pause in the tower was not completed, for it was going to building be built on to, and there was a pause in the building. And the six men commanded all the builders to retire a little and rest, but they commanded the maidens not to go away from the tower. And it seemed to me that the maidens had given up looking after the tower. 2. But after they had all gone away and were resting I said to the shepherd : " Why, Sir," said I, " was the building of the tower not completed ? " " The tower," said he, " cannot yet be completed unless its lord come and test this building, in order that if some stones prove to be

εὑρεθῶσιν, ἀλλάξῃ αὐτούς· πρὸς γὰρ τὸ ἐκείνου θέλημα οἰκοδομεῖται ὁ πύργος. 3. Ἤθελον, φημί,
κύριε, τούτου τοῦ πύργου γνῶναι τί ἐστιν ἡ
οἰκοδομὴ αὕτη, καὶ περὶ τῆς πέτρας καὶ πύλης
καὶ τῶν ὀρέων καὶ τῶν παρθένων καὶ τῶν λίθων
τῶν ἐκ τοῦ βυθοῦ ἀναβεβηκότων καὶ μὴ λελατο-
μημένων, ἀλλ' οὕτως ἀπελθόντων εἰς τὴν οἰκοδομήν. 4. καὶ διατί πρῶτον εἰς τὰ θεμέλια ι΄ λίθοι
ἐτέθησαν, εἶτα κ΄, εἶτα λε΄, εἶτα μ΄, καὶ περὶ τῶν
λίθων τῶν ἀπεληλυθότων εἰς τὴν οἰκοδομὴν καὶ
πάλιν ἠρμένων καὶ εἰς τόπον ἴδιον ἀποτεθειμένων·
περὶ πάντων τούτων ἀνάπαυσον τὴν ψυχήν μου,
κύριε, καὶ γνώρισόν μοι αὐτά. 5. Ἐάν, φησί, κενό-
σπουδος μὴ εὑρεθῇς, πάντα γνώσῃ· μετ' ὀλίγας γὰρ
ἡμέρας ἐλευσόμεθα ἐνθάδε, καὶ τὰ λοιπὰ ὄψει
τὰ ἐπερχόμενα τῷ πύργῳ τούτῳ καὶ πάσας τὰς
παραβολὰς ἀκριβῶς γνώσῃ. 6. καὶ μετ' ὀλίγας
ἡμέρας[1] ἤλθομεν εἰς τὸν τόπον, οὗ κεκαθίκαμεν,
καὶ λέγει μοι· Ἄγωμεν πρὸς τὸν πύργον· ὁ γὰρ
αὐθέντης τοῦ πύργου ἔρχεται κατανοῆσαι αὐτόν.
καὶ ἤλθομεν πρὸς τὸν πύργον· καὶ ὅλως οὐδεὶς ἦν
πρὸς αὐτὸν εἰ μὴ αἱ παρθένοι μόναι. 7. καὶ
ἐπερωτᾷ ὁ ποιμὴν τὰς παρθένους, εἰ ἄρα παρε-
γεγόνει ὁ δεσπότης τοῦ πύργου. αἱ δὲ ἔφησαν
μέλλειν αὐτὸν ἔρχεσθαι κατανοῆσαι τὴν οἰκοδομήν.

VI

1. Καὶ ἰδοὺ μετὰ μικρὸν βλέπω παράταξιν
πολλῶν ἀνδρῶν ἐρχομένων· καὶ εἰς τὸ μέσον ἀνὴρ

[1] ἐλευσόμεθα . . . ἡμέρας retranslated from LE, om. A.

rotten, he may change them, for the tower is being built according to his will." 3. "I should like, Sir," said I, "to know what is this building of the tower, and concerning the rock, and the gate, and the mountains and the maidens, and the stones which came up from the deep place, and were not hewn, but went as they were into the building. 4. And why ten stones were first laid for the foundation, then twenty, then thirty-five, then forty, and concerning the stones which went into the building, and were taken away again and put back in their own place. Give my soul rest concerning all these things, Sir, and let me know them." 5. "If," said he, " you are not found to be vainly zealous, you shall know all things. For after a few days we will come here, and you shall see the rest of what happens to this tower, and you will know all the parables accurately." 6. And after a few days we came to the place where we had sat, and he said to me : 'Let us go to the tower, for the master of the tower is coming to examine it." And we came to the tower, and there was nobody by it at all, except only the maidens. 7. And the shepherd asked the maidens if the Lord of the tower had come. And they said that he was about to come, to examine the building.

VI

1. AND lo, after a little time I saw an array of many men coming, and in the middle there was

τις ὑψηλὸς τῷ μεγέθει, ὥστε τὸν πύργον ὑπερέχειν. 2. καὶ οἱ ἐξ ἄνδρες οἱ εἰς τὴν οἰκοδομὴν ἐφεστῶτες ἐκ δεξιῶν τε καὶ ἀριστερῶν περιεπάτησαν μετ᾽ αὐτοῦ, καὶ πάντες οἱ εἰς τὴν οἰκοδομὴν[1] ἐργασάμενοι μετ᾽ αὐτοῦ ἦσαν καὶ ἕτεροι πολλοὶ κύκλῳ αὐτοῦ ἔνδοξοι. αἱ δὲ παρθένοι αἱ τηροῦσαι τὸν πύργον προσδραμοῦσαι κατεφίλησαν αὐτὸν καὶ ἤρξαντο ἐγγὺς αὐτοῦ περιπατεῖν κύκλῳ τοῦ πύργου. 3. κατενόει δὲ ὁ ἀνὴρ ἐκεῖνος τὴν οἰκοδομὴν ἀκριβῶς, ὥστε αὐτὸν καθ᾽ ἕνα λίθον ψηλαφᾶν. κρατῶν δέ τινα ῥάβδον τῇ χειρὶ κατὰ ἕνα λίθον τῶν ᾠκοδομημένων ἔτυπτε.[2] 4. καὶ ὅταν ἐπάτασσεν, ἐγένοντο αὐτῶν τινὲς μέλανες ὡσεὶ ἀσβόλη, τινὲς δὲ ἐψωριακότες, τινὲς δὲ σχισμὰς ἔχοντες, τινὲς δὲ κολοβοί, τινὲς δὲ οὔτε λευκοὶ οὔτε μέλανες, τινὲς δὲ τραχεῖς καὶ μὴ συμφωνοῦντες τοῖς ἑτέροις λίθοις, τινὲς δὲ σπίλους πολλοὺς ἔχοντες· αὗται ἦσαν αἱ ποικιλίαι τῶν λίθων τῶν σαπρῶν εὑρεθέντων εἰς τὴν οἰκοδομήν. 5. ἐκέλευσεν οὖν πάντας τούτους ἐκ τοῦ πύργου μετενεχθῆναι καὶ τεθῆναι παρὰ τὸν πύργον καὶ ἑτέρους ἐνεχθῆναι λίθους καὶ ἐμβληθῆναι εἰς τὸν τόπον αὐτῶν. 6. καὶ ἐπηρώτησαν αὐτὸν οἱ οἰκοδομοῦντες, ἐκ τίνος ὄρους θέλῃ ἐνεχθῆναι λίθους καὶ ἐμβληθῆναι εἰς τὸν τόπον αὐτῶν.[3] καὶ ἐκ μὲν τῶν ὀρέων οὐκ ἐκέλευσεν ἐνεχθῆναι, ἐκ δέ τινος πεδίου ἐγγὺς ὄντος ἐκέλευσεν ἐνεχθῆναι.[4] 7. καὶ ὠρύγη τὸ

---

[1] Retranslated from EL, om. A.
[2] ἔτυπτε LE, τρὶς ἔτυπτε A.
[3] Retranslated from EL, om. A.
[4] Retranslated from EL, om. A.

a man so tall, that he overtopped the tower. The coming
of the
Lord of
the Tower
2. And the six men, who had been in charge of the
building, were walking with him on the right hand
and on the left, and all who had worked at the
building were with him, and there were many other
glorious beings around him. And the maidens who
kept the tower ran to him and kissed him, and
began to walk near him round the tower. 3. And
that man examined the building carefully, so that
he felt each stone, and he held a staff in his
hand and hit each individual stone used in the
building. 4. And when he struck, some of them
became as black as pitch, and some rotten, and some
with cracks, and some short, and some neither white
nor black, and some rough and not fitting in with
the other stones, and some with many stains. These
were the varieties of the rotten stones which were
found in the building. 5. Therefore he commanded
all these to be taken away from the tower, and to
be put beside the tower, and other stones to be
brought and laid in their place. 6. And the
builders asked him from which mountains he wished
stones to be brought and laid in their place, and he
commanded them not to be brought from the
mountains, but he commanded them to be brought
from a certain plain near at hand. 7. And the plain

πεδίον, καὶ εὑρέθησαν λίθοι λαμπροὶ τετράγωνοι,
τινὲς δὲ καὶ στρογγύλοι. ὅσοι δέ ποτε ἦσαν
λίθοι ἐν τῷ πεδίῳ ἐκείνῳ, πάντες ἠνέχθησαν καὶ
διὰ τῆς πύλης ἐβαστάζοντο ὑπὸ τῶν παρθένων.
8. καὶ ἐλατομήθησαν οἱ τετράγωνοι λίθοι καὶ
ἐτέθησαν εἰς τὸν τόπον τῶν ἠρμένων· οἱ δὲ
στρογγύλοι οὐκ ἐτέθησαν εἰς τὴν οἰκοδομήν, ὅτι
σκληροὶ ἦσαν εἰς τὸ λατομηθῆναι αὐτοὺς καὶ
βραδέως ἐγένοντο. ἐτέθησαν δὲ παρὰ τὸν πύργον,
ὡς μελλόντων αὐτῶν λατομεῖσθαι καὶ τίθεσθαι
εἰς τὴν οἰκοδομήν· λίαν γὰρ λαμπροὶ ἦσαν.

VII

1. Ταῦτα οὖν συντελέσας ὁ ἀνὴρ ὁ ἔνδοξος καὶ
κύριος ὅλου τοῦ πύργου προσεκαλέσατο τὸν
ποιμένα καὶ παρέδωκεν αὐτῷ τοὺς λίθους πάντας
τοὺς παρὰ τὸν πύργον κειμένους, τοὺς ἀποβεβλημένους ἐκ τῆς οἰκοδομῆς, καὶ λέγει αὐτῷ· 2. Ἐπιμελῶς καθάρισον τοὺς λίθους τούτους καὶ θὲς
αὐτοὺς εἰς τὴν οἰκοδομὴν τοῦ πύργου, τοὺς
δυναμένους ἁρμόσαι τοῖς λοιποῖς· τοὺς δὲ μὴ ἁρμό-
ζοντας ῥῖψον μακρὰν ἀπὸ τοῦ πύργου. 3. ταῦτα
κελεύσας τῷ ποιμένι ἀπῄει ἀπὸ τοῦ πύργου[1]
μετὰ πάντων, μεθ' ὧν ἐληλύθει· αἱ δὲ παρθένοι
κύκλῳ τοῦ πύργου εἱστήκεισαν τηροῦσαι αὐτόν.
4. λέγω τῷ ποιμένι· Πῶς οὗτοι οἱ λίθοι δύνανται
εἰς τὴν οἰκοδομὴν τοῦ πύργου ἀπελθεῖν ἀποδεδοκι-
μασμένοι; ἀποκριθείς μοι λέγει· Βλέπεις, φησί, τοὺς
λίθους τούτους; Βλέπω, φημί, κύριε. Ἐγώ, φησί,

[1] Retranslated from LE, om. A.

was quarried, and splendid square stones were found, but some were also round. And all the stones that were found in that plain were brought and carried through the door by the maidens. 8. And the square stones were hewn and put into the place of those which had been taken out, but the round stones were not put into the building, because they were hard to hew, and it took a long time; but they were put beside the tower, as if they were going to be hewn and put into the building; for they were very splendid.

VII

1. WHEN the glorious man, the Lord of all the tower, had finished these things, he called the shepherd and gave over to him all the stones which were lying by the tower which had been taken out of the building, and said to him : 2. "Clean these stones carefully, and put into the building of the tower those which can fit in with the rest, and throw far away from the tower those which do not fit." 3. With these commands to the shepherd he went away from the tower, with all those with whom he had come. But the maidens stood round the tower guarding it. 4. I said to the shepherd : "How can these stones come again into the building of the tower after they have been rejected ?" He answered and said to me : "Do you see these

The injunctions of the Lord to the Shepherd

τὸ πλεῖστον μέρος τῶν λίθων τούτων λατομήσω καὶ
βαλῶ εἰς τὴν οἰκοδομήν, καὶ ἁρμόσουσι μετὰ τῶν
λοιπῶν λίθων. 5. Πῶς, φημί, κύριε, δύνανται
περικοπέντες τὸν αὐτὸν τόπον πληρῶσαι; ἀποκριθεὶς λέγει μοι· Ὅσοι μικροὶ εὑρεθήσονται, εἰς
μέσην τὴν οἰκοδομὴν βληθήσονται, ὅσοι δὲ μεί-
ζονες, ἐξώτεροι τεθήσονται καὶ συγκρατήσουσιν
αὐτούς. 6. ταῦτά μοι λαλήσας λέγει μοι· Ἄγωμεν καὶ μετὰ ἡμέρας δύο ἔλθωμεν καὶ καθαρίσωμεν
τοὺς λίθους τούτους καὶ βάλωμεν αὐτοὺς εἰς τὴν
οἰκοδομήν· τὰ γὰρ κύκλῳ τοῦ πύργου πάντα
καθαρισθῆναι δεῖ, μήποτε ὁ δεσπότης ἐξάπινα
ἔλθῃ καὶ τὰ περὶ τὸν πύργον ῥυπαρὰ εὕρῃ καὶ
προσοχθίσῃ, καὶ οὗτοι οἱ λίθοι οὐκ ἀπελεύσονται
εἰς τὴν οἰκοδομὴν τοῦ πύργου, κἀγὼ ἀμελὴς δόξω
εἶναι παρὰ τῷ δεσπότῃ. 7. καὶ μετὰ ἡμέρας δύο
ἤλθομεν πρὸς τὸν πύργον καὶ λέγει μοι· Κατανοήσωμεν τοὺς λίθους πάντας καὶ ἴδωμεν τοὺς
δυναμένους εἰς τὴν οἰκοδομὴν ἀπελθεῖν. λέγω
αὐτῷ· Κύριε, κατανοήσωμεν.

VIII

1. Καὶ ἀρξάμενοι πρῶτον τοὺς μέλανας κατενο-
οῦμεν λίθους. καὶ οἷοι ἐκ τῆς οἰκοδομῆς ἐτέθησαν,
τοιοῦτοι καὶ εὑρέθησαν. καὶ ἐκέλευσεν αὐτοὺς ὁ
ποιμὴν ἐκ τοῦ πύργου μετενεχθῆναι καὶ χωρισθῆ-
ναι. 2. εἶτα κατενόησε τοὺς ἐψωριακότας, καὶ
λαβὼν ἐλατόμησε πολλοὺς ἐξ αὐτῶν καὶ ἐκέλευσε
τὰς παρθένους ἆραι αὐτοὺς καὶ βαλεῖν εἰς τὴν
οἰκοδομήν. καὶ ἦραν αὐτοὺς αἱ παρθένοι καὶ
ἔθηκαν εἰς τὴν οἰκοδομὴν τοῦ πύργου μέσου. τοὺς

stones?" said he. "Yes, Sir, I see them," said I.
"I will hew," said he, "the greater part of these
stones, and put them into the building, and they
will fit in with the rest of the stones." 5. "How, Sir,"
said I, "can they fill the same room after they have
been hewn?" He answered and said to me:
"Those which turn out to be little will be put into
the middle of the building, and such as are bigger
will be put outside and will hold them together."
6. When he had said this he said to me: "Let us
go, and after two days let us come and cleanse these
stones and put them into the building, for everything
round the tower must be cleansed lest the Master
come suddenly and find it dirty round the tower
and he will be angry, and these stones will not go
into the building of the tower, and I shall seem
to be careless before the Master." 7. And after two
days we came to the tower, and he said to me: "Let
us look at all the stones, and let us see which
are able to come into the building." I said to him:
"Sir, let us look."

VIII

1. AND when we began we first looked at the
black stones, and these were found to be the same
as when they were put out of the building. And
the shepherd commanded them to be removed from
the tower and sent away. 2. Then he looked
at those which were rotten and he took and hewed
many of them and commanded the maidens to take
them and put them into the building, and the maidens
took them and put them into the building in the
middle of the tower. And the rest he commanded to

The Shepherd's treatment of the Stones

THE APOSTOLIC FATHERS

δὲ λοιποὺς ἐκέλευσε μετὰ τῶν μελάνων τεθῆναι·
καὶ γὰρ καὶ οὗτοι μέλανες εὑρέθησαν. 3. εἶτα
κατενόει τοὺς τὰς σχισμὰς ἔχοντας· καὶ ἐκ τούτων πολλοὺς ἐλατόμησε καὶ ἐκέλευσε διὰ τῶν
παρθένων εἰς τὴν οἰκοδομὴν ἀπενεχθῆναι· ἐξώτεροι
δὲ ἐτέθησαν, ὅτι ὑγιέστεροι εὑρέθησαν. οἱ δὲ λοιποὶ
διὰ τὸ πλῆθος τῶν σχισμάτων οὐκ ἠδυνήθησαν
λατομηθῆναι· διὰ ταύτην οὖν τὴν αἰτίαν ἀπεβλήθησαν ἀπὸ τῆς οἰκοδομῆς τοῦ πύργου. 4. εἶτα
κατενόει τοὺς κολοβούς, καὶ εὑρέθησαν πολλοὶ ἐν
αὐτοῖς μέλανες, τινὲς δὲ σχισμὰς μεγάλας πεποιη-
κότες· καὶ ἐκέλευσε καὶ τούτους τεθῆναι μετὰ
τῶν ἀποβεβλημένων. τοὺς δὲ περισσεύοντας
αὐτῶν καθαρίσας καὶ λατομήσας ἐκέλευσεν εἰς τὴν
οἰκοδομήν τεθῆναι. αἱ δὲ παρθένοι αὐτοὺς ἄρασαι
εἰς μέσην τὴν οἰκοδομὴν τοῦ πύργου ἥρμοσαν·
ἀσθενέστεροι γὰρ ἦσαν. 5. εἶτα κατενόει τοὺς
ἡμίσεις λευκούς, ἡμίσεις δὲ μέλανας· καὶ πολλοὶ
ἐξ αὐτῶν εὑρέθησαν μέλανες. ἐκέλευσε δὲ καὶ
τούτους ἀρθῆναι μετὰ τῶν ἀποβεβλημένων. οἱ δὲ
λοιποὶ πάντες ἤρθησαν ὑπὸ τῶν παρθένων·
λευκοὶ γὰρ ὄντες ἡρμόσθησαν ὑπ᾽ αὐτῶν τῶν
παρθένων εἰς τὴν οἰκοδομήν· ἐξώτεροι δὲ ἐτέθησαν,
ὅτι ὑγιεῖς εὑρέθησαν, ὥστε δύνασθαι αὐτοὺς
κρατεῖν τοὺς εἰς τὸ μέσον τεθέντας· ὅλως γὰρ ἐξ
αὐτῶν οὐδὲν ἐκολοβώθη. 6. εἶτα κατενόει τοὺς
τραχεῖς, καὶ σκληροὺς καὶ ὀλίγοι ἐξ αὐτῶν
ἀπεβλήθησαν διὰ τὸ μὴ δύνασθαι λατομηθῆναι·
σκληροὶ γὰρ λίαν εὑρέθησαν. οἱ δὲ λοιποὶ αὐτῶν
ἐλατομήθησαν καὶ ἤρθησαν ὑπὸ τῶν παρθένων
καὶ εἰς μέσην τὴν οἰκοδομὴν τοῦ πύργου ἡρμόσθη-

be put with the black ones, for these also were found to be black. 3. Then he began to look at those which had cracks, and of these he hewed many, and commanded them to be brought back by the maidens into the building. But they were put on the outside because they were found to be stronger. But the rest could not be hewn because of the number of the cracks. For this cause, therefore, they were thrown away from the building of the tower. 4. Then he began to look at those which were short, and many among them were found black, and some with great cracks, and he commanded these also to be put with the rejected. But the majority of them he cleaned and hewed and commanded to be put into the building. And the maidens took them, and fitted them into the middle of the building of the tower, for they were too weak.[1] 5. Then he began to look at those which were half white, and half black, and many of them were found to be black, and these also he commanded to be put away with the rejected. But the rest were all taken up by the maidens, for they were white and were fitted by the maidens themselves into the building. And they were put on the outside because they were found to be sound, so that they could support those that were put in the middle, for in no way were they too short. 6. Then he began to look at those which were hard and difficult, and a few of them were rejected, because they could not be hewn, for they proved to be very hard. But the rest of them were hewn, and were taken by the maidens and fitted into the middle of the building of the

[1] *i.e.* to endure the strain of the outside.

σαν· ἀσθενέστεροι γὰρ ἦσαν. 7. εἶτα κατενόει
τοὺς ἔχοντας τοὺς σπίλους, καὶ ἐκ τούτων ἐλά-
χιστοι ἐμελάνησαν καὶ ἀπεβλήθησαν πρὸς τοὺς
λοιπούς. οἱ δὲ περισσεύοντες λαμπροὶ καὶ ὑγιεῖς[1]
εὑρέθησαν· καὶ οὗτοι ἡρμόσθησαν ὑπὸ τῶν
παρθένων εἰς τὴν οἰκοδομήν, ἐξώτεροι δὲ ἐτέθησαν
διὰ τὴν ἰσχυρότητα αὐτῶν.

IX

1. Εἶτα ἦλθε κατανοῆσαι τοὺς λευκοὺς καὶ
στρογγύλους λίθους καὶ λέγει μοι· Τί ποιοῦμεν
περὶ τούτων τῶν λίθων; Τί, φημί, ἐγὼ γινώσκω,
κύριε; Οὐδὲν οὖν ἐπινοεῖς περὶ αὐτων; 2. Ἐγώ,
φημί, κύριε, ταύτην τὴν τέχνην οὐκ ἔχω, οὐδὲ
λατόμος εἰμὶ οὐδὲ δύναμαι νοῆσαι. Οὐ βλέπεις
αὐτούς, φησί, λίαν στρογγύλους ὄντας; καὶ ἐὰν
αὐτοὺς θελήσω τετραγώνους ποιῆσαι, πολὺ δεῖ ἀπ᾽
αὐτῶν ἀποκοπῆναι· δεῖ δὲ ἐξ αὐτῶν ἐξ ἀνάγκης
τινὰς εἰς τὴν οἰκοδομὴν τεθῆναι. 3. Εἰ οὖν, φημί,
κύριε, ἀνάγκη ἐστί, τί σεαυτὸν βασανίζεις καὶ οὐκ
ἐκλέγεις εἰς τὴν οἰκοδομὴν οὓς θέλεις καὶ ἁρμόζεις
εἰς αὐτήν; ἐξελέξατο ἐξ αὐτῶν τοὺς μείζονας καὶ
λαμπροὺς καὶ ἐλατόμησεν αὐτούς· αἱ δὲ παρθένοι
ἄρασαι ἥρμοσαν εἰς τὰ ἐξώτερα μέρη τῆς οἰκοδομῆς. 4. οἱ δὲ λοιποὶ οἱ περισσεύσαντες ἤρθησαν
καὶ ἀπετέθησαν εἰς τὸ πεδίον, ὅθεν ἠνέχθησαν·
οὐκ ἀπεβλήθησαν δέ, Ὅτι, φησί, λείπει τῷ πύργῳ
ἔτι μικρὸν οἰκοδομηθῆναι. πάντας[2] δὲ θέλει ὁ

---

[1] ὑγιεῖς L, ἐκεῖνοι A, om. E.
[2] πάντας A (probably, but it is difficult to read), 'forsitan'
L which in Sim. vii. 4 seems to represent πάντως.

tower; for they were too weak.   7. Then he began to look at those which had stains, and of these a very few were turned black, and were rejected with the rest, but most of them were found to be bright and sound, and these were fitted by the maidens into the building, but they were put on the outside because of their strength.

IX

1. NEXT he came to look at the white and round stones, and said to me : " What do we do with these stones ? "   " How should I know, Sir ? " said I. " Then do you not notice anything about them ? " 2. " I, Sir," said I, " have not this art, I am neither a stone-cutter, nor can I understand." " Do you not see," said he, " that they are very round, and if I wish to make them square, a great deal must be cut away from them ? Yet some of them must of necessity be put into the building." 3. " If then, Sir," said I, " it is necessary, why do you worry yourself, and not choose for the building those which you wish and fit them into it ? " He chose out from them the largest and bright ones and hewed them, and the maidens took and fitted them into the outside of the building. 4. And the rest which remained over were taken up and put back into the plain from which they had been brought. But they were not rejected, " Because," said he, " there remains still a little to be

THE APOSTOLIC FATHERS

δεσπότης τοῦ πύργου τούτους ἁρμοσθῆναι τοὺς
λίθους εἰς τὴν οἰκοδομήν, ὅτι λαμπροί εἰσι λίαν.
5. ἐκλήθησαν δὲ γυναῖκες δώδεκα, εὐειδέσταται
τῷ χαρακτῆρι, μέλανα ἐνδεδυμέναι, περιεζωσμέναι καὶ ἔξω τοὺς ὤμους ἔχουσαι[1] καὶ τὰς
τρίχας λελυμέναι· ἐδοκοῦσαν δέ μοι αἱ γυναῖκες
αὗται ἄγριαι εἶναι. ἐκέλευσε δὲ αὐτὰς ὁ ποιμὴν
ἆραι τοὺς λίθους τοὺς ἀποβεβλημένους ἐκ τῆς
οἰκοδομῆς καὶ ἀπενεγκεῖν αὐτοὺς εἰς τὰ ὄρη, ὅθεν
καὶ ἠνέχθησαν. 6. αἱ δὲ ἱλαραὶ ἦραν καὶ ἀπήνεγκαν πάντας τοὺς λίθους καὶ ἔθηκαν, ὅθεν ἐλήφθη-
σαν. καὶ μετὰ τὸ ἀρθῆναι πάντας τοὺς λίθους
καὶ μηκέτι κεῖσθαι λίθον κύκλῳ τοῦ πύργου,
λέγει μοι ὁ ποιμήν· Κυκλώσωμεν τὸν πύργον καὶ
ἴδωμεν, μή τι ἐλάττωμά ἐστιν ἐν αὐτῷ. καὶ
ἐκύκλευον ἐγὼ μετ' αὐτοῦ. 7. ἰδὼν δὲ ὁ ποιμὴν
τὸν πύργον εὐπρεπῆ ὄντα τῇ οἰκοδομῇ λίαν ἱλαρὸς
ἦν· ὁ γὰρ πύργος οὕτως ἦν ᾠκοδομημένος, ὥστε
με ἰδόντα ἐπιθυμεῖν τὴν οἰκοδομὴν αὐτοῦ· οὕτω
γὰρ ἦν ᾠκοδομημένος, ὡσὰν ἐξ ἑνὸς λίθου μὴ
ἔχων μίαν ἁρμογὴν ἐν ἑαυτῷ. ἐφαίνετο δὲ ὁ λίθος
ὡς ἐκ τῆς πέτρας ἐκκεκολαμμένος· μονόλιθος γάρ
μοι ἐδόκει εἶναι.

X

1. Κἀγὼ περιπατῶν μετ' αὐτοῦ ἱλαρὸς ἤμην
τοιαῦτα ἀγαθὰ βλέπων. λέγει δέ μοι ὁ ποιμήν·
Ὕπαγε καὶ φέρε ἄσβεστον καὶ ὄστρακον λεπτόν,
ἵνα τοὺς τύπους τῶν λίθων τῶν ἠρμένων καὶ

---

[1] Retranslated from LE, om. A.

built of the tower, and the master of the tower wishes that all these stones should be fitted into the building because they are very bright. 5. And there were called twelve women, very beautiful to look at, clothed in black, girded, and their shoulders bare, and their hair loose. And these women looked to me to be cruel. And the shepherd commanded them to take the stones which were rejected from the building, and take them back to the mountains, from which also they had been brought. 6. And they were glad and took them up, and took away all the stones, and put them whence they had been taken. And after all the stones had been taken up, and there no longer remained a stone round the tower, the shepherd said to me: "Let us go round the tower and see if there is any defect in it." And I went round it with him. 7. And when the shepherd saw that the tower was beautifully built, he was very joyful; for the tower was so built that when I saw it, I envied its building, for it was so built, as if it were all one stone, without a single joint in it, and the stone appeared as if it had been hewn out of a rock, for it seemed to me to be a single stone.

X

1. AND I also walked with him and was glad when I saw such good things. And the shepherd said to me: "Go and bring lime and a light clay, that I may fill up the marks of the stones[1] which have

The clearing of the neighbour-hood of the tower

[1] Apparently the meaning is that the holes left in the ground where stones had been taken out were to be filled up and levelled.

εἰς τὴν οἰκοδομὴν βεβλημένων[1] ἀναπληρώσω· δεῖ γὰρ τοῦ πύργου τὰ κύκλῳ πάντα ὁμαλὰ γενέσθαι. 2. καὶ ἐποίησα καθὼς ἐκέλευσε, καὶ ἤνεγκα πρὸς αὐτόν. Ὑπηρέτει μοι, φησί, καὶ ἐγγὺς τὸ ἔργον τελεσθήσεται. ἐπλήρωσεν οὖν τοὺς τύπους τῶν λίθων τῶν εἰς τὴν οἰκοδομὴν ἀπεληλυθότων καὶ ἐκέλευσε σαρωθῆναι τὰ κύκλῳ τοῦ πύργου καὶ καθαρὰ γενέσθαι· 3. αἱ δὲ παρθένοι λαβοῦσαι σάρους ἐσάρωσαν καὶ πάντα τὰ κόπρια ἦραν ἐκ τοῦ πύργου καὶ ἔρραναν ὕδωρ, καὶ ἐγένετο ὁ τόπος ἱλαρὸς καὶ εὐπρεπέστατος τοῦ πύργου. 4. λέγει μοι ὁ ποιμήν· Πάντα, φησί, κεκαθάρται· ἐὰν ἔλθῃ ὁ κύριος ἐπισκέψασθαι τὸν πύργον, οὐκ ἔχει ἡμῖν οὐδὲν μέμψασθαι. ταῦτα εἰπὼν ἤθελεν ὑπάγειν. 5. ἐγὼ δὲ ἐπελαβόμην αὐτοῦ τῆς πήρας καὶ ἠρξάμην αὐτὸν ὁρκίζειν κατὰ τοῦ κυρίου, ἵνα μοι ἐπιλύσῃ, ἃ ἔδειξέ μοι. λέγει μοι. Μικρὸν ἔχω ἀκαιρεθῆναι καὶ πάντα σοι ἐπιλύσω· ἔκδεξαί με ὧδε, ἕως ἔρχομαι. 6. λέγω αὐτῷ· Κύριε, μόνος ὢν ὧδε ἐγὼ τί ποιήσω; Οὐκ εἶ, φησί, μόνος· αἱ γὰρ παρθένοι αὗται μετὰ σοῦ εἰσί. Παράδος οὖν, φημί, αὐταῖς με. προσκαλεῖται αὐτὰς ὁ ποιμὴν καὶ λέγει αὐταῖς· Παρατίθεμαι ὑμῖν τοῦτον ἕως ἔρχομαι· καὶ ἀπῆλθεν. 7. ἐγὼ δὲ ἤμην μόνος μετὰ τῶν παρθένων· ἦσαν δὲ ἱλαρώτεραι καὶ πρὸς ἐμὲ εὖ εἶχον· μάλιστα δὲ αἱ τέσσαρες αἱ ἐνδοξότεραι αὐτῶν.

[1] ἠρημένων . . . βεβλημένων LE, ἡρμοσμένων εἰς τὴν οἰκοδυμὴν καὶ βεβλημένων A.

been taken up, and put into the building. For all the ground round the tower must be level." 2. And I did as he commanded and brought them to him. "Serve me," said he, "and the work will soon be completed." So he filled up the marks of the stones which had gone into the building, and commanded all round the tower to be swept, and be made clean. 3. And the maidens took brooms and swept, and they took away all the dirt from the tower and sprinkled water, and the place of the tower became joyful and very beautiful. 4. The shepherd said to me : "Everything," said he, "has been made clean. If the lord come to visit the tower, he has nothing with which to blame us." When he had said this he wished to go away. 5. But I took him by his wallet, and began to adjure him by the Lord to explain to me what he had shown me. He said to me : "I am busy for a little and then I will explain everything to you. Wait for me here till I come." 6. I said to him : "Sir, what shall I do here alone?" "You are not alone," he said, "for these maidens are here with you." "Give me then," said I, "into their charge." The shepherd called them and said to them : "I entrust him to you till I come," and he went away. 7. And I was alone with the maidens, and they were merry and gracious towards me, especially the four more glorious of them.

XI

1. Λέγουσί μοι αἱ παρθένοι· Σήμερον ὁ ποιμὴν
ὧδε οὐκ ἔρχεται. Τί οὖν, φημί, ποιήσω ἐγώ;
Μέχρις ὀψέ, φασίν, περίμεινον αὐτόν· καὶ ἐὰν
ἔλθῃ, λαλήσει μετὰ σοῦ, ἐὰν δὲ μὴ ἔλθῃ, μενεῖς
μεθ᾽ ἡμῶν ὧδε ἕως ἔρχεται. 2. λέγω αὐταῖς·
Ἐκδέξομαι αὐτὸν ἕως ὀψέ· ἐὰν δὲ μὴ ἔλθῃ,
ἀπελεύσομαι εἰς τὸν οἶκον καὶ πρωῒ ἐπανήξω.
αἱ δὲ ἀκοκριθεῖσαι λέγουσί μοι· Ἡμῖν παρεδόθης·
οὐ δύνασαι ἀφ᾽ ἡμῶν ἀναχωρῆσαι. 3. Ποῦ οὖν,
φημί, μενῶ; Μεθ᾽ ἡμῶν, φασί, κοιμηθήσῃ ὡς
ἀδελφός, καὶ οὐχ ὡς ἀνήρ· ἡμέτερος γὰρ ἀδελφὸς
εἶ, καὶ τοῦ λοιποῦ μέλλομεν μετὰ σοῦ κατοικεῖν·
λίαν γάρ σε ἀγαπῶμεν. ἐγὼ δὲ ᾐσχυνόμην μετ᾽
αὐτῶν μένειν. 4. καὶ ἡ δοκοῦσα πρώτη αὐτῶι
εἶναι ἤρξατό με καταφιλεῖν καὶ περιπλέκεσθαι.
αἱ δὲ ἄλλαι ὁρῶσαι ἐκείνην περιπλεκομένην μοι
καὶ αὐταὶ ἤρξαντό με καταφιλεῖν καὶ περιάγειν
κύκλῳ τοῦ πύργου καὶ παίζειν μετ᾽ ἐμοῦ. 5. κἀγὼ
ὡσεὶ νεώτερος ἐγεγόνειν καὶ ἠρξάμην καὶ αὐτὸς
παίζειν μετ᾽ αὐτῶν· αἱ μὲν γὰρ ἐχόρευον, αἱ δὲ ὠρ-
χοῦντο, αἱ δὲ ᾖδον· ἐγὼ δὲ σιγὴν ἔχων μετ᾽ αὐτῶν
κύκλῳ τοῦ πύργου περιεπάτουν καὶ ἱλαρὸς ἤμην
μετ᾽ αὐτῶν. 6. ὀψίας δὲ γενομένης ἤθελον εἰς
τὸν οἶκον ὑπάγειν· αἱ δὲ οὐκ ἀφῆκαν, ἀλλὰ κατέ-
σχον με. καὶ ἔμεινα μετ᾽ αὐτῶν τὴν νύκτα καὶ
ἐκοιμήθην παρὰ τὸν πύργον. 7. ἔστρωσαν γὰρ αἱ
παρθένοι τοὺς λινοῦς χιτῶνας ἑαυτῶν χαμαὶ καὶ
ἐμὲ ἀνέκλιναν εἰς τὸ μέσον αὐτῶν, καὶ οὐδὲν ὅλως
ἐποίουν εἰ μὴ προσηύχοντο· κἀγὼ μετ᾽ αὐτῶν

XI

1. THE maidens said to me : " To-day the shepherd is not coming here." " What then," said I, " shall I do ? " " Wait for him," said they, " until the evening, and if he come he will speak with you ; and if he come not you shall remain here with us until he come." 2. I said to them : " I will wait for him till evening, but if he come not I will go away home and return in the morning." But they answered and said to me : " You were given to our charge ; you cannot go away from us." 3. " Where shall I stay then ? " said I. " You shall sleep with us," said they, " as a brother and not as a husband, for you are our brother and for the future we are going to live with you, for we love you greatly." But I was ashamed to stay with them. 4. And she who seemed to be the first of them began to kiss and embrace me, and the others seeing her embracing me began to kiss me themselves, and to lead me round the tower, and to play with me. 5. I, too, had, as it were, become young again, and began to play with them myself, for some were dancing, others were gavotting, others were singing, and I walked in silence with them round the tower, and was merry with them. 6. But when evening came I wished to go home but they did not let me go, but kept me, and I stayed the night with them and slept by the tower. 7. For the maidens spread their linen tunics on the ground, and they made me lie down in the midst of them, and they did nothing else but pray, and I also prayed with

ἀδιαλείπτως προσηυχόμην καὶ οὐκ ἔλασσον
ἐκείνων. καὶ ἔχαιρον αἱ παρθένοι οὕτω μου
προσευχομένου. καὶ ἔμεινα ἐκεῖ μέχρι τῆς αὔριον
ἕως ὥρας δευτέρας μετὰ τῶν παρθένον. 8. εἶτα
παρῆν ὁ ποιμήν, καὶ λέγει ταῖς παρθένοις· Μή
τινα αὐτῷ ὕβριν πεποιήκατε; Ἐρώτα, φασίν,
αὐτόν. λέγω αὐτῷ· Κύριε, εὐφράνθην μετ᾽
αὐτῶν μείνας. Τί, φησίν, ἐδείπνησας; Ἐδεί-
πνησα, φημί, κύριε, ῥήματα κυρίου ὅλην τὴν
νύκτα. Καλῶς, φησίν, ἔλαβόν σε; Ναί, φημί,
κύριε. 9. Νῦν, φησί, τί θέλεις πρῶτον ἀκοῦσαι;
Καθώς, φημί, κύριε, ἀπ᾽ ἀρχῆς ἔδειξας· ἐρωτῶ
σε, κύριε, ἵνα, καθὼς ἄν σε ἐπερωτήσω, οὕτω μοι
καὶ δηλώσῃς. Καθὼς βούλει, φησίν, οὕτω σοι
καὶ ἐπιλύσω, καὶ οὐδὲν ὅλως ἀποκρύψω ἀπὸ σοῦ.

XII

1. Πρῶτον, φημί, πάντων, κύριε, τοῦτό μοι
δήλωσον· ἡ πέτρα καὶ ἡ πύλη τίς ἐστιν; Ἡ
πέτρα, φησίν, αὕτη καὶ ἡ πύλη ὁ υἱὸς τοῦ θεοῦ
ἐστί. Πῶς, φημί, κύριε, ἡ πέτρα παλαιά ἐστιν,
ἡ δὲ πύλη καινή; Ἄκουε, φησί, καὶ σύνιε, ἀσύνετε.
2. ὁ μὲν υἱὸς τοῦ θεοῦ πάσης τῆς κτίσεως αὐτοῦ
προγενέστερός ἐστιν, ὥστε σύμβουλον αὐτὸν
γενέσθαι τῷ πατρὶ τῆς κτίσεως αὐτοῦ· διὰ τοῦτο
καὶ παλαιὰ ἡ πέτρα.[1] Ἡ δὲ πύλη διατί καινή,
φημί, κύριε; 3. Ὅτι, φησίν, ἐπ᾽ ἐσχάτων τῶν
ἡμερῶν τῆς συντελείας φανερὸς ἐγένετο, διὰ τοῦτο

Prov. 8,
27–30

---

[1] παλαιὰ ἡ πέτρα P^am παλαιός ἐστι A, om. L.

them unceasingly and not less than they, and the maidens rejoiced when I was praying thus, and I stayed there until the morrow until the second hour with the maidens. 8. Then the shepherd came and said to the maidens: "Have you done him any despite?" "Ask him," said they. I said to him: "Sir, I rejoiced at remaining with them." "On what," said he, "did you sup?" "I supped, Sir," said I, "on the words of the Lord the whole night." "Did they receive you well?" said he, "Yes, Sir," said I. 9. "Now," said he, "what do you wish to hear first?" "Even as, Sir," said I, "you showed me from the beginning; I ask you, Sir, to declare things to me even as I ask them of you." "Even as you desire," said he, "so I will interpret to you, and hide from you nothing at all."

XII

1. "First of all, Sir," said I, "tell me this: What is the rock and the door?" "This rock and the door," said he, "is the Son of God." "How is it," said I, "Sir, that the rock is old, but the gate is new?" "Listen," said he, "and understand, foolish man. 2. The Son of God is older than all his creation, so that he was the counsellor of his Creation to the Father, therefore the rock is also old." "But why is the gate new, Sir?" said I. 3. "Because," said he, "He was manifested in the last days of the end[1]

The explanation of the parable

---

[1] The Greek means 'the consummation,' the time when this age or world-period is finished, and a new age will begin. (Cf. Mt. 13, 40.)

καινὴ ἐγένετο ἡ πύλη, ἵνα οἱ μέλλοντες σώζεσθαι δι᾽ αὐτῆς εἰς τὴν βασιλείαν εἰσέλθωσι τοῦ θεοῦ.

Jo. 3, 5 cf.
Mc. 9, 47;
10, 23-25;
Mt. 5, 20;
7, 21; 18, 3

4. εἶδες, φησίν, τοὺς λίθους τοὺς διὰ τῆς πύλης εἰσεληλυθότας εἰς τὴν οἰκοδομὴν τοῦ πύργου βεβλημένους,[1] τοὺς δὲ μὴ εἰσεληλυθότας πάλιν ἀποβεβλημένους εἰς τὸν ἴδιον τόπον; Εἶδον, φημί, κύριε. Οὕτω, φησίν, εἰς τὴν βασιλείαν τοῦ θεοῦ οὐδεὶς εἰσελεύσεται, εἰ μὴ λάβοι τὸ ὄνομα τὸ ἅγιον[2] αὐτοῦ. 5. ἐὰν γὰρ εἰς πόλιν θελήσῃς εἰσελθεῖν τινα κἀκείνη ἡ πόλις περιτετειχισμένη κύκλῳ καὶ μίαν ἔχει πύλην, μήτι δύνῃ εἰς ἐκείνην τὴν πόλιν εἰσελθεῖν, εἰ μὴ διὰ τῆς πύλης ἧς ἔχει; Πῶς γάρ, φημί, κύριε, δύναται γενέσθαι ἄλλως; Εἰ οὖν εἰς τὴν πόλιν οὐ δύνῃ εἰσελθεῖν εἰ μὴ διὰ τῆς πύλης ἧς ἔχει, οὕτω, φησί, καὶ

Jo. 3, 5

εἰς τὴν βασιλείαν τοῦ θεοῦ ἄλλως εἰσελθεῖν οὐ δύναται ἄνθρωπος εἰ μὴ διὰ τοῦ ὀνόματος τοῦ υἱοῦ αὐτοῦ τοῦ ἠγαπημένου ὑπ᾽ αὐτοῦ. 6. Εἶδες, φησί, τὸν ὄχλον τὸν οἰκοδομοῦντα τὸν πύργον; Εἶδον, φημί, κύριε. Ἐκεῖνοι, φησί, πάντες ἄγγελοι ἔνδοξοί εἰσι· τούτοις οὖν περιτετείχισται ὁ κύριος. ἡ δὲ πύλη ὁ υἱὸς τοῦ θεοῦ

Jo. 14, 6

ἐστιν· αὕτη μία εἴσοδός ἐστι πρὸς τὸν κύριον. ἄλλως οὖν οὐδεὶς εἰσελεύσεται πρὸς αὐτὸν εἰ μὴ διὰ τοῦ υἱοῦ αὐτοῦ. 7. Εἶδες, φησί, τοὺς ἐξ ἄνδρας καὶ τὸν μέσον αὐτῶν ἔνδοξον καὶ μέγαν ἄνδρα τὸν περιπατοῦντα περὶ τὸν πύργον καὶ τοὺς λίθους ἀποδοκιμάσαντα ἐκ τῆς οἰκοδομῆς; Εἶδον, φημί, κύριε. 8. Ὁ ἔνδοξος, φησίν, ἀνὴρ ὁ υἱὸς τοῦ θεοῦ ἐστι, κἀκεῖνοι οἱ ἐξ οἱ ἔνδοξοι ἄγγελοι

---

[1] βεβλημένους om. A.
[2] τὸ ἅγιον A, τοῦ υἱοῦ αὐτοῦ E, τοῦ υἱοῦ τοῦ θεοῦ L.

of the world, for this reason the gate is new, that those who are to be saved may 'enter' through it 'into the kingdom of God.' 4. Do you see," said he, "the stones which entered through the gate, were put into the building of the tower, but those which did not enter through it were put back again into their own place?" "I see, Sir," said I. "So," said he, "no man 'shall enter into the Kingdom of God,' except he take his holy name. 5. For if you wish to enter into a city, and that city has been walled round, and has one gate, can you enter into that city except through the gate which it has?" "No, Sir," said I, "for how is it possible otherwise?" "If then you are not able to enter into the city except through the gate which it has, so," said he, "a man 'cannot' otherwise 'enter into the kingdom of God,' except through the name of his Son, who was beloved by him. 6. Do you see," said he, "the crowd which is building the tower?" "Yes, Sir," said I, "I see it." "They," said he, "are all glorious angels; by these then the Lord[1] has been walled round. But the gate is the Son of God, this is the only entrance to the Lord. No man can enter in to him otherwise, than through his Son. 7. So you see," said he, "the six men, and the glorious and great man in their midst, who is walking round the tower and rejected the stones from the building?" "Yes, Sir," said I, "I see him." 8. "The glorious man," said he, "is the Son of God, and

The six men

The 'glorious man'

---

[1] It is noteworthy that here the Lord is for the moment identified with the tower.

εἰσι δεξιὰ καὶ εὐώνυμα συγκρατοῦντες αὐτόν.
τούτων, φησί, τῶν ἀγγέλων τῶν ἐνδόξων οὐδεὶς
εἰσελεύσεται πρὸς τὸν θεὸν ἄτερ αὐτοῦ· ὃς ἂν τὸ
ὄνομα αὐτοῦ μὴ λάβῃ, οὐκ εἰσελεύσεται εἰς τὴν
βασιλείαν τοῦ θεοῦ.

XIII

1. Ὁ δὲ πύργος, φημί, τίς ἐστιν; Ὁ πύργος,
φησίν, οὗτος ἡ ἐκκλησία ἐστίν. 2. Αἱ δὲ
παρθένοι αὗται τίνες εἰσίν; Αὗται, φησίν, ἅγια
πνεύματά εἰσι· καὶ ἄλλως ἄνθρωπος οὐ δύναται
εὑρεθῆναι εἰς τὴν βασιλείαν τοῦ θεοῦ, ἐὰν μὴ
αὗται αὐτὸν ἐνδύσωσι τὸ ἔνδυμα αὐτῶν· ἐὰν γὰρ
τὸ ὄνομα μόνον λάβῃς, τὸ δὲ ἔνδυμα παρὰ τούτων
μὴ λάβῃς, οὐδὲν ὠφελήσῃ· αὗται γὰρ αἱ παρθένοι
δυνάμεις εἰσὶ τοῦ υἱοῦ τοῦ θεοῦ. ἐὰν τὸ ὄνομα
φορῇς, τὴν δὲ δύναμιν μὴ φορῇς αὐτοῦ, εἰς μάτην
ἔσῃ τὸ ὄνομα αὐτοῦ φορῶν. 3. τοὺς δὲ λίθους,
φησίν, οὓς εἶδες ἀποβεβλημένους, οὗτοι τὸ μὲν
ὄνομα ἐφόρεσαν, τὸν δὲ ἱματισμὸν τῶν παρθένων
οὐκ ἐνεδύσαντο. Ποῖος, φημί, ἱματισμὸς αὐτῶν
ἐστί, κύριε; Αὐτὰ τὰ ὀνόματα, φησίν, ἱματισμός
ἐστιν αὐτῶν. ὃς ἂν τὸ ὄνομα τοῦ υἱοῦ τοῦ θεοῦ
φορῇ, καὶ τούτων ὀφείλει τὰ ὀνόματα φορεῖν· καὶ
γὰρ αὐτὸς ὁ υἱὸς τὰ ὀνόματα τῶν παρθένων τούτων φορεῖ. 4. ὅσους, φησί, λίθους εἶδες εἰς τὴν
οἰκοδομὴν τοῦ πύργου εἰσεληλυθότας, ἐπιδεδο-
μένους διὰ τῶν χειρῶν αὐτῶν καὶ μείναντας εἰς
τὴν οἰκοδομήν,[1] τούτων τῶν παρθένων τὴν δύνα-

---

[1] Retranslated from LE, om. A.

those six are glorious angels supporting him on the right hand and on the left. None of these glorious angels," said he, "can enter into God's presence without him. Whoever receives not his name 'shall not enter into the kingdom of God.'"

XIII

1. "BUT," said I, "what is the tower? "This The Tower tower," said he, "is the Church." 2. "And what The are these maidens?" "They," said he, "are holy Maidens spirits. And a man cannot be found in the kingdom of God in any other way, except they clothe him with their clothing. For if you receive the name alone but do not receive the clothing from them, you will benefit nothing, for these maidens are the powers of the Son of God. If you bear the name, but do not bear his power you will be bearing his name in vain. 3. And the stones," said he, "which you saw rejected, these are they who bore the name, but were not clothed with the raiment of the maidens." "What," said I, "is their raiment, Sir?" "Their names themselves," said he, "are their raiment. Whoever bears the name of the Son of God must also bear their names; for even the Son himself bears the names of these maidens.[1] 4. All the stones," said he, "which you saw enter into the building of the tower, given by their hands and remaining in the building, had put on the power of

[1] The explanation is given in Sim. ix. 15.

μιν ἐνδεδυμένοι εἰσί. 5. διὰ τοῦτο βλέπεις τὸν
πύργον μονόλιθον γεγονότα μετὰ τῆς πέτρας·
οὕτω καὶ οἱ πιστεύσαντες τῷ κυρίῳ διὰ τοῦ υἱοῦ
αὐτοῦ καὶ ἐνδιδυσκόμενοι τὰ πνεύματα ταῦτα
ἔσονται εἰς ἓν πνεῦμα, ἓν σῶμα, καὶ μία χρόα τῶν
ἱματίων αὐτῶν. τῶν τοιούτων δὲ τῶν φορούντων
τὰ ὀνόματα τῶν παρθένων ἐστὶν ἡ κατοικία εἰς τὸν
πύργον. 6. Οἱ οὖν, φημί, κύριε, ἀποβεβλημένοι
λίθοι διατί ἀπεβλήθησαν; διῆλθον γὰρ διὰ τῆς
πύλης, καὶ διὰ τῶν χειρῶν τῶν παρθένων ἐτέθησαν εἰς τὴν οἰκοδομὴν τοῦ πύργου. Ἐπειδὴ
πάντα σοι, φησί, μέλει, καὶ ἀκριβῶς ἐξετάζεις,
ἄκουε περὶ τῶν ἀποβεβλημένων λίθων. 7. οὗτοι,
φησί, πάντες τὸ ὄνομα τοῦ υἱοῦ τοῦ θεοῦ
ἔλαβον, ἔλαβον δὲ καὶ τὴν δύναμιν τῶν παρθένων
τούτων. λαβόντες οὖν τὰ πνεύματα ταῦτα ἐνε-
δυναμώθησαν καὶ ἦσαν μετὰ τῶν δούλων τοῦ
θεοῦ, καὶ ἦν αὐτῶν ἓν πνεῦμα καὶ ἓν σῶμα καὶ ἓν
ἔνδυμα· τὰ γὰρ αὐτὰ ἐφρόνουν καὶ δικαιοσύνην
εἰργάζοντο. 8. μετὰ οὖν χρόνον τινὰ ἀνεπεί-
σθησαν ὑπὸ τῶν γυναικῶν ὧν εἶδες μέλανα ἱμάτια
ἐνδεδυμένων, τοὺς ὤμους ἔξω ἐχουσῶν καὶ τὰς
τρίχας λελυμένας καὶ εὐμόρφων· ταύτας ἰδόντες
ἐπεθύμησαν αὐτῶν καὶ ἐνεδύσαντο τὴν δύναμιν
αὐτῶν, τῶν δὲ παρθένων ἀπεδύσαντο τὸ ἔνδυμα
καὶ τὴν δύναμιν.[1] 9. οὗτοι οὖν ἀπεβλήθησαν
ἀπὸ τοῦ οἴκου τοῦ θεοῦ καὶ ἐκείναις παρεδόθησαν·
οἱ δὲ μὴ ἀπατηθέντες τῷ κάλλει τῶν γυναικῶν
τούτων ἔμειναν ἐν τῷ οἴκῳ τοῦ θεοῦ. ἔχεις, φησί,
τὴν ἐπίλυσιν τῶν ἀποβεβλημένων.

Eph. 4, 4

Eph. 4, 4
II Cor. 13,
11 ; Philipp
2, 2 ; 3, 16 ;
4, 2 ; Rom.
12, 16

Ps. 14, 2 ;
Acts 10, 35 ;
Heb. 11, 33

[1] τὴν δύναμιν ΑL₂, τὸ ἔνδυμα L₁ τὸ ἔνδυμα καὶ τὴν δύναμιν Α.

these maidens. 5. For this reason you see that the tower has become one solid stone with the rock. So also those who believe on the Lord through his Son, and put on these spirits will become 'one spirit and one body,' and the colour of their raiment will be one. And the dwelling of such as bear the names of the maidens is in the tower." 6. "Why, Sir," said I, "were the rejected stones rejected? For they came in through the gate and were put into the building of the tower by the hands of the maidens." "Since," said he, "you care for everything, and enquire accurately, listen concerning the rejected stones. 7. These," said he, "all bore the name of the Son of God, and they also received the power of these maidens. By receiving these spirits, then, they were strengthened and were with the servants of God, and they had 'one spirit and one body,' and one raiment, for they 'had the same mind' and 'wrought righteousness.' 8. After some time, then, they were made disobedient by the women whom you saw clothed in black raiment, who had their shoulders bare, and their hair loose, and were beautiful. When they saw them they desired them, and put on their power, and put off the clothing and power of the maidens. 9. They were therefore rejected from the house of God and were handed over to those women. But those who were not deceived by the beauty of these women remained in the house of God. You have here," said he, "the explanation of those who were rejected."

The rejected stones

XIV

1. Τί οὖν, φημί, κύριε, ἐὰν οὗτοι οἱ ἄνθρωποι, τοιοῦτοι ὄντες, μετανοήσωσι καὶ ἀποβάλωσι τὰς ἐπιθυμίας τῶν γυναικῶν τούτων, καὶ ἐπανακάμψωσιν ἐπὶ τὰς παρθένους καὶ ἐν τῇ δυνάμει αὐτῶν καὶ ἐν τοῖς ἔργοις αὐτῶν πορευθῶσιν, οὐκ εἰσελεύσονται εἰς τὸν οἶκον τοῦ θεοῦ; 2. Εἰσελεύσονται, φησίν, ἐὰν τούτων τῶν γυναικῶν ἀποβάλωσι τὰ ἔργα, τῶν δὲ παρθένων ἀναλάβωσι τὴν δύναμιν καὶ ἐν τοῖς ἔργοις αὐτῶν πορευθῶσι· διὰ τοῦτο γὰρ καὶ τῆς οἰκοδομῆς ἀνοχὴ ἐγένετο, ἵνα, ἐὰν μετανοήσωσιν οὗτοι, ἀπέλθωσιν εἰς τὴν οἰκοδομὴν τοῦ πύργου. ἐὰν δὲ μὴ μετανοήσωσι, τότε ἄλλοι εἰσελεύσονται,[1] καὶ οὗτοι εἰς τέλος ἐκβληθήσονται. 3. ἐπὶ τούτοις πᾶσιν ηὐχαρίστησα τῷ κυρίῳ, ὅτι ἐσπλαγχνίσθη ἐπὶ πᾶσι τοῖς ἐπικαλουμένοις τῷ ὀνόματι αὐτοῦ καὶ ἐξαπέστειλε τὸν ἄγγελον τῆς μετανοίας εἰς ἡμᾶς τοὺς ἁμαρτήσαντας εἰς αὐτὸν καὶ ἀνεκαίνισεν ἡμῶν τὸ πνεῦμα καὶ ἤδη κατεφθαρμένων ἡμῶν καὶ μὴ ἐχόντων ἐλπίδα τοῦ ζῆν ἀνενέωσε τὴν ζωὴν ἡμῶν. 4. Νῦν, φημί, κύριε, δήλωσόν μοι, διατί ὁ πύργος χαμαὶ οὐκ ᾠκοδόμηται, ἀλλ' ἐπὶ τὴν πέτραν καὶ ἐπὶ τὴν πύλην. Ἔτι, φησίν, ἄφρων εἶ καὶ ἀσύνετος; Ἀνάγκην ἔχω, φημί, κύριε, πάντα ἐπερωτᾶν σε, ὅτι οὐδ' ὅλως οὐδὲν δύναμαι νοῆσαι· τὰ γὰρ πάντα μεγάλα καὶ ἔνδοξά ἐστι καὶ δυσνόητα τοῖς ἀνθρώποις. 5. Ἄκουε, φησί· τὸ ὄνομα τοῦ υἱοῦ τοῦ θεοῦ μέγα ἐστὶ καὶ ἀχώρητον καὶ τὸν κόσμον ὅλον βαστάζει.

Is. 43, 7

---

[1] εἰσελεύσονται LE, ἀπελεύσονται A.

XIV

1. "How will it then be, Sir," said I, "if these men, such as they are, repent and put away tne lusts of these women, and return to the maidens and walk in their power and in their deeds? Will they not enter into the house of God?" 2. "They will enter," said he, "if they put away the works of these women, and take back the power of the maidens and walk in their deeds. For this cause also there was a pause in the building, in order that, if they repent, they may go away into the building of the tower. But if they do not repent then others will enter and they will be finally rejected." 3. I thanked the Lord for all these things, that he had mercy on all who call upon his name, and sent the angel of repentance to us who have sinned against him, and renewed our spirit, even when we were already corrupted, and restored our life, when we had no hope of living. 4. "Now, Sir," said I, "explain to me why the tower was not built on the ground but on the rock and on the gate." "Are you still," said he, "silly and foolish?" "I need, Sir," said I, "to ask everything from you, because I am wholly without power of understanding anything. For all things great and glorious are also difficult for men to understand." 5. "Listen," said he, "the name of the Son of God is great and incomprehensible, and supports the whole world. If

εἰ οὖν πᾶσα ἡ κτίσις διὰ τοῦ υἱοῦ τοῦ θεοῦ
βαστάζεται, τί δοκεῖς τοὺς κεκλημένους ὑπ' αὐτοῦ
καὶ τὸ ὄνομα φοροῦντας τοῦ υἱοῦ τοῦ θεοῦ καὶ
πορευομένους ταῖς ἐντολαῖς αὐτοῦ; 6. βλέπεις
οὖν, ποίους βαστάζει; τοὺς ἐξ ὅλης καρδίας φοροῦντας τὸ ὄνομα αὐτοῦ. αὐτὸς οὖν θεμέλιος
αὐτοῖς ἐγένετο καὶ ἡδέως αὐτοὺς βαστάζει, ὅτι
οὐκ ἐπαισχύνονται τὸ ὄνομα αὐτοῦ φορεῖν.

XV

1. Δήλωσόν μοι, φημί, κύριε, τῶν παρθένων τὰ ὀνόματα καὶ τῶν γυναικῶν τῶν τὰ μέλανα
ἱμάτια ἐνδεδυμένων. Ἄκουε, φησίν, τῶν παρθένων[1] τὰ ὀνόματα τῶν ἰσχυροτέρων, τῶν εἰς τὰς
γωνίας σταθεισῶν. 2. ἡ μὲν πρώτη Πίστις, ἡ δὲ
δευτέρα Ἐγκράτεια, ἡ δὲ τρίτη Δύναμις, ἡ δὲ
τετάρτη Μακροθυμία· αἱ δὲ ἕτεραι ἀνὰ μέσον
τούτων σταθεῖσαι ταῦτα ἔχουσι τὰ ὀνόματα·
Ἁπλότης, Ἀκακία, Ἁγνεία, Ἱλαρότης, Ἀλήθεια,
Σύνεσις, Ὁμόνοια, Ἀγάπη. ταῦτα τὰ ὀνόματα
Jo. 3, 5 ὁ φορῶν καὶ τὸ ὄνομα τοῦ υἱοῦ τοῦ θεοῦ δυνήσεται
εἰς τὴν βασιλείαν τοῦ θεοῦ εἰσελθεῖν. 3. ἄκουε,
φησί, καὶ τὰ ὀνόματα τῶν γυναικῶν τῶν τὰ ἱμάτια
μέλανα ἐχουσῶν. καὶ ἐκ τούτων τέσσαρές εἰσι
δυνατώτεραι. ἡ πρώτη Ἀπιστία, ἡ δευτέρα Ἀκ-
ρασία, ἡ δὲ τρίτη Ἀπείθεια, ἡ δὲ τετάρτη Ἀπάτη.
αἱ δὲ ἀκόλουθοι αὐτῶν καλοῦνται Λύπη, Πονηρία,
Ἀσέλγεια, Ὀξυχολία, Ψεῦδος, Ἀφροσύνη, Κατα-
λαλιά, Μῖσος. ταῦτα τὰ ὀνόματα ὁ φορῶν τοῦ

---

[1] τὰ ὀνόματα . . . παρθένων, retranslated from LE, om. A.

258

then the whole creation is supported by the Son of God, what do you think of those who are called by him, and bear the name of the Son of God, and walk in his commandments? 6. Do you see then whom he supports? Those who bear his name with their whole heart. He then was their foundation and he supports them joyfully, because they are not ashamed to bear his name."

XV

1. "EXPLAIN to me, Sir," said I, "the names of the maidens, and of the women who are clothed in black raiment." "Listen," said he, "to the names of the stronger maidens who stand at the corners. 2. The first is Faith, the second is Temperance, the third is Power, the fourth is Long-suffering, and the others who stand between them have these names:— Simplicity, Guilelessness, Holiness, Joyfulness, Truth, Understanding, Concord, Love. He who bears these names and the name of the Son of God, 'shall be able to enter into the Kingdom of God.' 3. Hear, also," said he, "the names of the women who have black raiment. Of these also four are more powerful. The first is Unbelief, the second Impurity, the third Disobedience, and the fourth Deceit; and those who follow them are called Grief, Wickedness, Licentiousness, Bitterness, Lying, Foolishness, Evilspeaking, Hate. The servant of God who bears

θεοῦ δοῦλος τὴν βασιλείαν μὲν ὄψεται τοῦ θεοῦ,
Deut. 34, 4 εἰς αὐτὴν δὲ οὐκ εἰσελεύσεται. 4. Οἱ λίθοι δέ,
φημί, κύριε, οἱ ἐκ τοῦ βυθοῦ ἡρμοσμένοι εἰς τὴν
οἰκοδομὴν τίνες εἰσίν; Οἱ μὲν πρῶτοι, φησίν, οἱ ι´
οἱ εἰς τὰ θεμέλια τεθειμένοι, πρώτη γενεά· οἱ δὲ
κε´¹ δευτέρα γενεὰ ἀνδρῶν δικαίων· οἱ δὲ λε´ προφῆται τοῦ θεοῦ καὶ διάκονοι αὐτοῦ· οἱ δὲ μ´
ἀπόστολοι καὶ διδάσκαλοι τοῦ κηρύγματος τοῦ
υἱοῦ τοῦ θεοῦ. 5. Διατί οὖν, φημί, κύριε, αἱ
παρθένοι καὶ τούτους τοὺς λίθους ἐπέδωκαν εἰς
τὴν οἰκοδομὴν τοῦ πύργου, διενέγκασαι διὰ τῆς
πύλης; 6. Οὗτοι γάρ, φησί, πρῶτοι ταῦτα τὰ
πνεύματα ἐφόρεσαν καὶ ὅλως ἀπ᾽ ἀλλήλων οὐκ
ἀπέστησαν, οὔτε τὰ πνεύματα ἀπὸ τῶν ἀνθρώπων
οὔτε οἱ ἄνθρωποι ἀπὸ τῶν πνευμάτων, ἀλλὰ παρέ-
μειναν τὰ πνεύματα αὐτοῖς μέχρι τῆς κοιμήσεως
αὐτῶν. καὶ εἰ μὴ ταῦτα τὰ πνεύματα μετ᾽ αὐτῶν
ἐσχήκεισαν, οὐκ ἂν εὔχρηστοι γεγόνεισαν τῇ
οἰκοδομῇ τοῦ πύργου τούτου.

XVI

1. Ἔτι μοι, φημί, κύριε, δήλωσον. Τί, φησίν,
ἐπιζητεῖς; Διατί, φημί, κύριε, οἱ λίθοι ἐκ τοῦ
βυθοῦ ἀνέβησαν καὶ εἰς τὴν οἰκοδομὴν τοῦ
πύργου² ἐτέθησαν, πεφορηκότες τὰ πνεύματα
ταῦτα; 2. Ἀνάγκην, φησίν, εἶχον δι᾽ ὕδατος ἀνα-
Jo. 3, 5 βῆναι, ἵνα ζωοποιηθῶσιν· οὐκ ἠδύναντο γὰρ ἄλλως

---

¹ κε´ AL, xv E.   ² τοῦ πύργου LE, om. A.

these names shall see the Kingdom of God, but shall not enter into it." 4. "But, Sir," said I, "what are the stones which were fitted into the building from the deep?" "The first," said he, "the ten which were placed in the foundation, are the first generation; and the twenty-five are the second generation of righteous men; and the thirty-five are the prophets of God and his servants, and the forty[1] are prophets and teachers of the preaching of the Son of God." 5. "Why, then, Sir," said I, "did the maidens give these stones also for the building of the tower, and brought them through the gate?" 6. "Because," said he, "these first bore these spirits, and they did not depart from one another at all; neither the spirits from the men nor the men from the spirits, but the spirits remained with them until they fell asleep. And if they had not had these spirits with them they would not have been useful for the building of this tower." The stones of the foundation

XVI

1. "EXPLAIN to me, Sir," said I, "still more." "What," said he, "are you asking further?" "Why Sir," said I, "did the stones come up from the deep and were put into the building of the tower, after they had borne these spirits?" 2. "They had need," said he, "to come up through the water that they might be made alive, for 'they could not' The stones from the deep

---

[1] It must be noted that the numbers given here do not quite agree with those in Sim. ix. 4, and no satisfactory hypothesis has ever been suggested as to any hidden meaning which the numbers may conceal.

εἰσελθεῖν εἰς τὴν βασιλείαν τοῦ θεοῦ, εἰ μὴ τὴν
νέκρωσιν ἀπέθεντο τῆς ζωῆς αὐτῶν τῆς προτέρας.[1] 3. ἔλαβον οὖν καὶ οὗτοι οἱ κεκοιμημένοι
τὴν σφραγῖδα τοῦ υἱοῦ τοῦ θεοῦ καὶ εἰσῆλθον

Jo. 3, 5   εἰς τὴν βασιλείαν τοῦ θεοῦ.[2] πρὶν γάρ, φησί,
φορέσαι τὸν ἄνθρωπον τὸ ὄνομα τοῦ υἱοῦ τοῦ
θεοῦ, νεκρός ἐστιν· ὅταν δὲ λάβῃ τὴν σφραγῖδα,
ἀποτίθεται τὴν νέκρωσιν καὶ ἀναλαμβάνει τὴν
ζωήν. 4. ἡ σφραγὶς οὖν τὸ ὕδωρ ἐστίν· εἰς τὸ
ὕδωρ οὖν καταβαίνουσι νεκροὶ καὶ ἀναβαίνουσι
ζῶντες. κἀκείνοις οὖν ἐκηρύχθη ἡ σφραγὶς αὕτη
καὶ ἐχρήσαντο αὐτῇ, ἵνα εἰσέλθωσιν εἰς τὴν

Jo. 3, 5   βασιλείαν τοῦ θεοῦ. 5. Διατί, φημί, κύριε, καὶ
οἱ μ΄ λίθοι μετ᾽ αὐτῶν ἀνέβησαν ἐκ τοῦ βυθοῦ,
ἤδη ἐσχηκότες τὴν σφαγῖδα; Ὅτι, φησίν, οὗτοι
οἱ ἀπόστολοι καὶ οἱ διδάσκαλοι οἱ κηρύξαντες τὸ
ὄνομα τοῦ υἱοῦ τοῦ θεοῦ, κοιμηθέντες ἐν δυνάμει
καὶ πίστει τοῦ υἱοῦ τοῦ θεοῦ ἐκήρυξαν καὶ τοῖς
προκεκοιμημένοις[3] καὶ αὐτοὶ ἔδωκαν αὐτοῖς τὴν
σφραγῖδα τοῦ κηρύγματος. 6. κατέβησαν οὖν
μετ᾽ αὐτῶν εἰς τὸ ὕδωρ καὶ πάλιν ἀνέβησαν·
ἀλλ᾽ οὗτοι μὲν ζῶντες κατέβησαν καὶ ζῶντες
ἀνέβησαν· ἐκεῖνοι δὲ οἱ προκεκοιμημένοι νεκροὶ
κατέβησαν, ζῶντες δὲ ἀνέβησαν.[4] 7. διὰ τούτων
οὖν ἐζωοποιήθησαν καὶ ἐπέγνωσαν τὸ ὄνομα τοῦ
υἱοῦ τοῦ θεοῦ· διὰ τοῦτο καὶ συνανέβησαν μετ᾽
αὐτῶν, καὶ συνηρμόσθησαν εἰς τὴν οἰκοδομὴν τοῦ

---

[1] τῆς προτέρας LE, om. A.
[2] καὶ . . . θεοῦ retranslated from LE, om. A.
[3] προκεκοιμημένοις Clem. L₁E, κεκοιμημένοις AL₂.
[4] ἀλλ᾽ οὗτοι . . . ἀνέβησαν Clem. (LE) . . ., om. A.

otherwise 'enter into the kingdom of God' unless they put away the mortality of their former life. 3. So these also who had fallen asleep received the seal of the Son of God and " entered into the kingdom of God.' For before," said he, " a man bears the name of the Son of God, he is dead. But when he receives the seal he puts away mortality and receives life. 4. The seal, then, is the water. They go down then into the water dead, and come up alive. This seal, then, was preached to them also, and they made use of it ' to enter into the kingdom of God.' " 5. " Why, Sir," said I, " did the forty stones also come up with them from the deep, although they had received the seal already?" " Because," said he, " these apostles and teachers, who preached the name of the Son of God, having fallen asleep in the power and faith of the Son of God, preached also to those who had fallen asleep before them,[1] and themselves gave to them the seal of the preaching. 6. They went down therefore with them into the water and came up again, but the latter went down alive and came up alive, while the former, who had fallen asleep before, went down dead but came up alive. 7. Through them, therefore, they were made alive, and received the knowledge of the name of the Son of God. For this cause they also came up with them and were joined into the building of the tower, and were used

---

[1] Cf. 1, Pet. 3, 19, Gospel of Peter ix. and the Descensus ad inferos in the Acta Pilati. The idea that hearing the gospel and baptism is necessary for the salvation of the righteous dead of pre-Christian times is common, but it is more usually the Christ himself who descends to Hades for the purpose.

πύργου, καὶ ἀλατόμητοι συνῳκοδομήθησαν· ἐν
δικαιοσύνῃ γὰρ ἐκοιμήθησαν καὶ ἐν μεγάλῃ ἁγνείᾳ·
μόνον δὲ τὴν σφραγῖδα ταύτην οὐκ εἶχον. ἔχεις
οὖν καὶ τὴν τούτων ἐπίλυσιν. Ἔχω, φημί,
κύριε.

XVII

1. Νῦν οὖν, κύριε, περὶ τῶν ὀρέων μοι δήλωσον·
διατί ἄλλαι καὶ ἄλλαι εἰσὶν αἱ ἰδέαι καὶ ποικίλαι; Ἄκουε, φησί· τὰ ὄρη ταῦτα τὰ δώδεκα
φυλαί[1] εἰσιν αἱ κατοικοῦσαι ὅλον τὸν κόσμον.
ἐκηρύχθη οὖν εἰς ταύτας ὁ υἱὸς τοῦ θεοῦ διὰ τῶν
ἀποστόλων. 2. Διατί δὲ ποικίλα καὶ ἄλλη καὶ
ἄλλη ἰδέα ἐστὶ τὰ ὄρη, δήλωσόν μοι, κύριε.
Ἄκουε, φησίν· αἱ δώδεκα φυλαὶ αὗται αἱ κατοικοῦσαι ὅλον τὸν κόσμον δώδεκα ἔθνη εἰσί· ποικίλα
δέ εἰσι τῇ φρονήσει καὶ τῷ νοΐ· οἷα οὖν εἶδες τὰ
ὄρη ποικίλα, τοιαῦταί εἰσι καὶ τούτων αἱ ποικιλίαι
τοῦ νοὸς τῶν ἐθνῶν καὶ ἡ φρόνησις. δηλώσω δέ
σοι καὶ ἑνὸς ἑκάστου τὴν πρᾶξιν. 3. Πρῶτον,
φημί, κύριε, τοῦτο δήλωσον, διατί οὕτω ποικίλα
ὄντα τὰ ὄρη, εἰς τὴν οἰκοδομὴν ὅταν ἐτέθησαν οἱ
λίθοι αὐτῶν, μιᾷ χρόᾳ ἐγένοντο λαμπροί, ὡς καὶ
οἱ ἐκ τοῦ βυθοῦ ἀναβεβηκότες λίθοι; 4. Ὅτι,
φησί, πάντα τὰ ἔθνη τὰ ὑπὸ τὸν οὐρανὸν κατοικοῦντα, ἀκούσαντα καὶ πιστεύσαντα ἐπὶ τῷ
ὀνόματι ἐκλήθησαν τοῦ υἱοῦ[2] τοῦ θεοῦ. λαβόντες
Eph. 4, 3-6 οὖν τὴν σφραγῖδα μίαν φρόνησιν ἔσχον καὶ ἕνα

---

[1] φυλαί Α, φυλαὶ δώδεκα L. E connects δώδεκα with φυλαί,
but omits it with ὄρη. The original text may have been
τὰ ὄρη ταῦτα δώδεκα φυλαί etc.   [2] τοῦ υἱοῦ LE, om. A.

together with them for the building without being hewn. For they had fallen asleep in righteousness and in great purity, only they had not received this seal. You have then the explanation of these things also." "Yes, Sir," said I, "I have."

XVII

1. "Now therefore, Sir, explain to me about the mountains. Why is their appearance different from one another and various?" "Listen," said he, "these twelve mountains are the tribes which inhabit the whole world. The Son of God, then, was preached to them by the Apostles." 2. "But tell me, Sir," said I, "why the appearance of the mountains differs one from another and is various." "Listen," said he, "these twelve tribes wiich inhabit the whole world are twelve nations, but they are various in understanding and mind. Just as, then, you saw that the mountains are various, so also are there varieties in the mind and understanding of the nations. And I will explain to you the action of each one." 3. "First of all, Sir," said I, "explain this to me, why though these mountains were so various, when the stones from them were put into the building they became bright with a single colour, like the stones which had come up from the deep." 4. "Because," said he, "all the nations which dwell under heaven, when they heard and believed were called after the name of the Son of God. So then when they received the seal they

The mountains

265

νοῦν, καὶ μία πίστις αὐτῶν ἐγένετο καὶ μία ἀγάπη,
καὶ τὰ πνεύματα τῶν παρθένων μετὰ τοῦ ὀνόματος
ἐφόρεσαν· διὰ τοῦτο ἡ οἰκοδομὴ τοῦ πύργου μιᾷ
χρόᾳ ἐγένετο λαμπρὰ ὡς ὁ ἥλιος. 5. μετὰ δὲ τὸ
εἰσελθεῖν αὐτοὺς ἐπὶ τὸ αὐτὸ καὶ γενέσθαι ἓν
σῶμα, τινὲς ἐξ αὐτῶν ἐμίαναν ἑαυτοὺς καὶ ἐξεβλή-
θησαν ἐκ τοῦ γένους τῶν δικαίων καὶ πάλιν
ἐγένοντο, οἷοι πρότερον ἦσαν, μᾶλλον δὲ καὶ χείρονες.

XVIII

1. Πῶς, φημί, κύριε, ἐγένοντο χείρονες, θεὸν
ἐπεγνωκότες; Ὁ μὴ γινώσκων, φησί, θεὸν καὶ
πονηρευόμενος ἔχει κόλασίν τινα τῆς πονηρίας
αὐτοῦ, ὁ δὲ θεὸν ἐπιγνοὺς οὐκέτι ὀφείλει πονηρεύ-
εσθαι, ἀλλ' ἀγαθοποιεῖν. 2. ἐὰν οὖν ὁ ὀφείλων
ἀγαθοποιεῖν πονηρεύηται, οὐ δοκεῖ πλείονα πονηρίαν ποιεῖν παρὰ τὸν μὴ γινώσκοντα τὸν θεόν;
διὰ τοῦτο οἱ μὴ ἐγνωκότες θεὸν καὶ πονηρευόμενοι κεκριμένοι εἰσὶν εἰς θάνατον, οἱ δὲ τὸν θεὸν
ἐγνωκότες καὶ τὰ μεγαλεῖα αὐτοῦ ἑωρακότες καὶ
πονηρευόμενοι δισσῶς κολασθήσονται καὶ ἀποθανοῦνται εἰς τὸν αἰῶνα. οὕτως οὖν καθαρισθή-
σεται ἡ ἐκκλησία τοῦ θεοῦ. 3. ὡς δὲ εἶδες ἐκ τοῦ
πύργου τοὺς λίθους ἠρμένους καὶ παραδεδομέ-
νους τοῖς πνεύμασι τοῖς πονηροῖς καὶ ἐκεῖθεν
ἐκβληθέντας· (καὶ ἔσται ἓν σῶμα τῶν κεκαθαρ-
μένων, ὥσπερ καὶ ὁ πύργος ἐγένετο ὡς ἐξ ἑνὸς
λίθου γεγονὼς μετὰ τὸ καθαρισθῆναι αὐτόν·) οὕτως
ἔσται καὶ ἡ ἐκκλησία τοῦ θεοῦ μετὰ τὸ καθαρισ-

had one understanding and one mind, and their faith became one, and their love one, and they bore the spirits of the maidens together with the name. For this cause the building of the tower became bright with one colour like the sun. 5. But after they entered in together and became one body, some of them defiled themselves and were cast out from the family of the righteous, and became again what they had been before, or rather even worse."

XVIII

1. "How, Sir," said I, "did they become worse, after they had attained to the knowledge of God?" "He who does not know God," said he, "and does wickedly, incurs some punishment for his wickedness, but he who has knowledge of God, is bound no more to do wickedly, but to do good. 2. If then he who is bound to do good do wickedly, does he not seem to do more wickedly than he who does not know God? For this reason, those who have no knowledge of God and do wickedly, are condemned to death, but those who have knowledge of God and have seen his great deeds, and do wickedly, shall be punished doubly, and shall die for ever. Thus therefore the Church of God shall be cleansed. 3. But just as you saw that the stones were taken from the tower, and handed over to the evil spirits and cast out from it (and there shall be one body of those who are purified, just as also the tower became as if it were made of a single stone, after it was purified), so the Church of God also shall be, after it

Why the backsliders are worse than the unconverted

267

θῆναι αὐτὴν καὶ ἀποβληθῆναι τοὺς πονηροὺς καὶ
ὑποκριτὰς καὶ βλασφήμους καὶ διψύχους καὶ
πονηρευομένους ποικίλαις πονηρίαις. 4. μετὰ τὸ
τούτους ἀποβληθῆναι ἔσται ἡ ἐκκλησία τοῦ θεοῦ
ἓν σῶμα, μία φρόνησις, εἷς νοῦς, μία πίστις, μία
ἀγάπη· καὶ τότε ὁ υἱὸς τοῦ θεοῦ ἀγαλλιάσεται καὶ
εὐφρανθήσεται ἐν αὐτοῖς ἀπειληφὼς τὸν λαὸν
αὐτοῦ καθαρόν. Μεγάλως, φημί, κύριε, καὶ ἐνδόξως πάντα ἔχει. 5. Ἔτι, φημί, κύριε, τῶν ὀρέων
ἑνὸς ἑκάστου δήλωσόν μοι τὴν δύναμιν καὶ τὰς
πράξεις, ἵνα πᾶσα ψυχὴ πεποιθυῖα ἐπὶ τὸν
κύριον ἀκούσασα δοξάσῃ τὸ μέγα καὶ θαυμαστὸν
καὶ ἔνδοξον ὄνομα αὐτοῦ. Ἄκουε, φησί, τῶν
ὀρέων τὴν ποικιλίαν καὶ τῶν δώδεκα ἐθνῶν.

Ps. 9, 2 ;
86, 9, 12 ;
99, 3

XIX

1. Ἐκ τοῦ πρώτου ὄρους τοῦ μέλανος οἱ πιστεύσαντες τοιοῦτοί εἰσιν· ἀποστάται καὶ βλάσφημοι
εἰς τὸν κύριον καὶ προδόται τῶν δούλων τοῦ θεοῦ.
τούτοις δὲ μετάνοια οὐκ ἔστι, θάνατος δὲ ἔστι, καὶ
διὰ τοῦτο καὶ μέλανές εἰσι· καὶ γὰρ τὸ γένος
αὐτῶν ἄνομόν ἐστιν. 2. ἐκ δὲ τοῦ δευτέρου ὄρους
τοῦ ψιλοῦ οἱ πιστεύσαντες τοιοῦτοί εἰσιν· ὑποκριταὶ καὶ διδάσκαλοι πονηρίας. καὶ οὗτοι οὖν τοῖς
προτέροις ὅμοιοί εἰσι, μὴ ἔχοντες καρπὸν δικαιο-
σύνης· ὡς γὰρ τὸ ὄρος αὐτῶν ἄκαρπον, οὕτω καὶ
οἱ ἄνθρωποι οἱ τοιοῦτοι ὄνομα μὲν ἔχουσιν, ἀπὸ δὲ
τῆς πίστεως κενοί εἰσι καὶ οὐδεὶς ἐν αὐτοῖς καρπὸς
ἀληθείας. τούτοις οὖν μετάνοια κεῖται, ἐὰν ταχὺ
μετανοήσωσιν· ἐὰν δὲ βραδύνωσι, μετὰ τῶν

Philipp. 1,
11 ; Heb. 12,
11 ; Jam. 3,
18 ;

has been purified, and the wicked and hypocrites and blasphemers and double-minded, and doers of various wickedness, have been rejected from it. 4. After these have been rejected the Church of God shall be one body, one mind, one spirit, one faith, one love, and then the Son of God shall rejoice and be glad in them, when he has received his people in purity." "All this, Sir," said I, "is great and wonderful. 5. Yet, Sir," said I, "explain to me the power and the action of each one of the mountains, that every soul that has believed on the Lord, may hear and glorify His great and wonderful and glorious name." "Listen," said he, "to the variety of the mountains and the twelve nations.

XIX

1. "From the first mountain, the black one, are such believers as these: apostates and blasphemers against the Lord, and betrayers of the servants of God. For these there is no repentance, but there is death, and for this cause they also are black, for their race is lawless. 2. And from the second mountain, the bare one, are such believers as these: hypocrites and teachers of wickedness. These then also are like unto the first, having no 'fruit of righteousness,' for just as their mountain is unfruitful, so also such men have the name, but are devoid of faith, and there is no fruit of truth in them. For these then repentance is ready if they repent quickly. but if they delay their death will be with the former ones."

The characteristics of the mountains

The first mountain

The second mountain

THE APOSTOLIC FATHERS

προτέρων ἔσται ὁ θάνατος αὐτῶν. 3. Διατί,
φημί, κύριε, τούτοις μετάνοιά ἐστι, τοῖς δὲ πρώτοις
οὐκ ἔστι; παρά τι γὰρ αἱ αὐταὶ αἱ πράξεις αὐτῶν
εἰσί. Διὰ τοῦτο, φησί, τούτοις μετάνοια κεῖται,
ὅτι οὐκ ἐβλασφήμησαν τὸν κύριον αὐτῶν οὐδὲ
ἐγένοντο προδόται τῶν δούλων τοῦ θεοῦ· διὰ δὲ
τὴν ἐπιθυμίαν τοῦ λήμματος ὑπεκρίθησαν καὶ
ἐδίδαξεν ἕκαστος κατὰ[1] τὰς ἐπιθυμίας τῶν
ἀνθρώπων τῶν ἁμαρτανόντων. ἀλλὰ τίσουσι
δίκην τινά· κεῖται δὲ αὐτοῖς μετάνοια διὰ τὸ μὴ
γενέσθαι αὐτοὺς βλασφήμους μηδὲ προδότας.

XX

1. Ἐκ δὲ τοῦ ὄρους τοῦ τρίτου τοῦ ἔχοντος
ἀκάνθας καὶ τριβόλους οἱ πιστεύσαντες τοιοῦτοί
εἰσιν. ἐξ αὐτῶν οἱ μὲν πλούσιοι, οἱ δὲ πραγματείαις πολλαῖς ἐμπεφυρμένοι. οἱ μὲν τρίβολοί
εἰσιν οἱ πλούσιοι, αἱ δὲ ἄκανθαι οἱ ἐν ταῖς πραγματείαις ταῖς ποικίλαις ἐμπεφυρμένοι. 2. οὗτοι
οὖν, οἱ ἐν πολλαῖς καὶ ποικίλαις πραγματείαις
ἐμπεφυρμένοι, οὐ[2] κολλῶνται τοῖς δούλοις τοῦ
θεοῦ, ἀλλ᾽ ἀποπλανῶνται πνιγόμενοι ὑπὸ τῶν
πράξεων αὐτῶν· οἱ δὲ πλούσιοι δυσκόλως κολλῶνται τοῖς δούλοις τοῦ θεοῦ, φοβούμενοι, μή τι
αἰτισθῶσιν ὑπ᾽ αὐτῶν· οἱ τοιοῦτοι οὖν δυσκόλως
εἰσελεύσονται εἰς τὴν βασιλείαν τοῦ θεοῦ. 3. ὥσπερ γὰρ ἐν τριβόλοις γυμνοῖς ποσὶ περιπατεῖν δύσκολόν ἐστιν, οὕτω καὶ τοῖς τοιούτοις

Mt. 13, 22; Mc. 4, 18. 19

Mt. 19, 23; Mc. 10, 23; Luk. 18, 24

[1] κατά LE, om. A.
[2] οὖν . . . οὐ retranslated from LE, om. A.

270

3. "Why, Sir," said I, "is there repentance for these but not for the first, for their deeds are almost the same?" "For this reason," said he, "there is repentance for these, because they did not deceive their Lord and were not betrayers of the servants of God; but because of the lust of gain, they played the hypocrite, and each taught according to the lusts of sinful men. But they will be punished in some way, yet repentance is open to them because they did not become blasphemers or traitors.

XX

1. "AND from the third mountain, which has thorns and thistles, are such believers as these. Of them are those who are rich and are mixed up with many affairs of business, for the thistles are the rich, and the thorns are those who are mixed up with various affairs of business. 2. These then who are engaged in many and various businesses do not cleave to the servants of God, but are choked by their work and go astray. And the rich cleave with difficulty to the servants of God, fearing that they will be asked for something by them. Such then 'will enter with difficulty the kingdom of God.' 3. For just as it is difficult to walk with naked feet among thistles, so it is

The third mountain

Mc. 10, 24 δύσκολόν ἐστιν εἰς τὴν βασιλείαν τοῦ θεοῦ εἰσελθεῖν. 4. ἀλλὰ τούτοις πᾶσι μετάνοιά ἐστι, ταχινὴ
δέ, ἵν' ὃ τοῖς προτέροις χρόνοις οὐκ εἰργάσαντο
νῦν ἀναδράμωσιν ταῖς ἡμέραις καὶ ἀγαθόν τι ποιήσωσιν. ἐὰν οὖν μετανοήσωσι καὶ ἀγαθόν τι
ποιήσωσι,[1] ζήσονται τῷ θεῷ· ἐὰν δὲ ἐπιμείνωσι
ταῖς πράξεσιν αὐτῶν, παραδοθήσονται ταῖς
γυναιξὶν ἐκείναις, αἵτινες αὐτοὺς θανατώσουσιν.

XXI

1. Ἐκ δὲ τοῦ τετάρτου ὄρους τοῦ ἔχοντος
βοτάνας πολλάς, τὰ μὲν ἐπάνω τῶν βοτανῶν
χλωρά, τὰ δὲ πρὸς ταῖς ῥίζαις ξηρά, τινὲς δὲ καὶ
ἀπὸ τοῦ ἡλίου ξηραινόμεναι, οἱ πιστεύσαντες
τοιοῦτοί εἰσιν· οἱ μὲν δίψυχοι, οἱ δὲ τὸν κύριον
ἔχοντες ἐπὶ τὰ χείλη, ἐπὶ τὴν καρδίαν δὲ μὴ
ἔχοντες. 2. διὰ τοῦτο τὰ θεμέλια αὐτῶν ξηρά
ἐστι καὶ δύναμιν μὴ ἔχοντα, καὶ τὰ ῥήματα αὐτῶν
μόνα ζῶσι, τὰ δὲ ἔργα αὐτῶν νεκρά ἐστιν. οἱ
τοιοῦτοι οὔτε ζῶσιν οὔτε[2] τεθνήκασιν. ὅμοιοι
οὖν εἰσὶ τοῖς διψύχοις· καὶ γὰρ οἱ δίψυχοι οὔτε
χλωροί εἰσιν οὔτε ξηροί· οὔτε γὰρ ζῶσιν οὔτε
τεθνήκασιν. 3. ὥσπερ γὰρ αὗται[3] αἱ βοτάναι ἥλιον
ἰδοῦσαι ἐξηράνθησαν, οὕτω καὶ οἱ δίψυχοι, ὅταν
θλῖψιν ἀκούσωσι, διὰ τὴν δειλίαν αὐτῶν εἰδωλολα-
τροῦσι καὶ τὸ ὄνομα ἐπαισχύνονται τοῦ κυρίου
αὐτῶν. 4. οἱ τοιοῦτοι οὖν οὔτε ζῶσιν[4] οὔτε

---

[1] ἐὰν .. - ποιήσωσι retranslated from LE, καί A.
[2] οὔτε ζῶσιν, οὔτε LE, om. A.
[3] αὗται LE, αὐτῶν A.   [4] οὔτε ζῶσιν LE, om. A.

also 'difficult' for such men 'to enter into the Kingdom of God.' 4. But for all these there is repentance,
but it must be speedy, that they may now retrace
their days and the omissions of former years, and
do some good. If then they repent and do some
good they will live to God, but if they remain in
their deeds they will be delivered to those women,
and they will put them to death.

XXI

1. " AND from the fourth mountain which has many The fourth
herbs, with the top of the herbs green but the parts mountain
by the roots dry, and some dried up by the sun, are
such believers as these: the double-minded, and
those who have the Lord on their lips but do not
have him in their hearts. 2. For this cause their
foundations are dry and have no power, and only
their words are alive but their deeds are dead.
Such are neither alive nor dead. Therefore
they are like the double-minded, for the double-
minded are neither green nor dry, for they
are neither alive nor dead. 3. For just as these
herbs, when they saw the sun, were dried up, so also
the double-minded when they hear of affliction, become idolators through their cowardice, and they are
ashamed of the name of their Lord. 4. Such men

τεθνήκασιν. ἀλλὰ καὶ οὗτοι ἐὰν ταχὺ μετανοήσωσιν, δυνήσονται ζῆσαι· ἐὰν δὲ μὴ μετανοήσωσιν,[1] ἤδη παραδεδομένοι εἰσὶ ταῖς γυναιξὶ ταῖς
ἀποφερομέναις τὴν ζωὴν αὐτῶν.

XXII

1. Ἐκ δὲ τοῦ ὄρους τοῦ πέμπτου τοῦ ἔχοντος
βοτάνας χλωρὰς καὶ τραχέος ὄντος οἱ πιστεύσαντες τοιοῦτοί εἰσι· πιστοὶ μέν, δυσμαθεῖς δὲ
καὶ αὐθάδεις καὶ ἑαυτοῖς ἀρέσκοντες, θέλοντες
πάντα γινώσκειν, καὶ οὐδὲν ὅλως γινώσκουσι.
2. διὰ τὴν αὐθάδειαν αὐτῶν ταύτην ἀπέστη ἀπ᾿
αὐτῶν ἡ σύνεσις, καὶ εἰσῆλθεν εἰς αὐτοὺς ἀφροσύνη μωρά. ἐπαινοῦσι δὲ ἑαυτοὺς ὡς σύνεσιν
ἔχοντας καὶ θέλουσιν ἐθελοδιδάσκαλοι[2] εἶναι,
ἄφρονες ὄντες. 3. διὰ ταύτην οὖν τὴν ὑψηλο-
φροσύνην πολλοὶ ἐκενώθησαν ὑψοῦντες ἑαυτούς·
μέγα γὰρ δαιμόνιόν ἐστιν ἡ αὐθάδεια καὶ ἡ κενὴ
πεποίθησις· ἐκ τούτων οὖν πολλοὶ ἀπεβλήθησαν,
τινὲς δὲ μετενόησαν καὶ ἐπίστευσαν καὶ ὑπέταξαν
ἑαυτοὺς τοῖς ἔχουσι σύνεσιν, γνόντες τὴν ἑαυτῶν
ἀφροσύνην. 4. καὶ τοῖς λοιποῖς δὲ τοῖς τοιούτοις κεῖται μετάνοια· οὐκ ἐγένοντο γὰρ πονηροί,
μᾶλλον δὲ μωροὶ καὶ ἀσύνετοι. οὗτοι οὖν ἐὰν[3]
μετανοήσωσι, ζήσονται τῷ θεῷ· ἐὰν δὲ μὴ μετανοήσωσι, κατοικήσουσι μετὰ τῶν γυναικῶν τῶν
πονηρευομένων εἰς αὐτούς.

[1] δυνήσονται . . . μετανοήσωσιν retranslated from LE, om. A.
[2] ἐθελοδιδάσκαλοι A, but LE seem to represent διδάσκαλοι.
[3] μωροὶ καὶ . . . ἐάν retranslated from LE. A is illegible,
but seems to read πονηρ(ότατοι ?) instead of μωροί.

therefore are neither alive nor dead; but these also will be able to live if they repent quickly, but if they do not repent they have already been given over to the women who take away their life.

XXII

1. "AND from the fifth mountain, which has green herbage and is rough, are such believers as these: believers, but slow to learn and presumptuous, and pleasing themselves, wishing to know everything, and yet they know nothing at all. 2. Because of this presumption of theirs understanding has departed from them, and senseless folly has entered into them, and they praise themselves for having understanding and they wish to be teachers[1] in spite of their folly. 3. For this high-mindedness therefore many have been made worthless by exalting themselves,[2] for presumption and vain confidence is a great demon. Many therefore of these were rejected, but some repented and believed, and submitted themselves to those who have understanding, recognising their own folly. 4. And for the rest of such men repentance is waiting, for they were not wicked, but rather foolish and without understanding. If therefore these repent they will live to God, but if they do not repent they will dwell with the women who devise evil against them.

The fifth mountain

[1] ἐθελοδιδάσκαλοι is not found elsewhere. If it be right it must mean a teacher who unduly magnifies his office. Cf. ἐθελοθρησκεία in Col. 2, 23.

[2] There may be here a reference to Philipp. 2, 9 in which κένωσις and ὕψωσις are contrasted: the point being that as the κένωσις of Christ led to his ὕψωσις, so the ὕψωσις of these men results in their ultimate κένωσις.

XXIII

1. Οἱ δὲ ἐκ τοῦ ὄρους τοῦ ἕκτου τοῦ ἔχοντος σχισμὰς μεγάλας καὶ μικρὰς καὶ ἐν ταῖς σχισμαῖς βοτάνας μεμαραμμένας πιστεύσαντες τοιοῦτοί εἰσιν. 2. οἱ μὲν τὰς σχισμὰς τὰς μικρὰς ἔχοντες, οὗτοί εἰσιν οἱ κατ᾽ ἀλλήλων ἔχοντες, καὶ ἀπὸ τῶν καταλαλιῶν ἑαυτῶν μεμαραμμένοι εἰσὶν ἐν τῇ πίστει· ἀλλὰ μετενόησαν ἐκ τούτων πολλοί. καὶ οἱ λοιποὶ δὲ μετανοήσουσιν, ὅταν ἀκούσωσί μου τὰς ἐντολάς· μικραὶ γὰρ αὐτῶν εἰσιν αἱ καταλαλιαί, καὶ ταχὺ μετανοήσουσιν.   3. οἱ δὲ μεγάλας ἔχοντες σχισμάς, οὗτοι παράμονοί εἰσι ταῖς καταλαλιαῖς αὐτῶν καὶ μνησίκακοι γίνονται μηνιῶντες ἀλλήλοις· οὗτοι οὖν ἀπὸ τοῦ πύργου ἀπερρίφησαν καὶ ἀπεδοκιμάσθησαν τῆς οἰκοδομῆς αὐτοῦ. οἱ τοιοῦτοι οὖν δυσκόλως ζήσονται. 4. εἰ ὁ θεὸς καὶ ὁ κύριος ἡμῶν ὁ πάντων κυριεύων καὶ ἔχων πάσης τῆς κτίσεως αὐτοῦ τὴν ἐξουσίαν οὐ μνησικακεῖ τοῖς ἐξομολογουμένοις τὰς ἁμαρτίας αὐτῶν, ἀλλ᾽ ἵλεως γίνεται, ἄνθρωπος φθαρτὸς ὢν καὶ πλήρης ἁμαρτιῶν ἀνθρώπῳ μνησικακεῖ ὡς δυνάμενος ἀπολέσαι ἢ σῶσαι αὐτόν; 5. λέγω δὲ ὑμῖν, ὁ ἄγγελος τῆς μετανοίας· ὅσοι ταύτην ἔχετε τὴν αἵρεσιν ἀπόθεσθε αὐτὴν καὶ μετανήσατε, καὶ ὁ κύριος ἰάσεται ὑμῶν τὰ πρότερα ἁμαρτήματα, ἐὰν καθαρίσητε ἑαυτοὺς ἀπὸ τούτου τοῦ δαιμονίου· εἰ δὲ μή, παραδοθήσεσθε αὐτῷ εἰς θάνατον.

Jam. 4, 12

XXIII

1. "AND those of the sixth mountain which has The sixth
cracks, great and small, and withered plants in the mountain
cracks, are such believers as these. 2. Those who
have the small cracks are those who have quarrels
with one another, and are withered in the faith
from their evil speaking. But many of these
repented, and the rest shall also repent when they
hear my commandments, for their evil-speaking was
small and they will quickly repent. 3. But those
who have great cracks are those who are persistent
in their evil-speaking, and are become malicious in
their rage against one another. These then were
cast away from the tower and were rejected from its
building. Such men then will live with difficulty.
4. If God and our Lord who rules over all and has
power over all his creation bear no malice against
those who confess their sins, but is merciful, shall
man who is mortal and full of sin bear malice against
man, as though he were 'able to destroy or to save
him.'? 5. And I, the angel of repentance, say to
you, do all you, who have this heresy, put it aside
and repent, and the Lord will heal your former sins,
if you cleanse yourselves from this demon. But if
not you shall be delivered to him to death.

THE APOSTOLIC FATHERS

XXIV

1. Ἐκ δὲ τοῦ ἑβδόμου ὄρους, ἐν ᾧ βοτάναι χλωραὶ καὶ ἱλαραί, καὶ ὅλον τὸ ὄρος εὐθηνοῦν καὶ πᾶν γένος κτηνῶν καὶ τὰ πετεινὰ τοῦ οὐρανοῦ ἐνέμοντο τὰς βοτάνας ἐκ τούτῳ τῷ ὄρει, καὶ αἱ βοτάναι, ἃς ἐνέμοντο, μᾶλλον εὐθαλεῖς ἐγίνοντο, οἱ πιστεύσαντες τοιοῦτοί εἰσι. 2. πάντοτε ἁπλοῖ καὶ ἄκακοι καὶ μακάριοι ἐγίνοντο, μηδὲν κατ' ἀλλήλων ἔχοντες, ἀλλὰ πάντοτε ἀγαλλιώμενοι ἐπὶ τοῖς δούλοις τοῦ θεοῦ καὶ ἐνδεδυμένοι τὸ πνεῦμα τὸ ἅγιον τούτων τῶν παρθένων καὶ πάντοτε σπλάγχνον ἔχοντες ἐπὶ πάντα ἄνθρωπον, καὶ ἐκ τῶν κόπων αὐτῶν παντὶ ἀνθρώπῳ ἐχορήγησαν ἀνονειδίστως καὶ ἀδιστάκτως. 3. ὁ οὖν κύριος ἰδὼν τὴν ἁπλότητα αὐτῶν καὶ πᾶσαν νηπιότητα ἐπλήθυνεν αὐτοὺς ἐν τοῖς κόποις τῶν χειρῶν αὐτῶν καὶ ἐχαρίτωσεν αὐτοὺς ἐν πάσῃ πράξει αὐτῶν. 4. λέγω δὲ ὑμῖν τοῖς τοιούτοις οὖσιν ἐγὼ ὁ ἄγγελος τῆς μετανοίας· διαμείνατε τοιοῦτοι, καὶ οὐκ ἐξαλειφθήσεται τὸ σπέρμα ὑμῶν ἕως αἰῶνος· ἐδοκίμασε γὰρ ὑμᾶς ὁ κύριος καὶ ἐνέγραψεν ὑμᾶς εἰς τὸν ἀριθμὸν τὸν ἡμέτερον, καὶ ὅλον τὸ σπέρμα ὑμῶν κατοικήσει μετὰ τοῦ υἱοῦ τοῦ θεοῦ· ἐκ γὰρ τοῦ πνεύματος αὐτοῦ ἐλάβετε.

XXV

1. Ἐκ δὲ τοῦ ὄρους τοῦ ὀγδόου, οὗ ἦσαν αἱ πολλαὶ πηγαὶ καὶ πᾶσα ἡ κτίσις τοῦ κυρίου ἐποτίζετο ἐκ τῶν πηγῶν, οἱ πιστεύσαντες τοιοῦτοί

XXIV

1. " AND from the seventh mountain, on which were The seventh mountain green and joyful herbs, and the whole mountain was fair and every kind of cattle and the birds of heaven were feeding on the herbs on this mountain, and the herbs on which they were feeding became yet more luxuriant, are such believers as these. 2. They were ever simple and guileless and blessed and had nothing against one another, but ever rejoiced in the servants of God and were clothed in the holy spirit of these maidens, and were ever merciful to every man, and helped every man from the fruit of their labours without upbraiding or doubting. 3. The Lord, therefore, seeing their simplicity and all their innocence, filled them with the labours of their hand, and was gracious to them in all their doings. 4. And I, the angel of repentance, say to you who are such :— Remain such as you are, and your seed shall not be blotted out for ever, for the Lord has proved you and written you in among our number, and all your seed shall dwell with the Son of God, for of his spirit have you received.

XXV

1. " AND from the eighth mountain, where there The eighth mountain were many springs and all the creation of the Lord was given to drink from the springs, are such

εἰσιν· 2. ἀπόστολοι καὶ διδάσκαλοι οἱ κηρύξαντες εἰς ὅλον τὸν κόσμον καὶ οἱ διδάξαντες
σεμνῶς καὶ ἁγνῶς τὸν λόγον τοῦ κυρίου καὶ μηδὲν
ὅλως νοσφισάμενοι εἰς ἐπιθυμίαν πονηράν, ἀλλὰ
πάντοτε ἐν δικαιοσύνῃ καὶ ἀληθείᾳ πορευθέντες,
καθὼς καὶ παρέλαβον τὸ πνεῦμα τὸ ἅγιον. τῶν
τοιούτων οὖν ἡ πάροδος μετὰ τῶν ἀγγέλων ἐστίν.

XXVI

1. Ἐκ δὲ τοῦ ὄρους τοῦ ἐνάτου τοῦ ἐρημώδους,
τοῦ τὰ ἑρπετὰ καὶ θηρία ἐν αὐτῷ ἔχοντος τὰ
διαφθείροντα τοὺς ἀνθρώπους, οἱ πιστεύσαντες
τοιοῦτοί εἰσιν· 2. οἱ μὲν τοὺς σπίλους ἔχοντες
διάκονοί εἰσι κακῶς διακονήσαντες καὶ διαρπά-
σαντες χηρῶν καὶ ὀρφανῶν τὴν ζωὴν καὶ ἑαυτοῖς
περιποιησάμενοι ἐκ τῆς διακονίας ἧς ἔλαβον
διακονῆσαι· ἐὰν οὖν ἐπιμείνωσι τῇ αὐτῇ ἐπιθυμίᾳ, ἀπέθανον καὶ οὐδεμία αὐτοῖς ἐλπὶς ζωῆς·
ἐὰν δὲ ἐπιστρέψωσι καὶ ἁγνῶς τελειώσωσι τὴν
διακονίαν αὐτῶν, δυνήσονται ζῆσαι. 3. οἱ δὲ
ἐψωριακότες, οὗτοι οἱ ἀρνησάμενοί εἰσι καὶ μὴ
ἐπιστρέψαντες ἐπὶ τὸν κύριον ἑαυτῶν, ἀλλὰ
χερσωθέντες καὶ γενόμενοι ἐρημώδεις· μὴ κολλώμενοι τοῖς δούλοις τοῦ θεοῦ, ἀλλὰ μονάζοντες
ἀπολλύουσι τὰς ἑαυτῶν ψυχάς. 4. ὡς γὰρ
ἄμπελος ἐν φραγμῷ τινι καταλειφθεῖσα ἀμελείας
τυγχάνουσα καταφθείρεται καὶ ὑπὸ τῶν βοτανῶν
ἐρημοῦται καὶ τῷ χρόνῳ ἀγρία γίνεται, καὶ οὐκέτι

Mt. 10, 39;
Luk. 9, 24;
17, 33; Joh.
12, 25

believers as these : 2. Apostles and teachers who preached to all the world, and taught reverently and purely the word of the Lord, and kept nothing back for evil desire, but always walked in righteousness and truth, even as they had received the Holy Spirit. The passing of such is with the angels.[1]

XXVI

1. "And from the ninth mountain, which was desert, and had in it creeping things and wild beasts which devour men, are such believers as these : 2. Those with spots are ministers who ministered amiss, and devoured the living of widows and orphans, and made gain for themselves from the ministry which they had received to administer. If then they remain in the same covetousness they are dead and they have no hope of life. But if they turn and fulfil their ministry in holiness they shall be able to live. 3. And those with scabs, these are they who have denied and have not turned to their Lord, but have become barren and deserted ; by not cleaving to the servants of God, but keeping alone, they are destroying their own souls. 4. For just as a vine left alone within a fence and neglected is spoilt and is wasted by weeds, and in time becomes wild and is no longer

The ninth mountain

---

[1] That is, after death they will be with the angels. Cf. notes on Herm. *Vis.* ii. 2, 7 and on Martyr. Polycarp. ii. 3.

εὔχρηστός ἐστι τῷ δεσπότῃ ἑαυτῆς, οὕτω καὶ
οἱ τοιοῦτοι ἄνθρωποι ἑαυτοὺς ἀπεγνώκασι καὶ
γίνονται ἄχρηστοι τῷ κυρίῳ ἑαυτῶν ἀγριωθέντες.
5. τούτοις οὖν μετάνοια γίνεται, ἐὰν μὴ ἐκ καρδίας
εὑρεθῶσιν ἠρνημένοι· ἐὰν δὲ ἐκ καρδίας εὑρεθῇ
ἠρνημένος τις, οὐκ οἶδα, εἰ δύναται ζῆσαι. 6. καὶ
τοῦτο οὐκ εἰς ταύτας τὰς ἡμέρας λέγω, ἵνα τις
ἀρνησάμενος μετάνοιαν λάβῃ· ἀδύνατον γάρ ἐστι
σωθῆναι τὸν μέλλοντα νῦν ἀρνεῖσθαι τὸν κύριον
ἑαυτοῦ· ἀλλ' ἐκείνοις τοῖς πάλαι ἠρνημένοις δοκεῖ
κεῖσθαι μετάνοια. εἴ τις οὖν μέλλει μετανοεῖν,
ταχινὸς γενέσθω πρὶν τὸν πύργον ἀποτελεσθῆναι·
εἰ δὲ μή, ὑπὸ τῶν γυναικῶν καταφθαρήσεται εἰς
θάνατον. 7. καὶ οἱ κολοβοί, οὗτοι δόλιοί εἰσι
καὶ κατάλαλοι· καὶ τὰ θηρία, ἃ εἶδες εἰς τὸ ὄρος,
οὗτοί εἰσιν. ὥσπερ γὰρ τὰ θηρία διαφθείρει τῷ
ἑαυτῶν ἰῷ τὸν ἄνθρωπον καὶ ἀπολλύει, οὕτω καὶ
τῶν τοιούτων ἀνθρώπων τὰ ῥήματα διαφθείρει
τὸν ἄνθρωπον καὶ ἀπολλύει. 8. οὗτοι οὖν κολοβοί
εἰσιν ἀπὸ τῆς πίστεως αὐτῶν διὰ τὴν πρᾶξιν, ἣν
ἔχουσιν ἐν ἑαυτοῖς· τινὲς δὲ μετενόησαν καὶ
ἐσώθησαν. καὶ οἱ λοιποὶ οἱ τοιοῦτοι ὄντες δύνανται σωθῆναι, ἐὰν μετανοήσωσιν· ἐὰν δὲ μὴ
μετανοήσωσιν, ἀπὸ τῶν γυναικῶν ἐκείνων, ὧν τὴν
δύναμιν ἔχουσιν, ἀποθανοῦνται.

XXVII

1. Ἐκ δὲ τοῦ ὄρους τοῦ δεκάτου, οὗ ἦσαν δένδρα
σκεπάζοντα πρόβατά τινα, οἱ πιστεύσαντες

useful to its master, so also such men as these have renounced themselves and have become wild and valueless to their Lord. 5. To these then there is repentance, if they be not found to have denied from their hearts. But if one be found to have denied from his heart I do not know whether he can live. 6. And I do not speak this for these days, in order that one may deny and receive repentance, for it is impossible for him to be saved who shall now deny his Lord. But there seems to be repentance waiting for those who have denied in time past. If then any be about to repent, let him make haste before the tower be finished, otherwise he will be destroyed by the women unto death. 7. And the stunted ones, these are deceitful and evil-speaking men, and the wild beasts which you saw on the mountains are these. For just as the wild beasts destroy man by their poison [1] and kill him, so also the words of such men destroy man and kill him. 8. These then are stunted in their faith through their conduct which they have in themselves, but some repented and were saved. And the rest who are such can be saved if they repent; but if they repent not they will be put to death by those women whose quality [2] they have.

XXVII

1. "And from the tenth mountain, where were trees sheltering some sheep, are such believers as these: The tenth mountain

---

[1] Apparently θηρίον, as often in later Greek, means "snake."
[2] Lit. "power."

τοιοῦτοί εἰσιν· 2. ἐπίσκοποι καὶ φιλόξενοι, οἵτινες ἡδέως εἰς τοὺς οἴκους ἑαυτῶν πάντοτε ὑπεδέξαντο τοὺς δούλους τοῦ θεοῦ ἄτερ ὑποκρίσεως· οἱ
δὲ ἐπίσκοποι πάντοτε τοὺς ὑστερημένους καὶ τὰς
χήρας τῇ διακονίᾳ ἑαυτῶν ἀδιαλείπτως ἐσκέπασαν
καὶ ἁγνῶς ἀνεστράφησαν πάντοτε. 3. οὗτοι οὖν
πάντες σκεπασθήσονται ὑπὸ τοῦ κυρίου διαπαντός.
οἱ οὖν ταῦτα ἐργασάμενοι ἔνδοξοί εἰσι παρὰ τῷ
θεῷ καὶ ἤδη ὁ τόπος αὐτῶν μετὰ τῶν ἀγγέλων
ἐστίν, ἐὰν ἐπιμείνωσιν ἕως τέλους λειτουργοῦντες
τῷ κυρίῳ.

XXVIII

1. Ἐκ δὲ τοῦ ὄρους τοῦ ἑνδεκάτου, οὗ ἦσαν
δένδρα καρπῶν πλήρη, ἄλλοις καὶ ἄλλοις καρποῖς
κεκοσμημένα, οἱ πιστεύσαντες τοιοῦτοί εἰσιν.
2. οἱ παθόντες ὑπὲρ τοῦ ὀνόματος τοῦ υἱοῦ τοῦ
θεοῦ, οἱ καὶ προθύμως ἔπαθον ἐξ ὅλης τῆς καρδίας
Acts 15, 26 καὶ παρέδωκαν τὰς ψυχὰς αὐτῶν. 3. Διατί οὖν,
φημί, κύριε, πάντα μὲν τὰ δένδρα καρποὺς ἔχει,
τινὲς δὲ ἐξ αὐτῶν καρποὶ εὐειδέστεροί εἰσιν;
Ἄκουε, φησίν· ὅσοι ποτὲ ἔπαθον διὰ τὸ ὄνομα,
ἔνδοξοί εἰσι παρὰ τῷ θεῷ, καὶ πάντων αἱ ἁμαρτίαι
ἀφῃρέθησαν, ὅτι ἔπαθον διὰ τὸ ὄνομα τοῦ υἱοῦ τοῦ
θεοῦ. διατί δὲ οἱ καρποὶ αὐτῶν ποικίλοι εἰσίν,
τινὲς δὲ ὑπερέχοντες, ἄκουε. 4. ὅσοι, φησίν, ἐπ᾽
ἐξουσίαν ἀχθέντες ἐξητάσθησαν καὶ οὐκ ἠρνή-
σαντο, ἀλλ᾽ ἔπαθον προθύμως, οὗτοι μᾶλλον
ἐνδοξότεροί εἰσι παρὰ τῷ κυρίῳ· τούτων ὁ καρπός
ἐστιν ὁ ὑπερέχων· ὅσοι δὲ δειλοὶ καὶ ἐν δι
σταγμῷ
ἐγένοντο καὶ ἐλογίσαντω ἐν ταῖς καρδίαις αὐτῶν,

2. Bishops and hospitable men who at all times received the servants of God into their houses gladly and without hypocrisy; and the bishops ever ceaselessly sheltered the destitute and the widows by their ministration, and ever behaved with holiness. 3. These then shall all be always sheltered by the Lord. They then who have done these things are glorious with God, and their place is already with the angels, if they continue serving the Lord unto the end.

XXVIII

1. " AND from the eleventh mountain, where were The eleventh trees full of fruit, each adorned with different fruit, mountain are such believers as these: 2. they who have suffered for the name of the Son of God, who also suffered readily with all their heart and 'gave up their lives.'" 3. "Why then, Sir," said I, " have all the trees fruit, but the fruit of some of them is more beautiful?" "Listen," said he, "as many as ever suffered for the name are glorious before God, and the sins of all these have been taken away because they suffered for the name of the Son of God. But listen why their fruits are different and some better than others. 4. As many," said he, "as were brought under authority and were questioned and did not deny, but suffered readily, these are especially glorious before the Lord; the fruit of these is excellent. But as many as were fearful, were in doubt, and considered

πότερον ἀρνήσονται ἢ ὁμολογήσουσι, καὶ ἔπαθον,
τούτων οἱ καρποὶ ἐλάττους εἰσίν, ὅτι ἀνέβη ἐπὶ
τὴν καρδίαν αὐτῶν ἡ βουλὴ αὕτη· πονηρὰ γὰρ ἡ
βουλὴ αὕτη, ἵνα δοῦλος κύριον ἴδιον ἀρνήσηται.
5. βλέπετε οὖν ὑμεῖς οἱ ταῦτα βουλευόμενοι,
μήποτε ἡ βουλὴ αὕτη διαμείνῃ ἐν ταῖς καρδίαις

I Pet. 4, 13.
15, 16 ;

ὑμῶν καὶ ἀποθάνητε τῷ θεῷ. ὑμεῖς δὲ οἱ πάσχοντες ἕνεκεν τοῦ ὀνόματος δοξάζειν ὀφείλετε
τὸν θεόν, ὅτι ἀξίους ὑμᾶς ἡγήσατο ὁ θεός, ἵνα
τοῦτο[1] τὸ ὄνομα βαστάζητε καὶ πᾶσαι ὑμῶν

Mt. 5, 11. 12;
Luk. 6, 22 ;
I Pet. 4, 14

αἱ ἁμαρτίαι ἰαθῶσιν. 6. οὐκοῦν μακαρίζετε
ἑαυτούς· ἀλλὰ δοκεῖτε ἔργον μέγα πεποιηκέναι,
ἐάν τις ὑμῶν διὰ τὸν θεὸν πάθῃ. ζωὴν ὑμῖν ὁ
κύριος χαρίζεται, καὶ οὐ νοεῖτε· αἱ γὰρ ἁμαρτίαι
ὑμῶν κατεβάρησαν, καὶ εἰ μὴ πεπόνθατε ἕνεκεν
τοῦ ὀνόματος κυρίου, διὰ τὰς ἁμαρτίας ὑμῶν
τεθνήκειτε ἂν τῷ θεῷ. 7. ταῦτα ὑμῖν λέγω
τοῖς διστάζουσι περὶ ἀρνήσεως ἢ ὁμολογήσεως·
ὁμολογεῖτε, ὅτι κύριον ἔχετε, μήποτε ἀρνούμενοι
παραδοθήσησθε εἰς δεσμωτήριον. 8. εἰ τὰ
ἔθνη τοὺς δούλους αὐτῶν κολάζουσιν, ἐάν τις
ἀρνήσηται τὸν κύριον ἑαυτοῦ, τί δοκεῖτε ποιήσει
ὁ κύριος ὑμῖν, ὃς ἔχει πάντων τὴν ἐξουσίαν;
ἄρατε τὰς βουλὰς ταύτας ἀπὸ τῶν καρδιῶν ὑμῶν,
ἵνα διαπαντὸς ζήσητε τῷ θεῷ.

XXIX

1. Ἐκ δὲ τοῦ ὄρους τοῦ δωδεκάτου τοῦ λευκοῦ
οἱ πιστεύσαντες τοιοῦτοί εἰσιν· ὡς νήπια βρέφη

---

[1] τοῦτο L₂, τούτου A, αὐτοῦ L₁E.

in their hearts whether they should deny or confess, and suffered, the fruits of these are inferior because this thought entered into their hearts, for this is an evil thought, that a servant should deny his own Lord. 5. See to it, then, you who have these thoughts, lest this thought remain in your hearts and you die to God. But you who are suffering for the name, ought to glorify God, that God deemed you worthy to bear this name and that all your sins should be healed. 6. So then count yourselves blessed; but think that you have done a great deed, if any of you suffer for God's sake. The Lord is giving you life, and you do not consider it; for your sins have weighed you down, and except you had suffered for the name of the Lord you would have died to God because of your sins. 7. I say this to you who are hesitating as to denial or confession. Confess that you have a Lord, lest you deny him and be delivered into prison. 8. If the heathen punish their servants, if one deny his lord, what think you will the Lord, who has power over all, do to you ? Put away these thoughts from your heart that you may live for ever to God.

XXIX

1. " And from the twelfth mountain, the white one, The twelfth mountain
are such believers as these: They are as innocent

287

εἰσίν, οἷς οὐδεμία κακια ἀναβαίνει ἐπὶ τὴν καρδίαν
οὐδὲ ἔγνωσαν, τί ἐστι πονηρία, ἀλλὰ πάντοτε
ἐν νηπιότητι διέμειναν. 2. οἱ τοιοῦτοι οὖν ἀδιστάκτως κατοικήσουσιν ἐν τῇ βασιλείᾳ τοῦ θεοῦ,
ὅτι ἐν οὐδενὶ πράγματι ἐμίαναν τὰς ἐντολὰς τοῦ
θεοῦ, ἀλλὰ μετὰ νηπιότητος διέμειναν πάσας τὰς
ἡμέρας τῆς ζωῆς αὐτῶν ἐν τῇ αὐτῇ φρονήσει.

Mt. 18, 3

3. ὅσοι οὖν διαμενεῖτε, φησί, καὶ ἔσεσθε ὡς τὰ
βρέφη, κακίαν μὴ ἔχοντες, πάντων τῶν προειρημένων ἐνδοξότεροι ἔσεσθε· πάντα γὰρ τὰ βρέφη
ἔνδοξά ἐστι παρὰ τῷ θεῷ καὶ πρῶτα παρ'
αὐτῷ.[1] μακάριοι οὖν ὑμεῖς, ὅσοι ἂν ἄρητε ἀφ'
ἑαυτῶν τὴν πονηρίαν, ἐνδύσησθε δὲ τὴν ἀκακίαν·
πρῶτοι πάντων ζήσεσθε τῷ θεῷ. 4. μετὰ τὸ
συντελέσαι αὐτὸν τὰς παραβολὰς τῶν ὀρέων
λέγω αὐτῷ· Κύριε, νῦν μοι δήλωσον περὶ τῶν
λίθων τῶν ἠρμένων ἐκ τοῦ πεδίου καὶ εἰς τὴν
οἰκοδομὴν τεθειμένων ἀντὶ τῶν λίθων τῶν ἠρμένων
ἐκ τοῦ πύργου, καὶ τῶν στρογγύλων τῶν τε-
θέντων εἰς τὴν οἰκοδομήν, καὶ τῶν ἔτι στρογγύλων
ὄντων.

XXX

1. Ἄκουε, φησί, καὶ περὶ τούτων πάντων. οἱ
λίθοι οἱ τοῦ πεδίου ἠρμένοι καὶ τεθειμένοι εἰς
τὴν οἰκοδομὴν τοῦ πύργου ἀντὶ τῶν ἀποβεβλημένων, αἱ ῥίζαι εἰσὶ τοῦ ὄρους τοῦ λευκοῦ.[2] 2. ἐπεὶ
οὖν οἱ πιστεύσαντες, ἐκ τοῦ ὄρους τοῦ λευκοῦ

---

[1] πάντα γάρ . . . αὐτῷ AFL₁, om. L₂.
[2] λευκοῦ Pᵃᵐ, λευκοῦ τούτου AL.

babes, and no evil enters into their heart, nor have
they known what wickedness is, but have ever
remained in innocence. 2. Such then shall live
without doubt in the kingdom of God, because by no
act did they defile the commandments of God, but
remained in innocence all the days of their lives in
the same mind. 3. All of you, then, as many as shall
continue," said he, "and shall be as babes, with no
wickedness, shall be more glorious than all those
who have been mentioned before, for all babes
are glorious before God, and are in the first place
by him. Blessed then are you who put away
evil from yourselves, and put on guiltlessness, for
you shall be the first of all to live to God." 4. But The stones
after he had finished the parable of the moun- taken out of
tains I said to him : " Sir, now explain to me about
the stones which were taken out of the plain,
and put into the building instead of the stones which
were taken away from the tower, and the round
stones which were put into the building, and those
which are still round."

XXX

1. " LISTEN also," he said, " concerning all these.
The stones that are taken from the plain and put into
the building of the tower instead of those which are
rejected, are the roots of the white mountain.
2. Since then all the believers from the white

πάντες ἄκακοι εὑρέθησαν, ἐκέλευσεν ὁ κύριος τοῦ
πύργου τούτους ἐκ τῶν ῥιζῶν[1] τοῦ ὄρους τούτου
βληθῆναι εἰς τὴν οἰκοδομὴν τοῦ πύργου· ἔγνω
γάρ, ὅτι, ἐὰν ἀπέλθωσιν εἰς τὴν οἰκοδομὴν τοῦ
πύργου οἱ λίθοι οὗτοι, διαμενοῦσι λαμπροὶ καὶ
οὐδεὶς αὐτῶν μελανήσει.[2]   3. Quodsi de ceteris
montibus adiecisset, necesse habuisset rursus visitare
eam turrem atque purgare.   Hi autem omnes can-
didi inventi sunt, πιστεύσαντες καὶ οἱ μέλλοντες
πιστεύειν· ἐκ τοῦ αὐτοῦ γὰρ γένους εἰσίν. μακάριον τὸ γένος τοῦτο, ὅτι ἄκακόν ἐστιν. 4.
ἄκουε νῦν καὶ περὶ τῶν λίθων τῶν στρογγύλων
καὶ λαμπρῶν. καὶ αὐτοὶ πάντες ἐκ τοῦ ὄρους τοῦ
λευκοῦ εἰσίν.   Audi autem, quare rotundi sunt
reperti.   Divitiae suae eos pusillum obscuraverunt
a veritate atque obfuscaverunt, a deo vero nun-

Eph. 4, 29

quam recesserunt, nec ullum verbum malum pro-
cessit de ore eorum, sed omnis aequitas et virtus
veritatis.   5. Horum ergo mentem cum vidisset
dominus posse eos veritati favere, bonos quoque
permanere, iussit opes eorum circumcidi, non enim
in totum eorum tolli, ut possint aliquid boni
facere de eo, quod eis relictum est, et vivent deo,
quoniam ex bono genere sunt.   Ideo ergo pusillum
circumcisi sunt et positi sunt in structuram turris
huius.

---

[1] τῶν ῥιζῶν LE, om. A.

[2] At this point A ends, as the last leaf is missing. The
Latin text which follows is that of L₁. The few verses in
Greek are from Pᵃᵐ. Some words have been restored as the
Papyrus is in bad condition, but the reconstructions are
almost certain.

mountain were found guiltless, the lord of the tower commanded these to be brought from the roots of this mountain for the building of the tower. For he knew that if these stones go into the building of the tower they will remain bright and none of them will become black. 3. But if he had added them from the other mountains he would have been obliged to visit the tower again, and to purge it, for all these have been found white, both past and future believers, for they are of the same race. Blessed is this race, because it is innocent. 4. Listen now concerning the round and bright stones. They also are all from this white mountain. Listen then why they have been found round. Their riches have hidden them a little from the truth and darkened them, but they have never departed from God, nor has any evil word proceeded from their mouth, but all equity and virtue of truth. 5. When therefore the Lord saw their minds, that they are able to favour the truth and to remain good, he commanded their wealth to be cut down, yet not to be wholly taken away from them, that they may be able to do some good with that which was left them, and they shall live to God because they are of a good kind. Therefore they were cut down a little, and placed in the building of this tower.

XXXI

1. Ceteri vero, qui adhuc rotundi remanserunt neque aptati sunt in eam structuram, quia nondum acceperunt sigillum, repositi sunt suo loco; valde enim rotundi reperti sunt. 2. Oportet autem circumcidi hoc saeculum ab illis et vanitates opum suarum, et tunc convenient in dei regnum. Necesse est enim eos intrare in dei regnum; hoc enim genus innocuum benedixit dominus. Ex hoc ergo genere non intercidet quisquam. Etenim licet quis eorum temptatus a nequissimo diabolo aliquid deliquerit, cito recurret ad dominum suum. 3. Felices vos iudico omnes, ego nuntius paenitentiae, quicumque estis innocentes sicut infantes, quoniam pars vestra bona est et honorata apud deum. 4. Dico autem omnibus, vobis, quicumque sigillum hoc accepistis, simplicitatem habere neque offensarum memores esse neque in malitia vestra permanere aut in memoria offensarum amaritudinis, in unum quemque spiritum fieri et has malas scissuras permediare ac tollere a vobis, ut dominus pecorum gaudeat de his.[1] 5. χαρήσεται δέ, ἐὰν πάντα ὑγιῆ εὑρεθῇ, καὶ μὴ διαπεπτωκότα ἐξ αὐτῶν. ἐὰν δὲ εὑρεθῇ τινα ἐξ αὐτῶν διαπεπτωκότα, οὐαὶ τοῖς ποιμέσιν ἔσται. 6. ἐὰν δὲ καὶ αὐτοὶ οἱ ποιμένες εὑρεθῶσι διαπεπτωκότες, τί ἐροῦσι τῷ δεσπότῃ τοῦ ποιμνίου; ὅτι ἀπὸ τῶν προβάτων διέπεσαν; οὐ πιστευθήσονται· ἄπιστον γὰρ πρᾶγμά ἐστι ποιμένα ὑπὸ προβάτων παθεῖν τι· μᾶλλον δὲ κολασ-

---

[1] The Greek which follows is a quotation preserved in Antiochus.

XXXI.

1. " But the others which still remained round and were not fitted into the building, because they had not yet received the seal, were put back in their place, for they were found very round. 2. But this world and the vanities of their riches must be cut away from them, and then they will be meet for the kingdom of God. For they needs must 'enter into the kingdom of God'; for the Lord blessed this innocent kind. Therefore not one of this kind shall perish, for though one of them be tempted by the most wicked devil, and do some wrong, he will quickly return to his Lord. 3. I, the angel of repentance, judge you all happy who are innocent as babes, for your part is good and honourable with God. 4. But I say to you all, as many as have received the seal, keep simplicity and bear no malice, and do not remain in your guilt, or in remembrance of the bitterness of offences. Be of one spirit and put away these evil schisms, and take them away from yourselves that the lord of the sheep may rejoice over them. 5. But he will rejoice if all be found whole; but if he find some of them fallen away, it will be woe to the shepherds. 6. But if the shepherds themselves be found fallen away, what shall they answer to the Master of the flock? That they have fallen away because of the sheep? They will not be believed, for it is incredible that a shepherd should be harmed

The round stones

θήσονται διὰ τὸ ψεῦδος αὐτῶν. Et ego sum pastor, et validissime oportet me de vobis reddere rationem.

XXXII

1. Remediate ergo vos, dum adhuc turris aedificatur. 2. Dominus habitat in viris amantibus pacem; ei enimvero pax cara est; a litigiosis vero et perditis malitiae longe abest. Reddite igitur ei spiritum integrum, sicut accepistis. 3. Si enim dederis fulloni vestimentum novum integrum idque integrum iterum vis recipere, fullo autem scissum tibi illud reddet, recipies illud? Nonne statim scandesces[1] et eum convicio persequeris, dicens : Vestimentum integrum tibi dedi; quare scidisti illud et inutile redegisti? Et propter scissuram, quam in eo fecisti, in usu esse non potest. Nonne haec omnia verba dices fulloni ergo et de scissura, quam in vestimento tuo fecerit?[2] 4. Si sic igitur tu doles de vestimento tuo et quereris, quod non illud integrum recipias, quid putas dominum tibi facturum, qui spiritum integrum tibi dedit, et tu eum totum inutilem redegisti, ita ut in nullo usu esse possit domino suo? Inutilis enim esse coepit usus eius, cum sit corruptus a te. Nonne igitur dominus spiritus eius propter hoc factum tuum morte te adficiet? 5. Plane, inquam, omnes eos,

[1] Scandescis L₁, irasceris L₂.
[2] A great part of this paragraph is found in Greek in Antiochus, but he seems here to abbreviate and perhaps to paraphrase too much to render it wise to follow his text.

by the sheep, and they will rather be punished for their lie. And I am the shepherd, and am very exceedingly bound to give account for you.

XXXII

1. " THEREFORE, amend yourselves while the tower is still being built. 2. The Lord dwells among men who love peace, for of a truth peace is dear to him, but he is far away from the contentious and those who are destroyed by malice. Give back then to him your spirit whole as you received it. 3. For if you give to the dyer a new garment whole, and wish to receive it back from him whole, but the dyer gives it you back torn, will you accept it? Will you not at once grow hot [1] and pursue him with abuse, saying ' I gave you a whole garment, why have you torn it and given it me back useless? And because of the tear which you have made in it it cannot be used.' Will you not say all these things to the dyer about the rent which he has made in your garment? 4. If then you are grieved with your garment, and complain that you did not receive it back whole, what do you think the Lord will do to you, who gave you the spirit whole, and you have returned it altogether useless, so that it can be of no use to its Lord, for its use began to be useless when it had been corrupted by you. Will not therefore the Lord of that spirit punish you with death, because of this deed of yours?" 5. "Certainly," said I, "He will punish

The final exhortation of the shepherd

---

[1] Scandesco is probably a dialectic form of candesco, which is found in some MSS of L_1.

quoscumque invenerit in memoria offensarum permanere, adficiet. Clementiam, inquit, eius calcare
nolite, sed potius honorificate eum, quod tam patiens
est ad delicta vestra et non est sicut vos. Agite
enim paenitentiam utilem vobis.

XXXIII

1. Haec omnia, quae supra scripta sunt, ego pastor
nuntius paenitentiae ostendi et locutus sum dei
servis. Si credideritis ergo et audieritis verba mea
et ambulaveritis in his et correxeritis itinera vestra,
vivere poteritis. Sin autem permanseritis in malitia
et memoria offensarum, nullus ex huiusmodi vivet
deo. Haec omnia a me dicenda dicta sunt vobis.
2. Ait mihi ipse pastor: Omnia a me interrogasti?
Et dixi: Ita, domine. Quare ergo non interrogasti
me de forma lapidum in structura repositorum, quod
explevimus formas? Et dixi: Oblitus sum, domine.
3. Audi nunc, inquit, de illis. Hi sunt qui nunc
mandata mea audierunt et ex totis praecordiis
egerunt paenitentiam. Cumque vidisset dominus
bonam atque puram esse paenitentiam eorum et
posse eos in ea permanere, iussit priora peccata
eorum deleri. Hae enim formae peccata erant
eorum, et exaequata sunt, ne apparerent.

all those whom he finds keeping the memory of offences." "Do not then," said he, "trample on his mercy, but rather honour him that he is so patient to your offences and is not as you are. Repent therefore with the repentance that avails you.

XXXIII

1. "ALL these things which have been written above I, the shepherd, the angel of repentance, have declared and spoken to the servants of God. If then you shall believe and shall listen to my words and shall walk in them, and shall correct your ways, you shall be able to live. But if you shall remain in malice and in the memory of offences, none of such kind shall live to God. All these things that I must tell have been told to you." 2. The shepherd himself said to me, "Have you asked me about everything?" And I said: "Yes, Sir," "Why then did you not ask me about the marks of the stones which were placed in the building, why we filled up the marks?" And I said: "I forgot, Sir." 3. "Listen now," said he, "about them. These are those who heard my commandments, and repented with all their hearts. And when the Lord saw that their repentance was good and pure, and that they could remain in it, he commanded their former sins to be blotted out. For these marks were their sins, and they were made level that they should not appear."

Similitudo X

I

1. Postquam perscripseram librum hunc, venit nuntius ille, qui me tradiderat huic pastori, in domum, in qua eram, et consedit supra lectum, et adstitit ad dexteram hic pastor. Deinde vocavit me et haec mihi dixit: 2. Tradidi te, inquit, et domum tuam huic pastori, ut ab eo protegi possis. Ita, inquam, domine. Si vis ergo protegi, inquit, ab omni vexatione et ab omni saevitia, successum autem habere in omni opere bono atque verbo et omnem virtutem aequitatis, in mandatis huius ingredere, quae dedi tibi, et poteris dominari omni nequitiae. 3. Custodienti enim tibi mandata huius subiecta erit omnis cupiditas et dulcedo saeculi huius, successus vero in omni bono negotio te sequetur. Maturitatem huius et modestiam suscipe in te et dic omnibus, in magno honore esse eum et dignitate apud dominum et magnae potestatis eum praesidem esse et potentem in officio suo. Huic soli per totum orbem paenitentiae potestas tributa est. Potensne tibi videtur esse? Sed vos maturitatem huius et verecundiam, quam in vos habet, despicitis.

II

1. Dico ei: Interroga ipsum, domine, ex quo in domo mea est, an aliquid extra ordinem fecerim, ex

Parable 10

I

1. After I had written this book the angel who had handed me over to the shepherd came to the house in which I was, and sat on the couch, and the shepherd stood on his right hand. Then he called me and said to me : 2. " I have handed you over," said he, " and your house to this shepherd, that you may be protected by him." " Yes, Sir," said I. " If then," said he, " you wish to be protected from all vexation and all cruelty, and to have success in every good work and word, and every virtue of righteousness, walk in his commandments, which he gave you, and you will be able to overcome all wickedness. 3. For, if you keep his commandments, all the lusts and delight of this world will be subject to you, but success in every good undertaking will follow you. Take his perfection[1] and moderation[2] upon you, and say to all that he is in great honour and dignity with the Lord, and that he is set in great power and powerful in his office. To him alone throughout all the world is given the power of repentance. Does he not seem to you to be powerful ? But you despise his perfection and the modesty which he has towards you."

The final vision of the Angel

II

1. I said to him : " Ask him himself, Sir, whether since he has been in my house I have done anything

[1] Literally 'ripeness.'
[2] A translation either of σωφροσύνη or of εὐταξία = propriety of conduct, a word specially used by the Stoics.

quo eum offenderim. 2. Et ego, inquit, scio nihil extra ordinem fecisse te neque esse facturum. Et ideo haec loquor tecum, ut perseveres. Bene enim de te hic apud me existimavit. Tu autem ceteris haec verba dices, ut et illi, qui egerunt aut acturi sunt paenitentiam, eadem quae tu sentiant et hic apud me de his bene interpretetur et ego apud dominum. 3. Et ego, inquam, domine, omni homini indico magnalia domini ; spero autem, quia omnes, qui antea peccaverunt, si haec audiant, libenter acturi sunt paenitentiam vitam recuperantes. 4. Permane ergo, inquit, in hoc ministerio et consumma illud. Quicumque autem mandata huius efficiunt, habebunt vitam, et hic apud dominum magnum honorem. Quicumque vero huius mandata non servant, fugiunt a sua vita et illum adversus[1] ; nec mandata eius sequuntur, sed morti se tradunt et unusquisque eorum reus fit sanguinis sui. Tibi autem dico, ut servias mandatis his, et remedium peccatorum habebis.

Acts 2, 11

III

1. Misi autem tibi has virgines, ut habitent tecum ; vidi enim eas affabiles tibi esse. Habes ergo eas adiutrices, quo magis possis huius mandata servare ; non potest enim fieri, ut sine his virginibus haec mandata serventur. Video autem eas libenter esse tecum ; sed ego praecipiam eis, ut omnino a domo

---

[1] Hilgenfeld emends to "aversantur illum."

against his command, to offend against him?" 2. "I know myself," said he, "that you have done nothing and will do nothing against his command, and therefore I am speaking thus with you, that you may persevere; for he has given me a good account of you. But you shall tell these words to others, that they also who have repented, or shall repent, may have the same mind as you, and that he may give a good account to me of them, and I to the Lord." 3. "I myself, Sir," said I, "show the 'mighty acts' of the Lord to all men, but I hope that all who have sinned before, if they hear this, will willingly repent, and recover life." 4. "Remain then," said he, "in this ministry and carry it out. But whoever perform his commandments shall have life, and such a one has great honour with the Lord. But whoever do not keep his commands, are flying from their own life and against him, and they do not keep his commandments, but are delivering themselves to death, and each one of them is guilty of his own blood. But you I bid to keep these commandments, and you shall have healing for your sins.

III

1. "But I sent these maidens to you to dwell with you, for I saw that they were courteous to you. You have them therefore to help you, in order to keep his commandments the better, for it is not possible that these commandments be kept without these maidens. I see moreover that they are with you willingly; but I will enjoin on them not to depart at all from your

Hermas and the maidens

tua non discedant. 2. Tu tantum communda domum
tuam; in munda enim domo libenter habitabunt;
mundae enim sunt atque castae et industriae et
omnes habentes gratiam apud dominum. Igitur si
habuerint domum tuam puram, tecum permanebunt.
Sin autem pusillum aliquid inquinationis acciderit,
protinus a domo tua recedent; hae enim
virgines nullum omnino diligunt inquinationem.
3. Dico ei: Spero me, domine, placiturum eis,
ita ut in domo mea libenter habitent semper.
καὶ ὥσπερ οὗτος, ᾧ παρέδωκάς με, οὐ μέμ-
φεταί με, οὐδὲ αὗται μέμψονταί με. 4. λέγει
τῷ ποιμένι· Οἶδα, ὅτι ὁ δοῦλος τοῦ θεοῦ
θέλει ζῆν καὶ τηρήσει τὰς ἐντολὰς ταύτας
καὶ τὰς παρθένους ἐν καθαρότητι καταστήσει.
5. ταῦτα εἰπὼν τῷ ποιμένι πάλιν παρέ-
δωκέν με καὶ τὰς παρθένους καλέσας . . . .
λέγει αὐταῖς·[1] Quoniam video vos libenter in domo
huius habitare, commendo eum vobis et domum eius,
ut a domo eius non recedatis omnino. Illae vero
haec verba libenter audierunt.

IV

1. Ait deinde mihi: Viriliter in ministerio hoc
conversare, omni homini indica magnalia domini, et
habebis gratiam in hoc ministerio. Quicumque ergo
in his mandatis ambulaverit, vivet et felix erit in
vita sua; quicumque vero neglexerit, non vivet et
erit infelix in vita sua. 2. Dic omnibus, ut non

Acts 2, 1

---

[1] The Greek is from P^ox (Oxyrynchus Papyr. 404).

house. 2. Only do you make your house pure, for in a pure house they will willingly dwell, for they are pure and chaste and industrious and all have favour with the Lord.   If then they find your house pure they will remain with you.   But if ever so little corruption come to it they will at once depart from your home, for these maidens love no sort of impurity." 3. I said to him : "I hope, Sir, that I shall please them so that they may ever willingly dwell in my house. And just as he, to whom you handed me over, finds no fault in me, so they also shall find no fault in me." 4. He said to the shepherd : "I know that the servant of God wishes to live, and will keep these commandments, and will provide for the maidens in purity." 5. When he had said this he handed me over again to the shepherd, and called the maidens and said to them : " Since I see that you willingly dwell in his house I commend him and his house to you, that you depart not at all from his house."   But they heard these words willingly.

IV

1. THEN he said to me : " Behave manfully in this ministry, show to every man the ' mighty acts ' of the Lord, and you shall have favour in this ministry. Whoever therefore shall walk in these commandments shall live, and shall be happy in his life ; but whoever shall neglect them shall not live, and shall be unhappy in his life. 2. Say to all men who are

cessent, quicumque recte facere possunt; bona
opera exercere utile est illis. Dico autem, omnem
hominem de incommodis eripi oportere. Et is enim,
qui eget et in cotidiana vita patitur incommoda, in
magno tormento est ac necessitate. 3. Qui igitur
huiusmodi animam eripit de necessitate, magnum
gaudium sibi adquirit. Is enim, qui huiusmodi
vexatur incommodo, pari tormento cruciatur atque
torquet se qui in vincula est. Multi enim propter
huiusmodi calamitates, cum eas sufferre non possunt,
mortem sibi adducunt. Qui novit igitur calamitatem
huiusmodi hominis et non eripit eum, magnum
peccatum admittit et reus fit sanguinis eius. 4.
Facite igitur opera bona, quicumque accepistis a
domino, ne, dum tardatis facere, consummetur
structura turris. Propter vos enim intermissum est
opus aedificationis eius. Nisi festinetis igitur facere
recte, consummabitur turris, et excludemini. 5.
Postquam vero locutus est mecum, surrexit de lecto
et apprehenso pastore et virginibus abiit, dicens
autem mihi, remissurum se pastorem illum et virgines
in domum meam.

able to do right,[1] that they cease not; the exercise of good deeds is profitable to them. But I say that every man ought to be taken out from distress, for he who is destitute and suffers distress in his daily life is in great anguish and necessity. 3. Whoever therefore rescues the soul of such a man from necessity gains great joy for himself. For he who is vexed by such distress is tortured with such anguish as he suffers who is in chains. For many bring death on themselves by reason of such calamities when they cannot bear them. Whoever therefore knows the distress of such a man, and does not rescue him, incurs great sin and becomes guilty of his blood. 4. Therefore do good deeds, all you who have learnt of the Lord, lest the building of the tower be finished while you delay to do them. For the work of the building has been broken off for your sake. Unless therefore you hasten to do right the tower will be finished and you will be shut out."

5. Now after he had spoken this he rose from the couch, and took the shepherd and the maidens and departed, but said to me that he would send back the shepherd and the maidens to my house.

---

[1] 'recte facere' can hardly be translated otherwise: but from the context it seems probably to represent εὖ ποιεῖν, or some such phrase, meaning to do good in the sense of charitable acts.

THE MARTYRDOM OF POLYCARP

THE MARTYRDOM OF POLYCARP

THIS obviously genuine and contemporary account of the martyrdom of Polycarp, in the form of a letter from the Church of Smyrna to the Church of Philomelium, is the earliest known history of a Christian martyrdom, the genuineness of which is unquestionable, and its value is enhanced by the fact that in the extant MSS. a short account is given of the history of the text. From this it appears that Gaius, a contemporary of Irenaeus who had himself seen Polycarp when he was a boy, copied the text from a manuscript in the possession of Irenaeus. Later on Socrates in Corinth copied the text of Gaius, and finally Pionius copied the text of Socrates. Pionius, who is supposed to have lived in the 4th century, says that the existence of the document was revealed to him in a vision by Polycarp, and that when he found it the MS. was old and in bad condition.

Of the text of Pionius, the following five Greek MSS. are available and further research among hagiographical MSS. would probably reveal the existence of more, but there is no reason to suppose that such discovery would make any important addition to our knowledge of the text, which is quite good.

m, Codex Mosquensis 159 (13th century), now in
the Library of the Holy Synod at Moscow.

b, Codex Baroccianus 238 (11th century), now in
the Bodleian Library at Oxford.

p, Codex Parisinus Gr. 1452 (10th century), now
in the Bibliothèque nationale at Paris.

s, Codex Hierosolymitanus (10th century), now
in the monastery of the Holy Sepulchre at
Jerusalem.

v, Codex Vindobonensis Gr. Eccl. iii. (11th century), at Vienna.

Of these MSS. b p s v form a group as opposed
to m, which has often the better text.

We also have the greater part of the letter preserved by Eusebius in quotations in his Ecclesiastical
History IV. 15, quoted as E.

Besides these authorities there exists a Latin
version, quoted as L, and extracts from Eusebius in
Syriac and Coptic which have obviously no inde-
pendent value.

The date of the martyrdom of Polycarp is fixed by
the chronicle of Eusebius as 166–7, but this date has
now been almost universally abandoned, as according
to the letter to the church at Smyrna, Polycarp's
martyrdom was on Saturday, Xanthicus[1] 2, that is
Feb. 23, in the proconsulship of Statius Quadratus,
and from a reference in Aelius Aristides, Waddington
(Mémoire sur la chronologie de la vie du rhéteur,
Aelius Aristide, Paris, 1864) showed that Quadratus
became proconsul of Asia in 153–4. Now, Feb. 23
fell on a Saturday in 155. It is therefore suggested

---

[1] The name of the spring month in the Macedonian
Calendar which was commonly used in Smyrna.

that Feb. 23, 155, was the date of the martyrdom. The question however is complicated by the statement in the letter that the day of the martyrdom was a great Sabbath. This may mean the Jewish feast Purim, and Purim in 155 was not on Feb. 23. Mr. C. H. Turner has argued in *Studia Biblica* II., pp. 105 ff. that Purim, Feb. 22, 156, is the real date and that the Roman reckoning which regards Xanthicus 2 as equivalent to Feb. 23 is a mistake due to neglect to consider fully the complicated system of intercalation in the Asian calendar. More recently Prof. E. Schwartz has argued in the *Abhandlungen der königlichen Gesellschaft der Wissenschaften zu Göttingen* VIII. (1905), 6, pp. 125 ff. that the 'great Sabbath' can only mean the Sabbath after the Passover (cf. Jo. 19, 21), and that owing to the local customs of the Jews in Smyrna this was on Feb. 22 in the year 156 A.D. He thus reaches the same result as Turner, but by a different method.

ΜΑΡΤΥΡΙΟΝ ΤΟΥ ΑΓΙΟΥ ΠΟΛΥ-ΚΑΡΠΟΥ ΕΠΙΣΚΟΠΟΥ ΣΜΥΡΝΗΣ [1]

Jude 2

Ἡ ἐκκλησία τοῦ θεοῦ ἡ παροικοῦσα Σμύρναν
τῇ ἐκκλησίᾳ τοῦ θεοῦ τῇ παροικούσῃ ἐν
Φιλομηλίῳ καὶ πάσαις ταῖς κατὰ πάντα τόπον
τῆς ἁγίας καὶ καθολικῆς ἐκκλησίας παροι-
κίαις· ἔλεος, εἰρήνη καὶ ἀγάπη θεοῦ πατρὸς
καὶ κυρίου ἡμῶν Ἰησου Χριστοῦ πληθυνθείη.

I

1. Ἐγράψαμεν ὑμῖν, ἀδελφοί, τὰ κατὰ τοὺς
μαρτυρήσαντας καὶ τὸν μακάριον Πολύκαρπον,
ὅστις ὥσπερ ἐπισφραγίσας διὰ τῆς μαρτυρίας
αὐτοῦ κατέπαυσεν τὸν διωγμόν. σχεδὸν γὰρ
πάντα τὰ προάγοντα ἐγένετο, ἵνα ἡμῖν ὁ κύριος
ἄνωθεν ἐπιδείξῃ τὸ κατὰ τὸ εὐαγγέλιον μαρτύριον.
2. περιέμενεν γάρ, ἵνα παραδοθῇ, ὡς καὶ ὁ κύριος,

Phil. 2, 4

ἵνα μιμηταὶ καὶ ἡμεῖς αὐτοῦ γενώμεθα, μὴ μόνον
σκοποῦντες τὸ καθ' ἑαυτούς, ἀλλὰ καὶ τὸ κατὰ
τοὺς πέλας. ἀγάπης γὰρ ἀληθοῦς καὶ βεβαίας
ἐστίν, μὴ μόνον ἑαυτὸν θέλειν σώζεσθαι, ἀλλὰ
καὶ πάντας τοὺς ἀδελφούς.

---

[1] This title has no special support. Each MS. gives its
own title and though there is a general resemblance no
two are the same.

THE MARTYRDOM OF ST. POLY-CARP, BISHOP OF SMYRNA

THE Church of God which sojourns in Smyrna, to the Church of God which sojourns in Philomelium, and to all the sojournings of the Holy Catholic Church in every place. "Mercy, peace and love" of God the Father, and our Lord Jesus Christ be multiplied.

I

1. WE write to you, brethren, the story of the martyrs and of the blessed Polycarp, who put an end to the persecution by his martyrdom as though adding the seal.[1] For one might almost say that all that had gone before happened in order that the Lord might show to us from above a martyrdom[2] in accordance with the Gospel. 2. For he waited to be betrayed as also the Lord had done, that we too might become his imitators, "not thinking of ourselves alone, but also of our neighbours." For it is the mark of true and steadfast love, not to wish that oneself may be saved alone, but all the brethren also.

Intro-duction

[1] He was the last to suffer and thus might be regarded as being the seal to the 'witness' or 'testimony' (μαρτύριον) of the Church. It is not clear whether μαρτυρία and μαρτύριον ought to be translated 'martyrdom' or 'witness': there is an untranslateable play on the words.

[2] Or perhaps "witness."

II

1. Μακάρια μὲν οὖν καὶ γενναῖα τὰ μαρτύρια πάντα τὰ κατὰ τὸ θέλημα τοῦ θεοῦ γεγονότα. δεῖ γὰρ εὐλαβεστέρους ἡμᾶς ὑπάρχοντας τῷ θεῷ τὴν κατὰ πάντων ἐξουσίαν ἀνατιθέναι. 2. τὸ γὰρ γενναῖον αὐτῶν καὶ ὑπομονητικὸν καὶ φιλοδέσποτον τίς οὐκ ἂν θαυμάσειεν; οἳ μάστιξιν μὲν καταξανθέντες, ὥστε μέχρι τῶν ἔσω φλεβῶν καὶ ἀρτηριῶν τὴν τῆς σαρκὸς οἰκονομίαν θεωρεῖσθαι, ὑπέμειναν, ὡς καὶ τοὺς περιεστῶτας ἐλεεῖν καὶ ὀδύρεσθαι· τοὺς δὲ καὶ εἰς τοσοῦτον γενναιότητος ἐλθεῖν, ὥστε μήτε γρύξαι μήτε στενάξαι τινὰ αὐτῶν, ἐπιδεικνυμένους ἅπασιν ἡμῖν, ὅτι ἐκείνῃ τῇ ὥρᾳ βασανιζόμενοι τῆς σαρκὸς ἀπεδήμουν οἱ γενναιότατοι[1] μάρτυρες τοῦ Χριστοῦ, μᾶλλον δέ, ὅτι παρεστὼς ὁ κύριος ὡμίλει αὐτοῖς. 3. καὶ προσέχοντες τῇ τοῦ Χριστοῦ χάριτι τῶν κοσμικῶν κατεφρόνουν βασάνων, διὰ μιᾶς ὥρας τὴν αἰώνιον ζωὴν[2] ἐξαγοραζόμενοι. καὶ τὸ πῦρ ἦν αὐτοῖς ψυχρὸν τὸ τῶν ἀπηνῶν βασανιστῶν. πρὸ ὀφθαλμῶν γὰρ εἶχον φυγεῖν τὸ αἰώνιον καὶ μηδέποτε σβεννύμενον, καὶ τοῖς τῆς καρδίας ὀφθαλμοῖς ἀνέβλεπον τὰ τηρούμενα τοῖς ὑπομείνασιν ἀγαθά, ἃ οὔτε οὖς ἤκουσεν οὔτε ὀφθαλμὸς εἶδεν οὔτε ἐπὶ καρδίαν ἀνθρώπου ἀνέβη, ἐκείνοις δὲ ὑπεδείκνυτο ὑπὸ τοῦ κυρίου, οἵπερ μηκέτι ἄνθρωποι, ἀλλ᾽ ἤδη ἄγγελοι ἦσαν.

1 Cor. 2, 9
(Is. 64, 4;
65, 16)

---

[1] γενναιόταται mps, om. bv.

[2] ζωὴν m, κόλασιν bpsv. The reading of bpsv would have to be translated "buying off eternal punishment" and this rendering of ἐξαγοράζεσθαι is doubtful.

II

1. BLESSED then and noble are all the martyrdoms which took place according to the will of God, for we must be very careful to assign the power over all to God. 2. For who would not admire their nobility and patience and love of their Master? For some were torn by scourging until the mechanism of their flesh was seen even to the lower veins and arteries, and they endured so that even the bystanders pitied them and mourned. And some even reached such a pitch of nobility that none of them groaned or wailed, showing to all of us that at that hour of their torture the noble martyrs of Christ were absent from the flesh, or rather that the Lord was standing by and talking with them. 3. And paying heed to the grace of Christ they despised worldly tortures, by a single hour purchasing everlasting life. And the fire of their cruel torturers had no heat for them, for they set before their eyes an escape from the fire which is everlasting and is never quenched, and with the eyes of their heart they looked up to the good things which are preserved for those who have endured, 'which neither ear hath heard nor hath eye seen, nor hath it entered into the heart of man,' but it was shown by the Lord to them who were no longer men but already angels.[1]

The sufferings of the Martyrs

---

[1] This passage, combined with Hermas Vis. II. ii. 7 and Sim. IX. xxv. 2, shows that the identification of the dead with angels existed in the second century in Christian circles.

4. ὁμοίως δὲ καὶ οἱ εἰς τὰ θηρία κατακριθέντες ὑπέμειναν δεινὰς κολάσεις, κήρυκας ὑποστρωννύμενοι καὶ ἄλλαις ποικίλων βασάνων ἰδέαις κολαζόμενοι, ἵνα, εἰ δυνηθείη, ὁ τύραννος διὰ τῆς ἐπιμόνου κολάσεως εἰς ἄρνησιν αὐτοὺς τρέψῃ. πολλὰ γὰρ ἐμηχανᾶτο κατ᾽ αὐτῶν ὁ διάβολος.

III

1. Ἀλλὰ χάρις τῷ θεῷ· κατὰ πάντων γὰρ οὐκ ἴσχυσεν. ὁ γὰρ γενναιότατος Γερμανικὸς ἐπερρώννυεν αὐτῶν τὴν δειλίαν διὰ τῆς ἐν αὐτῷ ὑπομονῆς· ὃς καὶ ἐπισήμως ἐθηριομάχησεν. βουλομένου γὰρ τοῦ ἀνθυπάτου πείθειν αὐτὸν καὶ λέγοντος, τὴν ἡλικίαν αὐτοῦ κατοικτεῖραι, ἑαυτῷ ἐπεσπάσατο τὸ θηρίον προσβιασάμενος, τάχιον τοῦ ἀδίκου καὶ ἀνόμου βίου αὐτῶν ἀπαλλαγῆναι βουλόμενος. 2. ἐκ τούτου οὖν πᾶν τὸ πλῆθος, θαυμάσαν τὴν γενναιότητα τοῦ θεοφιλοῦς καὶ θεοσεβοῦς γένους τῶν Χριστιανῶν, ἐπεβόησεν· Αἶρε τοὺς ἀθέους· ζητείσθω Πολύκαρπος.

IV

1. Εἷς δέ, ὀνόματι Κόϊντος, Φρὺξ προσφάτως ἐληλυθὼς ἀπὸ τῆς Φρυγίας, ἰδὼν τὰ θηρία ἐδειλίασεν. οὗτος δὲ ἦν ὁ παραβιασάμενος ἑαυτόν τε καί τινας προσελθεῖν ἑκόντας. τοῦτον ὁ ἀνθύπατος πολλὰ ἐκλιπαρήσας ἔπεισεν ὀμόσαι καὶ ἐπιθῦσαι. διὰ τοῦτο οὖν, ἀδελφοί, οὐκ ἐπαινοῦμεν τοὺς προδιδόντας ἑαυτούς, ἐπειδὴ οὐχ οὕτως διδάσκει τὸ εὐαγγέλιον.

Mt. 10, 23

4. And in the same way also those who were condemned to the beasts endured terrible torment, being stretched on sharp shells and buffeted with other kinds of various torments, that if it were possible the tyrant might bring them to a denial by continuous torture. For the devil used many wiles against them.

III

1. But thanks be to God, for he had no power over any. For the most noble Germanicus encouraged their fears by the endurance which was in him, and he fought gloriously with the wild beasts. For when the Pro-Consul wished to persuade him and bade him have pity on his youth, he violently dragged the beast towards himself, wishing to be released more quickly from their unrighteous and lawless life. 2. So after this all the crowd, wondering at the nobility of the God-loving and God-fearing people of the Christians, cried out: "Away with the Atheists; let Polycarp be searched for."

Germanicus

IV

1. But one, named Quintus, a Phrygian lately come from Phrygia, when he saw the wild beasts played the coward. Now it was he who had forced himself and some others to come forward of their own accord. Him the Pro-Consul persuaded with many entreaties to take the oath and offer sacrifice. For this reason, therefore, brethren, we do not commend those who give themselves up, since the Gospel does not give this teaching.

Quintus

THE APOSTOLIC FATHERS

V

1. Ὁ δὲ θαυμασιώτατος Πολύκαρπος τὸ μὲν
πρῶτον ἀκούσας οὐκ ἐταράχθη, ἀλλ' ἐβούλετο
κατὰ πόλιν μένειν· οἱ δὲ πλείους ἔπειθον αὐτὸν
ὑπεξελθεῖν. καὶ ὑπεξῆλθεν εἰς ἀγρίδιον οὐ μακρὰν ἀπέχον ἀπὸ τῆς πόλεως καὶ διέτριβεν μετ'
ὀλίγων, νύκτα καὶ ἡμέραν οὐδὲν ἕτερον ποιῶν ἢ
προσευχόμενος περὶ πάντων καὶ τῶν κατὰ τὴν
οἰκουμένην ἐκκλησιῶν, ὅπερ ἦν σύνηθες αὐτῷ.
2. καὶ προσευχόμενος ἐν ὀπτασίᾳ γέγονεν πρὸ
τριῶν ἡμερῶν τοῦ συλληφθῆναι αὐτόν, καὶ εἶδεν
τὸ προσκεφάλαιον αὐτοῦ ὑπὸ πυρὸς κατακαιό-
μενον· καὶ στραφεὶς εἶπεν πρὸς τοὺς σὺν αὐτῷ·
Δεῖ με ζῶντα καῆναι.[1]

VI

1. Καὶ ἐπιμενόντων τῶν ζητούντων αὐτὸν μετέβη
εἰς ἕτερον ἀγρίδιον, καὶ εὐθέως ἐπέστησαν οἱ
ζητοῦντες αὐτόν· καὶ μὴ εὑρόντες συνελάβοντο
παιδάρια δύο, ὧν τὸ ἕτερον βασανιζόμενον
Mt. 10, 36   ὡμολόγησεν. 2. ἦν γὰρ καὶ ἀδύνατον λαθεῖν
αὐτόν, ἐπεὶ καὶ οἱ προδιδόντες αὐτὸν οἰκεῖοι
ὑπῆρχον, καὶ ὁ εἰρήναρχος, ὁ κεκληρωμένος τὸ
αὐτὸ ὄνομα, Ἡρώδης ἐπιλεγόμενος, ἔσπευδεν εἰς
τὸ στάδιον αὐτὸν εἰσαγαγεῖν, ἵνα ἐκεῖνος μὲν τὸν

---

[1] καῆναι m, κανθῆναι bpsv.

V

1. But the most wonderful Polycarp, when he first heard it, was not disturbed, but wished to remain in the city; but the majority persuaded him to go away quietly, and he went out quietly to a farm, not far distant from the city, and stayed with a few friends, doing nothing but pray night and day for all, and for the Churches throughout the world, as was his custom.   2. And while he was praying he fell into a trance three days before he was arrested, and saw the pillow under his head burning with fire, and he turned and said to those who were with him: "I must be burnt alive."

Polycarp's retreat to the country

VI

1. And when the searching for him persisted he went to another farm; and those who were searching for him came up at once, and when they did not find him, they arrested young slaves,[1] and one of them confessed under torture.   2. For it was indeed impossible for him to remain hid, since those who betrayed him were of his own house, and the police captain who had been allotted the very name, being called Herod,[2] hastened to bring him to the arena

His betrayal

---

[1] Literally 'children,' but constantly used for slaves; the South African use of 'boy' is an almost exact parallel.

[2] The writer desires to bring out the points of resemblance to the Passion of Christ. The coincidences are remarkable, but none are in themselves at all improbable.

ἴδιον κλῆρον ἀπαρτίσῃ Χριστοῦ κοινωνὸς γενόμενος, οἱ δὲ προδόντες αὐτὸν τὴν αὐτοῦ τοῦ Ἰούδα
ὑπόσχοιεν τιμωρίαν.

VII

1. Ἔχοντες οὖν τὸ παιδάριον, τῇ παρασκευῇ
περὶ δείπνου ὥραν ἐξῆλθον διωγμῖται καὶ ἱππεῖς
μετὰ τῶν συνήθων αὐτοῖς ὅπλων ὡς ἐπὶ λῃστὴν
τρέχοντες.   καὶ ὀψὲ τῆς ὥρας συνεπελθόντες
ἐκεῖνον μὲν εὗρον ἐν ὑπερῴῳ κατακείμενον·[1] κἀ-
κεῖθεν δὲ ἠδύνατο εἰς ἕτερον χωρίον ἀπελθεῖν,
ἀλλ᾽ οὐκ ἠβουλήθη εἰπών· Τὸ θέλημα τοῦ θεοῦ
γενέσθω. 2. ἀκούσας οὖν παρόντας αὐτούς, κα-
ταβὰς διελέχθη αὐτοῖς, θαυμαζόντων τῶν παρόν-
των τὴν ἡλικίαν αὐτοῦ καὶ τὸ εὐσταθές, καὶ εἰ
τοσαύτη σπουδὴ ἦν τοῦ συλληφθῆναι τοιοῦτον
πρεσβύτην ἄνδρα. εὐθέως οὖν αὐτοῖς ἐκέλευσεν
παρατεθῆναι φαγεῖν καὶ πιεῖν ἐν ἐκείνῃ τῇ ὥρᾳ,
ὅσον ἂν βούλωνται, ἐξῃτήσατο δὲ αὐτούς, ἵνα
δῶσιν αὐτῷ ὥραν πρὸς τὸ προσεύξασθαι ἀδεῶς.
3. τῶν δὲ ἐπιτρεψάντων, σταθεὶς προσηύξατο
πλήρης ὢν τῆς χάριτος τοῦ θεοῦ οὕτως ὥστε ἐπὶ
δύο ὥρας μὴ δύνασθαι σιγῆσαι καὶ ἐκπλήττεσθαι
τοὺς ἀκούοντας, πολλούς τε μετανοεῖν ἐπὶ τῷ
ἐληλυθέναι ἐπὶ τοιοῦτον θεοπρεπῆ πρεσβύτην.

Mt. 26, 55

Acts 21, 14
cf. Mt. 6, 10

---

[1] ἐν ὑπερῴῳ κατακείμενον E, ἔν τινι δωματίῳ ἐν ὑπερῴῳ
κατακείμενον m, ἔν τινι δωματίῳ κατακείμενον ἐν ὑπερῴῳ bpsv.

that he might fulfil his appointed lot by becoming a partaker of Christ, while they who betrayed him should undergo the same punishment as Judas.

VII

1. TAKING the slave then police and cavalry went out on Friday[1] about supper-time, with their usual arms, as if they were advancing against a robber.[2] And late in the evening they came up together against him and found him lying in an upper room. And he might have departed to another place, but would not, saying, "the will of God be done." 2. So when he heard that they had arrived he went down and talked with them, while those who were present wondered at his age and courage, and whether there was so much haste for the arrest of an old man of such a kind. Therefore he ordered food and drink to be set before them at that hour, whatever they should wish, and he asked them to give him an hour to pray without hindrance. 3. To this they assented, and he stood and prayed—thus filled with the grace of God— so that for two hours he could not be silent, and those who listened were astounded, and many repented that they had come against such a venerable old man.

The arrival of the police

Their reception by Polycarp

His prayer

---

[1] παρασκευή is literally Preparation (i.e. for the Sabbath) and has always been used in the Greek Church for Friday.
[2] "robber" is the traditional translation : but "brigand" is nearer the real meaning.

VIII

1. Ἐπεὶ δε ποτε κατέπαυσεν τὴν προσευχήν, μνημονεύσας ἁπάντων καὶ τῶν πώποτε συμβεβληκότων αὐτῷ, μικρῶν τε καὶ μεγάλων, ἐνδόξων τε καὶ ἀδόξων καὶ πάσης τῆς κατὰ τὴν οἰκουμένην καθολικῆς ἐκκλησίας, τῆς ὥρας ἐλθούσης τοῦ ἐξιέναι, ὄνῳ καθίσαντες αὐτὸν ἤγαγον εἰς τὴν πόλιν, ὄντος σαββάτου μεγάλου. 2. καὶ ὑπήντα αὐτῷ ὁ εἰρήναρχος Ἡρώδης καὶ ὁ πατὴρ αὐτοῦ Νικήτης, οἳ καὶ μεταθέντες αὐτὸν ἐπὶ τὴν καρούχαν¹ ἔπειθον παρακαθεζόμενοι καὶ λέγοντες· Τί γὰρ κακόν ἐστιν εἰπεῖν· Κύριος καῖσαρ, καὶ ἐπιθῦσαι καὶ τὰ τούτοις ἀκόλουθα καὶ διασώζεσθαι; ὁ δὲ τὰ μὲν πρῶτα οὐκ ἀπεκρίνατο αὐτοῖς, ἐπιμενόντων δὲ αὐτῶν ἔφη· Οὐ μέλλω ποιεῖν, ὃ συμβουλεύετέ μοι. 3. οἱ δὲ ἀποτυχόντες τοῦ πεῖσαι αὐτὸν δεινὰ ῥήματα ἔλεγον αὐτῷ καὶ μετὰ σπουδῆς καθῄρουν αὐτόν, ὡς κατιόντα ἀπὸ τῆς καρούχας ἀποσῦραι τὸ ἀντικνήμιον. καὶ μὴ ἐπιστραφείς, ὡς οὐδὲν πεπονθὼς προθύμως μετὰ σπουδῆς ἐπορεύετο, ἀγόμενος εἰς τὸ στάδιον, θορύβου τηλικούτου ὄντος ἐν τῷ σταδίῳ, ὡς μηδὲ ἀκουσθῆναί τινα δύνασθαι.

Jo. 19, 31

IX

1. Τῷ δὲ Πολυκάρπῳ εἰσιόντι εἰς τὸ στάδιον φωνὴ ἐξ οὐρανοῦ ἐγένετο· Ἴσχυε, Πολύκαρπε, καὶ ἀνδρίζου. καὶ τὸν μὲν εἰπόντα οὐδεὶς εἶδεν,

Jos. 1, 6

---

¹ καρούχα (cf. *Corpus Inscr. Lat.* iii. p. 835) is the Latin 'carucca,' a closed carriage used by ladies and high officials.

VIII

1. Now when he had at last finished his prayer, after remembering all who had ever even come his way, both small and great, high and low, and the whole Catholic Church throughout the world, the hour came for departure, and they set him on an ass, and led him into the city, on a "great Sabbath day."[1] 2. And the police captain Herod and his father Niketas met him and removed him into their carriage, and sat by his side trying to persuade him and saying: "But what harm is it to say, 'Lord Caesar,' and to offer sacrifice, and so forth, and to be saved?" But he at first did not answer them, but when they continued he said: "I am not going to do what you counsel me." 3. And they gave up the attempt to persuade him, and began to speak fiercely to him, and turned him out in such a hurry that in getting down from the carriage he scraped his shin; and without turning round, as though he had suffered nothing, he walked on promptly and quickly, and was taken to the arena, while the uproar in the arena was so great that no one could even be heard.

His arrival in Smyrna

And in the arena

IX

1. Now when Polycarp entered into the arena there came a voice from heaven: "Be strong, Polycarp, and play the man." And no one saw the

Polycarp's examination

[1] This may have been the Jewish feast Purim, which, according to tradition, celebrates the triumph of the Jews in Persia over their enemies, as is related in the book of Esther, or else the Sabbath in the Passover week (see p. 311).

τὴν δὲ φωνὴν τῶν ἡμετέρων οἱ παρόντες ἤκουσαν.
καὶ λοιπὸν προσαχθέντος αὐτοῦ, θόρυβος ἦν
μέγας ἀκουσάντων, ὅτι Πολύκαρπος συνείληπται.
2. προσαχθέντα οὖν αὐτὸν ἀνηρώτα ὁ ἀνθύπατος,
εἰ αὐτὸς εἴη Πολύκαρπος. τοῦ δὲ ὁμολογοῦντος,
ἔπειθεν ἀρνεῖσθαι λέγων· Αἰδέσθητί σου τὴν
ἡλικίαν, καὶ ἕτερα τούτοις ἀκόλουθα, ὡς ἔθος
αὐτοῖς λέγειν· Ὄμοσον τὴν Καίσαρος τύχην,[1]
μετανόησον, εἰπόν· Αἶρε τοὺς ἀθέους. ὁ δὲ
Πολύκαρπος ἐμβριθεῖ τῷ προσώπῳ εἰς πάντα τὸν
ὄχλον τὸν ἐν τῷ σταδίῳ ἀνόμων ἐθνῶν ἐμβλέψας
καὶ ἐπισείσας αὐτοῖς τὴν χεῖρα, στενάξας τε καὶ
ἀναβλέψας εἰς τὸν οὐρανὸν εἶπεν· Αἶρε τοὺς
ἀθέους. 3. ἐγκειμένου δὲ τοῦ ἀνθυπάτου καὶ
λέγοντος· Ὄμοσον, καὶ ἀπολύω σε, λοιδόρησον
τὸν Χριστόν, ἔφη ὁ Πολύκαρπος· Ὀγδοήκοντα
καὶ ἓξ ἔτη δουλεύω αὐτῷ, καὶ οὐδέν με ἠδίκησεν·
καὶ πῶς δύναμαι βλασφημῆσαι τὸν βασιλέα μου
τὸν σώσαντά με;

X

1. Ἐπιμένοντος δὲ πάλιν αὐτοῦ καὶ λέγοντος·
Ὄμοσον τὴν Καίσαρος τύχην, ἀπεκρίνατο· Εἰ
κενοδοξεῖς, ἵνα ὁμόσω τὴν καίσαρος τυχην, ὡς σὺ
λέγεις, προσποιεῖ δὲ ἀγνοεῖν με, τίς εἰμι, μετὰ
παρρησίας ἄκουε· Χριστιανός εἰμι. εἰ δὲ θέλεις
τὸν τοῦ Χριστιανισμοῦ μαθεῖν λόγον, δὸς ἡμέραν

---

[1] The customary Greek for the oath 'per genium' (or
sometimes 'fortunam,' hence τύχην) Caesaris which Christians rejected. Per salutem Caesaris (σωτηρίαν) they
accepted. (Cf Tertullian *Apol.* 32.)

speaker, but our friends who were there heard the voice. And next he was brought forward, and there was a great uproar of those who heard that Polycarp had been arrested. 2. Therefore when he was brought forward the Pro-Consul asked him if he were Polycarp, and when he admitted it he tried to persuade him to deny, saying : " Respect your age," and so forth, as they are accustomed to say : " Swear by the genius of Caesar, repent, say : ' Away with the Atheists ' " ; but Polycarp, with a stern countenance looked on all the crowd of lawless heathen in the arena, and waving his hand at them, he groaned and looked up to heaven and said : " Away with the Atheists." 3. But when the Pro-Consul pressed him and said : " Take the oath and I let you go, revile Christ," Polycarp said : " For eighty and six years [1] have I been his servant, and he has done me no wrong, and how can I blaspheme my King [2] who saved me ? "

X

1. But when he persisted again, and said : " Swear by the genius of Caesar," he answered him : " If you vainly suppose that I will swear by the genius of Caesar, as you say, and pretend that you are ignorant who I am, listen plainly : I am a Christian. And if you wish to learn the doctrine of Christianity fix a

[1] He was therefore probably a Christian born, unless we ascribe to him a quite improbable age.

[2] βασιλεύς represents ' imperator ' not ' rex,' and though it can hardly be translated ' Emperor,' the antithesis to Caesar is clearly implied.

καὶ ἄκουσον. 2. ἔφη ὁ ἀνθύπατος· Πεῖσον τὸν
δῆμον. ὁ δὲ Πολύκαρπος εἶπεν· Σὲ μὲν κᾶν
λόγου ἠξίωσα· δεδιδάγμεθα γὰρ ἀρχαῖς καὶ
ἐξουσίαις ὑπὸ τοῦ θεοῦ τεταγμέναις τιμὴν κατὰ
τὸ προσῆκον, τὴν μὴ βλάπτουσαν ἡμᾶς, ἀπονέ-
μειν· ἐκείνους δὲ οὐχ ἡγοῦμαι ἀξίους τοῦ ἀπολο
γεῖσθαι αὐτοῖς.

Rom. 13, 1
1 Pet. 2, 13

XI

1. Ὁ δὲ ἀνθύπατος εἶπεν· Θηρία ἔχω, τούτοις
σε παραβαλῶ, ἐὰν μὴ μετανοήσῃς. ὁ δὲ εἶπεν·
Κάλει, ἀμετάθετος γὰρ ἡμῖν ἡ ἀπὸ τῶν κρειττόνων
ἐπὶ τὰ χείρω μετάνοια· καλὸν δὲ μετατίθεσθαι
ἀπὸ τῶν χαλεπῶν ἐπὶ τὰ δίκαια. 2. ὁ δὲ πάλιν
πρὸς αὐτόν· Πυρί σε ποιήσω δαπανηθῆναι, εἰ τῶν
θηρίων καταφρονεῖς, ἐὰν μὴ μετανοήσῃς. ὁ δὲ
Πολύκαρπος εἶπεν· Πῦρ ἀπειλεῖς τὸ πρὸς ὥραν
καιόμενον καὶ μετ᾽ ὀλίγον σβεννύμενον· ἀγνοεῖς
γὰρ τὸ τῆς μελλούσης κρίσεως καὶ αἰωνίου κολάσεως τοῖς ἀσεβέσι τηρούμενον πῦρ. ἀλλὰ τί
βραδύνεις; φέρε, ὃ βούλει.

XII

1. Ταῦτα δὲ καὶ ἕτερα πλείονα λέγων θάρσους
καὶ χαρᾶς ἐνεπίμπλατο, καὶ τὸ πρόσωπον αὐτοῦ
χάριτος ἐπληροῦτο, ὥστε οὐ μόνον μὴ συμπεσεῖν
ταραχθέντα ὑπὸ τῶν λεγομένων πρὸς αὐτόν, ἀλλὰ
τοὐναντίον τὸν ἀνθύπατον ἐκστῆναι, πέμψαι τε
τὸν ἑαυτοῦ κήρυκα ἐν μέσῳ τοῦ σταδίου κηρύξαι

day and listen." 2. The Pro-Consul said: "Persuade the people." And Polycarp said: "You I should have held worthy of discussion, for we have been taught to render honour, as is meet, if it hurt us not, to princes and authorities appointed by God. But as for those, I do not count them worthy that a defence should be made to them.

XI

1. AND the Pro-Consul said: "I have wild beasts, I will deliver you to them, unless you repent." And he said: "Call for them, for repentance from better to worse is not allowed us; but it is good to change from evil to righteousness." 2. And he said again to him: "I will cause you to be consumed by fire, if you despise the beasts, unless you repent." But Polycarp said: "You threaten with the fire that burns for a time, and is quickly quenched, for you do not know the fire which awaits the wicked in the judgment to come and in everlasting punishment. But why are you waiting? Come, do what you will."

The Pro-Consul's threats

XII

1. AND with these and many other words he was filled with courage and joy, and his face was full of grace so that it not only did not fall with trouble at the things said to him, but that the Pro-Consul, on the other hand, was astounded and sent his herald into the midst of the arena to announce three

327

τρίς· Πολύκαρπος ὡμολόγησεν ἑαυτὸν Χριστιανὸν
εἶναι. 2. τούτου λεχθέντος ὑπὸ τοῦ κήρυκος,
ἅπαν τὸ πλῆθος ἐθνῶν τε καὶ Ἰουδαίων τῶν τὴν
Σμύρναν κατοικούντων ἀκατασχέτῳ θυμῷ καὶ
μεγάλῃ φωνῇ ἐπεβόα· Οὗτός ἐστιν ὁ τῆς Ἀσίας
διδάσκαλος, ὁ πατὴρ τῶν Χριστιανῶν, ὁ τῶν ἡμετέρων θεῶν καθαιρέτης, ὁ πολλοὺς διδάσκων μὴ θύειν
μηδὲ προσκυνεῖν. ταῦτα λέγοντες ἐπεβόων καὶ
ἠρώτων τὸν Ἀσιάρχην Φίλιππον, ἵνα ἐπαφῇ τῷ
Πολυκάρπῳ λέοντα. ὁ δὲ ἔφη, μὴ εἶναι ἐξὸν
αὐτῷ, ἐπειδὴ πεπληρώκει τὰ κυνηγέσια. 3. τότε
ἔδοξεν αὐτοῖς ὁμοθυμαδὸν ἐπιβοῆσαι, ὥστε τὸν
Πολύκαρπον ζῶντα κατακαῦσαι. ἔδει γὰρ τὸ τῆς
φανερωθείσης αὐτῷ ἐπὶ τοῦ προσκεφαλαίου ὀπ-
τασίας πληρωθῆναι, ὅτε ἰδὼν αὐτὸ καιόμενον
προσευχόμενος εἶπεν ἐπιστραφεὶς τοῖς σὺν αὐτῷ
πιστοῖς προφητικῶς· Δεῖ με ζῶντα καῆναι.

XIII

1. Ταῦτα οὖν μετὰ τοσούτου τάχους ἐγένετο,
θᾶττον ἢ ἐλέγετο, τῶν ὄχλων παραχρῆμα συνα-
γόντων ἔκ τε τῶν ἐργαστηρίων καὶ βαλανείων
ξύλα καὶ φρύγανα, μάλιστα Ἰουδαίων προθύμως,
ὡς ἔθος αὐτοῖς, εἰς ταῦτα ὑπουργούντων. 2. ὅτε
δὲ ἡ πυρκαϊὰ ἡτοιμάσθη, ἀποθέμενος ἑαυτῷ πάντα
τὰ ἱμάτια καὶ λύσας τὴν ζώνην ἐπειρᾶτο καὶ
ὑπολύειν ἑαυτόν, μὴ πρότερον τοῦτο ποιῶν διὰ τὸ
ἀεὶ ἕκαστον τῶν πιστῶν σπουδάζειν, ὅστις τάχιον
τοῦ χρωτὸς αὐτοῦ ἅψηται· παντὶ γὰρ καλῷ
ἀγαθῆς ἕνεκεν πολιτείας καὶ πρὸ τῆς μαρτυρίας

times : "Polycarp has confessed that he is a Christian."
2. When this had been said by the herald, all the
multitude of heathen and Jews living in Smyrna The anger
of the Jews
cried out with uncontrollable wrath and a loud
shout : "This is the teacher of Asia, the father of
the Christians, the destroyer of our Gods, who teaches
many neither to offer sacrifice nor to worship." And
when they said this, they cried out and asked Philip
the Asiarch to let loose a lion on Polycarp. But he
said he could not legally do this, since he had closed
the Sports.[1] 3. Then they found it good to cry out
with one mind that he should burn Polycarp alive, for
the vision which had appeared to him on his pillow
must be fulfilled, when he saw it burning, while he
was praying, and he turned and said prophetically
to those of the faithful who were with him, " I must
be burnt alive."

XIII

1. THESE things then happened with so great speed, The pre-
parations
for burning
him
quicker than it takes to tell, and the crowd came to-
gether immediately, and prepared wood and faggots
from the work-shops and baths and the Jews were
extremely zealous, as is their custom, in assisting
at this. 2. Now when the fire was ready he put off
all his clothes, and loosened his girdle and tried also
to take off his shoes, though he did not do this before,
because each of the faithful was always zealous, which
of them might the more quickly touch his flesh. For
he had been treated with all respect because of his

---

[1] Literally 'hunting,' the Latin 'venatio.'

ἐκεκόσμητο. 3. εὐθέως οὖν αὐτῷ περιετίθετο
τὰ πρὸς τὴν πυρὰν ἡρμοσμένα ὄργανα. μελλόντων
δὲ αὐτῶν καὶ προσηλοῦν, εἶπεν· Ἄφετέ με οὕτως·
ὁ γὰρ δοὺς ὑπομεῖναι τὸ πῦρ δώσει χωρὶς τῆς
ὑμετέρας ἐκ τῶν ἥλων ἀσφαλείας ἄσκυλτον
ἐπιμεῖναι τῇ πυρᾷ.

XIV

1. Οἱ δὲ οὐ καθήλωσαν μέν, προσέδησαν δὲ
αὐτόν. ὁ δὲ ὀπίσω τὰς χεῖρας ποιήσας καὶ
προσδεθείς, ὥσπερ κριὸς ἐπίσημος ἐκ μεγάλου
ποιμνίου εἰς προσφοράν, ὁλοκαύτωμα δεκτὸν τῷ
θεῷ ἡτοιμασμένον, ἀναβλέψας εἰς τὸν οὐρανὸν
εἶπεν· Κύριε ὁ θεὸς ὁ παντοκράτωρ, ὁ τοῦ ἀγαπητοῦ καὶ εὐλογητοῦ παιδός σου Ἰησοῦ Χριστοῦ
πατήρ, δι' οὗ τὴν περὶ σοῦ ἐπίγνωσιν εἰλήφαμεν,
ὁ θεὸς ἀγγέλων καὶ δυνάμεων καὶ πάσης τῆς
κτίσεως παντός τε τοῦ γένους τῶν δικαίων, οἳ
ζῶσιν ἐνώπιόν σου· 2. εὐλογῶ σε, ὅτι ἠξίωσάς με
τῆς ἡμέρας καὶ ὥρας ταύτης, τοῦ λαβεῖν με μέρος
ἐν ἀριθμῷ τῶν μαρτύρων ἐν τῷ ποτηρίῳ τοῦ

Joh. 5, 29

Χριστοῦ σου[1] εἰς ἀνάστασιν ζωῆς αἰωνίου ψυχῆς
τε καὶ σώματος ἐν ἀφθαρσίᾳ πνεύματος ἁγίου·
ἐν οἷς προσδεχθείην ἐνώπιόν σου σήμερον ἐν
θυσίᾳ πίονι καὶ προσδεκτῇ, καθὼς προητοίμασας

---

[1] σου mbvs, om. E p.

noble life,[1] even before his martyrdom. 3. Immediately therefore, he was fastened to the instruments which had been prepared for the fire, but when they were going to nail him as well he said: " Leave me thus, for He who gives me power to endure the fire, will grant me to remain in the flames unmoved even without the security you will give by the nails."

XIV

1. So they did not nail him, but bound him, and he put his hands behind him and was bound, as a noble ram out of a great flock, for an oblation, a whole burnt offering made ready and acceptable to God ; and he looked up to heaven and said: " O Lord God Almighty, Father of thy beloved and blessed Child,[2] Jesus Christ, through Whom we have received full knowledge of thee, the God of Angels and powers, and of all creation, and of the whole family of the righteous, who live before thee ! 2. I bless thee, that Thou hast granted me this day and hour, that I may share, among the number of the martyrs, in the cup of thy Christ, for the Resurrection to everlasting life, both of soul and body in the immortality of the Holy Spirit. And may I, to-day, be received among them before Thee, as a rich and acceptable sacrifice,

His last prayers

---

[1] Lit. "citizenship," but it is used in a special sense of Christian life.

[2] This use of παῖς as applied to Jesus is rare, and usually found in prayers ; cf. *Ep. ad Diogn.* viii. 9. 11, ix. 1, Didache 9, 2, I Clement 59, 2 (the " Prayer "), and Acts 3, 13. 26. 4, 27. 30. Here it is clearly " Child ": in Acts it may mean " Servant " with reference to Is. 53, etc.

331

καὶ προεφανέρωσας καὶ ἐπλήρωσας, ὁ ἀψευδὴς
καὶ ἀληθινὸς θεός. 3. διὰ τοῦτο καὶ περὶ πάντων
σὲ αἰνῶ, σὲ εὐλογῶ, σὲ δοξάζω διὰ τοῦ αἰωνίου
καὶ ἐπουρανίου ἀρχιερέως Ἰησοῦ Χριστοῦ, ἀγαπητοῦ σου παιδός, δι' οὗ σοὶ σὺν αὐτῷ καὶ πνεύματι ἁγίῳ δόξα καὶ νῦν καὶ εἰς τοὺς μέλλοντας
αἰῶνας. ἀμήν.

XV

1. Ἀναπέμψαντος δὲ αὐτοῦ τὸ ἀμὴν καὶ πλη-
ρώσαντος τὴν εὐχήν, οἱ τοῦ πυρὸς ἄνθρωποι
ἐξῆψαν τὸ πῦρ. μεγάλης δὲ ἐκλαμψάσης φλογός,
θαῦμα εἴδομεν, οἷς ἰδεῖν ἐδόθη· οἳ καὶ ἐτηρήθημεν
εἰς τὸ ἀναγγεῖλαι τοῖς λοιποῖς τὰ γενόμενα. 2. τὸ
γὰρ πῦρ καμάρας εἶδος ποιῆσαν, ὥσπερ ὀθόνη
πλοίου ὑπὸ πνεύματος πληρουμένη, κύκλῳ περιε-
τείχισεν τὸ σῶμα τοῦ μάρτυρος· καὶ ἦν μέσον
οὐχ ὡς σὰρξ καιομένη, ἀλλ' ὡς ἄρτος ὀπτώμενος ἢ
ὡς χρυσὸς καὶ ἄργυρος ἐν καμίνῳ πυρούμενος.
καὶ γὰρ εὐωδίας τοσαύτης ἀντελαβόμεθα, ὡς
λιβανωτοῦ πνέοντος ἢ ἄλλου τινὸς τῶν τιμίων
ἀρωμάτων·

XVI

1. Πέρας γοῦν ἰδόντες οἱ ἄνομοι μὴ δυνάμενον
αὐτοῦ τὸ σῶμα ὑπὸ τοῦ πυρὸς δαπανηθῆναι,
ἐκέλευσαν προσελθόντα αὐτῷ κομφέκτορα παρα-
βῦσαι ξιφίδιον. καὶ τοῦτο ποιήσαντος, ἐξῆλθεν

as Thou, the God who lies not and is truth, hast prepared beforehand, and shown forth, and fulfilled. 3. For this reason I also praise Thee for all things, I bless Thee, I glorify Thee through the everlasting and heavenly high Priest, Jesus Christ, thy beloved Child, through whom be glory to Thee with him and the Holy Spirit, both now and for the ages that are to come, Amen."

XV

1. Now when he had uttered his Amen and finished his prayer, the men in charge of the fire lit it, and a great flame blazed up and we, to whom it was given to see, saw a marvel. And we have been preserved to report to others what befell. 2. For the fire made the likeness of a room, like the sail of a vessel filled with wind, and surrounded the body of the martyr as with a wall, and he was within it not as burning flesh, but as bread that is being baked, or as gold and silver being refined in a furnace. And we perceived such a fragrant smell as the scent of incense or other costly spices.

The fire is lighted

XVI

1. At length the lawless men, seeing that his body could not be consumed by the fire, commanded an executioner to go up and stab him with a dagger, and when he did this, there came out a dove,[1] and

Polycarp's death

---

[1] This no doubt points to the belief that the spirit appears at death in the form of a bird. Cf. Prudentius *Peristeph. Hymn.* iii. 33 (other references are also given by Lightfoot).

περιστερὰ καὶ[1] πλῆθος αἵματος, ὥστε κατασβέσαι
τὸ πῦρ καὶ θαυμάσαι πάντα τὸν ὄχλον, εἰ τοσαύτη
τις διαφορὰ μεταξὺ τῶν τε ἀπίστων καὶ τῶν
ἐκλεκτῶν· 2. ὧν εἷς καὶ οὗτος γεγόνει ὁ θαυμασιώτατος μάρτυς Πολύκαρπος, ἐν τοῖς καθ᾿ ἡμᾶς
χρόνοις διδάσκαλος ἀποστολικὸς καὶ προφητικὸς
γενόμενος, ἐπίσκοπος τῆς ἐν Σμύρνῃ καθολικῆς[2]
ἐκκλησίας. πᾶν γὰρ ῥῆμα, ὃ ἀφῆκεν ἐκ τοῦ
στόματος αὐτοῦ, καὶ ἐτελειώθη καὶ τελειωθήσεται.

XVII

1. Ὁ δὲ ἀντίζηλος καὶ βάσκανος καὶ πονηρός,
ὁ ἀντικείμενος τῷ γένει τῶν δικαίων, ἰδὼν τό τε
μέγεθος αὐτοῦ τῆς μαρτυρίας καὶ τὴν ἀπ᾿ ἀρχῆς
ἀνεπίληπτον πολιτείαν, ἐστεφανωμένον τε τὸν τῆς
ἀφθαρσίας στέφανον καὶ βραβεῖον ἀναντίρρητον
ἀπενηνεγμένον, ἐπετήδευσεν, ὡς μηδὲ τὸ σωμάτιον
αὐτοῦ ὑφ᾿ ἡμῶν ληφθῆναι, καίπερ πολλῶν ἐπι-
θυμούντων τοῦτο ποιῆσαι καὶ κοινωνῆσαι τῷ ἁγίῳ
αὐτοῦ σαρκίῳ. 2. ὑπέβαλεν γοῦν Νικήτην τὸν
τοῦ Ἡρώδου πατέρα, ἀδελφὸν δὲ Ἄλκης,[3] ἐντυχεῖν
τῷ ἄρχοντι, ὥστε μὴ δοῦναι αὐτοῦ τὸ σῶμα· μή,
φησίν, ἀφέντες τὸν ἐσταυρωμένον τοῦτον ἄρξωνται
σέβεσθαι. καὶ ταῦτα εἶπον ὑποβαλλόντων καὶ
ἐνισχυόντων τῶν Ἰουδαίων, οἳ καὶ ἐτήρησαν,
μελλόντων ἡμῶν ἐκ τοῦ πυρὸς αὐτὸν λαμβάνειν·
ἀγνοοῦντες, ὅτι οὔτε τὸν Χριστόν ποτε καταλιπεῖν
δυνησόμεθα, τὸν ὑπὲρ τῆς τοῦ παντὸς κόσμου

---

[1] περιστερὰ καὶ om. E, Wordsworth emends to περὶ στύρακα
(round the sword-haft).

[2] καθολικῆς E bs, ἁγίας (holy) m(L).   [3] Δάλκης E.

much blood, so that the fire was quenched and all
the crowd marvelled that there was such a difference
between the unbelievers and the elect. 2. And of
the elect was he indeed one, the wonderful martyr,
Polycarp, who in our days was an apostolic and
prophetic teacher, bishop of the Catholic[1] Church in
Smyrna. For every word which he uttered from his
mouth both was fulfilled and will be fulfilled.

XVII

1. But the jealous and envious evil one who resists
the family of the righteous, when he saw the greatness
of his martyrdom, and his blameless career from the
beginning, and that he was crowned with the crown
of immortality, and had carried off the unspeakable
prize, took care that not even his poor body should
be taken away by us, though many desired to do
this, and to have fellowship with his holy flesh.
2. Therefore he put forward Niketas, the father of
Herod, and the brother of Alce, to ask the Governor
not to give his body, "Lest," he said, "they leave the
crucified one and begin to worship this man." And
they said this owing to the suggestions and pressure
of the Jews, who also watched when we were going
to take it from the fire, for they do not know that
we shall not ever be able either to abandon Christ,
who suffered for the salvation of those who are being

The treatment of the corpse

---

[1] If the reading "Catholic" be right, this and the instance
on p. 322 are the earliest clear examples of this use of the
word (but cf. Ignatius, *Symrn.* viii.).

335

τῶν σωζομένων σωτηρίας παθόντα ἄμωμον ὑπὲρ
ἁμαρτωλῶν, οὔτε ἕτερόν τινα σέβεσθαι. 3. τοῦτον
μὲν γὰρ υἱὸν ὄντα τοῦ θεοῦ προσκυνοῦμεν, τοὺς δὲ
μάρτυρας ὡς μαθητὰς καὶ μιμητὰς τοῦ κυρίου
ἀγαπῶμεν ἀξίως ἕνεκα εὐνοίας ἀνυπερβλήτου τῆς
εἰς τὸν ἴδιον βασιλέα καὶ διδάσκαλον· ὧν γένοιτο
καὶ ἡμᾶς κοινωνούς τε καὶ συμμαθητὰς γενέσθαι.

XVIII

1. Ἰδὼν οὖν ὁ κεντυρίων τὴν τῶν Ἰουδαίων
γενομένην φιλονεικίαν, θεὶς αὐτὸν ἐν μέσῳ, ὡς
ἔθος αὐτοῖς, ἔκαυσεν. 2. οὕτως τε ἡμεῖς ὕστερον
ἀνελόμενοι τὰ τιμιώτερα λίθων πολυτελῶν καὶ
δοκιμώτερα ὑπὲρ χρυσίον ὀστᾶ αὐτοῦ ἀπεθέμεθα,
ὅπου καὶ ἀκόλουθον ἦν. 3. ἔνθα ὡς δυνατὸν ἡμῖν
συναγομένοις ἐν ἀγαλλιάσει καὶ χαρᾷ παρέξει ὁ
κύριος ἐπιτελεῖν τὴν τοῦ μαρτυρίου αὐτοῦ ἡμέραν
γενέθλιον, εἴς τε τὴν τῶν προηθληκότων μνήμην
καὶ τῶν μελλόντων ἄσκησίν τε καὶ ἑτοιμασίαν.

XIX

1. Τοιαῦτα τὰ κατὰ τὸν μακάριον Πολύκαρπον,
ὃς σὺν τοῖς ἀπὸ Φιλαδελφίας δωδέκατος ἐν Σμύρνῃ
μαρτυρήσας, μόνος ὑπὸ πάντων μᾶλλον μνημο-
νεύεται, ὥστε καὶ ὑπὸ τῶν ἐθνῶν ἐν παντὶ τόπῳ
λαλεῖσθαι· οὐ μόνον διδάσκαλος γενόμενος ἐπίσημος, ἀλλὰ καὶ μάρτυς ἔξοχος, οὗ τὸ μαρτύριον

saved in the whole world, the innocent for sinners,
or to worship any other. 3. For him we worship as
the Son of God, but the martyrs we love as disciples
and imitators of the Lord ; and rightly, because of
their unsurpassable affection toward their own King
and Teacher. God grant that we too may be their
companions and fellow-disciples.

XVIII

1. When therefore the centurion saw the conten- The
tiousness caused by the Jews, he put the body in the Christians
midst, as was their custom, and burnt it. 2. Thus ashes
we, at last, took up his bones, more precious than
precious stones, and finer than gold, and put them
where it was meet. 3. There the Lord will permit us
to come together according to our power in gladness
and joy, and celebrate the birthday of his martyrdom,
both in memory of those who have already contested,[1]
and for the practice and training of those whose fate
it shall be.

XIX

1. Such was the lot of the blessed Polycarp, who Conclusion
though he was, together with those from Philadelphia, the twelfth martyr in Smyrna, is alone
especially remembered by all, so that he is spoken of
in every place, even by the heathen. He was not
only a famous teacher, but also a notable martyr,

---

[1] This is almost a technical term for martyrdom, cf.
Ignatius's epistle to Polycarp 1, 3.

πάντες ἐπιθυμοῦσιν μιμεῖσθαι κατὰ τὸ εὐαγγέλιον
Χριστοῦ γενόμενον. 2. διὰ τῆς ὑπομονῆς κατα-
γωνισάμενος τὸν ἄδικον ἄρχοντα καὶ οὕτως τὸν
τῆς ἀφθαρσίας στέφανον ἀπολαβών, σὺν τοῖς
ἀποστόλοις καὶ πᾶσιν δικαίοις ἀγαλλιώμενος
δοξάζει τὸν θεὸν καὶ πατέρα παντοκράτορα καὶ
εὐλογεῖ τὸν κύριον ἡμῶν[1] Ἰησοῦν Χριστόν, τὸν
σωτῆρα τῶν ψυχῶν ἡμῶν καὶ κυβερνήτην τῶν
σωμάτων ἡμῶν καὶ ποιμένα τῆς κατὰ τὴν οἰκουμένην καθολικῆς ἐκκλησίας.

XX

1. Ὑμεῖς μὲν οὖν ἠξιώσατε διὰ πλειόνων δηλωθῆναι ὑμῖν τὰ γενόμενα, ἡμεῖς δὲ κατὰ τὸ παρὸν
ἐπὶ κεφαλαίῳ μεμηνύκαμεν διὰ τοῦ ἀδελφοῦ ἡμῶν
Μαρκίωνος.[2] μαθόντες οὖν ταῦτα καὶ τοῖς ἐπέ-
κεινα ἀδελφοῖς τὴν ἐπιστολὴν διαπέμψασθε, ἵνα
καὶ ἐκεῖνοι δοξάζωσιν τὸν κύριον τὸν ἐκλογὰς
ποιοῦντα ἀπὸ[3] τῶν ἰδίων δούλων.
2. Τῷ δὲ δυναμένῳ πάντας ἡμᾶς εἰσαγαγεῖν ἐν
τῇ αὐτοῦ χάριτι καὶ δωρεᾷ εἰς τὴν ἐπουράνιον[4]
αὐτοῦ βασιλείαν διὰ τοῦ μονογενοῦς[5] παιδὸς αὐτοῦ
Ἰησοῦ Χριστοῦ, δόξα,[6] τιμή, κράτος, μεγαλωσύνη εἰς τοὺς αἰῶνας. προσαγορεύετε πάντας

---

[1] ἡμῶν bpvs, om. m.

[2] Μαρκίωνος m, Μάρκου bps (v ends with chap. xix.), Mar-
cianum L. Lightfoot prefers Μαρκιανοῦ

[3] ποιοῦντα ἀπό bps, ποιούμενον m.

[4] ἐπουράνιον m, αἰώνιον bps.

[5] τοῦ μονογενοῦς αὐτοῦ παιδός m, παιδὸς αὐτοῦ τοῦ μονογενοῦς
b, τοῦ παιδὸς αὐτοῦ τοῦ μονογενοῦς ps.

[6] δόξα m, ᾧ ἡ δόξα bps.

whose martyrdom all desire to imitate, for it followed the Gospel of Christ. 2. By his endurance he overcame the unrighteous ruler, and thus gained the crown of immortality, and he is glorifying God and the Almighty Father, rejoicing with the Apostles and all the righteous, and he is blessing our Lord Jesus Christ, the Saviour of our souls, and Governor of our bodies, and the Shepherd of the Catholic Church throughout the world.

XX

1. You, indeed, asked that the events should be explained to you at length, but we have for the present explained them in summary by our brother Marcion[1]; therefore when you have heard these things, send the letter to the brethren further on, that they also may glorify the Lord, who takes his chosen ones from his own servants.

2. And to him who is able to bring us all in his grace and bounty, to his heavenly kingdom, by his only begotten Child, Jesus Christ, be glory, honour, might, and majesty for ever. Greet all the saints. Those who are with us, and

---

[1] Not of course to be identified with the famous heretic. If Marcianus be the right text, it is noteworthy that Irenaeus sent his treatise on the "The Apostolic Preaching" to a certain Marcianus. But this was probably forty years later than Polycarp's death.

τοὺς ἁγίους. ὑμᾶς οἱ σὺν ἡμῖν προσαγορεύουσιν
καὶ Εὐάρεστος ὁ γράψας πανοικεί.[1]

XXI

1. Μαρτυρεῖ δὲ ὁ μακάριος Πολύκαρπος μηνὸς
Ξανθικοῦ[2] δευτέρᾳ ἱσταμένου, πρὸ ἑπτὰ καλανδῶν
Μαρτίων, σαββάτῳ μεγάλῳ, ὥρᾳ ὀγδόῃ. συνε-
λήφθη δὲ ὑπὸ Ἡρώδου ἐπὶ ἀρχιερέως Φιλίππου
Τραλλιανοῦ, ἀνθυπατεύοντος Στατίου Κοδράτου,
βασιλεύοντος δὲ εἰς τοὺς αἰῶνας Ἰησοῦ Χριστοῦ·
ᾧ ἡ δόξα, τιμή, μεγαλωσύνη, θρόνος αἰώνιος ἀπὸ
γενεᾶς εἰς γενεάν. ἀμήν.

XXII

1. Ἐρρῶσθαι ὑμᾶς εὐχόμεθα, ἀδελφοί, στοι-
χοῦντας τῷ κατὰ τὸ εὐαγγέλιον λόγῳ Ἰησοῦ
Χριστοῦ, μεθ᾽ οὗ δόξα τῷ θεῷ καὶ πατρὶ καὶ ἁγίῳ
πνεύματι, ἐπὶ σωτηρίᾳ τῇ τῶν ἁγίων ἐκλεκτῶν,
καθὼς ἐμαρτύρησεν ὁ μακάριος Πολύκαρπος, οὗ
γένοιτο ἐν τῇ βασιλείᾳ Ἰησοῦ Χριστοῦ πρὸς τὰ
ἴχνη εὑρεθῆναι ἡμᾶς.[3]
2. Ταῦτα μετεγράψατο μὲν Γάϊος ἐκ τῶν
Εἰρηναίου, μαθητοῦ τοῦ Πολυκάρπου, ὃς καὶ
συνεπολιτεύσατο τῷ Εἰρηναίῳ. ἐγὼ δὲ Σωκράτης
ἐν Κορίνθῳ ἐκ τῶν Γαΐου ἀντιγράφων ἔγραψα.
ἡ χάρις μετὰ πάντων.

[1] This is really the end of the book. What follows is a
series of notes, which have been taken into the text.

[2] The more correct spelling, according to inscriptions, is
Ξανδικοῦ.

[3] The whole of this paragraph is omitted by L m.

Evarestus, who wrote the letter, with his whole house, greet you.

XXI

1. Now the blessed Polycarp was martyred on the second day of the first half of the month of Xanthicus, the seventh day before the kalends of March,[1] a great sabbath, at the eighth hour. And he was arrested by Herod, when Philip of Tralles was High Priest, when Statius Quadratus was Pro-Consul, but Jesus Christ was reigning[2] for ever, to whom be glory, honour, majesty and an eternal throne, from generation to generation, Amen.

The date

XXII.

1. WE bid you God-speed, brethren, who walk according to the Gospel, in the word of Jesus Christ (with whom be glory to God and the Father and the Holy Spirit), for the salvation of the Holy Elect, even as the blessed Polycarp suffered martyrdom, in whose footsteps may it be granted us to be found in the Kingdom of Jesus Christ.

Notes by a later scribe

2. Gaius copied this from the writing of Irenaeus, a disciple of Polycarp, and he lived with Irenaeus, and I, Socrates, wrote it out in Corinth, from the copies of Gaius. Grace be with you all. 3. And I,

---

[1] *I.e.* Feb. 23.
[2] This phrase is pointedly inserted instead of a reference to the reigning Emperor.

THE APOSTOLIC FATHERS

3. Ἐγὼ δὲ πάλιν Πιόνιος ἐκ τοῦ προγεγραμμένου
ἔγραψα ἀναζητήσας αὐτά, κατὰ ἀποκάλυψιν
φανερώσαντός μοι τοῦ μακαρίου Πολυκάρπου,
καθὼς δηλώσω ἐν τῷ καθεξῆς, συναγαγὼν αὐτὰ
ἤδη σχεδὸν ἐκ τοῦ χρόνου κεκμηκότα, ἵνα κἀμὲ
συναγάγῃ ὁ κύριος Ἰησοῦς Χριστὸς μετὰ τῶν
ἐκλεκτῶν αὐτοῦ εἰς τὴν οὐράνιον βασιλείαν αὐτοῦ,
ᾧ ἡ δόξα σὺν τῷ πατρὶ καὶ ἁγίῳ πνεύματι εἰς
τοὺς αἰῶνας τῶν αἰώνων. ἀμήν.[1]

EPILOGUS ALIUS

E CODICE MOSQUENSI DESCRIPTUS.

2. Ταῦτα μετεγράψατο μὲν Γάϊος ἐκ τῶν
Εἰρηναίου συγγραμμάτων, ὃς καὶ συνεπολιτεύσατο
τῷ Εἰρηναίῳ, μαθητῇ γεγονότι τοῦ ἁγίου Πολυκάρπου.   3. οὗτος γὰρ ὁ Εἰρηναῖος, κατὰ τὸν
καιρὸν τοῦ μαρτυρίου τοῦ ἐπισκόπου Πολυκάρπου
γενόμενος ἐν Ῥώμῃ, πολλοὺς ἐδίδαξεν· οὗ καὶ
πολλὰ συγγράμματα κάλλιστα καὶ ὀρθότατα
φέρεται, ἐν οἷς μέμνηται Πολυκάρπου, ὅτι παρ'
αὐτοῦ ἔμαθεν, ἱκανῶς τε πᾶσαν αἵρεσιν ἤλεγξεν καὶ

---

[1] Instead of the two paragraphs ταῦτα μετεγράψατο — ἀμήν
m has the alternative conclusion given below.

342

again, Pionius, wrote it out from the former writings, after searching for it, because the blessed Polycarp showed it me in a vision, as I will explain in what follows,[1] and I gathered it together when it was almost worn out by age, that the Lord Jesus Christ may also gather me together with his elect into his heavenly kingdom, to whom be glory with the Father and the Holy Spirit, for ever and ever, Amen.

ANOTHER CONCLUSION FROM THE MOSCOW MANUSCRIPT.

2. THIS account Gaius copied from the writings of Irenaeus, and he also had lived with Irenaeus, who was a disciple of the holy Polycarp. 3. For this Irenaeus, at the time of the martydom of the bishop Polycarp was in Rome, and taught many, and many most excellent and correct writings are extant, in which he mentions Polycarp,[2] saying that he had been his pupil, and he ably refuted every heresy, and

---

[1] No explanation is given: probably because the "Pionian" text was part of a larger "Acts of Polycarp." Either these Acts have entirely disappeared except for this letter of the church of Smyrna, or a fragment preserved in p may perhaps belong to them.

[2] Irenaeus *Haer*. iii. 3. 4, *Ep. ad Florinum* (in Eusebius *H.E.* v. 20) and *Ep. ad Victorem* (in Eusebius *H.E.* v. 24). The story of Marcion is in *Haer*. iii. 3. 4.

THE APOSTOLIC FATHERS

τὸν ἐκκλησιαστικὸν κανόνα καὶ καθολικόν, ὡς παρέλαβεν παρὰ τοῦ ἁγίου, καὶ παρέδωκεν. 4. λέγει δὲ καὶ τοῦτο· ὅτι συναντήσαντός ποτε τῷ ἁγίῳ Πολυκάρπῳ Μαρκίωνος, ἀφ' οὗ οἱ λεγόμενοι Μαρκιωνισταί, καὶ εἰπόντος· Ἐπιγίνωσκε ἡμᾶς, Πολύκαρπε, εἶπεν αὐτὸς τῷ Μαρκίωνι· Ἐπιγινώσκω, ἐπιγινώσκω τὸν πρωτότοκον τοῦ σατανᾶ. 5. καὶ τοῦτο δὲ φέρεται ἐν τοῖς τοῦ Εἰρηναίου συγγράμμασιν, ὅτι ᾗ ἡμέρᾳ καὶ ὥρᾳ ἐν Σμύρνῃ ἐμαρτύρησεν ὁ Πολύκαρπος, ἤκουσεν φωνὴν ἐν τῇ Ῥωμαίων πόλει ὑπάρχων ὁ Εἰρηναῖος ὡς σάλπιγγος λεγούσης· Πολύκαρπος ἐμαρτύρησεν.

6. Ἐκ τούτων οὖν, ὡς προλέλεκται, τῶν τοῦ Εἰρηναίου συγγραμμάτων Γάϊος μετεγράψατο, ἐκ δὲ τῶν Γαΐου ἀντιγράφων Ἰσοκράτης ἐν Κορίνθῳ. ἐγὼ δὲ πάλιν Πιόνιος ἐκ τῶν Ἰσοκράτους ἀντιγράφων ἔγραψα κατὰ ἀποκάλυψιν τοῦ ἁγίου Πολυκάρπου ζητήσας αὐτά, συναγαγὼν αὐτὰ ἤδη σχεδὸν ἐκ τοῦ χρόνου κεκμηκότα, ἵνα κἀμὲ συναγάγῃ ὁ κύριος Ἰησοῦς Χριστὸς μετὰ τῶν ἐκλεκτῶν αὐτοῦ εἰς τὴν ἐπουράνιον αὐτοῦ βασιλείαν· ᾧ ἡ δόξα σὺν τῷ πατρὶ καὶ τῷ υἱῷ καὶ τῷ ἁγίῳ πνεύματι εἰς τοὺς αἰῶνας τῶν αἰώνων. ἀμήν.

he also handed on the ecclesiastical and catholic rule, as he had received it from the saint. 4. And he also says this that once Marcion,[1] from whom come the so-called Marcionites, met the holy Polycarp and said: "Recognise us, Polycarp," and he said to Marcion, "I do recognise you, I recognise the first-born of Satan." 5. And this is also recorded in the writings of Irenaeus, that at the day and hour when Polycarp suffered in Smyrna Irenaeus, who was in the city of Rome, heard a voice like a trumpet saying: "Polycarp has suffered martyrdom."

6. From these papers of Irenaeus, then, as was stated above, Gaius made a copy, and Isocrates used in Corinth the copy of Gaius. And again I, Pionius, wrote from the copies of Isocrates, according to the revelation of the holy Polycarp, after searching for them, and gathering them together when they were almost worn out from age, that the Lord Jesus Christ may also gather me into his Heavenly Kingdom together with his Elect. To him be glory, with the Father and the Son and the Holy Spirit, for ever and ever, Amen.

---

[1] Marcion was the most famous heretic of the second century. He was a native of Pontus and afterwards came to Rome. The main points of his teaching were the rejection of the Old Testament and a distinction between the Supreme God of goodness and an inferior God of justice, who was the Creator, and the God of the Jews. He regarded Christ as the messenger of the Supreme God.

THE EPISTLE TO DIOGNETUS

THE EPISTLE TO DIOGNETUS

THE epistle to Diognetus is an anonymous writing of uncertain date. The Diognetus to whom it is addressed is unknown, though some scholars have sought to identify him with a Diognetus who was a teacher of Marcus Aurelius. Its claim to be included among the apostolic fathers rests on custom rather than right, for it is probably later than any of the other writings in this group, and if it were judged by the character of its contents would more probably be placed among the works of the Apologists.

Like most early apologies for Christianity it begins by expounding the foolishness of the worship of idols, and the inadequacy of the Jewish religion and then proceeds to give a short sketch of Christian belief, a panegyric on Christian character and a description of the benefit which it offers to converts. In this respect it resembles the apology of Aristides, and somewhat less closely those of Justin and Tatian, and the suggestion has been made that it may have been written by Aristides. Its style is, however, rhetorical in the extreme and it may be doubted whether it was not an academic treatise or possibly the exercise of some young theologian rather than an actual apology sent to a living person. The general impression made by the document is unfavourable to any theory of an early date and quite decisive against the tradition which seems to have been preserved in the lost MS. in which the epistle was found, attributing it to Justin Martyr. Harnack thinks that it more probably belongs to the

third than to the second century, but early tradition does not mention the epistle and there is nothing in the internal evidence to justify any certainty of opinion.

The concluding chapters (xi–xii) have clearly no connection with the preceding ones, and it is generally conceded that they belong to a different document, probably an Epiphany homily, though possibly, as Otto thought, an Easter homily. Bonwetsch has shown very strong reasons for thinking that Hippolytus was the author. (*Nachrichten d. Gesellschaft d. Wissenschaften zu Göttingen*, 1902.)

The best authority for the text is the third edition of Otto's *Corpus Apologeticum*, vol. 3, published in 1879, as the unique MS. of the epistle in the library at Strasburg was twice collated for Otto's edition but was destroyed by fire in 1870. This MS., probably written in the thirteenth or fourteenth century, was formerly the property of Reuchlin, passed about 1560 to the Alsatian monastery of Maursmunster, and between 1793 and 1795 came to Strasburg. It was collated for the first edition of Otto by Cunitz and for the third edition by Reuss. Earlier copies were made by Stephanus in 1586 (now preserved in Leiden, Cod. Voss. Gr. 30) and about 1590 by Beurer and (a collation of this copy which is no longer extant was published by Stephanus at the end of his edition of 1592). A third copy was made by Hausius about 1580 for Martin Crucius and is now preserved in Tübigen (Cod. Misc. M.b. 17). The fullest account of these MSS. and the proof that none of them are more than copies of the Strasburg MS. is given in O. von Gebhardt's edition of the Apostolic Fathers, vol. i., part 2, published in 1878.

ΕΠΙΣΤΟΛΗ ΠΡΟΣ ΔΙΟΓΝΗΤΟΝ

I

Ἐπειδὴ ὁρῶ, κράτιστε Διόγνητε, ὑπερεσπουδακότα σε τὴν θεοσέβειαν τῶν Χριστιανῶν μαθεῖν καὶ πάνυ σαφῶς καὶ ἐπιμελῶς πυνθανόμενον περὶ αὐτῶν, τίνι τε θεῷ πεποιθότες καὶ πῶς θρησκεύοντες αὐτὸν τόν τε κόσμον ὑπερορῶσι πάντες καὶ θανάτου καταφρονοῦσι καὶ οὔτε τοὺς νομιζομένους ὑπὸ τῶν Ἑλλήνων θεοὺς λογίζονται οὔτε τὴν Ἰουδαίων δεισιδαιμονίαν φυλάσσουσι, καὶ τίνα τὴν φιλοστοργίαν ἔχουσι πρὸς ἀλλήλους, καὶ τί δή ποτε καινὸν τοῦτο γένος ἢ ἐπιτήδευμα εἰσῆλθεν εἰς τὸν βίον νῦν καὶ οὐ πρότερον· ἀποδέχομαί γε τῆς προθυμίας σε ταύτης καὶ παρὰ τοῦ θεοῦ, τοῦ καὶ τὸ λέγειν καὶ τὸ ἀκούειν ἡμῖν χορηγοῦντος, αἰτοῦμαι δοθῆναι ἐμοὶ μὲν εἰπεῖν οὕτως, ὡς μάλιστα ἂν ἀκούσαντά σε βελτίω γενέσθαι, σοί τε οὕτως ἀκοῦσαι, ὡς μὴ λυπηθῆναι τὸν εἰπόντα.

II

1. Ἄγε δή, καθάρας σεαυτὸν ἀπὸ πάντων τῶν προκατεχόντων σου τὴν διάνοιαν λογισμῶν καὶ τὴν ἀπατῶσάν σε συνήθειαν ἀποσκευασάμενος καὶ

350

THE EPISTLE TO DIOGNETUS

I

Intro-
duction

SINCE I perceive, most excellent Diognetus, that you are exceedingly zealous to learn the religion of the Christians and are asking very clear and careful questions concerning them, both who is the God in whom they believe, and how they worship him, so that all disregard the world and despise death, and do not reckon as Gods those who are considered to be so by the Greeks, nor keep the superstition of the Jews, and what is the love which they have for one another, and why this new race or practice has come to life at this time, and not formerly ; I indeed welcome this zeal in you, and I ask from God who bestows on us the power both of speaking and of hearing, that it may be granted to me so to speak that you may benefit so much as possible by your hearing, and to you so to hear that I may not be made sorry for my speech.

II

Discussion
of the Gods
of the
heathen

1. COME then, clear yourself of all the prejudice which occupies your mind, and throw aside the custom which deceives you, and become as it were

351

γενόμενος ὥσπερ ἐξ ἀρχῆς καινὸς ἄνθρωπος, ὡς ἂν
καὶ λόγου καινοῦ, καθάπερ καὶ αὐτὸς ὡμολόγησας,
ἀκροατὴς ἐσόμενος· ἴδε μὴ μόνον τοῖς ὀφθαλμοῖς,
ἀλλὰ καὶ τῇ φρονήσει, τίνος ὑποστάσεως ἢ τίνος
εἴδους τυγχάνουσιν, οὓς ἐρεῖτε καὶ νομίζετε θεούς.
2. οὐχ ὁ μέν τις λίθος ἐστίν, ὅμοιος τῷ πατουμένῳ,
ὁ δ᾽ ἐστὶ χαλκός, οὐ κρείσσων τῶν εἰς τὴν χρῆσιν
ἡμῖν κεχαλκευμένων σκευῶν, ὁ δὲ ξύλον, ἤδη καὶ
σεσηπός, ὁ δὲ ἄργυρος, χρήζων ἀνθρώπου τοῦ
φυλάξαντος, ἵνα μὴ κλαπῇ, ὁ δὲ σίδηρος, ὑπὸ ἰοῦ
διεφθαρμένος, ὁ δὲ ὄστρακον, οὐδὲν τοῦ κατεσκευα-
σμένου πρὸς τὴν ἀτιμοτάτην ὑπηρεσίαν εὐπρεπέσ-
τερον; 3. οὐ φθαρτῆς ὕλης ταῦτα πάντα; οὐχ ὑπὸ
σιδήρου καὶ πυρὸς κεχαλκευμένα; οὐχ ὁ μὲν
αὐτῶν λιθοξόος, ὁ δὲ χαλκεύς, ὁ δὲ ἀργυροκόπος,
ὁ δὲ κεραμεὺς ἔπλασεν; οὐ πρὶν ἢ ταῖς τέχναις
τούτων εἰς τὴν μορφὴν τούτων ἐκτυπωθῆναι, ἦν
ἕκαστον αὐτῶν ἑκάστῳ, ἔτι καὶ νῦν, μεταμεμορ-
φωμένον; οὐ τὰ νῦν ἐκ τῆς αὐτῆς ὕλης ὄντα σκεύη
γένοιτ᾽ ἄν, εἰ τύχοι τῶν αὐτῶν τεχνιτῶν, ὅμοια τοιούτοις; 4. οὐ ταῦτα πάλιν, τὰ νῦν ὑφ᾽ ὑμῶν προσ-
κυνούμενα, δύναιτ᾽ ἂν ὑπὸ ἀνθρώπων σκεύη ὅμοια
γενέσθαι τοῖς λοιποῖς; οὐ κωφὰ πάντα; οὐ τυφλά;
οὐκ ἄψυχα; οὐκ ἀναίσθητα; οὐκ ἀκίνητα; οὐ
πάντα σηπόμενα; οὐ πάντα φθειρόμενα; 5. ταῦτα
θεοὺς καλεῖτε; τούτοις δουλεύετε; τούτοις προσ-
κυνεῖτε, τέλεον δ᾽ αὐτοῖς ἐξομοιοῦσθε. 6. διὰ

a new man from the beginning, as one, as you yourself also admitted, who is about to listen to a new story. Look, not only with your eyes, but also with your intelligence, what substance or form they chance to have whom you call gods and regard as such. 2. Is not one a stone, like that on which we walk, another bronze, no better than the vessels which have been forged for our use, another wood already rotten, another silver, needing a man to guard it against theft, another iron, eaten by rust, another earthenware, not a whit more comely than that which is supplied for the most ordinary service? 3. Are not all these of perishable material? Were they not forged by iron and fire? Did not the wood-carver make one, the brass-founder another, the silversmith another, the potter another. Before they were moulded by their arts, into the shapes which they have, was it not possible and does it not still remain possible, for each of them to have been given a different shape? Might not vessels made out of the same material, if they met with the same artificers, be still made similar to such as they?[1] 4. Again, would it not be possible, for these, which are now worshipped by you, to be made by men into vessels like any others? Are they not all dumb? Are they not blind? Are they not without souls? Are they not without feeling? Are they not without movement? Are not they all rotting? Are they not all decaying? 5. Do you call these things gods? Are these what you serve? Are these what you worship and in the end become like them? 6. Is this the reason

---

[1] The meaning is that, given the requisite workers, the material used for ordinary vessels of wood or brass or silver might at any moment be turned into a 'god.'

τοῦτο μισεῖτε Χριστιανούς, ὅτι τούτους οὐχ
ἡγοῦνται θεούς; 7. ὑμεῖς γὰρ αἰνεῖν νομίζοντες
καὶ οἰόμενοι, οὐ πολὺ πλέον αὐτῶν καταφρονεῖτε;
οὐ πολὺ μᾶλλον αὐτοὺς χλευάζετε καὶ ὑβρίζετε,
τοὺς μὲν λιθίνους καὶ ὀστρακίνους σέβοντες
ἀφυλάκτους, τοὺς δὲ ἀργυρέους καὶ χρυσοῦς ἐγκλεί-
οντες ταῖς· νυξὶ καὶ ταῖς ἡμέραις φύλακας παρα-
καθιστάντες, ἵνα μὴ κλαπῶσιν; 8. αἷς δὲ δοκεῖτε
τιμαῖς προσφέρειν, εἰ μὲν αἰσθάνονται, κολάζετε
μᾶλλον αὐτούς· εἰ δὲ ἀναισθητοῦσιν, ἐλέγχοντες
αἵματι καὶ κνίσαις αὐτοὺς θρησκεύετε. 9. ταῦθ'
ὑμῶν τις ὑπομεινάτω, ταῦτα ἀνασχέσθω τις
ἑαυτῷ γενέσθαι. ἀλλὰ ἄνθρωπος μὲν οὐδὲ εἷς
ταύτης τῆς κολάσεως ἑκὼν ἀνέξεται, αἴσθησιν
γὰρ ἔχει καὶ λογισμόν· ὁ δὲ λίθος ἀνέχεται,
ἀναισθητεῖ γάρ. οὐκ οὖν τὴν αἴσθησιν αὐτοῦ
ἐλέγχετε; 10. περὶ μὲν οὖν τοῦ μὴ δεδουλῶσθαι
Χριστιανοὺς τοιούτοις θεοῖς πολλὰ μὲν ἂν καὶ
ἄλλα εἰπεῖν ἔχοιμι· εἰ δέ τινι μὴ δοκοίη κἂν
ταῦτα ἱκανά, περισσὸν ἡγοῦμαι καὶ τὸ πλείω
λέγειν.

III

1. Ἑξῆς δὲ περὶ τοῦ μὴ κατὰ τὰ αὐτὰ Ἰουδαίοις
θεοσεβεῖν αὐτοὺς οἶμαί σε μάλιστα ποθεῖν ἀκοῦσαι. 2. Ἰουδαῖοι τοίνυν, εἰ μὲν ἀπέχονται ταύτης τῆς προειρημένης λατρείας, καλῶς θεὸν ἕνα
τῶν πάντων σέβειν καὶ δεσπότην ἀξιοῦσι φρονεῖν·
εἰ δὲ τοῖς προειρημένοις ὁμοιοτρόπως τὴν θρη-
σκείαν προσάγουσιν αὐτῷ ταύτην, διαμαρτά-
νουσιν. 3. ἃ γὰρ τοῖς ἀναισθήτοις καὶ κωφοῖς

354

why you hate the Christians—that they do not think that these are gods? 7. For is it not you, who, though you think and believe that you are praising the gods, are much more despising them? Are you not much rather mocking and insulting them, when you worship those of stone and earthenware without guarding them; but lock up at night and in the day-time place guards over those of silver and gold, that they be not stolen away. 8. And, if they have powers of perception, by the honours which you think to pay them you are rather punishing them, and, if they are without perception, you are refuting them by worshipping them with blood and burnt fat. 9. Let one of you suffer these things, let him endure that it should be done to him. Why, there is not a single man who would willingly endure this punishment, for he has perception and reason. But the stone endures, for it has no perception. Do you not then refute its perception? 10. I could say much more as to the refusal of Christians to serve such gods, but if any one find these arguments insufficient, I think it useless to say more.

III

1. In the next place I think that you are especially anxious to hear why the Christians do not worship in the same way as the Jews. 2. The Jews indeed, by abstaining from the religion already discussed, may rightly claim that they worship the one God of the Universe, and regard him as master, but in offering service to him in like manner to those already dealt with they are quite wrong. 3. For just as the Greeks give a proof of foolishness

The difference between Jews and Christians

προσφέροντες οἱ Ἕλληνες ἀφροσύνης δεῖγμα παρέχουσι, ταῦθ᾿ οὗτοι καθάπερ προσδεομένῳ τῷ θεῷ λογιζόμενοι παρέχειν μωρίαν εἰκὸς μᾶλλον ἡγοῖντ᾿ ἄν, οὐ θεοσέβειαν. 4. ὁ γὰρ ποιήσας τὸν οὐρανὸν καὶ τὴν γῆν καὶ πάντα τὰ ἐν αὐτοῖς καὶ πᾶσιν ἡμῖν χορηγῶν, ὧν προσδεόμεθα, οὐδενὸς ἂν αὐτὸς προσδέοιτο τούτων ὧν τοῖς οἰομένοις διδόναι παρέχει αὐτός. 5. οἱ δέ γε θυσίας αὐτῷ δι᾿ αἵματος καὶ κνίσης καὶ ὁλοκαυτωμάτων ἐπιτελεῖν οἰόμενοι καὶ ταύταις ταῖς τιμαῖς αὐτὸν γεραίρειν, οὐδέν μοι δοκοῦσι διαφέρειν τῶν εἰς τὰ κωφὰ τὴν αὐτὴν ἐνδεικνυμένων φιλοτιμίαν· τῶν μὲν μὴ δυναμένοις τῆς τιμῆς μεταλαμβάνειν, τῶν δὲ δοκούντων παρέχειν τῷ μηδενὸς προσδεομένῳ.

Exod. 20.
11; Ps. 146,
6; Acts 14,
15

IV

1. Ἀλλὰ μὴν τό γε περὶ τὰς βρώσεις αὐτῶν ψοφοδεὲς καὶ τὴν περὶ τὰ σάββατα δεισιδαιμονίαν καὶ τὴν τῆς περιτομῆς ἀλαζονείαν καὶ τὴν τῆς νηστείας καὶ νουμηνίας εἰρωνείαν, καταγέλαστα καὶ οὐδενὸς ἄξια λόγου, οὐ νομίζω σε χρῄζειν παρ᾿ ἐμοῦ μαθεῖν. 2. τό τε γὰρ τῶν ὑπὸ τοῦ θεοῦ κτισθέντων εἰς χρῆσιν ἀνθρώπων ἃ μὲν ὡς καλῶς κτισθέντα παραδέχεσθαι, ἃ δ᾿ ὡς ἄχρηστα καὶ περισσὰ παραιτεῖσθαι, πῶς οὐκ ἀθέμιστον; 3. τὸ δὲ καταψεύδεσθαι θεοῦ ὡς κωλύοντος ἐν τῇ τῶν σαββάτων ἡμέρᾳ καλόν τι ποιεῖν, πῶς οὐκ ἀσεβές; 4. τὸ δὲ καὶ τὴν μείωσιν τῆς σαρκὸς μαρτύριον ἐκλογῆς ἀλαζονεύεσθαι ὡς

by making offerings to senseless and deaf images, so the Jews ought rather to consider that they are showing foolishness, not reverence, by regarding God as in need of these things. 4. For "He who made heaven and earth and all that is in them," and bestows on all of us that which we need, would not himself have need of any of these things which he himself supplies to those who think that they are giving them. 5. For after all, those who think that they are consecrating sacrifices to him by blood and burnt fat, and whole burnt offerings, and that they are reverencing him by these honours, seem to me to be in no way better than those who show the same respect to deaf images. For it seems that the one offer to those who cannot partake of the honour, the others to him who is in need of nothing.

IV

1. MOREOVER I do not suppose that you need to learn from me that, after all, their scruples about food and superstition about the Sabbath, and their pride in circumcision and the sham of their fasting and feast of the new moon, are ridiculous and unworthy of any argument. 2. For how can it be anything but unlawful to receive some of the things created by God for the use of man as if well created, and to reject others as if useless and superfluous? 3. And what can it be but impious falsely to accuse God of forbidding that a good deed should be done on the Sabbath day? 4. And what does it deserve but ridicule to be proud of the mutilation of the flesh as a proof of election, as if

357

διὰ τοῦτο ἐξαιρέτως ἠγαπημένους ὑπὸ θεοῦ, πῶς
οὐ χλεύης ἄξιον; 5. τὸ δὲ παρεδρεύοντας αὐτοὺς
ἄστροις καὶ σελήνῃ τὴν παρατήρησιν τῶν μηνῶν
καὶ τῶν ἡμερῶν ποιεῖσθαι καὶ τὰς οἰκονομίας θεοῦ
καὶ τὰς τῶν καιρῶν ἀλλαγὰς καταδιαιρεῖν πρὸς
τὰς αὐτῶν ὁρμάς, ἃς μὲν εἰς ἑορτάς, ἃς δὲ εἰς
πένθη· τίς ἂν θεοσεβείας καὶ οὐκ ἀφροσύνης
πολὺ πλέον ἡγήσαιτο δεῖγμα; 6. τῆς μὲν οὖν
κοινῆς εἰκαιότητος καὶ ἀπάτης καὶ τῆς Ἰουδαίων
πολυπραγμοσύνης καὶ ἀλαζονείας ὡς ὀρθῶς ἀπέχονται Χριστιανοί, ἀρκούντως σε νομίζω μεμαθη-
κέναι· τὸ δὲ τῆς ἰδίας αὐτῶν θεοσεβείας μυστή-
ριον μὴ προσδοκήσῃς δύνασθαι παρὰ ἀνθρώπου
μαθεῖν.

V

1. Χριστιανοὶ γὰρ οὔτε γῇ οὔτε φωνῇ οὔτε ἔθεσι
διακεκριμένοι τῶν λοιπῶν εἰσιν ἀνθρώπων. 2. οὔτε
γάρ που πόλεις ἰδίας κατοικοῦσιν οὔτε διαλέκτῳ
τινὶ παρηλλαγμένῃ χρῶνται οὔτε βίον παράσημον
ἀσκοῦσιν. 3. οὐ μὴν ἐπινοίᾳ τινὶ καὶ φροντίδι
πολυπραγμόνων ἀνθρώπων μάθημα τοῦτ' αὐτοῖς
ἐστιν εὑρημένον, οὐδὲ δόγματος ἀνθρωπίνου προε-
στᾶσιν, ὥσπερ ἔνιοι. 4. κατοικοῦντες δὲ πόλεις
ἑλληνίδας τε καὶ βαρβάρους, ὡς ἕκαστος ἐκλη-
ρώθη, καὶ τοῖς ἐγχωρίοις ἔθεσιν ἀκολουθοῦντες
ἔν τε ἐσθῆτι καὶ διαίτῃ καὶ τῷ λοιπῷ βίῳ θαυμα-
στὴν καὶ ὁμολογουμένως παράδοξον ἐνδείκνυνται
τὴν κατάστασιν τῆς ἑαυτῶν πολιτείας. 5. πατρί-
δας οἰκοῦσιν ἰδίας, ἀλλ' ὡς πάροικοι· μετέχουσι

they were, for this reason, especially beloved by God? 5. And their attention to the stars and moon, for the observance of months and days, and for their arbitrary distinctions between the changing seasons ordained by God, making some into feasts, and others into occasions of mourning;—who would regard this as a proof of piety, and not much more of foolishness? 6. So then I think that you have learnt sufficiently that the Christians do rightly in abstaining from the general silliness and deceit and fussiness and pride of the Jews. But do not suppose that you can learn from man the mystery of the Christians' own religion.

V

1. For the distinction between Christians and other men, is neither in country nor language nor customs. 2. For they do not dwell in cities in some place of their own, nor do they use any strange variety of dialect, nor practise an extraordinary kind of life. 3. This teaching of theirs has not been discovered by the intellect or thought of busy men, nor are they the advocates of any human doctrine as some men are. 4. Yet while living in Greek and barbarian cities, according as each obtained his lot, and following the local customs, both in clothing and food and in the rest of life, they show forth the wonderful and confessedly strange character of the constitution of their own citizenship. 5. They dwell in their own fatherlands, but as if sojourners in them; they share all things as citizens, and suffer

The true distinction of Christians

πάντων ὡς πολῖται, καὶ πάνθ᾽ ὑπομένουσιν ὡς
ξένοι· πᾶσα ξένη πατρίς ἐστιν αὐτῶν, καὶ πᾶσα
πατρὶς ξένη. 6. γαμοῦσιν ὡς πάντες, τεκνογον-
οῦσιν· ἀλλ᾽ οὐ ῥίπτουσι τὰ γεννώμενα. 7. τράπε-
ζαν κοινὴν παρατίθενται, ἀλλ᾽ οὐ κοίτην. 8. ἐν
σαρκὶ τυγχάνουσιν, ἀλλ᾽ οὐ κατὰ σάρκα ζῶσιν.
9. ἐπὶ γῆς διατρίβουσιν, ἀλλ᾽ ἐν οὐρανῷ πολι-
τεύονται. 10. πείθονται τοῖς ὡρισμένοις νόμοις,
καὶ τοῖς ἰδίοις βίοις νικῶσι τοὺς νόμους. 11. ἀγα-
πῶσι πάντας, καὶ ὑπὸ πάντων διώκονται.
12. ἀγνοοῦνται, καὶ κατακρίνονται· θανατοῦνται,
καὶ ζωοποιοῦνται. 13. πτωχεύουσι, καὶ πλουτί-
ζουσι πολλούς· πάντων ὑστεροῦνται, καὶ ἐν πᾶσι
περισσεύουσιν. 14. ἀτιμοῦνται, καὶ ἐν ταῖς
ἀτιμίαις δοξάζονται. βλασφημοῦνται, καὶ δικαι-
οῦνται. 15. λοιδοροῦνται, καὶ εὐλογοῦσιν· ὑβρί-
ζονται, καὶ τιμῶσιν. 16. ἀγαθοποιοῦντες ὡς
κακοὶ κολάζονται· κολαζόμενοι χαίρουσιν ὡς
ζωοποιούμενοι. 17. ὑπὸ Ἰουδαίων ὡς ἀλλόφυλοι
πολεμοῦνται καὶ ὑπὸ Ἑλλήνων διώκονται· καὶ
τὴν αἰτίαν τῆς ἔχθρας εἰπεῖν οἱ μισοῦντες οὐκ
ἔχουσιν.

VI

1. Ἁπλῶς δ᾽ εἰπεῖν, ὅπερ ἐστὶν σώματι ψυχή,
τοῦτ᾽ εἰσὶν ἐν κόσμῳ Χριστιανοί. 2. ἔσπαρται
κατὰ πάντων τῶν τοῦ σώματος μελῶν ἡ ψυχή,
καὶ Χριστιανοὶ κατὰ τὰς τοῦ κόσμου πόλεις.
3. οἰκεῖ μὲν ἐν τῷ σώματι ψυχή, οὐκ ἔστι δὲ ἐκ
τοῦ σώματος· καὶ Χριστιανοὶ ἐν κόσμῳ οἰκοῦσιν,

Marginal references:
II Cor. 10, 3; Rom. 8, 12. 13
Philipp. 3, 18-20
II Cor. 6, 9
II Cor. 6, 10
I Cor. 4, 12
II Cor. 6, 10
Jo. 17, 11. 14. 16

all things as strangers. Every foreign country is their fatherland, and every fatherland is a foreign country. \ 6. They marry as all men, they bear children, but they do not expose their offspring. 7. They offer free hospitality, but guard their purity. 8. Their lot is cast " in the flesh," but they do not live " after the flesh." ⌡9. They pass their time upon the earth, but they have their citizenship in heaven.⌉ 10. They obey the appointed laws, and they surpass the laws in their own lives. 11. They love all men and are persecuted by all men. 12. They are unknown and they are condemned. They are put to death and they gain life. 13. " They are poor and make many rich "; they lack all things and have all things in abundance. 14. They are dishonoured, and are glorified in their dishonour, they are spoken evil of and are justified. 15. " They are abused and give blessing," they are insulted and render honour. 16. When they do good they are buffeted as evil-doers, when they are buffeted they rejoice as men who receive life. 17. They are warred upon by the Jews as foreigners and are persecuted by the Greeks, and those who hate them cannot state the cause of their enmity.

VI.

1. To put it shortly what the soul is in the body, that the Christians are in the world. 2. The soul is spread through all members of the body, and Christians throughout the cities of the world. 3. The soul dwells in the body, but is not of the body, and Christians dwell in the world, but are not of the

The world and Christians

οὐκ εἰσὶ δὲ ἐκ τοῦ κόσμου. 4. ἀόρατος ἡ ψυχὴ
ἐν ὁρατῷ φρουρεῖται τῷ σώματι· καὶ Χριστιανοὶ
γινώσκονται μὲν ὄντες ἐν τῷ κόσμῳ, ἀόρατος δὲ

Gal. 5, 17   αὐτῶν ἡ θεοσέβεια μένει. 5. μισεῖ τὴν ψυχὴν ἡ
σὰρξ καὶ πολεμεῖ μηδὲν ἀδικουμένη, διότι ταῖς
ἡδοναῖς κωλύεται χρῆσθαι· μισεῖ καὶ Χριστιανοὺς
ὁ κόσμος μηδὲν ἀδικούμενος, ὅτι ταῖς ἡδοναῖς

Jo. 15, 18.
19
Mt. 5, 44 ;
Luk. 6, 27   ἀντιτάσσονται. 6. ἡ ψυχὴ τὴν μισοῦσαν ἀγαπᾷ
σάρκα καὶ τὰ μέλη· καὶ Χριστιανοὶ τοὺς μισοῦν-
τας ἀγαπῶσιν. 7. ἐγκέκλεισται μὲν ἡ ψυχὴ τῷ
σώματι, συνέχει δὲ αὐτὴ τὸ σῶμα· καὶ Χριστιανοὶ κατέχονται μὲν ὡς ἐν φρουρᾷ τῷ κόσμῳ,
αὐτοὶ δὲ συνέχουσι τὸν κόσμον. 8. ἀθάνατος ἡ
ψυχὴ ἐν θνητῷ σκηνώματι κατοικεῖ· καὶ Χριστιανοὶ παροικοῦσιν ἐν φθαρτοῖς, τὴν ἐν οὐρανοῖς
ἀφθαρσίαν προσδεχόμενοι. 9. κακουργουμένη
σιτίοις καὶ ποτοῖς ἡ ψυχὴ βελτιοῦται· καὶ
Χριστιανοὶ κολαζόμενοι καθ᾿ ἡμέραν πλεονάζουσι
μᾶλλον. 10. εἰς τοσαύτην αὐτοὺς τάξιν ἔθετο ὁ
θεός, ἣν οὐ θεμιτὸν αὐτοῖς παραιτήσασθαι.

VII

1. Οὐ γὰρ ἐπίγειον, ὡς ἔφην, εὕρημα τοῦτ᾿
αὐτοῖς παρεδόθη, οὐδὲ θνητὴν ἐπίνοιαν φυλάσσειν
οὕτως ἀξιοῦσιν ἐπιμελῶς, οὐδὲ ἀνθρωπίνων οἰ-

I Cor. 9, 17   κονομίαν μυστηρίων πεπίστευνται. 2. ἀλλ᾿ αὐτὸς
ἀληθῶς ὁ παντοκράτωρ καὶ παντοκτίστης καὶ

world. 4. The soul is invisible, and is guarded in a visible body, and Christians are recognised when they are in the world, but their religion remains invisible. 5. The flesh hates the soul, and wages war upon it, though it has suffered no evil, because it is prevented from gratifying its pleasures, and the world hates the Christians though it has suffered no evil, because they are opposed to its pleasures. 6. The soul loves the flesh which hates it and the limbs, and Christians love those that hate them. 7. The soul has been shut up in the body, but itself sustains the body; and Christians are confined in the world as in a prison, but themselves sustain the world.[1] 8. The soul dwells immortal in a mortal tabernacle, and Christians sojourn among corruptible things, waiting for the incorruptibility which is in heaven. 9. The soul when evil treated in food and drink becomes better, and Christians when buffeted day by day increase more. 10. God has appointed them to so great a post[2] and it is not right for them to decline it.

VII

1. For it is not, as I said, an earthly discovery which was given to them, nor do they take such pains to guard some mortal invention, nor have they been entrusted with the dispensation of human mysteries. 2. But in truth the Almighty and all-creating and invisible God himself founded among

The Christian revelation

[1] Cf. Aristides, *Apology* 16. 'I have no doubt but that the world stands through the intercession of Christians.'
[2] There is probably a recurrence of the idea of the church as the 'militia dei' (cf. note on Hermas, *Sim.* v. i. 1).

ἀόρατος θεός, αὐτὸς ἀπ᾿ οὐρανῶν τὴν ἀλήθειαν
καὶ τὸν λόγον τὸν ἅγιον καὶ ἀπερινόητον ἀνθρώποις ἐνίδρυσε καὶ ἐγκατεστήριξε ταῖς καρδίαις
αὐτῶν· οὐ, καθάπερ ἄν τις εἰκάσειεν, ἀνθρώποις
ὑπηρέτην τινὰ πέμψας ἢ ἄγγελον ἢ ἄρχοντα ἤ
τινα τῶν διεπόντων τὰ ἐπίγεια ἤ τινα τῶν
πεπιστευμένων τὰς ἐν οὐρανοῖς διοικήσεις, ἀλλ᾿
αὐτὸν τὸν τεχνίτην καὶ δημιουργὸν τῶν ὅλων,
ᾧ τοὺς οὐρανοὺς ἔκτισεν, ᾧ τὴν θάλασσαν
ἰδίοις ἐνέκλεισεν, οὗ τὰ μυστήρια πιστῶς πάντα
φυλάσσει τὰ στοιχεῖα, παρ᾿ οὗ τὰ μέτρα τῶν
τῆς ἡμέρας δρόμων ὁ ἥλιος εἴληφε φυλάσσειν, ᾧ
πειθαρχεῖ σελήνη νυκτὶ φαίνειν κελεύοντι, ᾧ
πειθαρχεῖ τὰ ἄστρα τῷ τῆς σελήνης ἀκολου-
θοῦντα δρόμῳ· ᾧ πάντα διατέτακται καὶ διώ-
ρισται καὶ ὑποτέτακται, οὐρανοὶ καὶ τὰ ἐν οὐρανοῖς, γῆ καὶ τὰ ἐν τῇ γῇ, θάλασσα καὶ τὰ ἐν τῇ
θαλάσσῃ, πῦρ, ἀήρ, ἄβυσσος, τὰ ἐν ὕψεσι, τὰ ἐν
βάθεσι, τὰ ἐν τῷ μεταξύ· τοῦτον πρὸς αὐτοὺς
ἀπέστειλεν. 3. ἆρά γε, ὡς ἀνθρώπων ἄν τις
λογίσαιτο, ἐπὶ τυραννίδι καὶ φόβῳ καὶ κατα-
πλήξει; 4. οὐ μὲν οὖν· ἀλλ᾿ ἐν ἐπιεικείᾳ καὶ
πραΰτητι ὡς βασιλεὺς πέμπων υἱὸν βασιλέα
ἔπεμψεν, ὡς θεὸν ἔπεμψεν, ὡς ἄνθρωπον πρὸς
ἀνθρώπους ἔπεμψεν, ὡς σῴζων ἔπεμψεν, ὡς
πείθων, οὐ βιαζόμενος· βία γὰρ οὐ πρόσεστι τῷ
θεῷ. 5. ἔπεμψεν ὡς καλῶν, οὐ διώκων· ἔπεμψεν
ὡς ἀγαπῶν, οὐ κρίνων. 6. πέμψει γὰρ αὐτὸν
κρίνοντα· καὶ τίς αὐτοῦ τὴν παρουσίαν ὑποστή-
σεται; . . . 7. . . . παραβαλλομένους θηρίοις,

Zech. 9, 9
Jo. 3, 17
Jo. 3, 17

Malach. 3, 2

men the truth from heaven, and the holy and incomprehensible word, and established it in their
hearts, not, as one might suppose, by sending some
minister to men, or an angel, or ruler, or one of
those who direct earthly things, or one of those who
are entrusted with the dispensations in heaven, but
the very artificer and Creator of the universe himself,
by whom he made the heavens, by whom he en-
closed the sea in its own bounds, whose mysteries
all the elements guard faithfully; from whom the
sun received the measure of the courses of the day,
to whose command the moon is obedient to give light
by night, whom the stars obey, following the course
of the moon, by whom all things were ordered, and
ordained, and placed in subjection, the heavens and
the things in the heavens, the earth and the things in
the earth, the sea and the things in the sea, fire, air,
abyss, the things in the heights, the things in the
depths, the things between them—him he sent to
them. 3. Yes, but did he send him, as a man might
suppose, in sovereignty and fear and terror? 4. Not
so, but in gentleness and meekness, as a king sending
a son, he sent him as King, he sent him as God, he
sent him as Man to men, he was saving and persuading
when he sent him, not compelling, for compulsion is
not an attribute of God. 5. When he sent him he
was calling, not pursuing; when he sent him he was
loving, not judging. 6. For he will send him as judge,
and who shall endure his coming?[1]   *   *   *
*   *   * 7. . . . they are thrown to wild beasts

[1] There is here a lacuna in the MS. Probably the next
sentence may be completed by prefixing " Do you not see
that " before " they are thrown."

ἵνα ἀρνήσωνται τὸν κύριον, καὶ μὴ νικωμένους;
8. οὐχ ὁρᾷς, ὅσῳ πλείονες κολάζονται, τοσούτῳ
πλεονάζοντας ἄλλους; 9. ταῦτα ἀνθρώπου οὐ
δοκεῖ τὰ ἔργα· ταῦτα δύναμίς ἐστι θεοῦ· ταῦτα
τῆς παρουσίας αὐτοῦ δείγματα.

VIII

1. Τίς γὰρ ὅλως ἀνθρώπων ἠπίστατο, τί ποτ᾽
ἐστὶ θεὸς πρὶν αὐτὸν ἐλθεῖν; 2. ἢ τοὺς κενοὺς καὶ
ληρώδεις ἐκείνων λόγους ἀποδέχῃ τῶν ἀξιοπίστων
φιλοσόφων, ὧν οἱ μέν τινες πῦρ ἔφασαν εἶναι τὸν
θεὸν (οὗ μέλλουσι χωρήσειν αὐτοί, τοῦτο καλοῦσι
θεόν), οἱ δὲ ὕδωρ, οἱ δ᾽ ἄλλο τι τῶν στοιχείων τῶν
ἐκτισμένων ὑπὸ θεοῦ; 3. καίτοι γε, εἴ τις τούτων
τῶν λόγων ἀποδεκτός ἐστι, δύναιτ᾽ ἂν καὶ τῶν
λοιπῶν κτισμάτων ἓν ἕκαστον ὁμοίως ἀποφαί-
νεσθαι θεόν. 4. ἀλλὰ ταῦτα μὲν τερατεία καὶ
πλάνη τῶν γοήτων ἐστίν· 5. ἀνθρώπων δὲ οὐδεὶς
οὔτε εἶδεν οὔτε ἐγνώρισεν, αὐτὸς δὲ ἑαυτὸν ἐπέδει-
ξεν. 6. ἐπέδειξε δὲ διὰ πίστεως, ᾗ μόνῃ θεὸν ἰδεῖν
συγκεχώρηται. 7. ὁ γὰρ δεσπότης καὶ δημιουργὸς
τῶν ὅλων θεός, ὁ ποιήσας τὰ πάντα καὶ κατὰ τάξιν
διακρίνας, οὐ μόνον φιλάνθρωπος ἐγένετο, ἀλλὰ
καὶ μακρόθυμος. 8. ἀλλ᾽ οὗτος ἦν μὲν ἀεὶ τοιοῦτος καὶ ἔστι καὶ ἔσται, χρηστὸς καὶ ἀγαθὸς
καὶ ἀόργητος καὶ ἀληθής, καὶ μόνος ἀγαθός ἐστιν·
9. ἐννοήσας δὲ μεγάλην καὶ ἄφραστον ἔννοιαν
ἀνεκοινώσατο μόνῳ τῷ παιδί. 10. ἐν ὅσῳ μὲν
οὖν κατεῖχεν ἐν μυστηρίῳ καὶ διετήρει τὴν σοφὴν
αὐτοῦ βουλήν, ἀμελεῖν ἡμῶν καὶ ἀφροντιστεῖν

that they may deny the lord, and are not overcome?
8. Do you not see that the more of them are punished,
the more do others multiply? 9. These things do
not seem to be the works of man; these things are a
miracle of God, these things are the proofs of his
coming.

VIII

1. For before he came what man had any knowledge at all of what God is? 2. Or do you accept
the vain and foolish statements of those pretentious
philosophers, of whom some said that God is fire
(they give the name of God to that to which they
shall go) and some water, and some one of the other
elements which were created by God. 3. And yet
if any of these arguments is acceptable it would be
possible for each one of the other created things to
be declared God. 4. Now these things are the miracle
mongering and deceit of the magicians; 5. but of
men there is none who has either seen him or known
him, but he himself manifested himself. 6. Now
he manifested himself through faith, by which alone
it is given to see God. 7. For God the Master and
Creator of the universe, who made all things and
arranged them in order was not only kind to man,
but also long-suffering. 8. Nay, he was ever so and
is and will be, kindly and good and free from wrath
and true, and he alone is good. 9. And having
formed a great and unspeakable design he commu-
nicated it to his Child alone. 10. And so long as he
kept it in a mystery and guarded his wise counsel,
he seemed to neglect us and to be careless; 11. but

Human knowledge of God

367

THE APOSTOLIC FATHERS

ἐδόκει· 11. ἐπεὶ δὲ ἀπεκάλυψε διὰ τοῦ ἀγαπητοῦ
παιδὸς καὶ ἐφανέρωσε τὰ ἐξ ἀρχῆς ἡτοιμασμένα,
πάνθ' ἅμα παρέσχεν ἡμῖν καὶ μετασχεῖν τῶν
εὐεργεσιῶν αὐτοῦ καὶ ἰδεῖν καὶ νοῆσαι, ἃ τίς
ἂν πώποτε προσεδόκησεν ἡμῶν;

IX

1. Πάντ' οὖν ἤδη παρ' ἑαυτῷ σὺν τῷ παιδὶ
οἰκονομηκώς, μέχρι μὲν τοῦ πρόσθεν χρόνου εἴασεν
ἡμᾶς, ὡς ἐβουλόμεθα, ἀτάκτοις φοραῖς φέρεσθαι,
ἡδοναῖς καὶ ἐπιθυμίαις ἀπαγομένους. οὐ πάντως
ἐφηδόμενος τοῖς ἁμαρτήμασιν ἡμῶν, ἀλλ' ἀνεχό-
μενος, οὐδὲ τῷ τότε τῆς ἀδικίας καιρῷ συνευδοκῶν,
ἀλλὰ τὸν νῦν τῆς δικαιοσύνης δημιουργῶν, ἵνα ἐν
τῷ τότε χρόνῳ ἐλεγχθέντες ἐκ τῶν ἰδίων ἔργων
ἀνάξιοι ζωῆς νῦν ὑπὸ τῆς τοῦ θεοῦ χρηστότητος
ἀξιωθῶμεν, καὶ τὸ καθ' ἑαυτοὺς φανερώσαντες
ἀδύνατον εἰσελθεῖν εἰς τὴν βασιλείαν τοῦ θεοῦ τῇ
δυνάμει τοῦ θεοῦ δυνατοὶ γενηθῶμεν. 2. ἐπεὶ δὲ
πεπλήρωτο μὲν ἡ ἡμετέρα ἀδικία καὶ τελείως
πεφανέρωτο, ὅτι ὁ μισθὸς αὐτῆς κόλασις καὶ
θάνατος προσεδοκᾶτο, ἦλθε δὲ ὁ καιρός, ὃν θεὸς
προέθετο λοιπὸν φανερῶσαι τὴν ἑαυτοῦ χρηστό-
τητα καὶ δύναμιν (ὢ τῆς ὑπερβαλλούσης φιλαν-
θρωπίας καὶ ἀγάπης τοῦ θεοῦ), οὐκ ἐμίσησεν
ἡμᾶς οὐδὲ ἀπώσατο οὐδὲ ἐμνησικάκησεν, ἀλλὰ
ἐμακροθύμησεν, ἠνέσχετο, ἐλεῶν αὐτὸς τὰς ἡμετέρας ἁμαρτίας ἀνεδέξατο, αὐτὸς τὸν ἴδιον υἱὸν
ἀπέδοτο λύτρον ὑπὲρ ἡμῶν, τὸν ἅγιον ὑπὲρ
ἀνόμων, τὸν ἄκακον ὑπὲρ τῶν κακῶν, τὸν δίκαιον

Rom. 3,
21-26

Tit. 3, 3

Jo. 3, 5

Tit. 3, 4. 5

Rom. 8, 32
Eph. 1, 7;
I Tim. 2, 6
I Pet. 3, 18

368

when he revealed it through his beloved Child, and manifested the things prepared from the beginning, he gave us all things at once, both to share in his benefits and to see and understand, and which of us would ever have expected these things?

IX

1. Having thus planned everything by himself with his Child he suffered us up to the former time to be borne along by unruly impulses as we willed, carried away by pleasures and lust. Not at all because he delighted in our sins, but in forbearance; not in approval of the time of iniquity which was then, but fashioning the time of righteousness which is now, that we, who at that time were proved by our own deeds to be unworthy of life, may now be granted it by the goodness of God, and that when we had made it plain that it was impossible for us by ourselves to enter into the kingdom of God, we might be made able by the power of God. 2. But when our iniquity was fulfilled and it had become fully manifest, that its reward of punishment and death waited for it, and the time came which God had appointed to manifest henceforth his kindliness and power (O the excellence of the kindness and the love of God!) he did not hate us nor reject us nor remember us for evil, but was long-suffering, endured us, himself in pity took our sin, himself gave his own Son as ransom for us, the Holy for the wicked, the innocent for the

The plan of Salvation

369

ὑπὲρ τῶν ἀδίκων, τὸν ἄφθαρτον ὑπὲρ τῶν φθαρτῶν,
τὸν ἀθάνατον ὑπὲρ τῶν θνητῶν. 3. τί γὰρ ἄλλο
τὰς ἁμαρτίας ἡμῶν ἠδυνήθη καλύψαι ἢ ἐκείνου
δικαιοσύνη; 4. ἐν τίνι δικαιωθῆναι δυνατὸν τοὺς
ἀνόμους ἡμᾶς καὶ ἀσεβεῖς ἢ ἐν μόνῳ τῷ υἱῷ τοῦ
θεοῦ; 5. ὦ τῆς γλυκείας ἀνταλλαγῆς, ὦ τῆς
ἀνεξιχνιάστου δημιουργίας, ὦ τῶν ἀπροσδοκήτων
εὐεργεσιῶν· ἵνα ἀνομία μὲν πολλῶν ἐν δικαίῳ
ἑνὶ κρυβῇ, δικαιοσύνη δὲ ἑνὸς πολλοὺς ἀνόμους
δικαιώσῃ. 6. ἐλέγξας οὖν ἐν μὲν τῷ πρόσθεν
χρόνῳ τὸ ἀδύνατον τῆς ἡμετέρας φύσεως εἰς τὸ
τυχεῖν ζωῆς, νῦν δὲ τὸν σωτῆρα δείξας δυνατὸν
σῴζειν καὶ τὰ ἀδύνατα, ἐξ ἀμφοτέρων ἐβουλήθη
πιστεύειν ἡμᾶς τῇ χρηστότητι αὐτοῦ, αὐτὸν
ἡγεῖσθαι τροφέα, πατέρα, διδάσκαλον, σύμβουλον,
Mt. 6, 25-31 ἰατρόν, νοῦν, φῶς, τιμήν, δόξαν, ἰσχύν, ζωήν, περὶ
ἐνδύσεως καὶ τροφῆς μὴ μεριμνᾶν.

X

1. Ταύτην καὶ σὺ τὴν πίστιν ἐὰν ποθήσῃς, καὶ
Jo. 3, 16; λάβῃς πρῶτον μὲν ἐπίγνωσιν πατρός. . . . 2. ὁ γὰρ
I Jo. 4, 9 θεὸς τοὺς ἀνθρώπους ἠγάπησε, δι' οὓς ἐποίησε τὸν
κόσμον, οἷς ὑπέταξε πάντα τὰ ἐν τῇ γῇ, οἷς λόγον
ἔδωκεν, οἷς νοῦν, οἷς μόνοις ἄνω πρὸς αὐτὸν ὁρᾶν
ἐπέτρεψεν, οὓς ἐκ τῆς ἰδίας εἰκόνος ἔπλασε, πρὸς
Gen. 1, 26. οὓς ἀπέστειλε τὸν υἱὸν αὐτοῦ τὸν μονογενῆ, οἷς
27
I Jo. 4, 9 τὴν ἐν οὐρανῷ βασιλείαν ἐπηγγείλατο, καὶ δώσει
τοῖς ἀγαπήσασιν αὐτόν. 3. ἐπιγνοὺς δὲ τίνος οἴει

370

guilty, the just for the unjust, the incorruptible for the corruptible, the immortal for the mortal. 3. For what else could cover our sins but his righteousness? 4. In whom was it possible for us, in our wickedness and impiety, to be made just, except in the son of God alone? 5. O the sweet exchange, O the inscrutable creation, O the unexpected benefits, that the wickedness of many should be concealed in the one righteous, and the righteousness of the one should make righteous many wicked! 6. Having convinced us then of the inability of our nature to attain life in time past, and now having shown the Saviour who is able to save, even where it was impossible, it was his will for both reasons that we should believe on his goodness, and regard him as nurse, father, teacher, counsellor, physician, mind, light, honour, glory, strength, life, and to have no care for clothing and food.

X

1. IF you also desire this faith, and receive first complete knowledge of the Father. . . .[1] 2. For God loved mankind for whose sake he made the world, to whom he subjected all things which are in the earth, to whom he gave reason, to whom he gave mind, on whom alone he enjoined that they should look upward to him, whom he made in his own image, to whom he sent his only-begotten Son, to whom he promised the kingdom in heaven,—and he will give it to them who loved him. 3. And when you

The benefits of conversion

---

[1] Here again there is apparently a lacuna in the text.

THE APOSTOLIC FATHERS

I Jo. 4, 19 πληρωθήσεσθαι χαρᾶς; ἢ πῶς ἀγαπήσεις τὸν
οὕτως προαγαπήσαντά σε; 4. ἀγαπήσας δὲ μιμητὴς ἔσῃ αὐτοῦ τῆς χρηστότητος. καὶ μὴ θαυμάσῃς,
εἰ δύναται μιμητὴς ἄνθρωπος γενέσθαι θεοῦ.
δύναται θέλοντος αὐτοῦ. 5. οὐ γὰρ τὸ καταδυναστεύειν τῶν πλησίον οὐδὲ τὸ πλέον ἔχειν βούλεσθαι
τῶν ἀσθενεστέρων οὐδὲ τὸ πλουτεῖν καὶ βιάζεσθαι
τοὺς ὑποδεεστέρους εὐδαιμονεῖν ἐστιν, οὐδὲ ἐν
τούτοις δύναταί τις μιμήσασθαι θεόν, ἀλλὰ ταῦτα
Gal. 6, 2 ἐκτὸς τῆς ἐκείνου μεγαλειότητος. 6. ἀλλ' ὅστις
τὸ τοῦ πλησίον ἀναδέχεται βάρος, ὃς ἐν ᾧ κρείσσων ἐστὶν ἕτερον τὸν ἐλαττούμενον εὐεργετεῖν
ἐθέλει, ὃς ἃ παρὰ τοῦ θεοῦ λαβὼν ἔχει, ταῦτα τοῖς
ἐπιδεομένοις χορηγῶν θεὸς γίνεται τῶν λαμβανόν-
Eph. 6, 9
Col. 4, 1 των, οὗτος μιμητής ἐστι θεοῦ. 7. τότε θεάσῃ
τυγχάνων ἐπὶ γῆς, ὅτι θεὸς ἐν οὐρανοῖς πολιτεύεται,
τότε μυστήρια θεοῦ λαλεῖν ἄρξῃ, τότε τοὺς κολα-
ζομένους ἐπὶ τῷ μὴ θέλειν ἀρνήσασθαι θεὸν καὶ
ἀγαπήσεις καὶ θαυμάσεις· τότε τῆς ἀπάτης τοῦ
κόσμου καὶ τῆς πλάνης καταγνώσῃ, ὅταν τὸ ἀληθῶς ἐν οὐρανῷ ζῆν ἐπιγνῷς, ὅταν τοῦ δοκοῦντος
ἐνθάδε θανάτου καταφρονήσῃς, ὅταν τὸν ὄντως
θάνατον φοβηθῇς, ὃς φυλάσσεται τοῖς κατακριθη-
σομένοις εἰς τὸ πῦρ τὸ αἰώνιον, ὃ τοὺς παραδο-
θέντας αὐτῷ μέχρι τέλους κολάσει. 8. τότε τοὺς
ὑπομένοντας ὑπὲρ δικαιοσύνης θαυμάσεις τὸ πῦρ
τὸ πρόσκαιρον καὶ μακαρίσεις, ὅταν ἐκεῖνο τὸ πῦρ
ἐπιγνῷς.

have this full knowledge, with that joy do you think that you will be filled, or how greatly will you love him who thus first loved you? 4. But by your love you will imitate the example of his goodness. And do not wonder that it is possible for man to be the imitator of God; it is possible when he will. 5. For happiness consists not in domination over neighbours, nor in wishing to have more than the weak, nor in wealth, and power to compel those who are poorer, nor can anyone be an imitator of God in doing these things, but these things are outside his majesty. 6. But whoever takes up the burden of his neighbour, and wishes to help another, who is worse off in that in which he is the stronger, and by ministering to those in need the things which he has received and holds from God becomes a god to those who receive them,—this man is an imitator of God. 7. Then, though your lot be placed on earth you will see that God lives in heaven, then you will begin to speak of the mysteries of God, then you will both love and admire those who are being punished because they will not deny God, then you will condemn the deceit and error of the world, when you know what is the true life of heaven, when you despise the apparent death of this world, when you fear the death which is real, which is kept for those that shall be condemned to the everlasting fire, which shall punish up to the end those that were delivered to it. 8. Then you will marvel at those who endure for the sake of righteousness the fire which is for a season, and you will count them blessed when you know that other fire.

XI

1. Οὐ ξένα ὁμιλῶ οὐδὲ παραλόγως ζητῶ, ἀλλὰ ἀποστόλων γενόμενος μαθητὴς γίνομαι διδάσκαλος ἐθνῶν· τὰ παραδοθέντα ἀξίως ὑπηρετῶ γινομένοις ἀληθείας μαθηταῖς. 2. τίς γὰρ ὀρθῶς διδαχθεὶς καὶ λόγῳ προσφιλὴς γενηθεὶς οὐκ ἐπιζητεῖ σαφῶς μαθεῖν τὰ διὰ λόγου δειχθέντα φανερῶς μαθηταῖς, οἷς ἐφανέρωσεν ὁ λόγος φανείς, παρρησίᾳ λαλῶν, ὑπὸ ἀπίστων μὴ νοούμενος, μαθηταῖς δὲ διηγούμενος, οἳ πιστοὶ λογισθέντες ὑπ᾽ αὐτοῦ ἔγνωσαν πατρὸς μυστήρια; 3. οὗ χάριν ἀπέστειλε λόγον, ἵνα κόσμῳ φανῇ, ὃς ὑπὸ λαοῦ ἀτιμασθείς, διὰ ἀποστόλων κηρυχθείς, ὑπὸ ἐθνῶν ἐπιστεύθη. 4. οὗτος ὁ ἀπ᾽ ἀρχῆς, ὁ καινὸς φανεὶς καὶ παλαιὸς εὑρεθεὶς καὶ πάντοτε νέος ἐν ἁγίων καρδίαις γεννώμενος. 5. οὗτος ὁ ἀεί, ὁ σήμερον υἱὸς λογισθείς, δι᾽ οὗ πλουτίζεται ἡ ἐκκλησία καὶ χάρις ἁπλουμένη ἐν ἁγίοις πληθύνεται, παρέχουσα νοῦν, φανεροῦσα μυστήρια, διαγγέλλουσα καιρούς, χαίρουσα ἐπὶ πιστοῖς, ἐπιζητοῦσι δωρουμένη, οἷς ὅρκια

Jo. 1, 9

I Tim. 3, 16

I Jo. 1, 1 ;

Ps. 2, 7 ;
Mt. 3, 17

XI

1. My speech is not strange, nor my inquiry Conclusion unreasonable, but as a disciple of apostles I am becoming a teacher of the heathen. I administer worthily that which has been handed down to those who are becoming disciples of the truth. 2. For who that has been properly taught, and has become a lover of the word does not seek to learn plainly the things which have been clearly shown by the word to disciples, to whom the Word appeared and revealed them, speaking boldly, not being perceived by the unbelieving, but relating them to disciples, who were held by him to be faithful and gained knowledge of the mysteries of the Father? 3. And for his sake he sent the Word to appear to the world, who was dishonoured by the chosen people,[1] was preached by apostles, was believed by the heathen. 4. He was from the beginning, and appeared new, and was proved to be old, and is ever young, as he is born in the hearts of the saints. 5. He is the eternal one, who to-day[2] is accounted a Son, through whom the Church is enriched, and grace is unfolded and multiplied among the saints, who confers understanding, manifests mysteries, announces seasons, rejoices in the faithful, is given to them that seek, that is, to those by whom the pledges of faith are

[1] λαός is here, as frequently, the chosen people of Israel, in contrast with τὰ ἔθνη, the heathen nations.
[2] This suggests that the homily belongs to a feast of the Nativity. In the time of Hippolytus this was probably not separated from the Epiphany or feast of the Baptism (see article on Christmas in Hastings *Dictionary of Religion and Ethics.*)

πίστεως οὐ θραύεται οὐδὲ ὅρια πατέρων παρορί-
ζεται.   6. εἶτα φόβος νόμου ᾄδεται, καὶ προφητῶν
χάρις γινώσκεται, καὶ εὐαγγελίων πίστις ἵδρυται,
καὶ ἀποστόλων παράδοσις φυλάσσεται, καὶ ἐκκλησίας χάρις σκιρτᾷ.   7. ἣν χάριν μὴ λυπῶν
ἐπιγνώσῃ, ἃ λόγος ὁμιλεῖ δι᾽ ὧν βούλεται, ὅτε
θέλει.   8. ὅσα γὰρ θελήματι τοῦ κελεύοντος λόγου
ἐκινήθημεν ἐξειπεῖν μετὰ πόνου, ἐξ ἀγάπης τῶν
ἀποκαλυφθέντων ἡμῖν γινόμεθα ὑμῖν κοινωνοί.

XII

1. Οἷς ἐντυχόντες καὶ ἀκούσαντες μετὰ σπουδῆς
εἴσεσθε, ὅσα παρέχει ὁ θεὸς τοῖς ἀγαπῶσιν ὀρθῶς,
οἱ γενόμενοι παράδεισος τρυφῆς, πάγκαρπον ξύλον
εὐθαλοῦν ἀνατείλαντες ἐν ἑαυτοῖς, ποικίλοις καρποῖς κεκοσμημένοι.   2. ἐν γὰρ τούτῳ τῷ χωρίῳ
ξύλον γνώσεως καὶ ξύλον ζωῆς πεφύτευται· ἀλλ᾽
οὐ τὸ τῆς γνώσεως ἀναιρεῖ, ἀλλ᾽ ἡ παρακοὴ
ἀναιρεῖ.   3. οὐδὲ γὰρ ἄσημα τὰ γεγραμμένα, ὡς
θεὸς ἀπ᾽ ἀρχῆς ξύλον γνώσεως καὶ ξύλον ζωῆς ἐν
μέσῳ παραδείσου ἐφύτευσε, διὰ γνώσεως ζωὴν
ἐπιδεικνύς· ᾗ μὴ καθαρῶς χρησάμενοι οἱ ἀπ᾽ ἀρχῆς
πλάνῃ τοῦ ὄφεως γεγύμνωνται.   4. οὐδὲ γὰρ ζωὴ
ἄνευ γνώσεως οὐδὲ γνῶσις ἀσφαλὴς ἄνευ ζωῆς
ἀληθοῦς· διὸ πλησίον ἑκάτερον πεφύτευται.   5. ἣν
δύναμιν ἐνιδὼν ὁ ἀπόστολος τήν τε ἄνευ ἀληθείας

Gen. 2, 15 ;
3, 24

Gen. 2, 9

not broken, nor the decrees of the Fathers transgressed. 6. Then is the fear of the Law sung, and the grace of the Prophets known, the faith of the Gospels is established, and the tradition of apostles is guarded, and the grace of the Church exults. 7. And if you do not grieve this grace you will understand what the word says through the agents of his choice, when he will. 8. For in all things which we were moved by the will of him who commands us to speak with pain, we become sharers with you through love of the things revealed to us.

XII

1. IF you consider and listen with zeal to these truths you will know what things God bestows on those that love him rightly, who are become " a Paradise of delight," raising up in themselves a fertile tree with all manner of fruits, and are adorned with divers fruits. 2. For in this garden has been planted " the tree of knowledge and the tree of life," but the tree of knowledge does not kill, but disobedience kills. 3. For that which was written is quite plain, that God in the beginning planted " a tree of knowledge and a tree of life in the midst of Paradise," and showed that life is through knowledge. But those who did not use it in purity were in the beginning deprived of it by the deceit of the serpent; 4. for neither is there life without knowledge, nor sound knowledge without true life; wherefore both are planted together. 5. And when the apostle saw the force of this, he blamed the

προστάγματος εἰς ζωὴν ἀσκουμένην γνῶσιν μεμφό-
μενος λέγει· Ἡ γνῶσις φυσιοῖ, ἡ δὲ ἀγάπη οἰκο-
δομεῖ.   6. ὁ γὰρ νομίζων εἰδέναι τι ἄνευ γνώσεως
ἀληθοῦς καὶ μαρτυρουμένης ὑπὸ τῆς ζωῆς οὐκ
ἔγνω, ὑπὸ τοῦ ὄφεως πλανᾶται, μὴ ἀγαπήσας τὸ
ζῆν.   ὁ δὲ μετὰ φόβου ἐπιγνοὺς καὶ ζωὴν ἐπι-
ζητῶν ἐπ᾽ ἐλπίδι φυτεύει, καρπὸν προσδοκῶν.
7. ἤτω σοὶ καρδία γνῶσις, ζωὴ δὲ λόγος ἀληθής,
χωρούμενος.   8. οὗ ξύλον φέρων καὶ καρπὸν
αἴρων τρυγήσεις ἀεὶ τὰ παρὰ θεῷ ποθούμενα, ὧν
ὄφις οὐχ ἅπτεται οὐδὲ πλάνη συγχρωτίζεται·
οὐδὲ Εὖα φθείρεται, ἀλλὰ παρθένος πιστεύεται·
9. καὶ σωτήριον δείκνυται, καὶ ἀπόστολοι συνετί-
ζονται, καὶ τὸ κυρίου πάσχα προέρχεται, καὶ
καιροὶ συνάγονται καὶ μετὰ κόσμου ἁρμόζονται,
καὶ διδάσκων ἁγίους ὁ λόγος εὐφραίνεται, δι᾽ οὗ
πατὴρ δοξάζεται· ᾧ ἡ δόξα εἰς τοὺς αἰῶνας.
ἀμήν.

I Cor. 8, 1

I Cor. 9, 10

knowledge which is exercised apart from the truth of the injunction which leads to life and said; "Knowledge puffeth up, but love edifieth." 6. For he who thinks that he knows anything without knowledge which is true and testified to by life, does not know, but is deceived by the serpent, not loving life. But he who has full knowledge with fear and seeks after life plants in hope, looking for fruit. 7. Let your heart be knowledge, and your life the true and comprehended word. 8. And if you bear the tree of this and pluck its fruit you will ever enjoy that which is desired by God, which the serpent does not touch, and deceit does not infect, and Eve is not corrupted but a virgin is trusted, 9. and salvation is set forth, and apostles are given understanding, and the Passover of the Lord advances, and the seasons are brought together, and are harmonised with the world, and the Word teaches the saints and rejoices, and through it the Father is glorified; to whom be glory for ever, Amen.

GENERAL INDEX

GENERAL INDEX

GENERAL INDEX

383

GENERAL INDEX

Israel,I . 83, 353, 355, 357, 369
——, chosen people of, II. 375

Jacob, I. 15, 61, 249, 369, 389
Jericho, I. 27
Jerusalem, I. 79
——, Patriarchal library of, I. 305
Jesse, I. 39
Jesus, Jesus Christ, the Lord Jesus
Christ, I. 9, and *passim*.
——, ascension of, I. 397
——, as High Priest, I. 117
——, as God, I. 191
——, as Judge, I. 129
——, as Life, I. 197
——, Resurrection of, I. 255, 261
——, words of, I. 31
Jesus–Joshua, I. 361
Jews, anger of, II. 329
Job, I. 39, 137
John, St., I. 168, 169, 280
John, the Presbyter, I. 280
Jonah, I. 21
Joseph, I. 15, 389
Joshua, I. 27, 385
Joyfulness, II. 115, 259
Judaism, I. 205, 207, 245
Judaistic practices, I. 167
Judas, II. 321
Judgment, the Day of, I. 155, 409
Judith, I. 103

Kennett, R. H., I. 6
Kingdom of God (or, of Christ),
I. 81, 95, 143, 147, 243, 291,
353; II. 261, 273, 289, 369
—— in Heaven, II. 371
Knopf, I. 9, 49
Knowledge, II. 47, 49

Laban, I. 61
Latin Church, I. 125
Law, I. 337; II. 141
——, Christian, II. 139
——, persecuted for the, II. 197
Law-breakers, II. 209
Leiden, II. 349
Leo, the Notary, I. 5
Leopards, I. 233
Leviathan, explanation of the, II. 65
——, the four Colours of, II. 67
Levites, I. 79
Licentiousness, II. 259
Life, Contest of, I. 139

Lightfoot, J. B., I. 5, 21, 32, 126,
136, 155, 168, 170, 171, 173, 182,
195, 200, 210, 218, 232, 251, 252,
276, 281; II. 338
Long-suffering, II. 87, 89, 93, 259
Lord's Day, I. 205, 331
Lot, I. 25, 27
Lot's wife, I. 27
Love, I. 93, 95; II. 47, 49, 259
Lueken, W., II. 197
Luxury, II. 179, 181
Lying, II. 259

Maeander, I. 197
Magic, I. 193
Magnesia, I. 166, 168, 197
Magnesia, bishop of, I. 199
Magnesians, Epistle of Ignatius to,
I. 196–211
Maidens, twelve, II. 221, 225, 245,
247, 249, 253, 255
Mammon, I. 137
Man, Son of, I. 387
Manasses, I. 389
Mandates, II. 71–137
Mandate, first, expansion of, II. 95
Maranatha, I. 325
Marcianus, II. 339
Marcion, I. 293; II. 339, 345
——, teaching of, II. 345
Marriages, second, II. 85
Martyrdom, II. 339
Martyrs, II. 197, 285, 337
——, place of the, II. 29
——, sufferings of the, II. 315
Mary of Cassobola, I. 167
Mary, Virgin, I. 168, 169, 221
Maursmunster, II. 349
Maximus, II. 23
Men, six young, II. 27, 31, 37, 223
Michael, II. 197
Milk and honey, I. 363
Minas, Bishop, I. 170
Ministers, evil, II. 281
Miriam, I. 17
Misael, I. 87
Modad (*see* Eldad and Modad)
Money-prize, II. 271
Monte Cavo, II. 219
Moon, new, II. 357
Morin, G., I. 6
Moses, I. 15, 17, 39, 81, 83, 97, 99,
101, 351, 361, 377, 379, 383, 385,
391, 393

385

GENERAL INDEX

Mountains, vision of, II. 219, 265
Muratorian Canon, II. 3.

Name, The (of the Lord), I. 149, 237; II. 35, 251, 257, 259, 273
Namur, I. 6
Neapolis, I. 277
Nero, I. 4
Nicodemus, Gospel of, I. 207; II. 263
Niketas, II. 335
Nineveh, I. 21
Noah, I. 21, 23, 137

Obedience, examples of, I. 23
—— to God, I. 31
Offerings, freewill, I. 79
——, sin, I. 79
——, trespass, I. 79
Onesimus, I. 175, 181
Ordinances, Church, I. 305, 306
Origen, I. 339
Otto, II. 349

Papyri, Amherst, II. 4
——, Berlin, II. 5
——, Oxyrynchus, II. 4
Paradise, I. 207; II. 377
Passion, I. 193
——, of God, I. 235
Passover, II. 379
Paul, St., I. 89, 187, 231, 287, 295, 297, 337
——, Martyrdom of, I. 17
Peacefulness, I. 33
Penance, II. 3
Penitence, I. 155
Persecution, great, II. 21
Peter, I. 17, 135, 231, 255
——, Gospel of, II. 263
——, Martyrdom of, I. 17
Petermann, I. 170
Petersburg, St., I. 338
Pharaoh, I. 15, 97
Philadelphia, I. 168, 239; II. 337
Philip of Tralles, II. 341
Philippi, I. 168
Philo, I. 251, 263, 267, 337
Philomelium, II. 309, 313
Phoenix, I. 53
Phrygia, II. 317
Pionius, II. 309, 343, 345
Pius, II. 3
Polybius, I. 213

Polycarp, I. 166, 169, 195, 211, 267, 338; II. 21, 309
——, Acts of, II. 343
——, arrival in Smyrna, II. 323
——, betrayal of, II. 319
——, dream of, II. 319
——, Epistle of, to the Philippians, I. 280-301
——, Epistle to, I. 169
——, examination of, II. 323-325
——, in Rome, II. 343
——, last prayers of, II. 331
——, martyrdom of, II. 309-345
——, retreat of, to country, II. 319
——, in the arena, II. 323
Pontius Pilate, I. 221, 253
Pontus, II. 345
Power, II. 259
Prayer, II. 109, 121, 145, 163
Prayer of Church in I Clem. I. 111-117
Prayers, I. 331
Preparation (for Sabbath), II. 321
Presbyter, Valens the, I. 297
Presbyters I. 47, 85, 107, 167, 199, 203, 239, 243, 249, 291
——, deposition of certain Corinthian, I. 3
Presbytery, I. 177, 209, 215, 219, 225, 261, 265
Priest, high, I. 79, 249
Prince of this World, I. 191, 197, 217, 235
Principalities, I. 217
Pro-Consul, II. 317, 325, 327
Promise, fulfilment of, to Jews, I. 391
Prophets, I. 249, 259, 291, 307, 325, 327, 343, 355, 359
——, Christian, I. 243
——, false and true, II. 117-125
Prudentius, II. 333
Punishment, time of, in relation to sin, II. 179-183
—— with torture, I. 159
Purim, II. 311, 323
Purity, I. 141; II. 77

Quintus, II. 317

Rachel, I. 367
Rahab, faith and hospitality of, I. 27
Ransom, II. 369

386

GENERAL INDEX

Readers (*see* Church, readers in)
Rebecca, I. 387
Redemption, I. 29
Repentance, I. 19, 141, 143, 149, 159; II. 2, 81, 83, 129, 179, 205, 207, 213, 277, 299
—— for sin after baptism, II. 83
—— in the Prophets, I. 21
Resurrection, I. 161, 207, 259, 261, 333, 355
——, hope of, I. 285
——, promised in the Scriptures, I. 55
——, proved by the crops, I. 51
——, proved by Phoenix, I. 53
——, proved by the seasons, I. 51
—— of the flesh, I. 141; II. 171
Reuchlin, II. 349
Revelation, Christian, II. 363
Reverence, II. 47, 49
Rheus Agathopous, I. 251, 263
Rhoda, II. 7
Rich, II. 211, 271
Righteousness, II. 129
Rock, the, as foundation of the Tower, II. 221 ff.
Romans, Epistle of Ignatius to, I. 169
Rome, I. 3, 166, 168, 197, 231; II. 7
——, catacombs in, I. 4
——, fight with beasts at, I. 175
Rosch, F., I. 6
Rufus, I. 295
Ruinart, I. 170
Rule, golden, in Didache, I. 309

Sabbath, I. 205, 393; II. 357
Sacrifice, argument against, II. 355
Sacrifices, I. 77, 345
——, daily, I. 79
Salonika, I. 277
Salvation, plan of, II. 369
Satan, I. 187, 401
Saul, I. 17
Saviour, II. 371
Scape-goat, I. 365
Scarlet-wool, II. 367, 369
Schism, I. 87, 89
Schismatics, II. 209, 211
Schisms, II. 207, 213
Schmidt, C., I. 6, 170
Schubert, W., I. 170
Schwartz, E., II. 311

Scriptures, I. 299
Seal, martyrdom as, II. 313
Seals, II. 193
Self-sacrifice, I. 101
Serpent, II. 379
Services, religious, I. 77
Shells, torment of, II. 317
Shepherd, the (the angel of repentance), II. 69; and afterwards throughout the book.
—— of luxury, II. 173
—— of punishment, II. 175, 185
Sibyl, the, II. 25
Similitudes, II. 139–
Simonides, II. 4
Simplicity, II. 47, 71, 259
Sinai, Mt., I. 381, 391, 393
Sincerity, I. 49
Smyrna, I. 168, 195, 211, 213, 223, 237, 267; II. 309, 310, 313, 329, 337, 345
Socrates, II. 309, 341
Sodom, I. 27
Son, the, I. 361; II. 215
——, as Spirit, II. 164
——, only begotten, II. 371
Son of God, name of (*see* Name)
Son of God, as servant, II. 165–169
Soothsaying, II. 119
Sorcerers, II. 51
Soter, Epistle of, to Corinth, I. 126, 127
Soul and body, II. 363
Spirit, Holy, I. 151, 183, 341, 383, 391, 393, 405; II. 87, 93, 119, 121, 125, 167, 281, 295
——, this flesh as anti-type of the, I. 153
——, prophetic, II. 121
——, as son, II. 164
Star, at birth of Christ, I. 193
Station, *i.e.* fast, II. 153
Statius Quadratus, II. 341
Stephanus, II. 349
Stichometry, II. 23
Stick, treatment of, by the shepherd, II. 195
Stoics, II. 299
Stones, various sorts used in the Tower or rejected, II. 31 ff., 37 ff., 225 ff., 253 ff.
Stone-throwing, metaphor of, II. 125
Strasburg, II. 349

387

GENERAL INDEX

Subordination, necessity for, I. 71
Succession, apostolic, I. 79
Sunday, worship on, I. 307
Synopsis, Athanasian, II. 23
Syria, I. 197, 211, 229, 231, 251
265, 275, 299
——, Church in, I. 237, 301
Syringe, metaphor of, II. 125

Tabernacle of Testimony, I. 83
Table of God, I. 83
Tables of stone, I. 351
Tarsus, I. 168
Tavia, I. 267
Teachers, II. 39, 281
Temperance, II. 103, 259
Temple, I. 397
——, rebuilding of, I. 338
Tertullian, II. 81
Testimony, tabernacle of, I. 83
Thegri, II. 65
Theophorus, I. 173
Tiber, II. 7
Tortures and punishments, II. 177
Tower, the, similitude of, II. 217 ff.
——, vision of, II. 31 ff.
    See also under Stones, Maidens,
        Mountains, Rock, Door,
        Water.
Traitors, II. 271
Trajan, I. 166
Tralles, I. 166, 168
Trallians, I. 211, 212–225
Tree of knowledge, II. 377
Tree of life, II. 377
Tree, nailed to a, I. 253
Trees, budding and withered, II. 149
——, leafless, II. 147
Troas, I. 166, 168, 251, 265, 277
Truth, II. 75, 259
Tübigen, II. 349
Turner, C. H., II. 311
Two ways, the, I. 306, 309, 401

Unbelief, II. 259
Understanding, II. 259
Unity, I. 177
Ussher, Archbishop, I. 133

Valens, I. 297
Valerius Vito, I. 121
Venatio, II. 329
Version, Armenian, of Ignatius, I.170
——, Coptic, of I Clement, I. 6
——, —— (Sahidic), of Ignatius,
I. 170
——, ——, of Hermas, II. 5
——, Latin, of I Clement, I. 6
——, ——, of Ignatius, I. 168, 170f.
——, ——, of Polycarp, I. 281
——, ——, of Didache, I. 305 f.
——, ——, of Hermas, II. 5
——, ——, of Martyrdom of Poly-
carp, II. 310
——, Syriac, of I. Clement, I. 5 f.
Via Campana, II. 61
Vine and Elm, metaphor of, II. 143
Virgin birth, I. 253
Virgins, I. 291
Virtues, power of, II. 47
Visions, reason for variety of, II. 217
Vossius, I. 170

Water, the tower built over, II.
31 f., 35
Way of Light, I. 405
Wealth, II. 43, 51
Wheat, God's, I. 231
Wickedness, II. 259
——, teachers of, II. 269
Widows, I. 271, 289
Willow trees, explanation of the
parable of, II. 195
——, parable of, II. 189
Wine-jars, metaphor of, II. 123
Winter and summer, metaphor of,
II. 149
Wives, immoral, II. 79
Word, II. 375
World, this, and the world to come,
I. 137

Xanthicus, II. 310, 341

Zahn, Th., I. 173; II. 5, 219
Zenobius, I. 231
Zosimus, I. 295

REFERENCE INDEX

REFERENCE INDEX